THE GASLIT BRAIN

Protect Your Brain from the Lies of Bullying,
Gaslighting, and Institutional Complicity

JENNIFER FRASER, PhD

Foreword by Michael Merzenich

PB Prometheus Books

Essex, Connecticut

Prometheus Books

An imprint of The Globe Pequot Publishing Group, Inc.
64 South Main St.
Essex, CT 06426
www.GlobePequot.com

British Library Cataloguing in Publication Information available

Library of Congress Cataloging-in-Publication Data Available

ISBN 978-1-4930-9092-1 (cloth)
ISBN 978-1-4930-9093-8 (ebook)

For Montgomery

"We must do what they fear—tell the truth, spread the truth."
—Alexei Navalny
June 19, 2023

CONTENTS

CONTENTS

FOREWORD

SOMETIMES OUR WORLD SEEMS BEDAZZLING, WITH GASLIGHTING COMing at us from all directions. Not too long ago, our human cultures held more reliably to ethical standards. Although it has always been challenging to bring those standards to bear, they appear to be disintegrating under the assault of an army of gaslighters, especially over the past several decades. Those increasingly more effective institutional and public fabricators are growing progressively stronger alliances to support their deceptions. In the all-too-rare instances when they are called on the carpet for supporting their ethically unsupportable opportunism, their first reaction is to demean or destroy those who actively oppose them.

The Gaslit Brain opposes them and teaches strategies to stop their damage.

Without those who speak up to defend the truth, sayonara, ethical standards. Good-bye, scientific guidance for social governance. In the third decade of the twenty-first century, opportunism rules, and science is suppressed.

In *The Gaslit Brain*—this book of discovery that will enlighten most modern citizens—Dr. Jennifer Fraser explains how this kind of cultural poisoning is impacting our modern lives. Although we have always lived with the neurological limitations that can favor the selfish fabulist over the altruistic truth teller, our modern communication networks and social media provide a powerful tool set for the purveyors of myths, conspiracies, and egoistic fantasies.

As Dr. Fraser explains—and neuroscientific studies have documented—gaslighting teams have well-established strategies for recruiting new members. In the right social setting and with the right social, emotional, and (alas) monetary rewards, membership in those teams of liars can be difficult to resist.

In the research laboratory, when we study the vulnerability of the brain to manipulation, individuals can be trained remarkably easily to adopt an utterly nonsensical perspective on the path to team membership. Alas, joining the crew on a gaslighting ship often comes with a requisite tolerance for what can be egregiously unethical, cruel, or collectively destructive behaviors. And with the exclusivity associated with team membership, crew members will turn a challenge to its nonsense to a call for vengeful reaction.

This rampant, opportunistic operationalism harms us all socially and neurologically in a world in which anything goes, if we can sell it and get away with it. Dr. Fraser relates experiences in her own life that were a source of long-standing personal stress and frustration in the face of institutional gaslighting. She also understands, and explains to us all, how our God and our mother, Nature, has provided us with a capacity to heal, as she has healed, after being subjected to vengeful gaslighting. Moreover, we have the capacity to resist lies when we know how to work *with* our brains.

The mental-health issues for gaslighters and their allies are more difficult to address because, as a rule, poor listening comes with the territory. Still, to be relieved of the burdens they carry in their hearts and souls would be a blessing for all concerned.

On some dark days, as a scientist for life, I have little hope for our human future, for the historically more stable ethical underpinnings that we appear to be so rapidly abandoning, or for planet Earth. *The Gaslit Brain* reminds us that the first step in solving our endemic weaknesses is to understand them, in social and neurological terms.

Dr. Fraser exposes your gaslit world. She explains how and why it is endemic in modern societies and outlines ways to prevent its harm. Consider *The Gaslit Brain* a call to action: First, if you have been a victim of vengeful gaslighters, use your powerful brain plasticity resources to address the neurological damage that they have engendered. And second, join Jennifer, me, and millions of other good citizens in doing our best to right the ship—to make America and the world science-guided, truthful, and ethical again.

There is not much hope for our descendants if we don't.

Michael Merzenich, PhD
Professor Emeritus, UCSF
Chief scientific officer, Posit Science
Founder and president, Brain Plasticity Institute

Introduction

When Your Workplace Is Constructed on Lies

IT'S SHOCKING TO DISCOVER THAT YOUR WORKPLACE—WHICH YOU believed was constructed on the bedrock of truth telling—is, in fact, more like a flimsy web of lies. It's so flimsy that those who call out the falsehoods and manipulations must be driven out. Telling the truth is the one forbidden act, and those who break this rule must be scapegoated. It's a highly effective deflection: everyone looks at the scapegoats as they walk away, rather than turning their questioning gaze on the institution.

In *The Gaslit Brain*, we will turn our questioning gaze directly on the institution. We will ask questions such as: Who is abusing and manipulating, and what is happening in their brains? Why are liars believed and truth tellers doubted? What's wrong with our brains? What happens to brains when they are manipulated by gaslighting? Why do good leaders cover up abuse, fraud, safety issues, and more? Why do good leaders drive out whistle-blowers, regardless of their high-level expertise and talent, to protect perpetrators who put the institution at risk? What kind of stress does this cause managers and human resources (HR)? What is happening in the leader's brain?

The most important question of the book is: Could we do things differently if we knew more about how our brains work? It is important for all workplaces to know that dishonesty increases with repetition as extensive psychological research documents in "The Brain Adapts to Dishonesty."[1] Institutions that allow some lies should be aware that they may dominate the workplace, creating a culture that condones falsehoods with "small transgressions gradually snowballing into larger ones." The research revealed that the more an individual tells self-serving lies, the less the brain's amygdala sounds the alarm. The amygdala is a brain region that is commonly thought of as a threat detection center, which gives us alerts and signals when we are at risk. Telling a lie usually puts us at serious societal risk as it undermines one of our most valued qualities as a person who can be believed and trusted. We are witnessing an unusual social phenomenon whereby lying has become mainstream. It is as if normalizing disinformation, misinformation, and self-serving lies have compromised the effectiveness of our collective amygdala so that it no longer jolts us when we issue falsehoods. Those who have lies told about them at work, lies so serious that they have cost them their job, knocked them off a hard-earned career path, hurt their place in the community, stripped them of physical and mental health are the casualties of institutions that normalize deceit.

The Gaslit Brain brings together contemporary stories of top employees who were exposed to the lies of bullying and gaslighting. A key defining feature of gaslighting's lies is that they are self-serving. We look at the stories of how lies impacted employees through the lens of brain science. If we don't understand how our brains create reality and the way it differs from illusion, we certainly will not understand when and how our brains fall for falsehoods. The book is designed to *prevent* crises in workplaces that revolve around the lies of bullying, gaslighting, and institutional complicity. The overarching goal is for leaders, managers, and HR to become experts in how to prevent the contagion of lies from infecting their institution to keep their workplaces healthy, productive, and profitable.

Throughout *The Gaslit Brain*, I refer to workplaces as "the institution" regardless of whether it's a corporation, company, not-for-profit, or something else. I use institution to examine institutional complicity with abuses. Likewise, I refer to abuses with the umbrella term "bullying" regardless of whether it's psychological, social-emotional, sexual harassment, cyberbullying, or any other of the many ways in which a person is targeted for maltreatment at work. The lies of bullying, in all its different forms, are contrasted with the truth telling of those who speak up. In chapter 8, we will hear from a lawyer—whose career has been dedicated to representing whistle-blowers—on why telling the truth is so important and yet so fraught with risk. Institutions that protect and enable those who bully are likely to scapegoat whistle-blowers. It is this normalized, counterintuitive workplace phenomenon we will examine from a host of neuroscientific angles in *The Gaslit Brain*.

When the penalty for speaking up impacts your livelihood, career, family, and health, it couldn't be more serious.[2] It's a bizarre sensation to be treated as if you have committed a grave crime—referred to in research as "committing the truth"—but it is exactly what happens to whistle-blowers in all kinds of workplaces.[3] Although the majority fall for (or choose to believe) the institution's gaslighting—which positions the truth teller as the villain—those who see through the illusion to the abusive, fraudulent, dangerous institutional reality and refuse to remain silent about it can teach us all a lesson about how to recognize and resist gaslighting.

GASLIGHTING IN THE WORKPLACE

As we examine in depth, gaslighting hinges on reversals. Its essential goal is to make the truth teller appear as a liar, the victims appear as perpetrators, the sane employees as crazy employees. Whistle-blowers—striving to save the institution and its integrity—are reversed into saboteurs who *apparently* are trying to ruin the institution's reputation. The motivation and evidence for wanting to sabotage the institution is *not* forthcoming, or worse: it is fabricated, which should cast doubt on the institution but rarely does.

Gaslighting has an agenda. It is a series of elaborate falsehoods, behind-closed-doors behaviors, smear campaigns shared in private. Gaslighting works hard to divide and conquer, not only populaces but even individuals. It seeks to divide its victims externally *and* internally to fulfill its own needs and drives. Those who gaslight ensure that victims are kept isolated, believing that they are the only one, always wondering if it's their own fault.[4] Gaslighting is self-serving. The one thing it cannot tolerate is those who pose questions within the institution, or from the outside, through investigative journalism and media scrutiny. Those who gaslight keep insiders quiet with nondisclosure agreements (NDAs). When asked to comment in the media, they reply, "No comment." When the media seek an official statement from the institution, officials can never give it because they have done "their own internal investigation"; they are "protecting" targets; they are maintaining "confidentiality." Note the reversals. The fact that the investigation is *internal* poses instant problems with conflict of interest and suggests cover-up. The institution is *destroying* targets but claims it's protecting them. It is *breaching* confidentiality for its own agenda but claims it cannot speak publicly.

The Gaslit Brain unpacks individual and institutional self-serving lies. It looks at ways to identify lies, protect your brain from their harmful impact, and maintain your safety and sanity. The book examines the way certain individuals and institutions strive to make you believe something that is *not* true for personal gain, whether psychological, financial, or reputational. They bully you because of their own psychological dysregulation. They try to manipulate you for money or embezzle your funds, posing as someone they're not, and lying each step of the way. When you speak up, report, call them out, the institution turns on you to protect itself, covers up for leadership's failure to prevent the crisis, and even sacrifices its best and most talented to maintain the institution's reputation. The irony is that their reputation is built on covering up wrongdoing. It doesn't have to be this way. Brain science can teach us a healthier, more productive, and more profitable way forward.

THE FIRST GASLIGHTER
In the Western tradition, the first recorded liar, hell-bent on destroying others and gaslighting to do it, is Satan. It's the twenty-first century, and surprisingly the lies that fuel gaslighting haven't changed much, if at all. This is good news for all of us who want to be informed about gaslighting *before* it happens to us or others in the workplace.

In Genesis, appearing to Eve as a snake, Satan—the personification of evil—gets information from her first that he can use to his advantage. Extracting information is textbook gaslighting. Satan learns that Adam and Eve are forbidden by God to eat or even touch the fruit of the tree in the garden. The risk is death. Satan takes this information and twists it, casting doubt, undermining God, making it appear that it is God who is in the wrong and not to be trusted. Although Satan seeks destructive power, he accuses God of his own crime. Such a reversal is classic gaslighting: the perpetrator of harm claims to be the victim of harm. It makes your head—more specifically, your brain—spin. But that's the whole point.

The lies at the heart of bullying are designed to unbalance you, destabilize you, make you think you deserve it, or someone else deserves it, because something is wrong with them. What's concerning is how much our institutions get trapped in the same faulty logic: somehow the one who reports abusive conduct is the one in the wrong, who must be expelled from the workplace and its community, while the perpetrator needs protection. It's mind-bending and has gone on for a very, very long time, but with brain science, hopefully that's about to change. Understanding how brains work, how they can detect lies, how they can be trained to identify gaslighting is the key to preventing the manipulation that occurs when we believe lies.

Back to the Bible. The snake says to Eve, "Ye shall not surely die: For God doth know that in the day ye eat thereof, then your eyes shall be opened, and ye shall be as gods, knowing good and evil." Note that Satan flat out tells Eve that her interpretation of reality and her essential relationship to her Maker are both incorrect and untrustworthy (Genesis 3: 1–24). Textbook destabilizing and confusing techniques, used by those who gaslit in biblical times, are still going on today. Abusive individuals still use the technique of isolating the targets from those who care about them such as family and friends. They cast doubt and aspersions on this caring community to constantly increase attention to *their* bond with the targets and the targets' dependence on them. Satan's method has not changed in its modern form. He offers his alternative reality constructed on conjured up half-truths that led to Eve and Adam losing their bond to God, being driven out of the garden, and setting off on a path of immense suffering where they do *know* good and evil, but rather than being "gods," they lose their connection to the divine.

The King James Bible credits Satan in his serpentine form as being "more subtil than any beast of the field." Gaslighting is frequently a subtle art that holds a mirror up to targets reflecting their own needs and wants. Eve wants to have her eyes opened; she wants to be godlike; she wants

Adam with her every step of the way; she seeks knowledge. Eve has no notion that these desires will be turned inside out by Satan, who seeks to have her ruined. "Subtle" is elusive, difficult to understand or analyze. It appeals to shadowy parts of the self, parts that lie within the dark chamber of the subconscious. All of us carry these vulnerabilities, and we can all be manipulated and blind to the betrayal taking place. How can you protect yourself against a betrayal that you can't even see?

Where Satan differs from present-day bullies and gaslighters is that he cannot manipulate God. In contrast, abusive individuals are adept at playing on the vulnerabilities and desires of targets *as well as* those in leadership positions.[5] They groom the targets while they groom the leaders, managers, HR, and others in the community. Think of all the times you've read stories about reports of bullying, disregard for safety, fraud being shared with leadership, management, and HR, yet nothing effective was done. It fell on deaf ears. How is it possible that bullying and corruption go on for years in established, respected institutions? As we examine in later chapters, it requires lies, gaslighting, and the fall of leaders, managers, and HR who go from being principled to complicit. Some leaders are so gaslit they don't even know what happened.

Notably in Christian iconography, the serpent who appears to gaslight Eve in the Garden of Eden was sculpted to appear as half-snake, half-woman. This artistic portrayal of the personification of evil associates Satan with Eve, engendering a misogynistic narrative whereby the woman brings original sin into the world. But from a psychological and neuroscientific angle, Satan reflecting Eve's wishes and desires by mirroring them is textbook gaslighting and is still being used effectively today. The psychopath not only puts on a fictional face to mirror what the victims want but also love bombs them, creating intimacy that lays the groundwork for manipulation and destruction. The perpetrator's allies— who fell for his gaslighting and followed his nefarious directives—might suffer serious penalties while the perpetrator walks away with impunity.

GASLIGHTING WAS *THE* WORD IN 2022

Merriam-Webster's Dictionary announced that 2022 saw a 1740 percent increase in searches for *gaslighting* "with high interest throughout the year." We're living in an age of overwhelming disinformation and apparently, people want to know why. What or who is the source? What is the motivation? Individuals want to learn more about gaslighting and how it uses lies to manipulate. Merriam-Webster refines the term for today:

> *The idea of a deliberate conspiracy to mislead has made gaslighting useful in describing lies that are part of a larger plan. Unlike lying, which tends to be between individuals, and fraud, which tends to involve organizations, gaslighting applies in both personal and political contexts.*[6]

The key line is "lies that are part of a larger plan." Lies that are part of a larger plan is the domain of the Dark Triad who spread "disinformation" throughout the institution as it succumbs to their "psychopathic fiction," as we discuss in greater detail in part 2.[7] Whether it's the macrocosm of political propaganda or the microcosm of institutional complicity, as we study lying and gaslighting, we see that asking questions about the agenda, the larger plan, can help in recognizing falsehoods and manipulation. Writer, historian, and activist Rebecca Solnit lasers in on the agenda: "What's striking about gaslighting is that it's an attempt to push a lie or a distortion by using advantages of power, including credibility and social status, to overwhelm the gaslit person or people—or populace. It's another kind of violence, not against bodies, but facts and truth."[8] What we need to know in the workplace is that those who attain positions of power, credibility, and social standing may also be part of the Dark Triad.

> *Narcissistic managers, in particular, tend to rise to management positions in organizations in disproportionately large numbers. Being particularly self-absorbed, they are known to use (and abuse) their subordinates and play up to their superiors to assure their own personal career success.*[9]

We tend to think that a person who has earned a position of power, credibility, and social standing is de facto trustworthy. However, as noted, the opposite is more likely to be true. As we will examine in part 2, narcissists,

Machiavellians, psychopaths rise up through the "use (and abuse)" of sub-ordinates. They gaslight and groom just as they gaslight and groom "their superiors." They are more likely to lie than to tell the truth.

Throughout *The Gaslit Brain*, we make a case—especially when draw-ing on the brain science—for the repeat error we make in mixing up posi-tion and person. We constantly fall for the power, credibility, and social standing of an individual's *position* that leads us to excuse or not even see destructive behavior done by the person. When we know powerful and prestigious positions may well be filled by narcissists and others in the Dark Triad, we need to become far more alert and aware about how they may operate in destructive ways.

Psychologists Drs. Robert Hare and Paul Babiak refer to the psycho-paths at work as "snakes in suits." They describe the impact of gaslighting, which perfectly outlines what happens to Eve: "victims will eventually come to doubt their own knowledge of the truth and change their own views to believe what the psychopath tells them rather than what they know to be true."[10] Imagine how you are likely to doubt yourself when in a courtroom with a judge who labels you with the ancient mythic crime of Eve.

BULLYING AND GASLIGHTING INFECT THE COURTROOM

As reported by Amrit Dhillon in August 2023, the Supreme Court in India created a handbook for judges "urging them to shun words like seductress, vamp, spinster, and harlot when talking about women."[11] Note, perpetrators are not using these misogynistic and derogatory terms. Judges are. In Indian courts, sexual harassment is trivialized as "Eve-teasing." This phrase positions Eve as weak, easily manipulated, carrying the taint of original sin, and along with it, Adam's downfall. Since biblical times, Eve apparently teases men to their demise. She is embodied in all women for thousands of years, and women are apparently still at it, teasing men who sexually assault them.

A man commits rape (perpetrator), but when you factor in "Eve-teasing," it's easy to use gaslighting to reposition him as the victim. At present in India, judges can give rapists the option to marry their victim (as if she is the perpetrator) to restore the woman's reputation. In this legal construct: she did the teasing and got raped; now the rapist can marry her to erase her teasing. According to this skewed way of thinking, the fault originally lies with her. In this reverse narrative, the rapist can heroically step in and remove her crime by offering his hand in marriage. It's hard to understand why the man is even in court if it's his decision whether to destroy or enhance the woman's reputation after he has raped her.

In the Supreme Court of India's new handbook, Chief Justice of India Dhananjaya Y. Chandrachud exposes the gaslighting at work. He writes that "marriage is not a remedy to the violence of rape." A remedy to the violence of rape—as noted above—is to do a brain scan and diagnose the empathy erosion in the rapist and assess whether he poses a danger of violating others. Instead, in India, the courts plan to cure rape with marriage. Let's unpack the manipulative reversal at work.

A perpetrator commits a crime against a target. The court does not penalize the perpetrator; instead, the perpetrator is offered an opportunity to cure or remedy the sickness of the violation. What speaks volumes to me about this legal transaction is the deafening silence of the victim. Not only is she not offered an opportunity to choose a cure for what has been done to her, she does not even have a space in which to speak about the violence done or how she wants to proceed. In a culture that describes sexual harassment as "Eve-teasing," one wonders what victims would say if they had voices. How many do you think would choose to marry their rapist? How many would feel thankful and relieved that their rapist had agreed to restore their reputation after raping them? How many of these twenty-first-century victims would argue that the rapist is "Tereus-teasing"? If ancient texts are relevant to contemporary crimes, then Indian women need to balance the "Eve-teasing" with an equivalent male predecessor. We are in a court of law, after all, and legal precedent is a way to understand and assign accountability.

TEREUS-TEASING

In Ovid's *Metamorphoses*, Tereus poses as a caring family member by law. He presents his good side and covers up his abusive side. He is married to Procne, who is the sister of Philomela. He has offered to accompany Philomela on a boat journey to see Procne at their home. On the journey, he drops the sheep's clothing and rapes his sister-in-law. Fully in abusive mode, he cuts off Philomela's tongue to ensure her silence about his crime of rape. Notice that his conduct provides a closer parallel to contemporary rapists than Eve does to female victims of a violent sexual assault. Both with the ancient rapist from Roman mythology and the contemporary rapist in today's courtroom, not only is there a violation of the female body, but this extreme harm is then followed by silencing the victim legally in court and literally in the myth. The mythic silencing is today's NDA when used to cover up the many rapes by a Harvey Weinstein, for instance (we will discuss this in more detail in chapter 4). Why is "Tereus-teasing" not institutionalized and precedent-setting like "Eve-teasing"? Why is it not used by the Indian legal institution to address rape?

Let's review one more time to cut through the normalizing. "Eve-teasing" in this new handbook for judges is textbook gaslighting. The symbolic woman "Eve" is positioned as the actual perpetrator, and the rapist is her victim. Note the reversal. The manipulation of justice by language—used to eliminate female civil rights and bestow them upon men who are offered the chance to save their woman victim through marriage—is a glaring sign of injustice. The judges now have a handbook that does not prohibit such language or rulings; it merely "urges" them to refrain from this archaic treatment of women because it may lead to a "distortion of the objective and impartial application of the law."

It appears that even in twenty-first-century courtrooms, where words determine innocence, guilt, and sentencing, the jury is still out on whether terms or word choice matter.[12] Language is critically important when you are exposed to the lies of bullying and gaslighting. You cannot recognize the manipulation without extreme clarity around word choice, as we will focus on in part 3.

What's *Not* Gaslighting

In 2023, Diane O'Leary reported that the term #medicalgaslighting had taken social media by storm, but this application of the term differs from how we'll use it. Thousands of posts by patients, mostly women, report that doctors have "ignored, minimized, or dismissed their symptoms," misdiagnosing them as anxiety or stress with serious consequences.[13]

Although this is awful, it is not precisely gaslighting in the way we are using the term. Doctors do not benefit from putting patients at risk. If anything, they open themselves to accusations of malpractice, loss of reputation, possible lawsuits. Although they may well be sexist or careless, they have no overarching agenda to misdiagnose female patients. Doctors receive lopsided education and training that has seen most research done into male health, and they make errors when diagnosing women's illnesses. Their misdiagnoses are unfortunate at best and dangerous at worst, but they aren't self-serving lies. It's a complex question because gaslighting in the courtrooms of India also doesn't directly benefit judges, but it forms part of an overarching misogynist approach to justice. We could say that this same flawed approach influences medicine in ways that put women's lives at risk.

The key point here is to understand that in our use of the term in *The Gaslit Brain*, gaslighting is carefully orchestrated, consciously done, and it serves the one using it. The book examines gaslighting among individuals and at the institutional level. The goal is to provide readers, wanting to understand how gaslighting works and why we're vulnerable to it, with an in-depth treatment of its seductive, malicious manipulation. Only when we understand intellectually, emotionally, and ethically how gaslighting works, and why it's used in bullying, can we begin to put in place neuroscience-informed protections to save our health, our sanity, our careers, and our lives.

THE MOVIE *GASLIGHT*

The term "gaslighting" entered the popular consciousness through a 1944 film, the American psychological thriller *Gaslight*, in which a husband wants to make his newlywed wife lose her mind to have her locked up in an asylum. His agenda is to steal jewels that he knows are hidden in her late aunt's house where they are living. The movie's name is symbolic of the many manipulations the husband undertakes to gaslight his wife into believing she's insane.

The film is set in London in the late nineteenth century when lamps were fueled by gas. The wife notices that their lamps randomly go dim. One way the husband destabilizes her is by denying that the gaslights are indeed dimming. It really is such a small manipulation. It's so minor that you might not make much of it. The husband has been showering his new wife with adoration—referred to in abusive relationships as "love bombing"—making it unlikely for her to think he's being deceptive. When the wife is told that the gaslights are *not* dimming, she chooses to believe her devoted husband and doubt her own perceptions. This is the beginning of what could be the end.

The wife not only notices that the gaslights are dimming, but also that sounds are coming from the attic. Her husband denies the sounds. She can't find her brooch even though she *knows* it was in her purse. He has removed it without her knowing. She finds a letter from one "Sergis Bauer," and her once-adoring husband becomes furious with her. Later, he explains that he became upset because *she* was upset (which she wasn't).

The husband tells his wife that the gaslights are *not* dimming; there are *no* sounds from the attic; she lost the brooch as it was *not* in her purse; she *didn't* see a letter from Sergis Bauer. On top of all that, he tells her that she stole a painting, and he has found out that her mother was put in an asylum. These are the textbook reversals and manipulations of gaslighting. He convinces his wife that not only is she fabricating things that don't exist, but also that she's a kleptomaniac, too high-strung and unwell to be in public. She must be crazy like her mother. Stealing the aunt's jewels is symbolic of a much more deadly crime: stealing his target's sanity. The husband is building a case for how his wife is obviously unstable and untrustworthy. Slowly but surely, the wife begins to lose her grip on what's real and what's false. She loses faith in her own perceptions. These are the textbook symptoms of the gaslit brain.

GASLIGHTING IS ALIVE AND WELL
In a hilarious recent reference to the film, political and sport commentator David Squires did a cartoon series on Luis Rubiales, president of the royal Spanish football federation who became an overnight social pariah by grabbing forward Jenni Hermosa at the FIFA World Cup awards ceremony and forcibly planting a kiss on her mouth. Rubiales, with a well-established reputation for doing what he likes with women, in a sport and country seething with issues around entrenched sexism

and sex abuse, tried to gaslight the world by saying the kiss was consensual. It was a valiant attempt, and he probably has used this technique effectively many times. He gave a rousing speech to his powerful football leadership community about how he would absolutely *not* be resigning, and the room full of men erupted in applause. You can well imagine that the tried-and-true technique of calling Jenni Hermosa a liar who consented, then tried to blame him for the kiss, would work its gaslighting magic, but this time, it didn't. Sometimes gaslighting doesn't work. David Squires in his cartoon encases Rubiales's head in a nineteenth-century glass lantern as he comically tries to convince the world to fault Jenni, his victim, not him.[14] Rubiales is lying while telling the world that Jenni Hermosa is a liar. Textbook.

Luckily for the 1944 wife in the movie *Gaslight*, it being a Hollywood movie and all, a policeman takes an interest in the unfolding manipulation. It turns out that the wife is merely useful to the husband, and he exploits her for his own means. Remember those who gaslight have an agenda. Their targets are merely pawns. A trademark of those who gaslight is to have no empathy for the target. In the movie, it turns out that *the husband* is the one who is untrustworthy and who steals, not his destabilized wife. Another trademark of those who gaslight is that they accuse their victim of possessing their own negative traits. They lie and accuse their targets of lying. They have dysregulated brains (as we will examine in detail) and accuse their targets of being dysregulated, and so on.

In the movie, it is then discovered that the husband had murdered his wife's aunt. Although he killed her, he failed to locate her jewels. Those who gaslight others are not fazed by those who suffer, or even die, in the wake of their destructive impulses. They do not feel guilt or experience regret. Another textbook aspect of gaslighting, the husband covers up his true identity with a fake one. He says he's pianist Gregory Anton—when, in fact, he's the murderer Sergis Bauer. This is the classic textbook split personality Dr. Jekyll and Mr. Hyde, which we will discuss in greater detail in chapter 6. In institutions, gaslighters use their position to cover up the harm they do, just like Dr. Jekyll exudes the qualities of a respectable, caring physician, an effective cover for his violent impulses.

The abuser must appear as "good" to cover up his plan to do "evil." Gaslighting in a marriage is disturbing. Gaslighting in an institution such as a corporation, church, school, sports club, courthouse, retirement home, government agency, news station, or political party is deeply disturbing. The target in the marriage may lose her mind and come to believe that she *is*, in fact, corrupt and insane. Her relationship to reality becomes unhinged. As has been demonstrated throughout history, the target in institutional gaslighting leads to whole segments of society losing their minds and coming to believe whatever alternative facts and fabricated events they are being fed by those in positions with power, credibility, and social status. This collective madness can occur in cults, even in nations. We are well-informed by history how incredibly dangerous and destructive this manipulation can be.

GASLIGHTING IN THE LAW

In 2022, the term "gaslighting" was published in a United Kingdom High Court judgment for the first time in what is being called a "milestone" hearing in a domestic abuse case. Describing the case, Maya Oppenheim defines the act as follows: "Gaslighting refers to manipulating someone by making them question their very grasp on reality by forcing them to doubt their memories and pushing a false narrative of events." Although this is being legally identified as manipulation in a marriage, it applies equally well to the workplace. Those who tell the lies of bullying and gaslighting at work make targets question their grasp on reality, force them to doubt their memories, and push a false narrative of events. This false narrative is often believed by higher-ups who have been carefully groomed over time to believe in the power, credibility, and social standing of the one bullying.

In this legal ruling, gaslighting is viewed as part of a campaign of psychological abuse that uses coercion and control to destabilize someone. Those who study workplace bullying frequently deplore the coercion and control leadership model entrenched in corporate culture. What's textbook in this case is that the husband—a mental-health worker—used the power, credibility, and social standing of his profession to tell his wife and others that she was "bipolar." Ironically, the gaslighting brain is the one that more closely resembles a dual personality disorder that shifts in mood from being the caring husband one moment to being the manipulative villain the next. Gaslighting works on reversals as we examine throughout our analysis of it, and this is a textbook reversal. The husband uses his position to appear to be a caring professional when he is harming his wife as an abusive husband.

As reported by Oppenheim, the wife's lawyer, Charlotte Proudman—a leading human rights barrister—said that the judge's use of the term gaslighting gives it "legitimacy and credibility." In her experience, she notes that "abusers have long been warping victims' 'realities' yet there has been no legal term to shed light on the problem." One of the most effective tools to identify and dismantle the siren song of gaslighting, whether in a marriage or a workplace, is language, as we discuss in detail further along. Gaslighting depends on language and cognition to manipulate; therefore, one of the most effective antidotes is attention to language and cognition.

Controlling the narrative, silencing questions and concerns, forcing the community to adhere to the institution's fabricated facts all prop up the harms of institutional complicity. Lawyer and workplace bullying expert Paul Pelletier finds that the lies of workplace bullying flourish when the leadership operates from a coercion and control model as identified in the manipulative and dysfunctional marriage under scrutiny in the UK High Court. Coercion and control as a leadership model sets the stage for the drama of bullying, gaslighting, and institutional complicity to unfold.[15] Psychiatrist Dr. Helen Riess discusses leaders who use "fear and intimidation" to exert their authority. As we see throughout *The Gaslit Brain*, she uses the concept of infection or contagion to describe its impact: "This type of failed leadership tends to spread across organizations like the plague."[16] As we will see, bullying and gaslighting, both techniques to exert coercion and control, are entwined and sicken workplaces in tandem.

GASLIGHTING, RETALIATION, AND INTIMIDATION
A year later, in 2023, a lawsuit was launched in New Jersey. Once again, "gaslighting" is one of the alleged behaviors that drove Joseph Nyre, for-

mer president of prestigious Seton Hall University, from his institution. As reported by Ted Sherman, Nyre alleges violations of the law against the former chairman of the board at Seton Hall, including the sexual harassment of Nyre's wife. As a whistle-blower, Nyre alleges he was targeted with "gaslighting, retaliation, and intimidation," which led him to resign. Attacks on those who speak up are textbook. Institutional complicity in silencing those who speak up uses textbook methods and gaslighting is long overdue to be understood as one of the weapons in their arsenal. Dr. Dorothy Suskind, an expert in workplace bullying, refers to the specific abuse meted out to those with "high ethical standards" as a "degradation ceremony."[17]

Although gaslighting is being recognized in the law, it is not fully understood from a psychological and brain science perspective, and it is rarely applied to workplace culture. In 2023, psychologists Priyam Kukreja and Jatin Pandey developed a "Gaslighting at Work Questionnaire" (GWQ) that revealed two key components in workplace gaslighting: "trivialization and affliction." According to psychologist Mark Travers, trivialization may take the form of "making promises that don't match their actions, twisting or misrepresenting things you've said and making degrading comments about you and pretending you have nothing to be offended about." Victims start down the path of wondering if they're being "too sensitive." Affliction may take the form of excessive control, making you self-critical, creating dependence, or being "very sweet to you and then flipp[ing] a switch, becoming hostile shortly after."[18] Again, this kind of maltreatment causes self-doubt. Kukreja and Pandey conclude:

The GWQ scale offers new opportunities to understand and measure gaslighting behaviors of a supervisor toward their subordinates in the work context. It adds to the existing literature on harmful leader behaviors, workplace abuse, and mistreatment by highlighting the importance of identifying and measuring gaslighting at work.[19]

Introducing a questionnaire on gaslighting is an effective way to draw attention to how this form of manipulation occurs. Equally important, it provides vocabulary for workplaces to understand and discuss this specific form of abuse. In recent years, *Forbes* began publishing articles on gaslighting in the workplace indicating that it is on the leadership radar.

Jonathan Westover advises on "How to Avoid and Counteract Gaslighting as a Leader," and his approach is insightful, but only if you are dealing with healthy brains. In terms of avoiding becoming a leader who gaslights, you could apply his approach:

- Practice regular self-reflection and foster intellectual humility.
- Actively listen to the perceptions of your team members.
- Practice vulnerability and own up to your mistakes.
- Develop and sustain authentic relationships of mutual accountability and trust.[20]

The problem is, as we will examine in detail in the following chapters, those who tell the lies of bullying and gaslighting do *not* experience self-reflection. They do *not* feel humility as an emotion, just like they don't feel guilt or remorse. They are disinterested in others' perceptions as their brain tends to objectify targets especially. They oftentimes experience a roller coaster of shame and grandiosity, and they deny vulnerability or the possibility that they have made a mistake. In short, they cannot have authentic relationships. They follow an abusive script that turns them—if not stopped—into a caricature who repeats bullying lies and gaslighting manipulations over and over. They avoid accountability and see trust as a game that they want to win. Using psychological research to understand how the brains of manipulators work hopefully will give us a better chance to prevent their negative impacts in the workplace.

Six Gaslighting Behaviors

Manzar Bashir describes six textbook gaslighting behaviors: "trivializing your feelings, shifting blame, projecting their behavior, insulting and belittling, creating confusion and contradictions," but he articulates one in particular—withholding information—that is very tricky to identify and yet can have devastating impacts. "Gaslighters often use a tactic of withholding information and keeping you in the dark about crucial matters. By selectively sharing or concealing facts, they manipulate your perception of reality and limit your ability to make informed decisions."[21] It's insightful: he shows that gaslighting, along with a great deal of psychological manipulation, is harmful in its omissions and passivity. In other words, it's the opposite of how we measure the harms of physical abuse. When you hurt someone's body, we assess severity by how much active damage was done. But when the brain is being manipulated, we need to find ways to figure out how much *lack of action* causes damage. Physical assaults are designed to weaken and harm the body; assaults via gaslighting are designed to weaken and destabilize the brain and the mind. Injuries to the body are far more likely to get immediate treatment, whereas neurological damage to brain architecture, disruption of the mind's ability to function healthily, are too often ignored.

Psychologists and brain scientists have developed extensive evidence about the way in which gaslighting brains operate, notably different from brains that do not manipulate. It's time we learned this key information to protect ourselves from gaslighting in institutional contexts. Knowledge of psychopathic brains and the way they work can better protect us from the gaslighters' domineering manipulation and their cruel capacity to exploit us for their own purposes.

BOOK STRUCTURE

The book is organized into three parts. Part 1 of *The Gaslit Brain* draws on the stories of recent targets of bullying and gaslighting in the workplace. I unpack my personal experience with the lies of bullying, gaslighting, and institutional complicity within the context of other victims who, like me, refused to conform to a corrupt workplace and now speak up publicly about how destructive and risky it is to allow a false narrative to dominate the truth. We hear from Megan Carle, a top executive at Nike; Jonathan Wilson, a detective superintendent in Scotland Yard; and Julie Macfarlane, a law professor at the University of Windsor. Stories are one of the best ways to educate as the brain remembers them effectively. As neuroeconomist Daniel Kahneman explains, "When learners are surprised with a statistical fact, they do not learn. But if you surprise them by an individual case, they can learn the key lesson or how to take the generalization from the individual scenario."[22] My individual case, put alongside the cases of Carle, Wilson, and Macfarlane, is surprising, and hopefully all encourage leaders, managers, and HR to take useful generalizations from our individual scenarios.

In part 2, we learn the psychology behind why we are blind to betrayal and who seeks to betray us. For educated, experienced, intelligent leaders in their field such as Carle, Wilson, and Macfarlane, it seems unbelievable that they, of all people, could have fallen for the manipulations of bullying and gaslighting. Why do we put on blinders to betrayal at work? What is going on? Equally surprising is to learn about those who betray and abuse. How and why do they lie so effectively that we fall for it? The science that explains the neuropsychology of abuse perpetrators is key information to help us stay safe and sane. It's a good way to take off workplace blinders and keep them off permanently.

Those who deal in the lies of bullying and gaslighting are so skilled at manipulation that they can even lead psychiatric experts to doubt themselves and subscribe to the manipulator's version of events. There's no shame in being tricked by them, but there are ways to protect yourself, your team, and your institution. There are ways to have leaders, managers, and HR educated and empowered to identify perpetrators early and effectively manage the mayhem and risk they bring to the institution.

Psychological research provides ample evidence of the many mistakes our brains can make when we are assessing and deciding what's real and what's false. Considering how high stakes the decisions are when it comes to bullying, abuse, corruption, gaslighting, and institutional complicity, we will be far better positioned to stay safe and sane when we learn how to manage our brains, avoid typical errors, and capitalize on our mental strengths.

Part 3 of *The Gaslit Brain* offers leaders, managers, and HR a way to apply brain science insights to recognize and resist the lies of bullying, gaslighting, and institutional complicity. We look at six proven ways, well-established in research, to learn how our brains construct "reality" and why they are susceptible to manipulation. Recognizing the self-serving lies of bullying and gaslighting begins with understanding how our brains differentiate "reality" from illusions. Knowing how your brain decides to believe one person and not another clearly will be helpful as you navigate the workplace and mitigate risks in your institution. Creating a culture and shared vocabulary around knowing how and why our brains fall prey to manipulation allows leaders, managers, and HR to prevent lies from infecting the institution.

SIX PROVEN WAYS TO IDENTIFY LIES AT WORK

The first proven way strengthens exteroception, which is how our brains make sense of incoming data from the environment. We discover why it's incredibly important to keep these fundamental pathways in the brain fit and strong. Neuroscientists have designed brain fitness for us, and for a healthy workplace it is key. The stronger and healthier the brain's ability to decode data, the stronger and healthier are its higher-level cognitive functions. You'd never go into the boxing ring without physically training to put up a good fight. Likewise, leaders, managers, and HR who want to battle efficiently against bullying and gaslighting in their institution need mental training.

The second proven way examines interoception, which is how we interpret information coming from our internal bodily systems. Applying this knowledge to the way we construct emotions from this information is a vital way to discern the manipulations of those doing harm. Those who tell the self-serving lies of bullying and gaslighting use our emotions against us as part of their repertoire for doing harm. Leaders, managers, and HR can ensure that their workplace is well-educated on how we construct emotions, how we articulate them, and how much a nuanced and doubled-up vocabulary can help protect us from perpetrators' attempts to confuse us. Gaslighting is all about making us replace our own relationship to "reality" with their lies. We learn how to resist this manipulation.

The third proven way unpacks why our threat detection system—our neuroception—fails us all too often when it comes to the self-serving lies of bullying and gaslighting. We build on previous insights into the dual presentation of abusers that leads us to drop our guard right when we should be on high alert. Becoming more skilled at reading our environment; informed about how our nervous system fuels our feelings of safety, supports an understanding of how vital connection and community are to the way we handle stress that inevitably comes when we're being manipulated. The goal for safe, healthy workplaces is to prioritize the balance that comes with homeostasis.

The fourth proven way trains us to resist our brain's tendency to habituate to almost every workplace environment regardless of how safe or sane. We learn in this chapter how to become a "dishabituation entrepreneur." Instead of normalizing our environment and the behaviors of our colleagues, we learn strategies to become far more perceptive. We learn to double up our vision so that we don't only fall for what's right in front of us but also consider what lies in the background that might pose risks.

The fifth proven way teaches about how our brain tends to take intuitive shortcuts that make us highly susceptible to manipulators. We need to apply the discipline of "thinking slow" to stay sane and safe. We call this technique proprioception as a way to stress the importance of balance in our brains and bodies when it comes to establishing a healthy, accurate understanding of what is "reality."

The sixth proven way looks at how our brains are double in their construction. The left and right hemisphere have different ways of constructing "reality," and knowing how they work together and separately is key. The left has an opportunist approach, whereas the right is more altruistic. Once again, we see the critical importance of balance as we are moving toward workplaces that tend to be dominated by the left hemisphere with its narrow focus and essential self-interest. We need to create workplaces that never ignore the right hemisphere and its bigger picture that cares about connection, relationship, and community.

KNOWLEDGE IS POWER

Most of us who are targeted for bullying at work are caught off guard. Because we are not trained to anticipate manipulation, we're easily victimized. I wish I knew then what I know now. The more aware we are of how abusive brains operate and how our brains are completely thrown off our game by them, the better able we are to prevent workplace bullying and gaslighting. The more leaders, managers, and HR are informed, the less likely they'll be drawn into institutional complicity.

Those who tell the self-serving lies of bullying and gaslighting—with ease—are part of a formidable trio referred to in psychology as the Dark Triad: narcissists, Machiavellians, and psychopaths.[23] Throughout *The Gaslit Brain*, we'll refer to them as the Dark Triad. If you're interested in their differing brains, see *The Bullied Brain*.[24] How can we identify these manipulative people more quickly and refuse to believe them? What if there were a way to protect ourselves and more specifically, our sanity from lies? What if there were proven strategies we could use to keep our minds safe from shattering? These are the questions that drove the researching and writing of *The Gaslit Brain*. I needed to answer them because I was being gaslit at work.

Notes

1. Neil Garrett, Stephanie Lazzaro, Dan Ariely, and Tali Sharot, "The Brain Adapts to Dishonesty," *Nature Neuroscience* (December 19, 2016): 1727–32, https://pmc.ncbi .nlm.nih.gov/articles/PMC5238933/.

2. Caroll Boydell, "Best Practices in Whistleblower Legislation: An Analysis of Federal and Provincial Legislation Relevant to Disclosures of Wrongdoing in British Columbia," *BC Freedom of Information and Privacy Association*, 2018, https://fipa.bc.ca/ wp-content/uploads/2018/11/FIPA_Whistleblower_Paper_web.pdf.

3. Dorothy Suskind, "How Whistleblowers Can Speak Up for Justice," *Psychology Today*, August 6, 2020, https://www.psychologytoday.com/ca/blog/bully-wise/202008/ how-whistleblowers-can-speak-up-for-justice.

4. Julie Macfarlane describes this phenomenon: "We did not share [our abuse experiences] even with our best friends, fearing the shame of being 'the only one' who experienced such behaviors." Abuse led to "suffocating shame" that left victims "isolated in our shame and fear." Macfarlane, *Going Public* (Toronto: Between the Lines, 2020), 5–6.

5. Paul Babiak and Robert Hare, *Snakes in Suits: When Psychopaths Go to Work* (New York: Harper, 2006), 48–49.

6. *Merriam-Webster Dictionary*, "Word of the Year 2022: 'Gaslighting,' plus 'Sentient,' 'Omicron,' 'Queen Consort,' and Other Top Lookups of 2022." https://www.merriam -webster.com/wordplay/word-of-the-year-2022.

7. Babiak and Hare, *Snakes in Suits*, 129.

8. For all reference to media, please see references.

9. Babiak and Hare, *Snakes in* Suits, 131.

10. Babiak and Hare, *Snakes in Suits*, 51.

11. For all reference to media, please see references.

12. India's normalization of violent rape has featured in the 2024 international news cycle multiple times. In September 2024, Subrata Choudhury reports on significant protests that have occurred in response to the rape and murder of a female doctor.

13. For all reference to media, please see references.

14. For all reference to media, please see references.

15. Paul Pelletier, *The Workplace Bullying Handbook: How to Identify, Prevent, and Stop Workplace Bullying* (Vancouver: Paul Pelletier Consulting, 2018).

16. Helen Riess, *The Empathy Effect: Seven Neuroscience-Based Keys for Transforming the Way We Live, Love, Work, and Connect Across Differences* (Boulder, CO: Sounds True, 2018), 58.

17. Dorothy Suskind, "Workplace Bullying: A Three-Part Degradation Ceremony," *Psychology Today*, April 2, 2021. https://www.psychologytoday.com/ca/blog/bully-wise/202104/workplace-bullying-a-three-part-degradation-ceremony.

18. Mark Travers, "Obvious Signs of 'Workplace Gaslighting,' from a Psychologist," *Forbes*, May 7, 2024. https://www.forbes.com/sites/traversmark/2024/05/07/2-obvious-signs-of-workplace-gaslighting-from-a-psychologist/.

19. Priyam Kukreja and Jatin Pandey, "Workplace Gaslighting: Conceptualization, Development, and Validation of a Scale," *Frontiers in Psychology* 14 (March 29, 2023). https://www.frontiersin.org/journals/psychology/articles/10.3389/fpsyg.2023.1099485/full.

20. Jonathan Westover, "How to Avoid and Counteract Gaslighting as a Leader," *Forbes*, October 28, 2021. https://www.forbes.com/sites/forbescoachescouncil/2021/10/28/how-to-avoid-and-counteract-gaslighting-as-a-leader/.

21. Manzar Bashir, "Six Signs That You Are Being Gaslighted and How to Break Free," *Forbes*, October 25, 2023. https://www.forbes.com/councils/forbescoachescouncil/2023/10/25/six-signs-that-you-are-being-gaslighted-and-how-to-break-free/.

22. Daniel Kahneman, *Thinking, Fast and Slow* (Toronto: Anchor Canada, 2013), 173–74.

23. Babiak and Hare, *Snakes in Suits*, 124–25.

24. Jennifer Fraser, *The Bullied Brain: Heal Your Scars and Restore Your Health* (Amherst, NY: Prometheus, 2022), 24–27.

PART ONE

GASLIGHTING SHATTERS BRAINS

CHAPTER ONE

My Story

WITHIN THE FIRST COUPLE OF YEARS AS TEACHER AT A VERY WEALTHY, established, private, international boarding school, I reported abuse being done by a colleague. He was a talented drama teacher who put on spectacular yearly musicals in a professional theater. He was also abusive—psychologically, sexually, and physically. Faculty, parents, and students were frequently in distress, with some reporting to the director and chaplain. I simply added my voice to this concerned group, not at all anticipating that I would be treated as if I were the one doing wrong.

I did not know the word *gaslighting*. It did not occur to me that the director would outright bully me and retaliate against me for bringing up serious concerns about student safety. The penny dropped when the director patted a big file on her desk and told me that it was about me. I might not have known that this was textbook gaslighting—using a reversal to confuse someone—but I knew it was wrong. I observed and heard reports about an abusive colleague. The director told me that *I* was the problem (for reporting my colleague). Gaslighting is designed to confuse your perceptions and mess up your sense of reality. It's highly effective.

I took my concerns to the institution's leader. I told him a simple anonymous survey would give him the information he needed to deal with the abuse crisis. Rather surprisingly, he yelled at me, "Do not tell me how to do my job!" I gave up. The teacher continued abusing. When faculty, parents, and students told me their concerns, I told them that I was powerless and that they needed to report to the director.

The school's chaplain was positioned as a moral leader but also as a kind of counselor, even an HR representative (because the school, with hundreds of employees, did not have an HR rep, let alone an HR department). He began commiserating with me about our abusive colleague. He acted as a counselor with students *and* faculty, enabling him to know privileged, vulnerable information. I don't know if he had any professional training or certification to take this role. For some reason, although in the leadership circle, he seemed as powerless as I was to protect students, but he assured me that he was very concerned and was keeping an eye on the abusive teacher. It never occurred to me that he had been dispatched to get information from me, assuage my worries, and act as a friend. He was betraying me, but I had no idea. As we will examine in greater detail in chapter 6, the chaplain's behavior is a textbook "psychopath-victim" bond based on "a convenient fabrication."

> *The persona of the psychopath—the "personality" the person is bonding with—does not really exist. It was built on lies, carefully woven together to entrap you. It is a mask, one of many, custom-made by the psychopath to fit your particular psychological needs and expectations.*[1]

The target—me in this case—thinks she's engaged in an actual relationship with a caring colleague, one who shares their serious concern about abuse, but she is being manipulated. I don't know if the chaplain is a psychopath, but he behaved like one. And the important takeaway from his conduct, and the abusive teacher, the leader, and the director, is to notice how psychopathology seems contagious in institutions. When workplaces enable abusive practices, they become like a virus that infects more and more people. We see this in history when enormous numbers of the populace behave in psychopathic ways once those in power establish it as necessary, normal, and accepted.

In part 2, we will look at how this happens and why we're vulnerable to this specific kind of betrayal. Within five years, the drama teacher would be fired, under the private school euphemism "retired early." By this time, a much bigger scandal was brewing that would rip the blinders from my eyes and put me on the whistle-blower's path.

POINT OF NO RETURN

When a director and leader cover up and enable abuse, when they comfortably use a figure such as the chaplain to further manipulate those who are appalled by the abuse and speak up, it's hardly surprising that another abuse scandal with a different set of colleagues jolted me out of my powerless state. I was going about my work with blinders on, collecting my salary, belonging to my cherished community, when once again abuse was reported directly to me. It was a whole other department, and this time it wasn't just one colleague. It was four. Two are discussed here; the others are another story.

The reason I became intrigued—in why some people's brains succumb to gaslighting, but others don't—was because this time so many of the targets spoke up. I watched with particular interest one target see right through director, leader, and even the chaplain's facade and outright reject their manipulations. Although I had heard directly about the abuse from multiple targets, he *was* one of the targets. He had been subjected to repeat bullying by two teachers—physical and psychological abuse, entwined with a kind of twisted sexual harassment—for two years. It began mildly in textbook fashion and became progressively more and more intense. It began with grooming. The younger teacher would lure him in with a kind, mentoring approach that slowly morphed into threatening, vicious attacks.

The grooming teacher recognized this student's talent and used it to make it seem normal that he would receive one-on-one time and mentoring. As a junior, the student was brought along to the year's culminating seniors' competition, which is a way to showcase the opportunities a teacher can provide to those who bow down. The grooming teacher, along with his colleague, said this target would be the "X factor" the following year because of his talent. Once he was lured in, once the honeymoon was over, his talent was used to publicly shame him over and over in front of his peers. Although his talent would be acknowledged, he'd be condemned for not using it because he "wasn't trying." He was repeatedly lambasted with public shaming, verbal abuse, and physical assaults. He and his team were repeatedly put down with slurs: "fucking retards," "fucking embarrassments," and "fucking pathetic."

The physical assaults were intensified by sexual harassment, which was layered into the repeat onslaught of humiliation. The team were all young men, and the teachers were also male, but this student was a special target. All work would be stopped by the teachers, the team would gather into an uneasy audience. The young teacher would yell rhetorical questions in his face about how he was so talented but wasn't trying. "Do you even like work?" The teacher questioned his commitment to the institution over and over. He asked him what he was worth. The other teacher would watch, and the team would have to watch. When the student couldn't take it anymore and tried to back away, the teacher who was yelling in his face, would grab him by the shirt or the arm and hold him for more. One member of the team reported that it was "vicious." Another reported that the team wanted to stop what was happening but couldn't because they didn't have power. The teachers did. These assaults happened hundreds of times.

SEXUAL POWER AND DOMINATION

The twisted sexual harassing began one day when the younger teacher—who had been doing the grooming—abruptly became violently angry. We noted in the introduction this textbook gaslighting behavior: going from kind and fun to demeaning and enraged. Prior to this moment was the honeymoon phase, the love bombing, the mentoring, and spending special one-on-one time. That all came to an ugly halt when the teacher yelled at the targeted student and a peer who were engaged and interacting in a joking manner: "Stop fucking touching each other." It was a shock—so shocking that no one said or did anything. It was the textbook jolt, the feeling of being electrocuted and paralyzed.

Bullying survivor, Nike executive, and author Megan Carle describes this kind of bullying as the "in-your-face-bully" who doesn't hesitate to drop "an F-bomb." This kind of bully depends on "explosive" attacks, "belittling," and "obvious aggression and volatility."[2] It is depressing how textbook bullying is, coupled with our endless enabling of it.

As is also textbook, this kind of homoerotic/homophobic behavior became more and more frequent. The teachers would call the all-male team "fucking pussies" and tell them to "grow some balls." It was misogynistic, perhaps with the goal of male bonding, creating a sense of superiority to women, a disgust with feminine weakness and anatomy to make the team strive to be invincible. But surely this is not a helpful way to improve the bottom line, make the team more competitive, earn more wins. It begs the question: Why was it happening?

Sex abuse survivor and lawyer Julie Macfarlane explains that "sexual violence is not about sex but about the use of power and domination."[3] These teachers were clearly desperate to establish power and domination over vulnerable targets; and although they claimed (on email) at one point that they didn't know it was harmful, they certainly were careful to keep it hidden. Considering that male teachers were targeting a team of young, vulnerable males—ones that lacked the power, credibility, and social standing of the teachers—you can't help but wonder whether the use of power and domination was in response to feeling threatened. Bullying is well-known to occur as a response to threat. Did the younger—perhaps more talented, more ethical, more likely to "win"—males threaten the older ones?

Or was the overarching agenda to use homophobic slurs and misogyny to make the team turn to the teachers and sexually engage with them? If being female and being associated with the female body were seen as insults, a disgusting, pathetic thing to be called as a team, was the idea to establish literal male bonding, students dependent on teachers, turning to them for guidance as well as sexual encounters? These are typical strategies in relationships that engage with those in the Dark Triad.

One teacher came right up to the targeted student's face in public and yelled that he was "fucking soft." This was a moment when the violent, vicious assaults were linked with the homophobic, misogynistic insults. Did the teacher want him to show just how "hard" he could be? What was he looking for in his dysregulated, abusive approach? How does this homophobic slur improve someone's performance?

Flipping back into the honeymoon phase, the teachers gifted the team with T-shirts but used the opportunity to layer in sexual harassment. The targeted student's T-shirt displayed the first part of his name blended with "-licious" as in "delicious." Delicious? To whom? How is this remotely normal or appropriate? A person's name is profoundly linked to their identity and how they are known in social-emotional and professional relationships. Mispronouncing a name, if done repeatedly, is well-recognized as an insult. But manipulating someone's name into a titillating, tantalizing name is a whole other level of harassment.

After intense competitions, the younger teacher would insist on one-on-one debriefs, the content of which the targeted student has fully blocked from memory. This teacher would send texts all the time and would be angry if the student's answers weren't expansive enough. He'd even send texts outside school hours. All these instances when they occurred could be dismissed, might seem part of an intense program, might seem normal somehow, not such a big deal. Not to me, though.

Because I had been exposed to the gaslighting approach to abuse with the initial colleague in the theater department, when I found out about this equally serious and harmful situation involving four other colleagues either yelling or muttering obscenities; publicly shaming; repeatedly assaulting a target who tried to get away; crossing all kinds of professional boundaries; creating a culture of fear, humiliation, and favoritism; using homophobia, homoeroticism, and misogyny, I bypassed the ineffective director and leader who were covering up. I wrote a letter directly to the secretary of the board (henceforth, I will refer to him simply as "the board"). He contacted the chair of the board, who then phoned me. I said in my letter that after I witnessed the way the director and leader handled the abusive behavior of my colleague in the theater department, I didn't think they would stop the abuse being reported from a different department. I said I would resign if it wasn't stopped. The chair told me on the phone that the drama teacher's abuse had been "taken care of." That teacher was fired a few months later.

Keep Your Enemies Close

The board asked me to gather information from parents for him. It did not occur to me that I was being used. I had no idea that by speaking up I was being positioned as an "enemy" to my institution. I thought I was being asked essentially to canvass those involved, survey their experiences. I was used throughout the crisis repeatedly in this way: asked to gather information by board and leader without knowing that a different story was being told behind my back.

I wrote parents and transparently told them about the board's request. I sent all their responses to him on email. The responses not only confirmed serious abuse but also implicated the director and the leader. Both had repeatedly heard reports of these teachers' abuses and had engaged in processes to address them for at least a year. Neither had effectively stopped the abuse or protected students or informed parents. They kept what was happening hidden within the institution. I also learned from these parents that the chaplain had also been informed and had intervened—as was his supposed expertise—in sorting out the crisis.

Believe it or not, I still did not clue in that the chaplain was part of the gaslighting. I did not understand that he was a double agent whose job was to get information and hand it over to the director and leader and board. He told me he was worried that I felt he had "betrayed" me, and I assured him that I didn't feel that way, that I knew his position was complex and that he was trying to be supportive. I cannot believe I was ever that naive. The board assured me that the leader would act immediately and in proper ways to address this latest abuse crisis in the workplace affecting children. I supported and tried to work once *again* with the leader.

I had a surreal feeling that all was not right, but once again I kept my blinders on to betrayal (as we will examine in greater detail in chapter 5). What worried me was that the initial abuser was fired like the chair of the board said, but as noted, it was announced publicly that he "retired early." It was once again a cover-up. It was gaslighting. It's like punching someone in the face, then giving them roses. Everyone's brain goes offline. You cannot make sense of these contradictory acts entwined together, forming a pattern, saying one thing but doing another. These leadership gestures are like apologies that hook you back in, make you feel that things are not so bad, improvement is happening, ethics are back in play, safety is respected, the vulnerable will receive protection. It was all a facade.

The board's stopping one abusive employee but faced with others was like the spouse who beats you up, then shows you he can change. He sees your pain and suffering and shows you it's over. He's different. He will do the right thing. What happens all too often is the opposite. The abuser intensifies his attacks, hurts you more. That is exactly what happened at my workplace. The firing of the first abuser was just to buy time to figure out how to shut me down—and all the others reporting rampant abuse, including children.

Brain Strength and Clarity

The intense phase of believing in leadership while they were lying to my face lasted five months. In contrast, the target of the abuse—the student who saw right through the gaslighting—was clear right from the day he reported. He saw that what was happening was manipulative and certainly not to be trusted. Along with at least thirteen other targeted victims, he gave detailed testimony about the abuse. He provided an interview to the leader. He then agreed to do an interview with a lawyer the leader hired with the support of the board. Unlike me, who wanted to help, he did what the leader asked of him but with a jaded, demoralized approach. I hoped for the best, whereas he despaired. I could not bring myself to believe that my colleagues, these leaders, the board, would behave in such a sickening manner, whereas he had resigned himself to their corruption. The chaplain offered to speak with him one-on-one to help, to offer support. The targeted student wouldn't go near the chaplain. He could see the snake, but all I could see was the suit (as we will examine in more detail in chapter 6).

The target, this victim—who for two years had been repeatedly abused with psychological and physical abuse, entwined with a strange mix of homophobic/homoerotic sexual harassment—was my teenage son, Montgomery.

Regardless of what his teachers had done to him, right from the beginning, Montgomery saw through the leader's gaslighting. He knew that the chaplain was *not* to be trusted. He was sixteen. Although it was an utter shock to me at the time to unpack layer after layer of the institutional complicity, it turns out to be all textbook. Macfarlane explains:

Abusers can easily hide inside institutions in which they hold status and power; for example as a teacher or a professor, a religious leader, or

33

a coach. Their institutional status allows easy access to large numbers of subordinates, enabling them to identify potential victims, groom them by flattering them with "special" attention, and then abuse and harass them.[4]

What is chilling is that the abusers are hidden from the next crop of subordinates (students) and their parents, but they are *not* hiding from the institution. It is known what they do. As I learned with the dramatic arts teacher and the physical education (PE) teachers, the leader, director, chaplain, and board were all well aware. No hiding was necessary. They had all received reports of abuse, who knows how many times and from how many sources. In the years that I was alerting them to the abuse, they received many, many complaints. The reports were from faculty, parents, students, past students. This would be shocking and scandalous material, but it's not. It's typical. We must stop being surprised and instead become informed about ways to change this unhealthy dynamic.

The institutional cover-up was not the only textbook component of the abuse at my workplace. The abusive behaviors were also textbook. The drama teacher, and the PE teachers who abused Montgomery and his peers—fully enabled by the leader, director, the chaplain, and board—fit the textbook profile of enabled abusers that Macfarlane outlined.

Typically, such individuals cultivate a high-profile and positive reputation created and reinforced by the institutional culture. It is not uncommon for this to take on a cult-like aura, sustained by inflation of their personal importance, power, and even qualifications; for example, the high school drama teacher who convinced students he was their gateway to fame and fortune. A predator will demand complete loyalty and obedience from "followers" who will protect him at all costs. He will also use intimidation and sometimes threats to silence those who question or challenge his authority and charisma. Another common strategy is "grooming" those targeted for harassment, extending to family members and immediate peers, employing various self-promotion techniques.[5]

Macfarlane learned about how abuse works from a drama teacher in Ontario where she waged an all-out battle to halt his abuse of students. Her experience is identical to mine. All you need to do is change the location from West Coast to East Coast as we will discuss further in chapter 4.

Theater is one way to cultivate a high profile and generate a cult-like aura. The PE teachers who Montgomery and many other students reported leaned on the older teacher having coached for a year a student who became a professional athlete some twenty years back. With this talented athlete on the team, the teacher won a provincial championship at the top level. During more than twenty years of coaching, he never won a top-level championship again and yet the myth of what an excellent coach he was seemed to be set in stone. His random coaching of a superstar for a year was harnessed by the teacher (and supported by the marketing department) to generate a cultlike aura, an opportunity to inflate his personal importance. It was all a facade. He established loyalty from his followers and obedience from players and used intimidation to keep his targets humiliated and silenced. He groomed certain useful families whose children received unearned opportunities and benefits. As per usual, it was textbook, as textbook as the abusive dramatic arts teacher. The institution enabled all of it regardless of the many reports of abuse.

Anticipating Abuse Reports

The key to those who target others for the lies of bullying and gaslighting is to notice how thoughtful and calculating they are. Nothing is left to chance. They are skilled at anticipating that abuse reports will come in, and they head them off at the pass adeptly. Montgomery's teachers gaslit players and parents to believe that they were trying to toughen them up for competition. This cover-up of abuse is used frequently in sports. If you didn't like being abused, it was a sign that you were not tough enough. Do you see the circular logic? If you don't like being called a "fucking pussy" and speak up, it means you are a fucking pussy. You're feminine, girly, pathetic, a snowflake, entitled, a millennial, a wuss. If you don't like having degrading questions yelled in your face in scenes of public shaming, it means you're "too sensitive." This was what the regulator, the commissioner for teacher regulation, ruled when he received the abuse reports from multiple students. Do you see the reversal? The teachers who are trying to toughen up athletes, motivate them, drive them to excel are fine; the weakness, the feminine sensitivity of the teenage boys are the real issues. Blink your eyes, and the powerful, adult perpetrators just became the victims of weak, whiny children. The teachers anticipated abuse reports and did an excellent job of turning them back on the kids who spoke up about their maltreatment.

Like everything else, thinking ahead by abusive individuals is textbook. As we will examine in greater detail in chapter 8, I interviewed lawyer Mary Inman, who has decades of experience representing those who speak up and report wrongdoing. One of her clients is Tyler Schultz, the whistle-blower on Elizabeth Holmes, the founder of the wildly successful blood-testing tech startup Theranos that ultimately fell apart when Schultz exposed that it was built on a house of cards. What's important to see here is the way in which manipulators such as Holmes are so adept at thinking ahead that they lay the groundwork for concerned questions about the ethics of what they are doing.

Inman told me that she and Schultz were presenting together at a conference on truth telling and accountability, and she was struck by his description of just "how methodical" Holmes was in setting the traps early for the lies she would later need to rely on.[6] When we learn more in part 2 about the brains of those who lie with ease, as they gaslight their believers to their doom, the methodical, anticipatory, cognitive skills are not surprising. Schultz shared the example of hearing Holmes position Theranos as "disrupters of the lab world and blood testing world," saying "traditional laboratories" were going to "come after us." As Inman explained to me, Holmes "would set this all up so that when they *did* come after them for fraud, people were like 'well yeah, she told us that was going to happen.'" Inman comments from a legal mind-set: "They are so premeditated in terms of how they can lay the traps."

We make the mistake of thinking that people who fall for gaslighting are ignorant and gullible. This mistaken interpretation leads us to be susceptible. The truth is that those who gaslight are often very smart and very articulate. They are masters of cognition and language, skills at the heart of lying, manipulating, and gaslighting. When they set out to hurt people, their chosen weapon is words. Inman reports that Schultz "was marvelling at how good [Elizabeth Holmes] was. She was just brilliant because she bamboozled all of the oversight people and there were many." Another sign of her premeditated way of operating, Inman notes that she put "only white men" who had "no biotech experience" on her board. They were savvy people who are supposed to ask hard questions, Inman explains, but they "didn't." You can imagine they did not want to look ill-informed or inexperienced in a new biotech entrepreneurial venture.

Holmes was adept at creating the conditions in which tough questions wouldn't be asked, but Inman stresses that it is we, the audience, who are ultimately at fault for being gaslit. Inman shares that in representing Theranos's whistle-blower Schultz, she realized just how much a manipulator like Holmes "preyed upon what the world wanted." Inman notes that Holmes was skilled at "whipping up the excitement and the enthusiasm" that replaced the brain's more skeptical approach that wants to look more cautiously at what's being offered. Holmes was able to draw the crowd into her circus tent with grand statements. Inman describes Holmes's enterprise as if it were "some sort of American myth, accompanied by big gestures that distracted her audience from the more boring, mundane small print of what she was doing and offering." Inman depicts our falling for the likes of Holmes.

> The world wanted a woman, a Stanford dropout to finally come and take Silicon Valley by storm and be all over the cover of Forbes. We all wanted to believe; we all wanted the myth and so I guess that's what their brain is good at, they're kind of a carnival barker or can be, at least she was.

We will examine this kind of brain behavior in more detail in both parts 2 and 3. We will look at how we think of reality as this phenomenon outside of us when, in fact, our brains create reality. Even more surprising, what we *want* to be true greatly influences how we experience what we believe to be true. Those who manipulate play on this tendency of our brains to be swayed by our beliefs, convictions, hopes, and desires. What is unfolding can be shockingly different. Those who believed in Theranos lost millions. Elizabeth Holmes's jail sentence is for eleven years and three months.

REFUSING TO BELIEVE THOSE WHO GASLIGHT

I became interested in gaslighting because I was a victim of it in the workplace, but more importantly, I watched Montgomery, a sixteen-year-old—equally exposed to its manipulative force—resist it every step of the way. One of the questions I strive to answer in *The Gaslit Brain* is why he did not succumb to manipulation. My struggle to stay sane and safe was mirrored by my son who put full effort into resistance. While I fell prey to manipulation, he taught me lesson after lesson about refusing to submit, making clarity and sanity the only things worth fighting for. While I was tricked, he was willing to endure the societal backlash for refusing to comply. While my brain tried to cling to the community, he consciously gave up the safety net of belonging and carved out his own path and constructed his own resilient mind-set. He even gave up what he loved most to reject the lies that abuse was normal, teacher-perpetrators of abuse should be commended for their "professionalism," and student victims should be branded with the leadership reversal that *they* were liars when the leaders were the ones lying.

Montgomery had attended and excelled at the school since fourth grade. He was on the headmaster's honor roll; he had won a number of major awards, but he had never been disciplined for anything. Now the school's leaders positioned him publicly as a liar who had issued false statements about his teachers. His track record disappeared as if it had never existed. In chapters 2, 3, and 4 we will see this pattern again and again. The leader paid for a lawyer's report saying that the students who reported being abused were—in the words of an anonymous student—"telling nasty lies." Attacking those who report abuse as being "liars" is textbook gaslighting.[7] It's one of the most typical reversals and classic reprisals for reporting. Threats to destroy your reputation are quick to follow abuse reports, even when you're a child. As we focus on in part 2, those in the Dark Triad are known to "spread considerable *disinformation* about their rivals."[8] Now imagine how much disinformation they spread about those who speak up about the abuse they do or the abuse they cover up.

No motivation for lying was attached to this character assassination from leader to students at Montgomery's school. Although it is a deadly serious accusation, no evidence was provided. It's the sort of accusation that results in suspension at least; and more likely, expulsion. It's the kind of accusation that could impact university acceptances, even one's career. The students weren't suspended or expelled. The teachers weren't suspended or fired. Instead of any kind of decisive action, there was just the soft glow of gaslighting.

The community—at this point, more like a cult—was simply being asked to believe the version of reality issued from the leader and not ask any questions. The leader's office with its advantages of power, social status, and credibility appeared to be enough to silence obvious questions, let alone vocal dissent. Not one of my colleagues publicly asked for proof or questioned the report. Two years later, the entire ten pages would be published in national news that exposed the private school colluding with the government regulator.[9] They were a textbook example of gaslighting and corruption. They came straight out of what Rebecca Solnit calls "the abuser's playbook."

Solnit explains that "the agenda at all scales is to control not just practical matters, but fact, truth, history; who can speak and what can be said." This is the agenda of coercion and control. As a dependent employee, my voice was not valued. What I had to report was dismissed by my colleagues who chose to believe the institution's leadership and their version of facts, truth, and the history of what had happened. It did not matter that I had a great deal of evidence spanning five years. It did not matter that the leader himself asked me to collect this evidence and give it to him, which I did. They did not care that he had already been informed from multiple other sources, and a full abuse report had been written by a lawyer a year before. All was seen as irrelevant. The leader's position of power, credibility, and social standing meant that only his voice was valued and only what he said was seen as true. Sociology professor Dr. Paige Sweet refers to those who fall for gaslighting as comparable to those falling under the "spells of power." She says that by "taking gaslighting seriously, we can learn about the relation between macro-level inequalities and the 'micro' forms of silencing and disempowerment that people experience in their everyday lives."[10]

BETRAYAL VIOLATES

The micro forms of silencing and disempowerment were done to me by the school's complicit leadership and by my colleagues who were at risk because students and parents reported them as abusive. The macro-level inequalities were between the teachers—perpetrators of abuse—and the students who were their victims.

Montgomery went from being an honor roll student who was widely popular, constantly praised by teachers, and an exceptional athlete in multiple sports to a student who, according to the leader, tells "nasty lies" about his teachers in eleventh grade, along with many other students, apparently all of them liars. It was hard to imagine what motivated them or what benefit they received from telling lies about teachers. It was especially hard to fathom how they coordinated with one another to produce very similar abuse reports when many didn't know each other, and they spanned five years. It's striking how obviously false gaslighting is and yet at the same time so seductive. It makes ethical, sane, caring people lose the courage to speak up about its illusory qualities and instead become complicit through their silence and lack of action.

This was my first encounter as an adult with gaslighting. Although I can identify it now, at the time, it put my brain into a fog. The mind struggles to understand reversals and lies. These kinds of manipulations do not make sense; and while the brain pours precious resources into trying to answer the question posed by the lie, it cannot, and the impact is like being shattered. I don't mean that metaphorically. I mean literally. The brain and its functions suffer a series of traumatic blows to a variety of systems when it cannot answer the question. As we unpack throughout this psychological study, asking questions, identifying the overarching agenda behind gaslighting, resisting the well-trained impulse to obey, rather than resist, are all critical to protecting yourself against the trauma of manipulation.

SEEING THROUGH LIES

Powerless, I watched Montgomery be labeled—with the other students who reported abuse—a liar. This reputational blow didn't take him out at the knees as planned. Instead, I witnessed him stand straighter, taller, and with nothing but disdain for those who tried to smear his reputation to cover up their own negligence. Although I wanted to believe those in power, who had social status and positions that conferred credibility, Montgomery had the mental strength and courage to see the lies for what they were, right from the beginning. He and the other students had reported the abusive teachers. Once the testimonies piled up, he told my husband and me that he had set himself one goal, which was "not to let them break me." While the teachers used day in and day out physical and psychological abuse, along with twisted sexual harassment, Montgomery responded with an iron will. Students do not have the power to push back against teachers, but he waged an inner battle of self-protection to stay safe and sane.

The reason my brain did *not* shatter is because he showed me in real time how to sculpt a mind with independence and clarity. His psychological strength and resistant mind-set remained safe and sane despite gaslighting—at higher and higher, more powerful and more prestigious levels. We ultimately learned that the private school had an agenda that drove their gaslighting: covering up negligence. The government regulator should have not only stopped the abuse but held leaders accountable for failure in their legal duty to report and protect children from abuse according to stringent rules of the commissioner for teacher regulation.[11] When government bureaucrats do not regulate but gaslight, it's hard to stay clearheaded.[12] When I read the commissioner's corrupt reports for the first time, knowing how much damage the teachers and leaders had done to Montgomery and so many students—I was literally brought to my knees. I am not one to cry easily but discovering that the gaslighting wasn't just in a corrupt school but had reached government institutions hit hard.[13]

Not for Montgomery.

His only comment was that he wanted to put the whole town where we lived "into the rearview mirror."

Walking Away
During this time of threats and manipulations, Montgomery intentionally withdrew from the school community. He did not go to classes. He

did not participate in sports. He did not go to his graduation ceremony. Withdrawal is extremely risky for the brain as it knows that it cannot survive without belonging, but now it's clear that Montgomery was drawing on the brain's greatest power: reinvention. He was using his neuroplasticity to imagine a new community, one that was *not* constructed on abuse being dished out from positions of credibility, social status, and power but, rather, a community of equals, friends, and educators. He was not confused and seduced by gaslighting. The teachers and leaders' promises rang hollow for him, and he sought authenticity.

Montgomery's retreat from the school might have looked like giving up. In fact, he was shoring up his strength. His suffering of depression, anxiety, and panic attacks could be rightly characterized as suffering "mental illness," but his brain was facing the threatening truth rather than collapsing into the gaslighters' lies. He was manifesting unbelievable mental strength and courage, which was very painful, but it brought him critical thinking, empathic reasoning, and mental resilience. It is hard to look in the dark corners of an institution, but that is what people with moral integrity and courage do.

In the spring of that truly terrible year of gaslighting and betrayal, he and I traveled to the United States on spring break to look at some universities. We had already visited some different American colleges as we knew we had to get him out of the country. If the private school could corrupt the government regulator, they could continue to harm Montgomery's reputation elsewhere in the country. To say that Montgomery was traumatized would be an understatement, and getting out of town was a key component of his reinvention.

It was cold and drizzling. We were walking across the University of Oregon campus, which had been the first college to send Montgomery an early acceptance the previous fall. As we cut across the campus, he came to a full stop. I followed his gaze and read carved into the northern entrance of the Knight Library, "Ye shall know the truth." He didn't say anything, and we resumed our walk through the rain. As we passed the library, again Montgomery stopped and turned around slowly. Above the library's northwestern entrance, the end of the quote was carved—"and the truth will make you free."

All he said was, "I choose University of Oregon," and that was the last college we toured.

SCULPTING YOUR BRAIN

Montgomery is an excellent example of how our minds are scripted or wired in childhood, but each of us is given, throughout our lifespan, the opportunity to take this wiring and change it. When the brain is wired by trauma at the hands of powerful adults, it can form into a fused block. Still, each of us has the capacity to chip away, carve, and sculpt past wiring into the kind of wiring that *we* practice and choose. Especially in childhood, we are wired by others and by our lot in life, but we always remain the sculptor of our own mind. Montgomery spent many years chipping away at the abuse, gaslighting, and institutional complicity to which he had been exposed.

Santiago Ramón y Cajal, born in 1852, winner of the Nobel Prize for neuroscience in 1906 wrote, "Any man could, if he were so inclined, be the sculptor of his own brain." A little more than a century later, with the use of noninvasive technology, neuroscientist Michael Merzenich's decades of research confirmed Cajal's insight into our brain's ability to change. In 2016, Merzenich, the "father of neuroplasticity," earned the Kavli Prize for Neuroscience. Although neuroplasticity was recognized by Cajal a hundred years ago and confirmed by decades of research today, few fully recognize the power of their own mind to unwire and rewire. They do not realize that they can sculpt their brain by what they choose and practice.

Montgomery had the choice as a teenager to remain wired by a private school system, supported by lawyers and governmental institutions, that normalized and enabled abusive teachers, *or* to refuse the destructive lessons and rewire his brain. He chose the latter. He was given the choice to believe the gaslighting of the abusive teachers and the leaders who protected them, *or* to take control of the information, follow his own path, and create the meaning of his own life. Again, he chose the latter.

Although potentially wired to abuse others from his abusive past, Montgomery chooses *not* to abuse others over whom he has power, and he chooses *not* to lie. He knows the truth and knows that it opens the door to freedom. Remaining subjected to those who wired your mind and shaped your mind-set in your formative years is no kind of freedom. You can continue to fire up those beliefs, those neural networks, and wire them in, or take the harder path of unwiring and rewiring. Every single one of us has neuroplasticity and thus the capacity to sculpt our *own* mind-set. If you think about it, psychology and neuroscience have taught us, especially in the past thirty years with noninvasive technology, that we can be sculptors of our own minds and their supporting brain functions. The changes in our mind-set from how we sculpt are visible on brain scans. It's empowering and inspiring, especially if we want to identify and resist the lies of bullying, gaslighting, and institutional complicity.

NOTES

1. Paul Babiak and Robert Hare, *Snakes in Suits: When Psychopaths Go to Work* (New York: Harper, 2006), 78.

2. Megan Carle, *Walk Away to Win* (New York: McGraw-Hill, 2023), 118–20.

3. Julie Macfarlane, *Going Public: A Survivor's Journey from Grief to Action* (Toronto: Between the Lines, 2020), 26.

4. Macfarlane, *Going Public*, 112.

5. Macfarlane, *Going Public*, 112.

6. All citations from Mary Inman are from my interview with her unless otherwise specified.

7. Macfarlane, *Going Public*, 32–33 and 37–38.

8. Babiak and Hare, *Snakes in Suits*, 240.

9. Robert Cribb, "Teachers' Bullying Scarred Us, Say Student Athletes," *Toronto Star*, March 14, 2015, https://www.thestar.com/news/canada/teachers-bullying-scarred-us-say -student-athletes/article_446e01ba-543b-5a01-8280-e5003dcd1c4b.html.

10. Paige Sweet, "How Gaslighting Manipulates Reality: Gaslighting Isn't Just be-tween People in a Relationship—It Involves Social Power, Too," *Scientific American*, Octo-ber 1, 2022, https://www.scientificamerican.com/article/how-gaslighting-manipulates -reality/.

11. I found many manipulations in the commissioner's reports, but one glaring exam-ple offered all the evidence anyone needs to recognize that he was corrupt. His task in making a determination about the teachers and administrators at the school is to adhere to the Teacher's Act and to the eight standards established by his office for teacher competency and conduct. He did not base his decisions on either. He offered links in his reports for the quotes he used to decide whether to hold the teachers accountable. The links did not take me to the Teacher's Act or to the Teacher Regulation Branch standards. Instead, one took me to "worksafe" rules and regulations that govern relation-ships between adult colleagues. And another took me to a 1990s government study on bullying between children in elementary school. Neither of these sources had any place in his reports and certainly should not be the key documents to which he turned for his

decisions. When the regulator is gaslighting, you really have nowhere to turn. I took this information to the ombudsman's office, and after three years, they dismissed it.

12. In a 2024 *Medical News Today* article, "Examples and Signs of Gaslighting and How to Respond" by Jennifer Huizen, https://www.medicalnewstoday.com/articles/gaslighting, she explains that abusive relationships intensify over time, reaching a point where the victim is told you're "being too sensitive" to undermine his sense of perception and emotion. The commissioner for teacher regulation used this tried-and-true abusive tactic to gaslight Montgomery and the other students who reported the abuse. He literally used the same phrase: "too sensitive." It's a stretch because it required him to decide that the fourteen students who reported abuse were *all* "too sensitive." Perhaps this is why he wanted to keep his reports confidential even from the victims and their families. The long-term effects of gaslighting as documented in the article are "anxiety, depression, isolation, psychological trauma."

13. As reported on by Justine Hunter in 2014, the B.C. Liberals had a long history with cutting hundreds of millions out of the public-school sector, which was reaching its biggest battle. Furthering the agenda begun by Christy Clark as minister of education in 2002, then premier in 2014, her Liberals pushed public school teachers to strike. According to the CBC, the three-month strike ushered five thousand more students into expensive private schools such as Montgomery's. The Liberals saved further millions in public school costs beyond the hundreds of millions they already took by increasing class size and cutting specialized teachers. According to Hunter, the Liberals tried to cover up court documents that exposed them as acting in bad faith with the teachers' union, but it was too late for vulnerable students. This was the political background to the Liberal-appointed commissioner for teacher regulation who insisted I keep his corrupt reports on abuse confidential. The one thing that could not be in the public domain was the truth. In 2016 as Katie Hyslop reported, public school teachers finally won their battle in the Supreme Court of Canada to return much-needed funding to public schools gutted by the Liberals. They fought on behalf of themselves as public school teachers and on behalf of families who couldn't afford, and may not have wanted, the risk of putting their child in a private school invested more in reputation than safety. If it put teachers, administrators, private schools, and even the government at risk, there needed to be a strategy to deal with students, like those at our son's private school, who reported abuses. The strategy that appeared to work was to confuse the enemy—the child victims—about what they had experienced and what it meant.

CHAPTER TWO

The Nike Executive

WHILE MONTGOMERY AND HIS TEAMMATES WERE BEING ABUSED WITH basketball being used as the cover-up for textbook bullying, Megan Carle was being bullied in comparable ways as a leader in basketball for Nike. More precisely, Carle was the vice president and general manager of North America Basketball. While Montgomery was in the powerless role of student at his "workplace," Carle was in the immensely powerful role of Nike's VP of all North America, and yet they were bullied in similar ways.

Both Montgomery and Carle left their beloved worlds of basketball to survive. This painful exit gets turned around by Carle who uses as the title of her book *Walk Away to Win* and reassigns her exit as a gesture of health and empowerment. It's important not to minimize what they sacrificed as they both lived and breathed basketball but reached a point where the abuse they were enduring was putting their safety and sanity at risk. I have found Carle's book to contain the most evocative description of the teachers who harmed Montgomery and the other athletes.

Listen to these quotes from her "Bully's Manifesto" that starts her book. Hear the voice of the abuser speaking to the target(s).

I know you're smarter, more imaginative, and more courageous than me. And deep down, that's what fuels my quiet rage: I know I'm a Lie and you're the Truth.[1]

The Dark Triad want to win their internal game more than anything else and see others as pawns. They cannot bear those who have talent and integrity. This is a brilliant insight into the Dark Triad, who pour all their energy into being a puppet master who pulls the strings making some follow them in adoration while others are made to suffer. They will make many happy but only to torment the few. The Dark Triad are playing a game, getting a psychological boost from manipulation, using their playbook that is all about how to tell lies and get away with it. As Carle expresses it in the voice of the abuser, "Deceit is my face paint."[2] But at the end of day, the Dark Triad know they are liars, and their victims are telling the truth. They know they are weak, and their targets are strong. Most of all, they pride themselves on power, but they don't even have courage.

INSIDE THE BULLY'S BRAIN
As the experts show, the Dark Triad have cognitive empathy so they are painfully aware of exactly what they are doing and the deficits they must cover up. Carle strengthens her insight into what is happening in the bully's brain by once again speaking in his voice, recording his "Manifesto."

Seeing you succeed amplifies my feelings of failure. Seeing you happy reminds me of my own misery. So I blow up whatever bridges I can see you're about to cross.[3]

These lines struck me as an apt way to describe the initial shocking blowup of the one teacher who had positioned himself as mentor, bestower of favors, sender of many texts, offering privileges, praising, and spending one-on-one time shooting hoops with Montgomery. Namely, the textbook grooming or honeymoon phase. When Montgomery was interacting playfully with a peer, as noted, the teacher screamed at them: "Stop fucking touching each other." Now let's look at this unhinged behavior through Carle's lens.

The bully cannot bear the boys' happiness as it exacerbates his feelings of misery, just like—as recorded in multiple athletes' testimonies—any athletic success by targets was swiftly punished. Targets could not fathom why the teachers penalized them for their skills and dominance on the court. They reported shooting three pointers and being benched for it. Not just one player; multiple players in different years. They did not know that for the Dark Triad who want to win their own inner game, *not* the actual game involving a team, every time a kid like Montgomery succeeds, the bully's feelings of failure are intensified. One time, when Montgomery had two players boxing him in, he seamlessly slid the ball behind his back to pass it to a teammate, who sank the ball. Montgomery got pulled off the court, and the teacher told him, "I don't want to see any of your Globetrotter shit." This kind of punishment for playing well was typical.

As Carle shows, the way to corrupt and subvert success for the target leads the Dark Triad to "blow up whatever bridges" the target is "about to cross." For Montgomery, this was a carefully constructed system of blocking him from success at every turn. Same thing for Carle in a highly sophisticated, goal-oriented company such as Nike. The bully's playbook doesn't change. Why? Because the bully has a mental illness that is as textbook as a chronic illness. Both have symptoms that can lead an expert to a diagnosis. It's just that we rarely look at mental illness in perpetrators, talk about it, or treat it that way. We don't bring in the experts to diagnose it, let alone cure it. We cover it up.

Here's another example of blowing up the bridge before Montgomery or the other talented but targeted athletes could cross it. If one of the beneficiaries—with their constant playing time—earned an award, it would be celebrated publicly in front of the whole school. One high-stakes game, Montgomery was allowed off the bench because one of the beneficiaries was injured. They were playing the best team in the league, which ultimately won the championship at the end of the season. With Montgomery allowed to play, his team won that game. Could they have won the championship? No one will know because Montgomery was benched for most of the championship games while one of the beneficiaries was missing shot after shot and visibly crying on the court. The teachers would not take him off—regardless of his obvious humiliation. Even the opposing team were demanding that the refs take him off the court. For both teams, it was psychotic.

In the earlier tournament, where Montgomery was allowed to play, the organizers awarded him MVP. His teachers couldn't stop him this time from getting the award, but they made sure no one knew. They gave it to him privately; there was no ceremony in front of the school. How is a teenage athlete supposed to understand this behavior? Carle's lived experience combined with her notable intelligence and ability to articulate complex dynamics gives voice to this psychosis, so it makes sense. She still couldn't stop it from harming her, sabotaging her career, and infiltrating Nike's culture.

Carle's first shock as a target was when she took on her new position as VP and general manager of North America Basketball. When joining her new team for the very first time at a board meeting, her bully did not even introduce her. So subtle, manipulative, confusing, hard to explain, easy to dismiss as unintentional, a mistake, not meant to harm. See the brain working double time to try to turn this microaggression into part of a coherent story? A coherent story that foregrounds a trustworthy, mentally healthy professional with power, credibility, and social standing who makes it almost impossible to recognize—simultaneously—that a shadowy other figure is at play who might just be an abusive liar.

If Montgomery's teachers wanted to win the championship, it's common sense to put their star player on the court, the kid who earns MVP at a tournament where they beat the powerhouse team that goes on to win the championship at season's end. But after this acknowledgment from the outside of his talent, Montgomery was benched again game after game. Carle describes this dynamic once again using the bully's voice: "I believe your pain is my gain."[4] Why do bullies inflict pain on their targets? Because for them it's a "win." That's not how healthy brains understand winning, which is why it's so confusing and hard to understand.

Blocking an athlete from playing his sport, forcing him to watch his team lose when he knows he could work with them for a win, is agony. Blocking the new VP from her team, shaming her as unworthy even of an introduction, exposing her to team members who try to understand why she was left in silence and silenced. What's wrong with her? Did she earn the position? Why is she being disrespected right out of the gate? Silence speaks volumes and is one of the most effective weapons in bullying, gaslighting, and institutional complicity. The psychopath gets a big hit of power and pleasure in creating this kind of pain in targets, and that sadistic pleasure is condoned and enabled over and over. As we noted, psychological abuse can take a deadly passive form that is at the other end of the spectrum from the active harm done by physical abuse. Pain here was inflicted through omission. The bridge was blown up before Carle could even be introduced.

THEY DON'T WANT TO WIN

My husband phoned me from Montgomery's championship tournament, and he sounded shocked to the core. He said, "They don't want to win." I couldn't understand why this was so horrifying to him until it dawned on me. If they're coaches and they're blocking their own team from winning, they're blowing up bridges that might lead to success, what's the real game they're playing? What's the agenda? The real game they are playing involves inflicting pain. It's in those moments that you see the psychopathology. It's the game of power and control. It's the game of propping up some to enable hurting others. It's not basketball they're coaching. It's a darker game played by intraspecies predators on the hunt. Not just this time, but always, year after year. Not just at this basketball tournament, but in the office of Nike's VP and general manager of North America Basketball. No one is immune.

Carle's next insight cuts to the core of what went on in her workplace, just as it did in Montgomery's school. These beliefs are what drive the psychopath-bully, *not* success and a win for the team. Instead, hear the bully's credo.

> *I believe in the magic of demeaning, devaluing, and dehumanizing. I believe in screaming, a smack on the ass, and a creepy whisper.*[5]

Carle's workplace bullies used a blend of psychological abuse and sexual harassment under the umbrella of misogyny. Women were in the "outgroup," which may have created a sense of superiority and provided male bonding for the bullies and boosts of psychotic triumph. Her insight applies to Montgomery's abuse as well in that it was done by males in positions of power, credibility, and social standing to boys who had no power. The boys were positioned as feminized, which was conveyed as disgusting and pathetic. Misogyny, like all hate, is frequently hammered into targets in their formative years.

In Montgomery and the other boys' abuse, the female body was blended with put-downs to express mental inferiority and unworthiness: "fucking pussies, fucking embarrassments, grow some balls, fucking retards, fucking soft, fucking pathetic." The abuse—as documented in multiple testimonies—was a day in and day out barrage of demeaning, devaluing, and dehumanizing directed at teenage targets. They endured screaming, and for Montgomery it was in his face. The smack on the ass is a normalized basketball-player gesture, but it got weird when it was linked with one of the teacher's repeated "creepy whispers." The older teacher was always muttering obscenities about the boys. When you have a middle-aged man whispering homophobic slurs while the boys are given T-shirts emblazoned with names like "Montylicious," the screaming and butt slapping all get entwined in creepy, destabilizing ways.

The female employees and executives at Nike got organized after Carle set in motion a movement by walking away, and Nike ultimately fired the abusive bullies.[6] In contrast, the commissioner for teacher regulation ruled at Montgomery's school that it was the students' fault for listening to the teacher's "creepy whispers." The commissioner ruled that when they were exposed to the teachers' obscenities, again it was their fault for being "too sensitive." Now, these are beautiful examples of gaslighting. The commissioner is reversing the terms that result in victim blaming. The perpetrator is not his focus. He does not examine what the perpetrator actively does. Instead, he homes in on the victims and conjures up examples of what is wrong with them. They are not the transmitters of psychological violence; the boys are passive recipients of abuse. The commissioner does not even reach for the straw of "insufficient evidence." He has so many students reporting that he has lots of evidence. So, he chooses the textbook gaslighting solution: reverse terms so that the perpetrators are positioned as victims and the victims are the ones faulted . . . which turns them into the perpetrators.

The commissioner writes in his reports that it is not the psychopath muttering obscenities that is the issue but the students who should *not* have been listening. The psychopath uses the same playbook. Carle exposes the Dark Triad and their ultimate skill, which is gaslighting. Listen to the voice of the bullying and gaslighting abuser in Carle's "Bully's Manifesto."

> *I believe in manipulation, exploitation, and Machiavelli. In short, I believe empathy and vulnerability are for losers.*[7]

The Dark Triad pour their energy into fluffing up their sheep's clothing so that no one can see the ravenous wolf within. They lean on their position, whether it's doctor, nurse, leader, teacher, manager, coach, professor, entrepreneur, or executive, not to create greatness but to exploit. They issue loud prophecies and repeat them over and over to cloud their inherent falsity. They don suits over their scales. They operate with reversals; the essential one is: I am the victim, and those who identify what I'm doing are perpetrators. I launch a smear campaign against those who see through my pontificating and have realized that I'm a false prophet. As I comfortably tell self-serving lies, I exclaim that those who report me are telling nasty lies. They're on a witch hunt. They're trying to hijack my work and my department. They're bullying me.

VULNERABILITY AND EMPATHY ARE FOR LOSERS

All this posturing as the wronged party is designed to head off any discoveries around the empathy erosion that drives the Dark Triad brain that manifests as an abusive individual. Empathy and vulnerability are kryptonite for the Dark Triad, so they play an elaborate game of beneficiaries and targets to avoid them.

Let's leave the microcosm of the workplace and look at this phenomenon on a macrocosmic scale. Dr. Gabor Maté brings his psychological insights to help us see that on an emotional level, "fascism," as it is driving international trauma in our present world, is also "a desperate escape from vulnerability."[8] He comments on the way children are traumatized in their formative years to show that it is a lack of empathy on the part of caregivers that leads to a fear of vulnerability.

Like all mammals, Maté explains, a human baby "enters the world with the implicit expectation of being safely held, seen, heard." Imagine homes where the infant does *not* get held, his needs are *not* seen, his words fall on deaf ears. Maté sees safety for this child in terms of being "physically protected and emotionally nourished." Imagine homes where the child is physically harmed and emotionally malnourished. Maté asserts that it is critically important that the child's "feelings" are "welcomed, recognized, validated and mirrored."[9] Now, imagine this child is being raised with food and shelter, but her feelings are not welcome, not recognized, certainly not validated or mirrored. This traumatizing disconnect can create the psychology that leads to the Dark Triad that cannot form healthy, empathic relationships but seeks others to mirror an invulnerably powerful, controlling, coercive, untouchable individual. How do they accomplish this? By positioning beneficiaries as mirrors who aggrandize their superiority and by positioning targets or enemies as mirrors who reflect their lack of empathy and unlimited power—the targets, the enemies who deserve their maltreatment because they are losers. If they are losers, then the Dark Triad are winners. That's how the gaslighting mirror works.

With fascism, the needs of the majority are not used to outweigh the suffering of the minority. It's just the opposite. The happiness of the few outweighs the suffering of the many. The many losers, the unhappy ones, the targets, the enemies are there to serve the winners, the happy ones, the beneficiaries, the in-group who live in fear that their leader will cast them into the out-group, and so they fawn and fabricate. Ursula K. Le Guin's short story "The Ones Who Walk Away from Omelas" depicts the world of winners whose lives are gorgeous beyond belief, but their whole world hinges on the brutal and abject suffering of a single chained child at the heart of their beautiful Omelas. Most are so overcome with happiness that they are OK with the suffering of the child. It is only one child after all, and everyone else is so happy. Le Guin's focus in the story is on those who can't stomach it. They walk away.

WHY WALK AWAY?
As Carle shares, having the psychopathic mirror put in front of you, rather than being face-to-face with an empathic, at times vulnerable, individual reverses your healthy attempts at human connection. The

bullying and gaslighting mirror is designed to make you believe that *you* are the one who is weak, at risk, and mentally ill. Amid being abused, Carle did not even have the term "bullying" available to apply to her trauma. She describes her declining mental state while being bullied: "It would mean questioning my values and doubting myself, not just as an employee, but as a human being on the edge of madness, some might say over the edge—and at my lowest point, putting my family risk."[10]

If an executive of twenty-five years can be seriously destabilized by abuse, imagine the damaging confusion that occurs in a student's brain. Few of us are trained at work to recognize the manipulations of the Dark Triad and how at first, they mirror us to draw us in, then demand that we mirror them back, aggrandizing their power. All it takes is some initial meetings before the Dark Triad identify our personal issues and concerns. "Using this information, the psychopath crafts a simulated persona—a mask—that mirrors or compliments these characteristics."[11] The Dark Triad then share personal and seemingly private insights into themselves that make the target feel heard and seen. They seem to have key issues and concerns in common. The target lets down her guard and then slowly but surely, this connection evaporates, and the target finds herself ignored and humiliated, which serves to mirror the power, credibility, and social standing of the perpetrator. We examine the dynamic of the Dark Triad in greater detail in part 2.

Carle has spent a twenty-five-year career being acknowledged and promoted for her hard work, her integrity, her brilliance, her expertise. All it takes is a textbook figure from the Dark Triad to dismantle her brain. His gaslighting and psychological torment are enough to make her doubt herself. The months he has access to her brain are so manipulative that it erases twenty-five years of experience and excellence in her company. Nonetheless, lawmakers, policy writers, corporate and government leaders do not see the urgency to protect employees from bullying in all forms. They don't seem to recognize that psychological safety is as important as physical safety. Harming the body surely is as serious as harming the brain. Physical illness is as serious as mental illness. Both can lead to intense suffering, ruined careers, loss of livelihood, mental illness, physical illness, and death. Why is one seen as requiring education and protection, whereas the other leaves targets to fend for themselves? This failure—in education and training, laws and regulations, institutional compliance designed to deter and prevent the lies of bullying, gaslighting, and the enabling role played by institutional complicity—can lead to an infectious cycle. The once bullied, abused, and neglected—who carry the virus—are far more likely to be facilitated in spreading the disease to others. It's a communicable disease but treated as a moral issue in our outdated system.

As Carle puts it, "Bullying is about one person dominating another. It's about dehumanizing, degrading, and devaluing targets. It's about power and control."[12] We can also alter this statement to encompass institutional complicity: Bullying is about the system (political, legal, economic, etc.) dominating an out-group. It's about dehumanizing, degrading, and devaluing targets.

Bullying takes myriad forms, but in general it can be put into the major categories of physical, psychological, and sexual abuse; physical and emotional neglect; financial abuse; cyberbullying; and social-relational bullying. As documented in *The Bullied Brain*, all forms of bullying can do significant damage to the brain, and the damage can be seen on brain scans.[13] Scientists have at least twenty years of extensive evidence on the impact of bullying on the brain, but this data is not reaching most of the populace. Although workplace protections, laws, and policy do not recognize the significant harm done by bullying that does *not* touch the body—namely, psychological, emotional, cyber and social-relational bullying—perpetrators use it frequently, and their mission is to do damage.

As Workplace Bullying Institute cofounder Dr. Gary Namie says, "Workplace bullying is a systemic laser-focused campaign of interpersonal destruction."[14] We are not legally permitted to physically destroy someone at work. Why are we legally permitted to psychologically and financially destroy someone? The systemic nature of bullying is well-documented, yet we are rarely prepared to be targeted. As Carle says, when she found herself being bullied after twenty-five years of exceptional service to her company: "It's confusing. It trips us up. It blindsides us."[15]

NAME BULLYING TO EXPOSE THE LIE

Carle stresses that being able to name what is happening as *bullying* is a critical first step in self-protection. "It's so important to understand that bullying is real, has a name, has perpetrators and targets. Why? Because unless you name it, you can't deal with it."[16] In part 3, we harness the neuroscience on naming emotions that puts us into an informed and powerful position regarding bullying, as opposed to being perpetually shocked and destabilized by it.

Carle describes her breakthrough session with a mental health counselor. Note the institutionalized reversal: victims of abuse seek therapy to find out what's wrong with them and how they can get better. Notice how the target is taking responsibility for the trauma that occurred. In contrast, perpetrators do *not* feel responsible for causing trauma and often disseminate the rumor that the victim's instability or mental illness is why they left the institution. Perpetrators of abuse do not seek therapy because they often believe their own lie that nothing's wrong with them and they have no need to change. What's mind-blowing about this reversal is that institutions frequently support it.

Carle feels "relief" when she hears her mental health counselor "name the behavior, name what was happening" to her. Because she does not trust her own perception of reality due to the bullying and gaslighting, it matters especially that the counselor is offering a "professional opinion." Carle has been faulting herself for "not being able to handle a difficult, diminishing boss." When we look in the next chapter at the bullying done to Jonathan Wilson, it's chilling that he suffers this same sense of failure. He thinks—being very accomplished, highly promoted, talented, dedicated after twenty-plus years just like Carle—that *he* is not successfully dealing with "difficult people." Those who bully and gaslight aren't difficult. They're deadly. Carle's breakthrough in this session with the counselor, where she discovers accurate language to cut through the lies and name her maltreatment as "bullying," makes her feel "maybe a little less crazy."[17]

Note the repetition of the act of naming by the counselor: "hearing her *name*," "*name* what was happening to me." And "by giving [bullying] a *name*" Carle regains "a tiny bit of control." The fact that a high-powered executive needs to go to a mental health professional to have her experience of maltreatment *named* as bullying tells us that we need to learn and be trained in how bullying works to distress and destabilize the brain. Carle says knowing that what had happened to her was "bullying," made her pause long enough to question her belief that she was "crazy." That is the overarching goal of gaslighting: make the targets believe that they are mentally unstable and can no longer trust their assessment of reality. This belief is poison for the brain. As Carle articulates it, "Everything is a test with a bully and especially with a gaslighter. The bully's reason for being is to push targets towards insanity."[18] Note that here she blends bullying and gaslighting.

Those who bully and gaslight test the waters. They are intentional, thoughtful, cautious in how they manipulate. Their goal is to exploit, and they are subtle. Leading another person to lose her mind and become unable to discern between reality and illusion is no simple task. The equivalent of the bully and gaslighter is the pedophile who uses micro-gestures of affection and thoughtful compliments. He offers minor opportunities and benefits. He invests time in the target. All these categories increase slowly but surely, deliberately. He's subtle and patient. It could take years, but with the overarching agenda to exploit, with the "gamelike fascination" abusers experience, it's worth it.

What is the result for the target who does not identify the manipulation in time? The target is exploited, mentally destabilized, knocked off her career path, stripped of her livelihood, deprived of her health. As Carle expresses the traumatizing experience: "a stressed brain gives a false reading of what's real and what isn't. A stressed brain struggles to perform until it can no longer perform."[19] Extensively documented in scientific studies, chronic or toxic stress that harms targets makes them struggle to tell the truth from a lie, know what's up and what's down, discern between illusion and reality, and thus, they can no longer perform. Carle's description here debunks the myth that abuse is a necessary evil for greatness. She *was* great, but then she was bullied and gaslit—enabled by her institution—into exiting her toxic workplace. We see the identical pattern with other career superstars: Jonathan Wilson and Julie Macfarlane. Institutions that want to be successful cannot afford to repeatedly lose their top talent.

LANGUAGE CAN DISEMPOWER AND EMPOWER

In workplace cultures that allow the lies of bullying, gaslighting, and institutional complicity, talent, work ethic, leadership are driven out while perpetrators and the damage they cause are protected. Worried about her sanity and health, Carle sets out on the path to repair and recover. Working with a counselor helps her on this journey. Although this is a normalized pattern in our society, note how backward it all is. Why do companies sacrifice their talent to abusers? Why does the victim need counseling from a mental health expert, but the perpetrator is positioned as stable and healthy? Why doesn't a high-level executive such as Carle not instantly recognize and name what she's dealing with and then tackle it? Why does she have to walk away to win?

It seems minor, but much of this chaos hinges on language. Words are part of the key to unlocking answers to these puzzling questions. Look at the way Carle describes the remedy to gaslighting that comes from the counselor naming the bullying: "I just felt validated, maybe a little less crazy." In many ways, Carle's crisis is a crisis of language. How is it possible that a highly sophisticated, successful executive resorts to almost childlike language—"crazy"—to describe what is being done to her?

I am hyperaware of this language breakdown because it is what led me astray with my son, Montgomery, when he and other students were being bullied by teachers. After the other victims had reported the pattern of abuse, making it explicit, I asked him why he didn't tell me what was happening. He looked me in the eye and said, "I *did* tell you." Then he repeated the phrases: "I hate those guys" and "They're freaks." Note the childlike language. He did not have the correct vocabulary to describe the abuse being done to him. I have felt painfully responsible as a parent for not teaching him how to properly articulate and narrate abuse to which he might be subjected. But when I read powerhouse Megan Carle, VP of North America basketball, I recognize that the issue is far bigger. Few of us, perhaps only the mental health professionals, have the correct language to describe and document bullying in all its insidious and explosive forms. A major focus of *The Gaslit Brain* is to build an effective operating vocabulary from psychological research to better identify and expose the lies of bullying, gaslighting, and institutional complicity. Our sanity hangs in the balance. We don't want to believe inaccurately that we are "crazy" and that the toxic environment we are in is healthy. This false reading by a stressed brain happens all too often.

Learning how to name bullying can't be something we do in a workshop or as a quick overview of policy and procedure at the start of the fiscal year. It needs to be taught over and over, identified immediately when it occurs, be summarily shut down by witnesses, and addressed effectively by leaders, managers, and HR. When we look at the prevalence of workplace bullying, which has affected almost eighty million US workers according to a 2021 survey by the Workplace Bullying Institute, it's amazing that this highly destructive yet preventable behavior is not abruptly stopped, and even more amazing, is frequently enabled.[20] One in two workers are targets of bullying, and one in three reports it; and yet, as the Workplace Bullying Institute states, "Workplace bullying remains 'the undiscussable.'"[21] You can't discuss something that either has no name outside of mental health expertise or is expressed by inaccurate language: freaks, hate, crazy. These words need to be replaced with psychologically informed vocabulary that is a requirement to know for employees, and certainly for leaders, managers, and HR.

Megan Carle's *crazy* becomes "the bullying, gaslighting, and institutional complicity I am faced with is dismantling my twenty-five years of exceptional work and repeat promotions which have earned me one of the most significant positions of responsibility and leadership at Nike. Instead of being able to contribute my expertise, I am being systematically attacked on a brain level. I am enduring psychological violence that is so harmful it is causing my brain to focus on threat and survival rather than all of the creative, important, vital work I need to do in my position."

As Carle puts it—and the injustice and cruelty are aptly conveyed—"The thing about workplace bullying is that it shatters what you know to be true. You start questioning your entire belief system."[22] Imagine being a top level executive and instead of doing your demanding work, you're reduced to questioning what's real and what's false, what's a lie and what's truth. In the next chapter, we hear Jonathan Wilson—as a counterterrorism expert for Scotland Yard with a law degree—describe a comparable collapse in his brain's way of working. This shattering is the legacy of enabled bullying and gaslighting in the workplace. Nike ultimately ousted the perpetrators, but how much damage to other targets had already occurred? There is a great deal more vocabulary we need to learn and have at the ready if we truly want to transform workplaces that normalize and enable bullying and gaslighting into work environments that normalize and enable speaking up and transparency.

CATCHING THE VIRUS OF BULLYING AND GASLIGHTING

Let us return to Gabor Maté's insights into the abuse and neglect that can create the Dark Triad. As the world tilts ominously back toward fascist regimes, he exposes the simple failure of child rearing that drives this dangerous impulse that becomes a plan to find an out-group, label them "enemy," demean, dehumanize, and destroy them. Leaders gaze upon the populace as strongmen and demand their power be mirrored back to them as if they are national, even religious saviors. It's remarkable that we find it so incredibly difficult to stop this same tired old playbook that fuels bullying and abuse in the home, the workplace, and in international politics.

> *The human infant enters the world with the implicit expectation of being safely held, seen, heard, physically protected and emotionally nourished, her feelings welcomed, recognized, validated and mirrored. Given such an "evolved nest," in the apt phrase of the psychologist Darcia Narvaez, we develop and maintain a strong connection to ourselves, a deeply rooted confidence in who we are, a trust in innate goodness present in the world and an openness to love within ourselves, as without. Trauma represents a disconnect from these healthy inclinations, in extreme cases a defensive denial of them as being too vulnerable to bear. And that, in essence, is what fascism is on the emotional level: a desperate escape from vulnerability.*

Neuroscientist Dr. Simon Baron-Cohen, whose research we will look at in detail in part 2, cannot fathom why we don't train and teach affective empathy at every stage from childhood to adulthood. Maté's life's work has been to do just that, and yet here we are. What will it take to put in place preventative measures and focus upstream on parenting, teaching, and coaching? Why do we bemoan the rise of populism, far-right demonizing of others, and fascism when we know that it is so often tied to a traumatic upbringing? Why not change how caretakers are educated and children are raised? Why allow whole swaths of the population to be dehumanized and degraded in their work and blocked from opportunities so that they must cover up their vulnerability and their families' vulnerability with grandiose gestures and a need to identify targets to blame? The blame goes to the target group, *not* to the higher-ups who are enablers of these unbearable conditions where opportunities for fair wages, decent workplaces, safety, and health are too often bridges blown up before they can be crossed.

Carle couldn't have been bullied out of her position at Nike if parents had raised the men with whom she worked to feel safe, held, seen, heard, physically protected and emotionally nourished, their feelings welcomed, recognized, validated, and mirrored; likewise for Wilson and Macfarlane. The tragedy of the Dark Triad is their endless hunt for mirroring. They didn't get it in childhood, and that lack is deeply traumatic. To compensate, they make others mirror their conquering potency (think misogyny, homophobia, sexual harassment, sexual assault) and their winning confidence (think humiliation, berating, threatening, punishing, blocking from opportunities, public shaming). Gazing into this mirror where the "losers" make them feel like winners, they can avoid acknowledging or feeling their eroded power and confidence. It does not matter to them that this mirror reflects nothing but falsehoods.

GASLIGHTING'S HALL OF MIRRORS
In October 1928, before fascism took hold of Europe, Virginia Woolf gave a lecture at Cambridge University on women and writing. She spoke about how women in fiction and in life were expected to hold a mirror up to men to aggrandize their image. She imagines that men aren't focused on female inferiority per se; rather, they're concerned about establishing and protecting their own superiority. They have a fragile self-image like glass that could easily be shattered.

Almost a century later, Megan Carle is suffocating in a workplace where misogyny has drained it of oxygen. The colleague who bullies her and "the executives" she thought she "could trust," who "turned their backs" when she asked for help, position her as a mirror that reflects back to them their power to ignore her, demean her, conduct business as if she's nothing, a nobody. She describes the impact of this treatment on her.

> *By the time I'd said goodbye to Nike, the key people I reported to didn't see me at all. And frankly, I no longer saw myself. When I looked in the mirror, it was blank. Nothing. Invisible.*[23]

When we go to work and instead of being in a healthy workplace we find ourselves lost in a hall of mirrors, the impact is deeply concerning. If we are targeted by someone who is in the Dark Triad, they can turn us into a mirror that reflects their psychological needs. When they feel small, we must reflect them back supersized. When they feel self-loathing, we must reflect them as adored. When they feel like a loser, we must show that they are winners. When they feel degraded, we must make them feel divine. When they feel rejected, we must reflect back to them their virility. When they feel impotent, we must reflect back to them their unlimited power. All this reflecting is not only disorienting, not only does it take us to the brink where we forget how to distinguish between truth and illusion, but we might just lose our own selves so that when we look in the mirror, nothing is there.

NOTES

1. Megan Carle, *Walk Away to Win: A Playbook to Combat Workplace Bullying* (New York: McGraw-Hill, 2023), vii.
2. Carle, *Walk Away to Win*, viii.
3. Carle, *Walk Away to Win*, viii.
4. Carle, *Walk Away to Win*, viii.
5. Carle, *Walk Away to Win*, viii.
6. Carle, *Walk Away to Win*, xii.
7. Carle, *Walk Away to Win*, viii.
8. Gabor Maté, "We Each Have a Nazi in Us. We Need to Understand the Psychological Roots of Authoritarianism," *The Guardian*, September 6, 2024. https://www.theguardian.com/commentisfree/article/2024/sep/06/authoritarianism-roots-origin. All quotes from Gabor Maté in this chapter are taken from this same article.
9. Simon Baron-Cohen reaches similar conclusions with his neuroscientific research into empathy erosion. He writes: "early secure attachment can promote the growth of

empathy, and early insecure empathy can erode empathy by making it hard to trust others or making one feel threatened." Baron-Cohen, *The Science of Evil: On Empathy and the Origins of Cruelty* (New York: Basic Books, 2011), 172.

10. Carle, *Walk Away to Win*, xx.

11. Paul Babiak and Robert Hare, *Snakes in Suits: When Psychopaths Go to Work* (New York: Harper, 2006), 76.

12. Carle, *Walk Away to Win*, 5.

13. Jennifer Fraser, *The Bullied Brain: Heal Your Scars and Restore Your Health* (Lanham, MD: Prometheus Books, 2022).

14. Carle, *Walk Away to Win*, 6.

15. Carle, *Walk Away to Win*, 4.

16. Carle, *Walk Away to Win*, 5.

17. Carle, *Walk Away to Win*, 5.

18. Carle, *Walk Away to Win*, 143.

19. Carle, *Walk Away to Win*, 109.

20. Carle, *Walk Away to Win*, 67 and 106.

21. Carle, *Walk Away to Win*, 6.

22. Carle, *Walk Away to Win*, 97.

23. Carle, *Walk Away to Win*, xiii.

Chapter Three

The Counterterrorism Expert

What happened with Nike executive Megan Carle, as we saw in the previous chapter, is concerningly similar to what happened to Detective Superintendent Jonathan Wilson. Textbook bullying, gaslighting, and institutional complicity strike again. Carle is in the United States and Wilson is in the United Kingdom. Carle is a top performer at a corporation; Wilson, a top performer with the police. Both are talented, recognized throughout their careers for excellence, repeatedly promoted, and yet when they are targeted for bullying, their respective institutions turn a blind eye. As reported by Michael Gillard and Fiona Hamilton, "Wilson, 56, who suffered a nervous breakdown, said the Met commissioner Sir Mark Rowley, who was then in charge of counterterrorism, turned a blind eye to his treatment."[1]

Far too many leaders turn a blind eye, think they're in control, believe it's a show of power, but really, they're blind to betrayal, and the betrayal does *not* come from the target. It comes from the Dark Triad. Both Carle and Wilson resigned and in both cases, a few years later, national news reported on their workplaces as enabling a bullying culture. The exact same pattern happened to me. So now we have the United States, United Kingdom, and Canada producing very similar case studies of bullying, gaslighting, and institutional complicity. The only real difference in these case studies appears to be the location.

In the bullying belief system, the victims are targeted because they are weak or have some obvious flaw or difference that makes it understandable why they become the focus of maltreatment. This myth spurs people to say to me all the time, "I was bullied because . . ." I stop them every time and set them straight. I tell them that the bullying had nothing to do with them. You should see quickly that this myth contains within it the essential lies that those who are bullied deserve it because they are not worthy and do not belong. They have some weakness or difference.

It's hard to see Detective Superintendent Jonathan Wilson as weak, being unworthy (based on any kind of trumped-up difference you can think of), and not belonging. If he had a history of these qualities, it might make more sense; but as we see with Carle, Macfarlane, Wilson, and me, it's the opposite history until the fateful moment when we are targeted. We have histories of strength, worth, and belonging that apparently become irrelevant when we speak up. All of us have differences, as does every human being, but no one was able to fault us for it or say that it resulted in our maltreatment.

As is well established, many are not so lucky. Their race, sexual orientation, class, lack of education, immigration status, religion, financial status, disability, age—*anything* that sticks—can make them traditional targets of maltreatment and slate them for unjust suffering. Some fall for the myth when they are put in the "out-group," but it gets harder to believe it when you examine white, educated, privileged individuals like Carle, Macfarlane, Wilson, and me. Of course, Carle, Macfarlane, and I belong to the "out-group" in which women are put, but we still had protective privileges many others do not enjoy. Our targeting puts in doubt the bullying myth that it is "X" that puts someone in the out-group. Apparently, anyone can be put in the out-group, which reminds us how false all the categories are that have justified—and still do—maltreatment.

BETRAYAL SPECIFICALLY HARMS BRAIN FUNCTIONING

As a white male who had proven himself in arguably the toughest profession, Wilson's mistake that brought the full force of bullying, gaslighting, and institutional complicity to his doorstep was the same as mine: reporting wrongdoing, exposing corrupt practices, calling out abuse and gaslighting. Institutions like Wilson's and mine rarely, if ever, advertise that they have zero tolerance for truth telling when it comes to abusive, corrupt practices. Part of succeeding in these kinds of workplaces requires you to look the other way. Then you are rewarded. I witnessed it firsthand, and so did Wilson.

Policing, police leadership, working in counterterrorism did not mentally unravel Wilson, but being exposed to the betrayal of his colleagues did. When our brains are certain who is an enemy and who is a colleague, they can perform effectively, but when our brains can't identify the threat, can't anticipate it, can't protect against it, can't strive to outwit it, can't employ strategies and techniques with our team to save others, we struggle to remain clearheaded and sane. When our brains cannot identify the threat because it's coming from *within* our team, when we have been trained for years to believe in our colleagues and leaders, only to discover they are lying and corrupt, the brain struggles to remain clear and steady. It's far more likely—even for those of us who have extreme mental strength such as Wilson—to suffer a nervous breakdown and succumb to such extreme mental suffering, it can lead to suicidal ideation. Working closely with others for decades at a workplace creates connection and community, both fundamental to brain health. As a leader in the counterterrorism command (CTC), when Wilson spoke up about the textbook culture of targets and beneficiaries—what he refers to as "a culture of bullying and nepotism"—he found himself "ostracized."[2] This word resonates painfully for me.

When my son, Montgomery, spoke up—along with many other students past and present—about the bullying by teachers with their beneficiaries and targets, he found himself ostracized. His shunning was carefully orchestrated by the leader and supported by the director, board, and chaplain. The leader promised confidentiality to all the students who reported the abuse, then he told one of the three abusers which boys had come forward. The leader promised new coaching the following year creating a sense that it was safe to speak up, but then he kept the abusers in position. They never missed a day regardless of their ongoing targeting and the supposedly "independent" investigations into their conduct. Many pitied the poor teachers who had multiple abuse reports about them because the leader carefully covered up the allegations every step of the way with the help of lawyers he hired and ultimately the educational regulator. Students, not knowing any better, aligned themselves with the aggressors kept in positions of power and took out their confusion on Montgomery and a few other boys. The rest of the students' identities were kept protected; so many were reporting abuse that it would have cast doubt on the leader's gaslighting.

As I drove Montgomery to a bogus interview that would be conducted by a "lawyer," hired by the leader to cover up, he asked me at sixteen if "ostracized" was the right word for what was happening to him. I told him it was. I knew that he was being singled out to shut me up. He didn't end up using the word because, as he told me, the "lawyer" didn't ask him about the abuse he had endured or witnessed done to others. Instead, he asked a few leading questions such as, "You don't really have to see the two teachers who you've complained about during the school day, do you?" A teenager, Montgomery knew the internal investigation was a sham. It was paid for by administrators who were heavily invested in ensuring that their knowledge of the abuse—of a year at least and on paper—was not uncovered. They did not want to be exposed as negligent with all the serious accountability that brings. The investigative report was such a sham that it was reproduced in full in national news.

The brain is wired for social connection; and an institution that blocks it, that ostracizes the victims, that scapegoats the truth tellers, is using a powerful, effective weapon to harm them. Montgomery suffered a severe depression, anxiety, and panic attacks. Megan Carle became desperately unwell to the point that she had to choose between her job and her health. I developed ulcers all over my throat. Jonathan Wilson had a nervous breakdown and became suicidal. Julie Macfarlane has cancer. All these mental and physical responses are extensively documented in research as correlated with the kind of maltreatment we endured in our workplaces.

It's important to understand that psychological safety also means physical, neurological, and physiological safety. Unsafe workplaces don't just crush toes that aren't in steel-toed boots, cause concussions to heads without helmets, result in accidents for those without reflective vests. Unsafe workplaces that enable and cover up the lies of bullying, gaslighting, and institutional complicity crush employees on equally serious and life-threatening levels. A lawyer arguing that psychological safety cannot be measured because it is about mind-set and integrity—and thus cannot be the legal responsibility of the institution—appears not to know that the impact of maltreatment can be measured on brain scans, with blood tests, through biomarkers, by taking blood pressure readings, checking the heart rate, and assessing gut health. It is hardly surprising that we have four concerningly similar case studies of individuals targeted in their workplace for maltreatment, repeatedly exposed to the lies of bullying, gaslighting, and institutional complicity, who all fall seriously ill. A child's "workplace" is school, so Montgomery makes five.

LYING REQUIRES BEING SKILLED WITH LANGUAGE AND COGNITION

In a bid to save his health and sanity, Wilson resigned from the force in 2020, humiliated and gaslit after he was told that his allegations lacked evidence and were meritless. He was positioned as someone who fabricated "bullying" because it just didn't happen. Three years later, the Baroness of Blackstock "published an excoriating report into the force" that exposed entrenched bullying. She investigated London's Metropolitan Police for a year and discovered rampant homophobic, racist, and misogynistic bullying. The carefully constructed narrative or smear campaign that 'Wilson was a complainer about behavior that was completely acceptable' suddenly collapsed. Casey discovered a police force ruled by "denial, hubris, and a lack of candour."[3] Leadership that denies bullying has occurred and is a serious threat in the workplace is formed by individuals too proud to admit failure even when necessary to protect their employees. They suffer from hubris. Leadership that refuses to take responsibility for harm taking place on their watch must resort to lack of candor or more forcefully, lies, cover-ups, and institutional complicity with bullying and gaslighting.

Let's circle back to the bullying mythology that something about the target makes them activate the maltreatment of perpetrators. Notice how the reversal has slipped into Casey's report. The focus is not on the perpetrator, the active transmitting agent of bullying, abuse, and harassment. The focus has strangely shifted to the passive receiver of bullying, abuse, and harassment. We would be surprised to read about *perpetrators* in the police being discussed in terms of their sexual orientation, their racial background, and their feelings around women. In contrast, we are not surprised—in fact, in many cases we completely normalize—this information as it applies to victims. It's like our brains need some reason to understand why those empowered to protect people are harming them. It doesn't make sense, so we seek information to explain it. We use categories, information about targets, to understand how cruel and destructive conduct occurred on the part of perpetrators. Wouldn't it make more sense to analyze what is it about the perpetrators—where they came from, their sexual orientation, their education or lack thereof, whether they are financially at risk, their racial background, religion, possible disability—that leads to bullying and gaslighting? Analyzing victims won't give us the information we need to understand destructive behavior.

Megan Carle saw misogyny as a focus of the bullying at Nike. At my workplace, it was a combination of homophobia and misogyny, with some racism, being used against teenaged boys. In Wilson's police force, it's homophobia, misogyny, and racism. In Macfarlane's workplace, an abuser is protected from public scrutiny who sexually targets female students, which we could categorize as misogyny. Granted, Macfarlane, Carle, and I are women, so we might say we were bullied and gaslit at work because we were women. But we hit a stumbling block with Montgomery and Wilson.

The myth fully breaks down at this point because Montgomery is white and male, on the headmaster's honor roll, an exceptional athlete, popular, six feet four, and a heterosexual. He isn't an immigrant or migrant. He isn't female or LGBTQ+. He's white, privileged, educated. They had no quick and easy way to push him into an out-group, but they did. Wilson is white and male, heterosexual, a leader in a high-stakes policing unit, a rugby player, popular, well-recognized after almost thirty years of service as being a likely choice for next in command at the highest level. No quick and easy way to shunt him into an out-group, but once again, they did. One of the key perpetrators in his maltreatment was a white woman in a position of power. How do we maintain our bullying myth in these contexts? These targets don't supply us with the answers we want to figure out how bullying and gaslighting work and why institutions are complicit in protecting and enabling perpetrators.

If it is true that being in the privileged position of educated, financially secure, white, straight male without a disability, and born in the country where they work, means you cannot be manipulated by the lies of bullying, gaslighting, and institutional complicity, Montgomery and Wilson cast doubt on the whole construct. They are crucial to my psychological study of lying because they highlight that all the other categories we use to explain and justify to ourselves why certain targets are singled out, or whole populaces are singled out, is the biggest lie of all. Nonetheless, far too many still believe this foundational lie.

If we want to halt rampant bullying, gaslighting, and institutional complicity in the workplace, we need to be laser focused on the perpetrators and stop trying to figure out what's wrong or weak or different about the target that led to the destructive manipulative conduct. Those who gaslight lean heavily on a conjured "enemy," whether it's women or migrants or visible minorities or people in poverty or LGBTQ+ or people with disabilities or targeted religions or people who laugh a certain way. Instead of examining the trumped-up target of bullying and gaslighting, we're more likely to solve this destructive issue in our workplaces by homing in on the perpetrators and why they need an enemy in the first place to define their own value or to mirror their untouchable power. In our focus on targets, we fail to examine the brains of perpetrators.

Even the laws expose our skewed way of thinking. Certain categories of victims are protected because they are seen as more vulnerable and are targeted more frequently. I am not saying that they don't need these protections. What I am saying is that the law needs to turn fully around and apply legal sanctions against perpetrators regardless of whom they target. All individuals have the right to safety, health, and fair treatment at work. All individuals who target others' rights to safety, health, and fair treatment need to be held legally accountable. If we had stringent laws, rules, regulations that created psychologically safe workplaces, they would demand compliance, act as a deterrent, spur education and training. Where are the laws for perpetrators of bullying, perpetrators of gaslighting, those who are pathological liars, and for those in institutions who are complicit in these extremely serious and harmful violations?

In Casey's report, her assessment makes crystal clear that bullying does not need a protected class of targets to do its harm. "Casey found a 'broader culture of bullying' with over one fifth (22%) of Met officers and staff surveyed having experienced it in the workplace." According to her report,

> *Those who do not conform to the prevailing culture face discrimination, bullying and barriers to thriving and progressing in their career. If they speak out they will be labelled a "troublemaker." But even if they walk the line, the organisation may still decide that their "face doesn't fit."*[4]

Montgomery's face didn't fit. Wilson's face didn't fit. Both of them spoke up about a prevailing culture of abuse. That was enough, like so many others, for them to be targeted for bullying behaviors that attacked them, blocked them from opportunities, lied to them and about them, and scrambled their relationship to others and even to their own reality. How do you avoid this fate in a bullying and gaslighting institution? You must conform to the prevailing culture even if it means compromising your sense of authenticity, your integrity, and your empathy. That's a lot to sacrifice, and the case studies in *The Gaslit Brain* look at individuals from my teenage son to superstar leaders in their fields such as Wilson, Carle, and Macfarlane who refuse to conform.

Pay Attention to the Pattern

Institutions that ignore reports by privileged (thus safer) individuals such as Montgomery and Wilson run a risk. Why? Because if these individuals speak up, chances are very good that many others aren't in as solid or protected a position to report the harm being done. If you are in a group typically targeted for injustice and maltreatment (women, LGBTQ+, visible minority, Jewish, Islamic, lacking in education, disabled, suffering from poverty, an immigrant etc.), you are more likely to keep a low profile and not run the risk of being singled out for even more maltreatment. Abusive individuals never only lie once, abuse one target, break one rule, financially do only one corrupt act; they are compelled to do these destructive acts over and over. They can be identified quickly by the pattern of their behavior. Institutions that choose to ignore reports of their maltreatment are wise to make this choice based on the fact that there is absolutely no pattern. All the case studies discussed in *The Gaslit Brain* include multiple reports of abuse. The patterns are glaring, but the institution still chooses to protect the perpetrators and revictimize the targets.

As Matt Dathan reports, after her yearlong investigation, Baroness Casey's findings on Wilson's workplace

> *"speak to a fundamental rupture in the bond of trust between the police and the public." She warned that the police's relationship with the public is "at breaking point" and the decline in trust among women and black people in London risks spreading to the rest of the country. Only "wholesale and radical reform" of policing can restore trust and confidence in the police, Casey said.*[5]

Notice that Casey uses the imagery of contagion. Maltreatment, injustice in the police—upholders of justice—who she finds are putting some into out-groups and not protecting them, all of it is like a virus that "risks spreading." Institutions are at risk of this virus as well, but we still see all too often, instead of containing it, doing the hard work to protect their employees, they allow it to spread. A glance at the news in the past few years reveals that the breakdown in trust in police forces is not unique to the United Kingdom. It is also a repeatedly pressing issue in the United States and Canada. It's a reminder that even the institutions empowered with the rule of law, the pursuit of justice, and the high-stakes mission to protect *all*, not just the beneficiaries, can succumb to cultures built on the falsehoods that fuel bullying, gaslighting, and institutional complicity. What does this ultimately lead to? A culture constructed on lies. The breakdown of trust. The only thing that stands between sanity and insanity is the truth. To remain healthy, we need to have trust in others with whom we share reality.

What was Wilson's reaction to Casey's investigation? A "huge sense of relief that he was not crazy."[6] Notice the identical sense of relief and even word choice used by Carle. Both were gaslit, and both worried they were "crazy." Wilson's statement exposes gaslighting in its essence. Gaslighting is all about making the targets lose trust in their own perceptions, their own sense of reality. This breakdown in trust expands and infects the institution. Those in power start controlling the narrative on what's true and what's false, which replaces reality with self-serving illusion. And as we saw with Casey's report, the breakdown in trust can infect whole nations at risk of destabilization through terrorism but lack a stable, trustworthy base from which to mount a defense.

RECOGNIZE INSTITUTIONAL COMPLICITY

Although it's challenging, potentially destabilizing, we will be healthier, saner, and safer if we admit that institutional complicity is possible and prepare ourselves to recognize the red flags. When you read the media coverage of Wilson's maltreatment, the signs are clear that institutional complicity is compounding the lies of bullying and gaslighting. Note that the internal investigation into his workplace complaint comes back with the strange assessment, "nothing to report here."[7] Right away, it begs the question. If nothing is going on, why are respected individuals going through the incredibly difficult and painful process of reporting maltreatment?

In brief, here's what was happening. Wilson reports

- striving to implement key changes as a leader and meeting resistance around sharing information;

- being told those he's in charge of are complaining about him—but when he checks with them, they don't know what he's referring to;

- being told he's lost the trust of MI5 and the home office to whom he regularly reports;

- having key resources such as whole teams of his officers being taken away without warning;

- being excluded from meetings he needs to attend;

- being pulled into ambush meetings repeatedly where there are no witnesses;

- reporting to a higher-up and being treated with contempt and ridicule; told that, in fact, "he is the problem."

If you didn't notice the textbook gaslighting at work in all the falsehoods used to manipulate Wilson and destabilize him, the final reversal ought to be obvious. When you report wrongdoing in a workplace constructed on the lies of bullying, gaslighting, and institutional complicity, reversal occurs: the perpetrator becomes the victim, and victim becomes the perpetrator. This brief list does not convey the impacts of bullying and gaslighting lies. Wilson says these allegations—which he didn't suspect were false—made him feel "mortified" and "none the wiser how to put it right." Then more "false allegations" of upsetting colleagues followed, which he says were an attempt to "destroy my confidence and my credibility."[8] Our laws prohibit us from destroying property, but they seem to fall apart when it comes to destroying a colleague with lies.

Now listen to how Met Commissioner Sir Mark Rowley tries to explain away the "nothing to report here" in the media, keeping in mind the list of reported maltreatment.

> *Rowley said he accepted the Met had not always been tough enough on building a positive culture, but added: "When disputes arise independent investigations, such as in this case, are the best way to find a fair resolution. Sadly, parties will not always agree with the outcome of these investigations. The findings of the independent review into Mr. Wilson's allegations at the time found insufficient evidence for them to be upheld."*

Note the strange phrase "not always been tough enough on building a positive culture." This odd phrasing insinuates that lack of toughness led to Wilson's demise. It insinuates a lack of toughness in Wilson who couldn't tough out the negative culture. Perhaps Crowley wants to say that the Met needs to get tough enough to hold perpetrators of abuse accountable. This statement would be accurate, except that he is using it in a series of phrases to discredit Wilson and prop up his culture of institutionally sanctioned bullying and gaslighting. It's not like Rowley didn't know Wilson or hadn't worked with him before. Rowley was assistant commissioner responsible for counterterrorism when Wilson raised concerns about bullying, but before, they had worked together in organized crime with the home secretary and held monthly meetings. As is typical in bullying scenarios, when targets speak up, their track record is erased, and a new reputation is constructed in the moment to discredit them.

Note that Crowley repeats "independent" twice. Repetition is often a signifier that regardless of the truth, the speaker wants you to become a believer. Crowley says the Met undertakes "independent investigations" and in Wilson's case conducted an "independent review." When I spoke with Wilson, he told me that this so-called independent review "was done by an ex-HR and was not independent." The use of partisan investigators is a tried-and-true trick used repeatedly where I worked. Wilson explained to me that he "was off sick," and the ex-HR had his email but he did not contact him, nor did the ex-HR get in touch with "two witnesses that he said he was going to come back to." In his investigation, the ex-HR took "'I don't remember' as legitimate responses without follow up." Wilson shares that "the investigation was completely inadequate."

If it was truly independent and fair, Rowley wouldn't have to keep repeating "independent." Note that he doesn't say it was done by an "ex-HR." Instead of facts, you get repetition of the narrative they want you to believe. If it was so accurate and so independent, how is it possible that Baroness Casey of Blackstock's investigation came to a glaringly opposite conclusion: abuse and failure were so rampant in the complaints it had the potential to infect the nation with lack of trust in the police force. Considering the reprehensible damage done to Wilson's career and health, Casey's truly independent investigation was pure vindication and exposure of the lies that proliferated around him. Not only did Casey's report find "a bullying culture," but it also highlighted the nightmare Wilson went through, "ridiculed" by those to whom he reported serious lies and manipulations. Casey refers to it as "an ineffective complaints process," but when you hear what it was like to suffer institutional betrayal as Wilson did, the official language seems inadequate to convey the damage done.

Wilson requested a meeting to report the bullying with Deputy Assistant Commander Helen Ball, whom he knew and respected.[9] Her public persona such as "speaking up in the past about women's rights" positioned her in Wilson's mind as someone who cares about human rights and was trustworthy. Her response to the request—noting that the

"Met didn't tolerate bullying" furthered those mistaken beliefs. A week later, confidently going alone without witnesses, Wilson encountered a shock. He describes the decision to go alone as "the biggest mistake of [his] service." Ball had already consulted the two officers who were bullying Wilson. As he tried to narrate the bullying being done to him, she repeatedly said contemptuously, "That is your view." The repetition that his interpretation is his alone, not shared, not part of the team, not trustworthy, reinforced by contempt—which conveys that he was unworthy of consideration—all screams gaslighting. Then she issues the purest gaslighting lie: "From everything I've heard, you're the problem." When a victim who reports bullying suddenly morphs into a perpetrator, then you have entered fully into gaslighting's hall of mirrors.

Now, if Wilson had a history of lying, wrongly accusing colleagues, being untrustworthy, Ball's reaction would be reasonable. But he has the opposite history. The fact that in this meeting it goes up in smoke while she accuses him of wrongdoing, you can easily recognize the lies of bullying and gaslighting. Notably, those he identifies as behaving in bullying, corrupt ways have concerning histories that, as usual, reveal the pattern of their complicated relationship with the truth.[10] Baroness Casey calls this an "ineffective complaints process." Wilson explains its actual impact on the victim: "I went in to that meeting a broken man and came out destroyed." Ball suggests that he "get some counselling," another glaring sign of gaslighting: your perceptions are not to be trusted; you don't know what's real and what's not; you're crazy; you need help. The perpetrators don't need counseling. The victims do.

Note that Crowley uses the condescending term "sadly" when he talks about the "independent" investigation. "Sadly, parties will not always agree with the outcome of these investigations." Is it sad or is it really worrisome that the assistant commissioner, in charge of the CTC, refers to credible reports of bullying lies and manipulations by one of his top leaders, compelled to formally report, because he's being further maltreated internally, and the commissioner does not seem clear on what is an effective investigation and what is further manipulation? He doesn't have concerns about a review that finds "nothing happened"? Does Crowley really want to say there was "insufficient evidence"? His language sounds official. It belongs to the world of police investigations. It's just that Baroness Casey's investigation revealed something deeply concerning that would have been covered up by leaders like Rowley without her report. The Met police appear to produce evidence when it suits them in cases of beneficiaries who belong to the in-group, but don't find evidence of wrongdoing when the target is not white, not male, not straight, not anything else they decide is fair game for dismissing and denying basic human rights of safety and security. And as noted, Wilson was white, male, and straight, but when psychopaths are at work, anyone can be a target. As we look at in greater detail, conjuring up or suppressing evidence—depending on what suits the agenda—are markers of the psychopathic brain. As we see in the workplaces under study in this book, the psychopathic brain appears able to infect whole workplaces.

When Crowley uses the manipulative term "disputes" to describe the bullying and gaslighting, and talks about the differing "parties," you should be on high alert that all is not right. Instead, the hazy, noisy, soft focus of institutional complicity is at work. When a perpetrator targets someone for bullying and gaslighting, it's *not* a dispute. The target is simply reporting abusive conduct. Either the conduct occurred or not. If it didn't occur, there needs to be evidence as to why it was falsely reported. None of this can be described as a "dispute."

This manipulation is what my gaslighting workplace tried to make me believe. I reported abuse being done to students by the drama teacher. They acted like we had an interpersonal issue to sort out and brought us to the table, face-to-face with the director, to do just that. It was a complete sham that enabled more and more abuse until the drama teacher was finally fired. Note that as usual, they were already well-informed about the drama teacher's pattern of abuse. I was merely one voice among many, but shutting me down, silencing me, sent a message to others that truth telling was unacceptable. Looking the other way would be rewarded.

Rowley's use of the term "sadly" serves to publicly dismiss and deny one of his top employees, one of his leaders in an elite unit, one of the best. Pretty strong message for the other employees at the Met who are not anywhere near the stature of Detective Superintendent Jonathan Wilson of the CTC who reports regularly to MI5 and the home office, and who has earned this position during a stellar twenty-eight-year career. Weigh those facts against Rowley's sadness that the review, as is textbook, found that Wilson must be at fault for bringing forth bullying allegations that were a figment of his imagination, or a lie, or a sign that he's mentally unhinged, or whatever. Just like Montgomery and the other students were telling "nasty lies," according to the slippery language—the anonymous quote—used by the "lawyer" hired by the leader to reach the result "nothing happened here."

Sadly, Rowley seems to emote, what Wilson experienced was not true or real. This is textbook gaslighting. Rowley is stating in public that Wilson cannot trust his own perception, needs to doubt his own sanity. It didn't matter that Wilson had twenty-eight years of not reverting to imaginings, not lying, not being unhinged. Is it surprising when institutions take out their top gun, or is it textbook? We see a pattern emerging with Carle, Macfarlane, Wilson, and me. In my workplace, I was one of two teachers who had earned a PhD. I was the only teacher published by both an American and a Canadian university press. I had earned an award for teaching excellence. But when I reported the abuse that I was hearing about directly from parents and students, I became instantly dismissible and worse. Why sacrifice your best and brightest?

I first witnessed this disturbing pattern with Montgomery where those who abuse target the best to keep everyone else in check, quiet, deferential, fawning, afraid. This is the "acquiescence culture" that Wilson's colleagues detail.

Even though it meant that the team could not win, the two teachers kept Montgomery on the bench. They used this same pattern with a junior team and with past senior teams. It wasn't new or startling. It was a pattern. The female teacher did the same, as multiple students reported from grade 11 to second-year university. It was well documented, par for the course. Talent was not allowed to play and was repeatedly put down. The school administrators and commissioner for teacher regulation dismissed all allegations. Ten years later, she is still facing serious allegations from athletes and their parents. It's a pattern. As the athletic director, she also targeted talented coaches. She used the same techniques dished out to Wilson. A coach would be kept from key meetings and would not be informed when her team was competing. The students told her how disappointed they were that she didn't show up.

Notice the disconnect, which is a red flag of gaslighting. On the one hand, the teachers put in writing that Montgomery was one of the best players ever seen in a school more than a hundred years old; on the other hand, he was almost never put on the court. Pretty strong message for the other players who don't have the same skills. If your top performer—not just in the moment, but in terms of the school's history—can be shot down through no fault of his own, it is an excellent, tried-and-true way to solidify your power base. You manifest coercion and control when you eliminate those who may threaten your "leadership" by their talent. Why else bully and drive out the likes of Montgomery, Carle, Macfarlane, and Wilson?

Those who bully and gaslight rarely feel secure; they know that their position hinges on wrongdoing, not meritocracy or healthy leadership, and thus they seem to suffer from paranoia. This isn't a new phenomenon. One of the most stunning portrayals of this dynamic is taught in schools like the one Montgomery attended. Shakespeare's *Macbeth* is a study of corrupt leadership that strives to eliminate all threats to power, only to find itself more and more insecure, paranoid, and destabilized. The witches are symbolic figures for gaslighting. Lady Macbeth's insane drive for power and prestige is a case study of the Dark Triad and what is going on in their dysregulated brains. The Macbeths try to destroy all competition, all threats to the king's position of which he is unworthy.

PARANOIA IS AS INFECTIOUS AS BULLYING

When Wilson realizes that he cannot trust his colleagues, he starts looking over his shoulder. He has lost trust in the police. His livelihood is entwined with the betrayal, and he is dependent on his employer for his career, which supports him and his family. As in all the case studies we look at that involve bullying, gaslighting, and institutional complicity, language is key. You cannot know that you are being lied to and betrayed by those you thought you could trust without the vocabulary to describe it. Wilson explains:

It all started to click and I realised what had happened with this bullying, these ambush meetings. It was gaslighting. I didn't even know the term gaslighting before. It really impacted on my confidence. It felt I was looking behind my back all the time. For someone with 25 years in I thought I'd seen the worst life could throw at you. I thought I was a pretty resilient guy.[11]

Wilson sees his demise as beginning after he called out corrupt practices. When he took a leadership position in the CTC, he was shocked to discover that a deal had been struck whereby detectives with full demands on their time due to the terrorist threat were, in fact, being used as free security guards at Wimbledon. "He said he angered colleagues when he questioned why detectives who had full workloads were being allowed to attend Wimbledon to work as paid stewards for a private security company." Wilson put a target on his back right out of the gate by shutting down this corrupt practice. Abusive workplaces that enable bullying and gaslighting have no stomach for integrity.

Rowley does not mention the corrupt Wimbledon deal. It's another fact he skips over. Wimbledon is a beautiful example of institutional complicity at the CTC. Wilson explained to me the details when we spoke.

When I first started, I found out that 40 of my officers, for the last 10–15 years were being used once a year as private security on public sector pay at Wimbledon. Senior level police were getting free tickets to Wimbledon as a thank-you. I said "this is outrageous, we've got senior level counter-terrorism police covering a private sporting match." I put a stop to it.

When Wilson is being bullied and gaslit, one wonders if senior level police looked the other way because they didn't like being called out on a glaringly corrupt practice. The key is to notice the agenda at work so that if betrayal occurs and you are targeted, you recognize that you are being sacrificed, as likely many before, to the "culture" of the institution.

Just look at the glowing language Rowley used when, in the context of Wilson and his maltreatment, he consciously chooses to sing the praises of the CTC. Skipping over Wimbledon and the way in which Wilson's first act as a counterterrorism leader was to shut down the corruption, this is how Rowley speaks to the media. "Those years were among the most challenging in my policing career as we confronted the very real threat of terrorism in the heart of London and across the UK. I am proud of my record and of the outstanding men and women I led who worked together in a professional and determined way to save lives." Saving lives did not seem to be priority during Wimbledon. Working under the radar for a private security company at a tennis tournament for the wealthy and privileged—while being paid by taxpayers—does not usually conjure up terms like "proud" or "professional" or "outstanding." His emphasis on the team, and how worthy they are, informs us through insinuation that Wilson deserves the bullying he endured. Here are the essential lies: Wilson is unworthy and doesn't belong. By sidestepping what was done to Wilson and instead singing the praises of his own leadership and the CTC, Rowley subtly suggests that Wilson wasn't a team player, wasn't able to get along with his colleagues. And as Rowley reminds us, these colleagues were "outstanding." They used their professionalism and determination to "save lives." Wilson's colleagues speaking to a journalist told a radically different story of their workplace.[12]

I am sorry to report that I can see right through the manipulative gaslighting here because it's so similar to what was said about me. The leader praised the teachers with multiple reports of abuse for their "professionalism" without saying what exactly it centered on. He did not ever share the facts of the abuse reports or the lies these teachers told to cover up what they had done, or the way they sat back and allowed the students—whom they had victimized—to be labeled by the leader as telling "nasty lies." Personally, I couldn't find any professionalism, just like I would struggle along with Wilson to find professionalism in the CTC that spent a few weeks at Wimbledon every year while the threat of terrorism loomed, and women and black people were at extreme risk. When I applied for another job, the leader told my potential employer that I was an excellent teacher but "couldn't get along with my colleagues." In gaslighting, a statement is designed to confuse. It insinuates rather than offer clear, factual commentary. It uses a hazy, veiled way of praising perpetrators to condemn and ostracize targets who have had the audacity to report what's really happening.

Cutting through Rowley's rhetoric for the media, we can reasonably assume that the "most challenging" years of his "policing career" in the CTC did *not* include watching the glitterati at a famed tennis competition. Rowley's failure to acknowledge that the Met police and their leaders were called out by Wilson for irresponsible and corrupt behavior like this—his sweeping such conduct under the carpet with a rousing comment on how dedicated the counterterrorism police are to citizen safety—smacks of gaslighting. Rowley presents us with the version of the Met police's elite unit that is associated with power, credibility, and social standing. He participates in the cover-up of maltreatment and corruption; the Met's risky, untrustworthy, and shameful culture that Baroness Casey exposed. Wilson rejected the cover-up and called out the truth at the CTC and as a result, was "destroyed." As Wilson's colleagues reported, "The CTC's 'clubby' culture, they say, prefers to promote internally and protects 'favourites' while punishing those who speak out about 'Spanish practises' involving perks, overtime and foreign trips."[13] Wimbledon was not a one-off corrupt practice. It never is. It is the smoke that tells you the fires of abuse and corruption burn brightly behind closed doors.

In textbook fashion, the one who reports bullying, abuse, or corruption is identified as the actual problem and is driven out. The perpetrators are protected, and the victim is revictimized. As Wilson put it in terms of the bullying, "I just wanted it to stop. I wasn't looking to get anyone in trouble but I was ridiculed when I raised my concerns. They saw me as the problem. I was told Rowley had suggested the solution was to move me out of CTC into a report-writing role and the next day I was gone." It's very difficult to connect this Rowley who—after a disturbing report on bullying practices—takes Wilson, one of his best, certainly one with far more integrity than the others, and moves him out of the most challenging unit, one with outstanding police, one that stands between citizen safety and serious threat. I mean if the counterterrorism unit was just about gigs such as watching over Wimbledon or other corrupt practices that Wilson and others report, that would be easier to understand. But if the counterterrorism unit is as Rowley describes, why would he scapegoat a talented, trusted police leader such as Wilson? These are the questions we must ask if we want to exit workplaces ruled by the lies of bullying, gaslighting, and institutional complicity. If we don't want a breakdown in the trust people have in institutions, we need to change this normalized abusive culture.

Rowley's comment about the counterterrorism unit does not mention Wilson's demands for it to have integrity. Instead, the glowing comment he provides to the media serves to further discredit Wilson, once a trusted leader in a high-stakes position, who was forced into early retirement and rendered dangerously ill when he should have been at the summit of his career. It appears from Rowley's comments that discredit him, Wilson may well have threatened Met higher-ups. He made them paranoid. If as Casey discovered, the force is corrupted by bullying and shameful practices such as Wimbledon, you can well imagine they're putting a lot of energy in keeping that ugly truth from the public.

If those who use bullying and gaslighting to keep a firm grip on their coercion and control style of leadership are exposed, threatened, questioned about their integrity—which could reveal a whole manner of breaking laws and rules—it ramps up their fears. They feel paranoid and through gaslighting reversal infect their victims with this painful sensation. The bullies who targeted Wilson reported to him "false complaints" about him. They lied. This was their strategy to manipulate him. They turned to the essential lies of bullying: you are unworthy; you do not belong. As noted and worth repeating, Wilson "was called to 'ambush meetings' and told that unnamed members of staff had complained about his interpersonal skills. Wilson claims that he faced further false allegations to 'destroy my confidence and my credibility,' including being told that he had lost the confidence of MI5 and the home office."[14]

He said he was excluded from meetings. They gave him "performance reviews" that had "no feedback." Textbook gaslighting, all of it. These officers are pouring cognition and language into creating an illusion of wrongdoing being done by an innocent victim, a colleague, a leader. If this kind of conduct is acceptable in the Met police, at the CTC, then we're all at risk. As Casey says, the nation is at risk. Where are the laws that hold these gaslighting employees accountable? Their conduct suggests that they may have seriously, dangerously dysregulated brains. Where are the neurological assessments and requirements by doctors giving them a clean bill of health before they return to their high-stakes positions?

Perpetrators lack accountability. The ones who destroyed Wilson's career and health apparently were conducting business as usual and making sure that a leader with integrity, committed to best practices, confident enough to call out leadership on corrupt practices, and worst of all, wanting to include others in "information sharing," was lied to, destabilized, and driven out. Controlling information, keeping what's really happening under the radar, ensuring that darkness covers dangerous practices such as sidelining elite police officers to Wimbledon, or allowing bullying, or failing to protect vulnerable groups—especially in need of police protection—cannot withstand any attention from others. Information must be kept closely guarded when it is suspect and corrupt. Transparency threatens the bullying and gaslighting culture that depends on institutional complicity to keep it hidden. Strict practices present power, credibility, and social standing to the media and use language and cognition to ensure that risk, untrustworthiness, and shameful practices are kept hidden.

GASLIGHTING STEALS YOUR SANITY

In our society, you are criminally charged if you steal from a shop, but you can steal colleagues' livelihoods, careers, and health, far too often, with impunity. Wilson not only lost a stellar career when he was at the top of his game, had immense amounts to contribute, and the kind of integrity that could have turned the Met police around and avoided the damning report by Baroness Casey and the erosion of trust in their critical role in society. Wilson also came close to losing his life through suicide.

His twenty-eight years of dedication to the police took place in London. After he was betrayed and ostracized, he chose to put distance between himself and the Met police to maintain his sanity. He told me, "I just had to get out. I felt relief. I needed to dissociate myself with all of it. This happened in 2014 and in 2020 I was still recovering." Targets of bullying, gaslighting, and institutional complicity often feel imprisoned by their betrayal. Although innocent, they can feel trapped and suffer the kind of trauma that makes a return to health and wellness a significant challenge.

For six years, Wilson did "trauma counseling." He told me about walking along the Thames and feeling the pull of suicidal ideation. Wilson shares that he experienced contrasting feelings. "I felt like if I go over there, I'll end it and it will show what they've done to me. But as soon as I thought that I thought that if I go over, they win. They'll still deny what they're doing and they'll win." Those who engage in institutional complicity with bullying in the workplace would be taken aback to hear that their behaviors are also bullying. When you dismiss and deny an employee's bullying trauma, you are bullying with an added layer of gaslighting. Wilson cannot stand that his leadership's response to his suicide would be further denial, further gaslighting, full on institutional complicity.

Wilson explained to me that a key thought process for him remaining safe from self-harm was to think *these people have already harmed you, don't let them harm you further, today is the first day of your recovery. Let's turn the tables.* Notice the sign for new community—"let's" as a team, as a group, as concerned citizens, as people who are trustworthy, "turn the tables." It is indicative of a conscious refusal to be ostracized and isolated. They might have driven out the truth teller, the one with integrity at the Met, but that does not mean for one minute Wilson is unworthy and does not belong. He can recognize those bullying lies and reject them. He can create new community beyond the abusive workplace.

Wilson's next expression of what went through his head after they took so much away from him—namely, his career, his salary, his community, his track record, his reputation, his health—is particularly poignant but also powerful.

You think this is the only way out when you're at the bottom. I knew this, I had to talk to lots of people in policing about suicide. When things feel like they're at their worst, they can only get better. I also link it to family because one of the things going through my head is my daughter is 8 years old and she needed me. At your worst, you need to remember there are people that love you, that rely on you, that need you. . . . Those perpetrators are not only harming you further, but they'll be harming those people who you care for. . . . They will be winning and they won't be held accountable.

85

Wilson expresses here the wisdom of a mental health professional, the love of a father, and the courage that drives a counterterrorism expert to refuse to let manipulation by destabilizing rule the day. As he did for almost three decades as a police officer, he won't rest while perpetrators are harming people. He won't let them win because he knows firsthand in the most painful way that with every victim they take down, they infect their family, friends, and community with grief, loss, and suffering. It's trauma that won't disappear anytime soon. The counterterrorism expert tells us that part of his mission is that perpetrators of terror may win and not be held accountable, but not on his watch. What's tragic is that his thoughts—that led him to counsel other suicidal police and that he applies to himself in this fraught moment—aren't about terrorists. They're in response to his colleagues.

NOTES

1. All references to Jonathan Wilson's bullying crisis are from a 2023 article in *The Times* written by Michael Galliard and Fiona Hamilton unless otherwise specified. See references.

2. There is a public website by "The Upsetter"— an investigative journalist—dedicated to Jonathan Wilson's appalling maltreatment at the Met. Henceforth, references to this site will be referred to as "The Upsetter." Wilson recognized that he had been relegated from the start to an "out-group" and was being sabotaged by a higher-up who ultimately called him out for not following proper procedure. He could not have known that the institution would also not follow proper procedure and instead would throw him under the bus. As reported in The Upsetter: "Wilson felt unsupported and undermined by his line manager, detective chief superintendent Duncan Ball, a respected CTC stalwart. At first Wilson put it down to not being one of the 'in crowd.' But by this time with over two decades at the Met he felt resilient enough to get on with the job in hand. However, Wilson came to suspect his boss was being 'wilfully obstructive' and dismissive of his attempt to integrate Prevent and work with agencies outside the CTC."

3. The Upsetter.

4. The Upsetter.

5. All references to Baroness Casey of Blackstock's yearlong report on the Met police are from a 2023 article in *The Times* written by Matt Dathan unless otherwise specified. See references.

6. The Upsetter.

7. Sir Mark Rowley would not provide comments or an interview to The Upsetter: "Rowley denies there was any bullying at CTC under his watch. But Wilson is supported by other counter-terrorism insiders who talk of a 'promotion culture of acquiescence' at the national security unit." This is a textbook example of bullying dynamics built on beneficia-

ries (those who look the other way when wrongdoing or abuse occurs and get promoted) and targets (those who are bullied, gaslit, and discarded by the institution). As soon as any leader states that his culture includes "no bullying," you should be on high alert.

8. The Upsetter.

9. This whole exchange with DAC Ball is recorded by The Upsetter.

10. The Upsetter.

11. The Upsetter.

12. As reported by The Upsetter: "One former CTC detective who'd served under Rowley said,

> CTC operates completely independently of the Met. It doesn't allow outside influence and does its own thing. There is a sickening culture of elitism and senior officers who abuse public money on foreign trips under the guise of national security.
>
> There is a massive culture of favouritism. People toe the line if they want overtime.
>
> Whistleblowing isn't an option. There's a fear of speaking out. Lots of nonsense gets squared up inside.

The insider gave an example of thousands of pounds of cash handed out to CTC officers during an overseas trip, which some spent on drink and prostitutes.

13. The Upsetter.

14. Wilson found these falsehoods some of the most destabilizing even after his colleagues debunked them. As reported by The Upsetter:

> The most memorable was when Wilson says he was accused of having lost the confidence of the Home Office and MI5 over a briefing on Prevent given to then Mayor of London, Boris Johnson. The spooks didn't want Johnson to have the briefing but didn't explain why, said Wilson. However, assistant commissioner Cressida Dick thought otherwise and ensured it went ahead. Wilson prided himself on good personal relationships with the handful of Home Office officials and MI5 officers he was liaising with and claims the security officials made it known to CTC that he had not lost their confidence.

CHAPTER FOUR

The Law Professor

JULIE MACFARLANE'S COURAGE TO SHARE HER STORY IS A GAME changer because it reveals the way in which brain wiring or scripting during our formative years may shape our responses, reactions, and assessments of ourselves and others in the workplace. I have grappled for years with this pressing question: Why do institutions protect perpetrators and not victims? Macfarlane's book *Going Public* gave me the answer in a shocking and heartrending way. I need to walk you through her story before I can share the insight that answers this puzzling question: Why are those who abuse often protected and enabled while those who are targeted and speak up often ostracized?

At the age of five, Macfarlane was raped by a teenage boy in the woods where she was alone and unsupervised. She had no words to tell her mother but gave enough of a child's version of the rape that her mother understood. As she explains, "I groped for the words to describe what happened to me."[1] The rape was never spoken of again. Macfarlane explains that the initial rape sets up the victim—on an exponential level—to suffer further assaults; the first assault lays the neurological groundwork for those that follow.

With the wisdom of hindsight, I can now see that each experience set me up for the next by further diminishing my self-esteem and my confidence in my ability to take care of myself. This is a common pattern. Research suggests that the chance of being sexually assaulted rises exponentially after the first incident, especially if it took place during childhood and the victim learned to keep silent.[2]

Silence is one of the most effective weapons in the perpetrator's arsenal. It works in the courtrooms of India, and it works in the homes, society, culture, and courtrooms of North America and beyond. Where it didn't work was at a highly successful company's workplace. Nike defined itself in 2018 by listening to the voices of victims, not silencing them. And even more powerful, it acted on the reports of victims rather than setting in motion the institutional complicity required to cover up and enable perpetrators of harm.

In the introduction, we noted the gaslighting that coach Luis Rubiales tried to use to claim that football player Jenni Hermoso consented to his forced public kiss. Spain has seen this moment—Hermoso pushing back and debunking the consent myth—as critically important in a nation rife with sexism. The consent myth is even used with children positioned in court as participants in sex abuse, ones who do not find the abuse "unwelcome," to use the word applied to Macfarlane who as a child was repeatedly abused by an Anglican minister, much to her fury as a law professor and disgust as an adult survivor.[3]

Macfarlane quotes from another victim of abuse by an Anglican minister. It's a memorable example of how our society trains us to trust *positions* of power, credibility, and social standing, which leads us to ignore signs that the person who inhabits the role may not be trustworthy. In a key step in gaslighting, as we saw with biblical Eve, the victim is encouraged to share her vulnerabilities. The minister's victim shares: "I told him all of this because I believed with my entire being that I was safe with a man of God."[4] The position is designed to convey safety, but there is no guarantee the human who occupies it is safe. These myths are prevalent in the workplace, and showing that they are even applied to children, assists in exposing the gaslighting at work.

Macfarlane explains that myths "remain pervasive, about malicious false reporting, women as temptresses, accusers seeking fame and fortune and—the most dangerous of all—the consent myth."[5] The victim must answer to anticipated character flaws mixed with corrupt desires for attention and money. Phrases don't appear to be attached to perpetrators, such as the "violence myth" or the "sexual assault myth." It's almost as if these are normalized, accepted behaviors. The victim reporting them is, in fact, the perpetrator who must defend her actions against the "rape myth" and the "consent myth." As Macfarlane notes, "This just adds to the feeling that we, the complainants, are in fact the ones being investigated."[6] It's one thing to be innocent until proven guilty. It's another to enter a realm of reversals where the perpetrator is treated as if he is the victim while the victim is under the investigative spotlight as if she is the perpetrator. These reversals occur even when the victim is a child, which is truly baffling.

BOWING DOWN TO THE AUTHORITY FIGURE

As noted, Macfarlane's first trauma was being raped as a five-year-old; the second, being sexually abused repeatedly by an Anglican minister. As a teenager questioning her relationship to God, Macfarlane sought the guidance of her small British town's minister. He began sexually abusing her. She writes: "The disconnect between what he made me do with him in private and his public role left me confused, terrified, and ashamed. As far as I knew, in the years after I left home, he was a minister still, holding a position of authority and power. Who was I to challenge this?"[7] The public, respected figure is a cover for the private, abusive figure. We are *not* taught to recognize this dual or split self-presentation.

Macfarlane cannot understand or name her abuse because she has no language for it: "I had no way of understanding or naming what was happening to me in those assaults that took place in the minister's study."[8] Remember that Carle did not have the vocabulary to name her maltreatment as "bullying." Wilson did not have the vocabulary to understand that he was being exposed to gaslighting. Macfarlane's trauma is not just the repeat abuses; it's the lack of vocabulary to understand and report. She is silenced. Instead of being clear, outraged, and demanding accountability, the victim is "confused, terrified, and ashamed." Because of the abuser's position, she internalizes the abuse and takes responsibility for it. Who was she to challenge him?

Macfarlane shuttles back and forth from the past to the present. She brings you into the traumatizing world of her teenage self with a sexually abusive minister, a girl uneducated in abuse, and her own mother who accuses her of being a "slut" when she seeks support. If she remained in the past, Macfarlane's book would be an upsetting but not a demanding read. In contrast, her book pushes the reader into an uncomfortable space by juxtaposing horrendous tales of childhood abuse with the present-day workplace abuse she encounters as a law professor.

Macfarlane recounts the contemporary crisis she's drawn into with a psychologically and sexually abusive colleague at an institution that covers up and facilitates his exit, allowing him access to other unwitting victims. It's concerning as we would like to believe that a university—especially the faculty of law—is highly advanced when it comes to establishing a just and safe society. Macfarlane makes her reader face the painful fact that her university and her law school are failing victims. As she explains, "In 2014, my law school had no internal processes for dealing with allegations of sexual assaults and harassment, and the central university processes were unwelcoming, bureaucratic, and inadequate." In short, "Silence was the status quo."[9] Silence was that status quo at my workplace. Silence was the status quo at Nike; silence was the status quo at the Met police department. When it comes to bullying, gaslighting, and institutional complicity, the one rule you can never break is to maintain silence about wrongdoing. Or put another way: Do not tell the truth.

When Macfarlane was a teen, she feared being attacked for reporting the abuse by the Anglican minister, so she kept silent. As a law professor, she speaks up about the risk her abusive colleague poses when asked by those who are considering hiring him. She tells them the truth about his predatory behavior as the reason he was fired. The abusive former colleague, which Macfarlane did not know was protected by an NDA, attacked *her* with a defamation lawsuit—a textbook example of how the perpetrator positions himself as the victim. The one who reports his wrongdoing suddenly becomes the perpetrator for committing the truth. *Not* maintaining silence, *not* participating in the institutional cover-up of abuse, is dangerous. In an email, Macfarlane described how she continues to be treated by her institution.

The ongoing gaslighting and ostracization from the institution I worked at for 30 years continues to amaze me. Despite the fact that the law has changed with regard to NDAs in universities in Ontario in a way that forbids the actions that [University of Windsor] took to protect my colleague and to set me up to be sued, I have heard nothing from the [university] or from any of my colleagues there that expresses the least bit of regret or personal support.

Imagine how incredibly harmful and hurtful it is to do the right thing and be penalized by your workplace leaders and colleagues. It is a particularly painful moral injury that demonstrates how mixed up we are in a work world whereby we protect those who hurt others and lie about it while we oust those who protect others and tell the truth about it.

What will it take to change this normalized scenario whereby when you report abuse, you are positioned as the perpetrator, and the perpetrator becomes the victim? How can we break the silence when we are too often trapped in the gaslighting hall of mirrors? A clear and powerful response is offered by Macfarlane, along with Zelda Perkins, who reported Harvey Weinstein's abuse twenty years before he was convicted but was silenced, like so many, with an NDA. Macfarlane and Perkins have joined forces to ban the use of nondisclosure agreements to cover up misconduct. They've called their advocacy campaign Can't Buy My Silence (see cantbuymy silence.com). Institutions can quickly and efficiently step out of bullying and gaslighting's hall of mirrors by changing the policies and culture that cover up, hide, and thereby enable abuse. Macfarlane and Perkins urge institutions to discontinue the use of NDAs, sign a public pledge that they have done so, and release all previous victims or reporters of abuse from any NDAs they might have signed. Macfarlane is clear that this one step alone would indicate an institutional commitment to safe workplaces and mark an effort to change a societal culture that revictimizes victims.

SOCIETAL SILENCING OF VICTIMS STARTS AT HOME
Macfarlane as a five-year-old was not taught any words to report the rape done to her. As a teenage girl, she still was not taught any words to understand the psychopathic split personality of the sexually abusive

Anglican minister. When our society does not teach us words to convey our experience, we have no way to understand it, let alone tell others. In part 3, we examine in depth the importance on a personal and institutional level to have shared emotion concepts of preventing and reporting abuse. Leaders, managers, and HR who know and teach these emotion concepts create far safer and healthier workplaces, which in turn creates more productive and profitable workplaces. Bullying and gaslighting depend on speaking lies. They commit violence against truth and facts. Speaking the truth with accuracy and accountability is an effective way to create a community where lies do not dominate.

As noted, a simple and effective strategy to find out the truth about what is going on is to send out anonymous surveys as the women did at Nike. This information-gathering tool heads off any attempts to attack or use reprisals against those who speak up. It reveals patterns of behavior and keeps the focus on perpetrators. It stops the institutional default to shoot the messenger because the messenger is irrelevant. The ones who are bullying and gaslighting are under scrutiny. Workplaces that use anonymous surveys may well prevent and deter harmful conduct because perpetrators know that victims can report them anonymously and therefore, cannot threaten them with retaliatory behaviors. If a workplace wants to level the playing field, anonymous surveys return power to those who lack official positions of power, credibility, and social standing. It surprises me that insurance companies require workplaces to be up to code when it comes to fire, but they do not require anonymous surveys from employees that inform leaders, managers, and HR, along with insurers, what is happening in terms of bullying and gaslighting, considering the significant risks they pose to psychological safety and the associated liabilities.

It surprises me that insurance companies do not join forces with Macfarlane and Perkins to insist that those institutions they insure discontinue the use of NDAs to cover up abuse. The risks and the costs to insurance companies of workplace bullying can be astronomical, yet they allow the cover-up and enabling of it through using NDAs that silence victims and truth tellers. From a business perspective, let alone a humane perspective, it does not make sense.

THE PRISON OF SELF-DOUBT

Macfarlane recognizes that similar to domestic abuse, sex abuse victims suffer from a "perception of inescapability" or "learned helplessness." She realizes that the Anglican minister's abuse, coupled with her society's lack of instruction on how to understand it let alone report it, trapped her in a "prison of self doubt."[10] Tapping into the mind-set of a teenager being abused provides insight into why so few victims—even in the workplace as adults—speak up when the abuse is occurring and often do not find the words or the comprehension until decades later. In part 2 of *The Gaslit Brain*, we will study the split personality, and examine it in more depth from a neuroscience perspective. Being informed will help us more quickly recognize the textbook confusion over an Anglican minister in a position of power, credibility, and social status who is simultaneously an abuser whose violence is against children, facts, and truth. Without studying this borderline personality phenomenon, how can a victim put these two contradictory figures into the same body? It baffles the brain.

Society, let alone workplaces, does not teach that this contradictory presentation can occur, and it does not provide accurate language, such as borderline personality disorder. In *The Gaslit Brain*, we can apply research and suspect that the Anglican minister is likely to have empathy erosion so that his brain defaults to language and cognition. The minister can harm children in his care at the same time as he parades about the community offering his blessing and guidance. To apply terminology, not just from ancient texts but also from contemporary psychological research, he can be understood as a wolf in sheep's clothing, an intraspecies predator, a snake dressed—not in a suit—but the robes of a man of God.

Why didn't Macfarlane have any of this vocabulary as a teenager? Why do few adults have this vocabulary? The victim quoted a few pages back who told another minister all her confidences—that made her vulnerable to his abuse—is an adult. I was an adult when I was being bullied and gaslit in my workplace. Megan Carle and Jonathan Wilson were adults. Why do we not teach children *and* adults to watch out for these perpetrators? Why do we leave victims to learn about perpetrators *after* they have become traumatized and are trying to find answers to what happened to them? Leaders, managers, and HR are often as confused and manipulated as the victims. As we saw with Wilson and Carle, it is only post-abuse, after forced retirement or resignation to save ourselves, that we finally learn from mental health experts what happened to us. With victims like hundreds of USA gymnasts, they learned in Judge Aquilina's courtroom what happened to them, in the larger context of what happened to others. They used their time in the courtroom to teach other potential victims how to protect themselves.

Macfarlane explains she could not *challenge* what the child abuser did to her in private because society acted as though his only true self was his public role as minister. What was done to her was societal, cultural, religious gaslighting. She is expected to discount her own personal experiences of abuse with the Anglican minister and act as if they are not real or not happening. Essentially, her society acts as if abusive acts are *not* possible, *not* worthy of warning potential victims about, *not* needing any kind of protection from, and thus, teen victims are expected to believe the lie that positions the Anglican minister as trustworthy, safe, and caring.

Although children don't know the history of rampant child abuse by perpetrators cloaked in religious positions, adults do. Religious authorities, lawmakers, policy writers, mental health professionals, educators know. Parents know. It's so rampant, you'd have to live on a different planet not to know. All too often child victims are handed over to perpetrators on a silver platter because of their ignorance. Amazingly enough, adults in the workplace can be as shocked and shattered by bullying and gaslighting behaviors as children. Privileged, educated, experienced adults like me, like Carle, like Wilson, can be victimized. Few of us are safe or immune. Extensive education about abuse and about the psychology of perpetrators *before* their onslaught and the resulting trauma can be a game changer.

It's hard to remain sane when you live in an insane society. It's hard to distinguish truth from lies when your society succumbs to collective gaslighting. Society might operate this way, but leaders, managers, and HR can create workplaces that reject the lies of bullying and gaslighting and instead, privilege truth and facts. With mental illness reaching epidemic proportions in today's society, organizations that prioritize workplace environments that are healthy for brains will enjoy mental strength and resilience, rather than mental weakness and illness.

Macfarlane strives to put her traumatizing abuse at the hands of the minister and her community's abject failure to protect her and other victims into a more contemporary context. She aims to show that what happened to her in a small rural town in Britain so many years ago is *no different* from what she witnesses decades later in a Canadian city as a law professor advocating for student safety from a serial abuser. It would have been an uphill battle for her as a child to stop the abuse of the Anglican minister; much more surprising, it is *still* an uphill battle for her as a legal professional to stop the abuse of a drama teacher in a public high-school in our time, and it is *still* an uphill battle for her to stop the abuse of a colleague being passed on to other unsuspecting victims legally protected by an NDA signed by his complicit institution.

CHOOSING SPECTACLE OVER REALITY

Imagine the jolt I felt when I read in Macfarlane's book about the way our society silences abuse: "For many years, rumours had swirled around the charismatic teacher of dramatic arts at a Windsor high school."[11] If you recall, I encountered this identical scenario a few years earlier. The dramatic arts teacher in Windsor was fired in 2017 and the dramatic arts teacher I referenced in Victoria was fired in 2012. Windsor is on the eastern side of Canada, whereas Victoria is on the western side. That is the only essential difference between these two tales of abuse. One other detail that differed was that the dramatic arts teacher at the public school in Windsor was publicly fired, whereas the one in Victoria, in the private school, apparently decided to "retire early." This is doublespeak in some private schools for he was *fired*, but it's being covered up.[12]

On the east and west sides of the country, both teachers used their positions of power, credibility, and social standing to physically, emotionally, sexually, and psychologically abuse students. Both continued in their positions for years while school leaders and boards were informed about the abuse but failed to protect students. Both drama teachers put on wonderful theatrical spectacles, which was enough to activate the institutional complicity required to enable their abuse.

The two teachers—thousands of miles apart—conducted the same abusive regimes, yet another example of the way in which maltreatment is textbook, follows a script (ironically here), and lacks imagination. Both these teachers even threw a chair! As is typical, in Windsor not only did the school leadership and board put on blinders to the abuse, so did some parents. Although they may have expressed concerns about "foul language directed at students" or "sudden angry outbursts," as Macfarlane says, "they for the most part ignored these."[13] In contrast with these parents who looked the other way, parents spoke up at the private school where I was working, but their complaints were repeatedly ignored. The leader, director, and chaplain did nothing effective to stop the abuse and ultimately tried to make it seem—as discussed—as if I was the problem for reporting it.

This is an excellent strategy to deflect attention away from the abuse and onto the one speaking up. Empathy is diverted from victims to the perpetrators who are being accused of wrongdoing and threatened with job action. Colleagues see themselves in these educators at risk and appear to forget what they have done to students that would result in multiple abuse reports. The teachers—whose empathy is for other teachers, not victimized students—feel like the institution should offer them protection. It's backward, but it often works in favor of perpetrators.

Parents spoke up in droves at the private school regarding the abuse affecting Montgomery and his peers in the PE department, but once again, the leader, director, chaplain, and ultimately the board shut them down and revictimized their children. How can you establish safety in these normalized scenarios, either the one where parents believe the teacher's expertise outweighs the abusive conduct, or the other where parents speak up and only succeed in bringing more suffering to their children? When I look at the reprisals Montgomery and his peers suffered, I wonder if the parents in the Windsor school didn't decide to keep quiet knowing that it would keep their kids safer. At least the abuse would be contained with the dramatic arts teacher and not become institutional with the revictimizing occurring through the offices of the leader, director, chaplain, and board.

Macfarlane reports that with the drama teacher in Windsor, some students were targeted for verbal abuse such as being called "retarded," some were targeted for "degrading and ridiculing" in front of other students, while others were targeted for "personal text messages."[14] I had to stop reading. If you recall, I learned in detail about how Montgomery was the target of *all* three of these exact abuses at the hands of *two other teachers*, beyond the drama department, protected in the private school despite multiple complaints. Note the contagion.

As Macfarlane comments, when it comes to abuse and attempts to stop it, "The stories we tell reflect depressing similarities."[15] Considering the remarkable damage with each instance of abuse, it's amazing that we have normalized it everywhere. Macfarlane reports that at Windsor "Students who made complaints were shunned by other students."[16] And that, too, was Montgomery's fate. Note the contagion and yet more depressing similarities. What saved Montgomery was that he did not respect the teachers who abused him or the students who shunned him, and he certainly did not respect the leader, chaplain, director, or the board. Even as a teenager, Montgomery watched boys mimic the abusive teachers. He watched boys his age hissing "pussy," one of the teachers' go-to insults, at him in economics class. His teacher wrote me to say she didn't know what was going on, but he had become very quiet in class. That is Montgomery's strength. He listens and observes. He would come home and discuss these boys and how pathetic he thought their actions were. If they wanted to call him a pussy, well, do it. Speak up. Why hiss and mutter like the teachers? Where was their courage and conviction?

Montgomery's disdain for the teachers who infected the boys with their own cowardly form of maltreatment reminds me of Megan Carle, who set in motion a healthy revolution at Nike headquarters by walking out. She didn't speak up. Even though she had become very unwell, her track record meant that her exit was the power move. Her silence spoke volumes and resulted in radical change for the better. In contrast, Macfarlane has put her legal expertise into blowing up silence, forcing workplaces and lawmakers to recognize that NDAs are being misused to silence abuse, not to protect intellectual property.

Abuse Communities Are Unevolved

When Macfarlane reported the allegations to the school board superintendent, he told her that "he would not take any further steps until he

98

heard directly from a student complainant." This is word for word what the school leader said to me when about thirty parents were reporting the teachers who abused Montgomery and his peers. Macfarlane supplied student testimonies, and so did I. More depressing similarities. The only difference was that the leader to whom I emailed student testimonies turned around and told the school community I was acting on my own, that he had *not* asked me to collect them. He put this blatant lie in writing, which indicates to me that he had told self-serving lies like this before and was accustomed to covering up abuse with impunity. As we learned in the introduction, it's quite possible that his brain was not sending him panicky alerts from the amygdala anymore as he lied. His brain had normalized such conduct, and he felt comfortable doing it. The lies of bullying are compounded by the lies of gaslighting and further compounded by those that prop up institutional complicity. The leader is an ideal example of a pathological liar.

Imagine the eastern teacher in drama, the western teacher in drama, and the two PE teachers enacting comparable abuse with Montgomery and the other students on the basketball court: obscene put-downs such as "retards" or "retarded," repeat scenes of public shaming, sending text messages to targets to love bomb them. I am fighting the normalized bullying and institutional complicity but failing. And while all this is happening, detective superintendent, head of Prevent at the counterterrorism command, Jonathan Wilson is being bullied and gaslit in Scotland Yard and Megan Carle, a top-of-the-line Nike basketball executive, is being daily abused in comparable ways. Imagine the expertise and leadership lost to organizations that allow their best and brightest to be targeted and driven out by those likely suffering from psychopathology who—after the dust settles from yet another round of abuse reports—will be on the hunt for the next victims, infecting their workplaces with violence against targets, facts and truth. It's inspiring to see that Nike fired the perpetrators harming the dedicated, talented women like Megan Carle in their organization. Far too often, the perpetrators are protected and the targets revictimized.

It's one thing to be twenty years or more into a fabulous career, where you've had opportunities to prove your work ethic and talent like Wilson, Carle, Macfarlane, and me, but abusers in one's formative years can crush that career before it even begins. Educators—whether they're high-school teachers, arts instructors, coaches, managers, corporate mentors, doctors, or professors—have enormous power over students or new hires. As law students said about reporting an abusive prof and are recorded in Macfarlane's book, "We felt that we were in a weak position. We felt that as bourgeoning law students, with no money to our name, and no careers to speak of, we were ending our careers before they started."[17] Imagine a workplace where to succeed in your career, you must keep quiet about the abuse being done to you or others.

A workplace that rewards abusers and penalizes those who speak up is on shaky ground. This is where leaders, managers, and HR can make the greatest difference. They can level the playing field and give power-less victims—who have not yet earned positions of credibility because of their age and stage, and who do not yet have power, credibility, and social standing—a right to speak and tell their facts and truth. As noted, the anonymous survey can do wonders to identify patterns of abuse. At present, all too often, the institution sides automatically with the perpe-trator due to her position of power, credibility, and social standing and thus allows for bullying, gaslighting, and retaliating a form of violence against facts and truth.

The Wiring of Brains

Macfarlane's brain was wired in her formative years by the lies of bul-lying and gaslighting from her mother. "I knew with certainty that if I described to my mother having been grabbed and groped at work that this would lead rapidly to her telling me I was a slut who must have been 'leading him on.'"[18] The mother, scripted by society, teaches her daughter that she is an "Eve-teaser" who leads men astray, causing them to abuse and assault her. Textbook reversal: when you are violated, the fault lies with you. You provoked the harm; therefore, you are the perpetrator. Note the psychosis of it. It's like saying your jewelry store was robbed, and you are at fault because you displayed the jewels. You (victim) caused the robbery, so you are the robber (perpetrator).

When Macfarlane was raped in university and had to get an abor-tion, her mother gaslit her again. "When she drove me home from the hospital the following day, she told me that I was a slut. I didn't even consider telling her that I had been raped. She would not have believed me. I was not sure I believed me."[19] Let's take a moment to fully absorb gaslighting in action. Can you imagine being a twentysomething who has been raped, has had to have an abortion, and instead of compassion for the violation, the violence, the loss of the infant, all the trauma, suffering, and heartbreak you are having to endure, you encounter blaming and shaming, namely bullying. Not from a stranger, but from your mother.

In this moment of bullying and gaslighting, the victim does not have an encounter with truth or reality between herself and her mother. Instead, she is met with the falsehood that she caused the violation done to her. She is falsely labeled a sexual manipulator who is unworthy of the mother's care, concern, and help. She does not deserve basic human empathy and compassion because—due to her mother labeling her a woman with many sexual partners, a "slut"—she does not belong. What is the impact of these repeat blows upon Macfarlane's young brain? She *believes* her mother's bullying and gaslighting lies and questions her own experience. "I was not sure I believed me." She is trapped in the prison of "self-doubt."

The scripting of a false reversal is being fired up and wired into Macfarlane's brain. She has become a young woman who believes the lies of her mother's bullying reversal—"you are a slut"—but *not* her own perception, *not* her own experience—"I was not sure I believed me." Macfarlane does not consider telling her mother the truth that she was raped because there are no words for it, no emotion concepts, only societal myths like the rape myth and the consent myth and the Eve-teasing myth. Lots of myths for the victims prevail, and yet, as noted, we don't find myths that convey the perpetrator's role or hold him accountable. The young, traumatized Macfarlane, recently raped, does not question her mother's lie, but we can. Let us ask her mother: If rapes are the result of manipulative sexual behavior, also known as being a "slut," then why was your daughter raped at the age of five when she was alone in the woods, when she had no maternal protection, no adults who felt a duty to keep her safe from intraspecies predators? Was she a slut at the age of five, too?

Only this context could provide insight for me into why a young law professor—brilliant, accomplished, highly educated Julie Macfarlane—

goes home nightly for eighteen months to a man who is on the verge of killing her.

GASLIGHTING AT HOME

"I lived a bizarre double-life between this nine-to-five world and the terror that engulfed me at home."[20] During the day, as a young woman, Macfarlane worked as a law professor. She went home to an extremely violent, psychotic partner. Dr. Bessel van der Kolk's psychiatric work has shown in decisive ways: the violated, harmed, traumatized individual is trying to survive and finding any method to do it. The reaction of dissociating is a reasonable, normal brain-body survival strategy.[21] As Macfarlane told me on email, "The split between my work life as a professor and my home life in a lethally violent relationship required me to dissociate from the experience I was having."

Even the potency of her survival instinct has been crushed, and we see that she has succumbed to the maternal and social lies that when she is abused it is *her* fault. It's like a codependency so deep and entrenched that Macfarlane thinks *she* is the abuser, the perpetrator. Since childhood, Macfarlane has been bullied and gaslit into having little sense of self-worth or sense of belonging. She has been repeatedly told that she is the cause of harm done to her. She provoked it. She is guilty. It is her fault. She deserved it. Like all messaging and wiring into neural networks, the more it's fired up and repeated, the more it wires in. It became the lens through which Macfarlane saw her reality. This wiring was so powerful that it made feeble the intellectual and experiential wiring of being a law professor.

Imagine the mental strength it took to leave her abuser.

Macfarlane shares this gut-wrenching story of domestic abuse with her readers displaying an almost breathtaking courage. "I was trapped with no idea what was happening to me and with no one to turn to for help."[22] Notice she has no language still. She cannot put into words the violence, or the fact that her life is at risk, or the manipulation of believing that the person who beats you does it because you deserve it. She does not believe she's worthy or that she belongs, so no one can help. You cannot reach your hand out to someone if no one is there because you are unworthy of their presence. Her abuser is not only violent, he's also a master at gaslighting, just like her mother. "He told me the violence was all my fault, and incredible though it sounds, I believed him."[23]

For us as readers, it's *not* incredible. Macfarlane has given us the lens we need to see what her mother's bullying and gaslighting had done to her brain. If her mother broke both her legs and did not send her to a doctor to get them set in a cast, we would *not* find it incredible that she was unable to walk. Legs walk, and the brain makes sense of a large amount of data constantly coming at it from the environment, the body, and interactions with others. Her brain is not working properly. It cannot mentally hold her upright, let alone walk.

When I interviewed Macfarlane, she told me that the man who came close to violently murdering her multiple times had a book written by Erin Pizzey called *Prone to Violence*. Pizzey's view of domestic violence was highly controversial, and Macfarlane's abuser argued that Pizzey's thesis was that female victims courted violence because they enjoyed it. Note once again that the perpetrator's agency is not the focus, as usual; the focus is on the receiver of the violence. The perpetrator does the act, but the victim is held responsible. The perpetrator rapes, but it is the Eve-teasing that caused him to violate her. In every case, the perpetrator's action is sidestepped to focus on the victim's provocation. Why else do victims constantly say, "I was bullied because . . ." This reversal has been taught by society. If we lived in a society where perpetrators were frequently held accountable, victims would say: "The perpetrator bullied me because . . ."

Macfarlane's mother wired into her brain the idea that she was abused because she was a "slut." Macfarlane's domestic abuser fired up this wiring by telling her about a book that argues women like to be beaten up. They make it happen. They're the perpetrators. He used Erin Pizzey's *Prone to Violence*, a published book no less—with its power, credibility, and social standing—to convince young law professor Macfarlane the reverse of the truth. His violence was against her body, and against facts and truth. When you lack the needed language, when you have been told that your reality does not exist, your brain can no longer be trusted to tell the story of your experience. Your perceptions and pain are ignored. It can put your life at risk.

Crime of Passion?

The man who nightly rained terror and harm on Macfarlane was careful not to ever wound her face.[24] She could cover up all his nightly violence with clothing and be a law professor by day. Rape, sex abuse, abortion, are wounds that can be covered up, and she was trained to act as if she was not suffering, not in pain, not at risk, and everything was fine. These horrendous traumas need to be covered up because they are her fault. According to her mother's gaslighting, they weren't done to her; she caused them. Trying to articulate the danger she was in, or the agony she was suffering, only brought her more bullying and gaslighting from her mother. Macfarlane learned *not* to set in motion further harm to herself by speaking up, asking for help, turning to her family for support and protection. It makes perfect sense that she applied these deeply ingrained life lessons to her relationship with the violent offender.

Notice that her abuser put on the pantomime of a crime of passion each night, a full-on spectacle of rage, but his careful avoidance of her face shows that he's thinking rationally and reasonably about covering up and not getting exposed. He intentionally keeps the abuse behind closed doors. He's *thinking* about consequences. He's using his cognition to do this, not his out-of-control emotions. He uses a book—a signifier of cognition—to reinforce the mother's messaging that Macfarlane is simply a slut who has it coming to her. She likes being beaten up.

Why Protect the Perpetrator and Not the Victim?

Why does the mother fault her daughter and fail to hold the perpetrator accountable? The mother reverses from her role as caregiver into bully and gaslighter. The layers of gaslighting that lead victims' brains to replace their own perceptions, experiences, and truths with those of manipulators also fuel workplaces that enable perpetrators, silence those who report abuse, and revictimize victims. When you look at these layers occurring through society, it's not all that surprising that we have institutional complicity with abusive practices. It still doesn't answer the psychological question: Why do we protect perpetrators in society, starting with parenting, that is reinforced by the education system so that this backward system occurs in the workplace?

Here is my realization. If the victim is at fault, then the mother did *not* fail to protect her five-year-old daughter alone in the woods when she was raped. If the victim is at fault, the mother was *not* negligent in the abuse done to her teenager—repeatedly—by the Anglican minister, men in the workplace, a university student who raped her, resulting in an abortion. The mother is *not* responsible. Is this why some institutions mimic this way of handling abuse in the workplace? How else do we explain abusers protected for decades while abuse reports pile up year after year? It appears that an impulse to shirk responsibility is at the heart of protecting perpetrators and revictimizing victims.

If the victim is, in fact, the perpetrator, then nothing must be done except remove the one reporting (who is positioned as the perpetrator). The victims are scapegoated and expected to take all the confusion, emotional upheaval, contradiction and destabilizing away from the institution. The pattern is established in society long before it enters workplace culture. The parent does not have to face her failure to protect her child. Educators and educational leaders do not have to face their failure to protect their vulnerable population of students who get abused. Sports and arts organizations who fail their duty can also fault the victims, avoiding responsibility for decades. Institutions and institutional leaders do not have to face their negligence in allowing abuse to occur on their watch. In fact, they can use this lack of accountability to actively cover up the harm done, believing that their true job is to protect the institution (and, therefore, themselves). They gaslight themselves into believing the happiness of the institution, the majority, trumps the rights of the victims, the unhappy minority.

Remember, Ursula K. Le Guin's parable "The Ones Who Walk Away from Omelas," which questions the utilitarian philosophy that we examine in more depth in part 2. Le Guin depicts a fictional society where the greatest good for the greatest number excuses the suffering of the single abused child. We see the institution thinking along these lines when it labels the abuse victim and truth teller a "perpetrator" and scapegoats them to protect everyone else (including the actual perpetrators). If we take it one step further into totalitarian dictatorships, then a happy minority of superior beings who do not suffer vulnerability or empathy can rightly rule over and benefit from a majority of enemies and losers defined by their vulnerability and empathy. These enemies and losers are despised by the strongman who protects the happy minority from being tainted by the out-group's inferiority, their desperation, their weakness. This kind of thinking can infect institutions and whole nations.

SCAPEGOATING THE VICTIM DOES NOT REMOVE THE PLAGUE

Faulting the victim and ousting the victim (as if he's the perpetrator) might not ultimately work because it is, in fact, the actual split-personality perpetrator who creates all this trauma. After each victim is sacrificed, the perpetrator simply starts up the predatory ritual again. Apparently, this repeat strategy is still preferable to Macfarlane's mother and to institutions such as the Met police, the Anglican Church, high schools, sports programs such as USA Gymnastics, Hollywood, Nike until recently, the University of Windsor, and more. They would rather the cycle of abuse keeps turning than be exposed as failing their duty. Enabling abuse wins out over facing the fact that they have been negligent, and harm has occurred on their watch. Macfarlane makes crystal clear what exactly is predatory in these scenarios.

> "Predatory" is commonly defined as behaviour intended to exploit, injure, or oppress. At the core of predatory behaviour inside institutions is the exploitation of power bestowed by the institution, either formally—for example a teacher, professor, coach, or cleric—or informally—for example a student athlete or "popular" guy. This power is used to intimidate and silence those who would complain, and to manipulate and take advantage of those who feel they have no choice but to comply. This pattern allows many predators to continue their behaviours over many years, often in the face of credible complaints.[25]

We can take the predatory power one step further. When the institution confers power in good faith on a leader or manager and starts to hear reports that he is an abusive individual, panic ensues. It appears that institutional leaders feel at extreme risk and think fast about ways to save themselves and the institution. They use quick thinking to make the problem go away, oftentimes directing the help of HR, which Wilson calls the institution's "black ops." This approach leads to ousting the victim, not the perpetrator. Exposing the perpetrator requires admitting failure, acknowledging that one was groomed by the abuser and fell for her facade. Perpetrators often groom higher-ups as much as they groom targets. It must be mortifying when abuse reports flow in from credible sources exposing that one was tricked into believing in the perpetrator's power, credibility, and social standing. Leaders, managers, and HR may believe so much in the manipulator's fabricated presentation that they ignore the warning signs that behind the facade resides an abuser.

Recognizing these painful truths requires coming face-to-face with harm done by empowering a predatory individual, recognizing the hurt and potentially devastating harm done to victims. It requires full disclosure that this awful manipulative occurrence happened on one's watch. All this immense discomfort can be avoided by ignoring, then faulting, and finally, ousting victims. It doesn't matter how much knowledge, expertise, dedication, talent they have. They must go. With the next round of reports and complaints, the whole crisis intensifies and then the leader, managers, and HR are even more complicit and *must* cover up or are truly exposed to risk and liability. Abuse by the predators may continue from this point forward for decades until the institution blows up as we have all read documented in many media exposés.

Gaslighting fully enhances the crisis. The victims in these scenarios, especially when the bullying and gaslighting start in childhood, do not want to report that they are at fault. They've been exposed to language that tells them *they* are the perpetrator. They have not been acquainted with terminology that would allow them to remain more clearheaded and report with more force and efficacy. So, they don't report for years, decades, sometimes never.

When Macfarlane is fighting via a lawsuit for her teen self and for future victims against the institutionalized cover-up of rampant abuse in the Anglican church, she recalls her mother asking why she didn't report when it was occurring. She explains that the initial teen rapist when she was alone in the woods told her to keep it quiet. "I was told 'you mustn't tell, you mustn't tell.'"[26] The traumatized five-year-old Macfarlane *told* her mother, but this is where the silencing seeps back in. Her parents never mentioned the rape. They did not take her to a doctor or mental health expert. The thinking may have been that she's too young to understand what happened. It's best to let her forget, but we now know from mental health experts, this kind of suppression of trauma can be extremely unhealthy. Whether in a domestic or workplace arena, the impulse might be to protect, but silencing the victim further harms the victim. While I use institutional complicity, Macfarlane uses "institutional protectionism."[27] I have learned in reading of her appalling repeat abuses that the mother and the institution *do* offer protection. They offer it to themselves. And this means they offer it to the perpetrator of abuse because this means that there is no victim. This erasure of the victim silences the victim.

No negligence occurred because there are no victims. According to those who want to shirk accountability, there are perpetrators who claim to be victims and there are perpetrators who report abuses. No abuse has been done. There is *no* perpetrator of abuse. The victims bear responsibility for their own suffering, which means that the parent and the institution have *not* failed in their duty. The one who speaks up must be silenced and condemned. As Macfarlane puts it succinctly, "The needs of the institution trump the needs of victims."[28]

REMEDY FOR GASLIGHTING: SPEAKING UP

According to Macfarlane, speaking up *can* be a powerful antidote to the manipulations of gaslighting and the betrayal of institutional complicity. Macfarlane feels a responsibility to protect other victims. She shares: "I was particularly haunted by the thought that the Anglican Minister who had abused me would continue to have access to young girls from a position of power and authority."[29] Macfarlane is well aware of her position of power, being white and highly educated, which intensifies her sense of responsibility. I share this awareness with her of my privilege and feel equally compelled—despite the challenges—to speak up about abuse. Likewise, Wilson and Carle are tireless advocates to reform our normalized culture of workplace bullying and cover-ups. They take their exceptional skill sets and apply them to ensuring that others do not have to suffer the kind of maltreatment they endured at institutions to which they had dedicated themselves. In all our cases, speaking up brings health and clarity, which ignite an empathic impulse to protect others from our career-wrecking experiences.

Macfarlane shares that speaking up "would mean that I could live up to my own strongly held principles about using my privilege for good and challenging social constructs of shame. I was also beginning to realize that speaking up would empower me too."[30] It's easy to imagine that the repeat disempowerment Macfarlane endured in her life would make a bid to take back power for good very appealing. Macfarlane's legal experience revealed to her the "power of authenticity and open disclosure," clearly the polar opposites of manipulation and cover-ups. Authenticity is the opposite of being two-faced, a wolf in sheep's clothing, a false prophet, a snake in a suit. Open disclosure is the opposite of telling the self-serving lies of bullying, gaslighting, and institutional complicity. Open disclosure is the opposite of abuse behind closed doors. If self-serving lies fuel bullying and gaslighting, authenticity and open disclosure offer a remedy, a way to cure this sickening and infectious pattern.

Macfarlane identifies the way in which authenticity and truth telling can "undermine patterns of hatred and presumption."[31] The fact that some individuals are offered more believability status than others signals patterns of hatred and presumption. Macfarlane's drive is to speak up about "something assumed to be shameful" to cause a reckoning whereby the "dominant culture is forced to re-evaluate the shame historically associated with prejudices and change attitudes."[32] As is well-documented, there are believability privileges, especially to being an educated, white male, but it still does not mean that even this seemingly protected class is safe from bullying, gaslighting, and institutional complicity as we see with the case of Montgomery, and more intensely with Wilson.

DISMANTLING DUALITY
Instead of covering up the traumas that shaped her past and present, Macfarlane foregrounds them in a context that allows for her professional

expertise to address them.[33] Instead of using power, credibility, and social standing to create a fabricated persona that covers up an exploitative harmful persona, Macfarlane harnesses her professional attributes to proactively protect and empower victims. She names her approach "academic activism," which reminds us that bullying and gaslighting pressure the target to be passive, simply a mirror upon which the perpetrators project their psychological, financial, or reputational agenda.

Macfarlane articulates her approach as a "journey from victim to change agent."[34] The victim suffers from learned helplessness due to the manipulative lies of bullying: you are at fault; you deserve to be abused; you cannot escape; you have nowhere to go; no one cares. These manipulations hinge on bullying's essential lies, which, remember, are that the target is unworthy and does not belong. These manipulations are compounded by gaslighting, which insinuates that you cannot trust your own perceptions and don't understand what's right and wrong, what's true and what's false, who's safe and who's dangerous, whether it's your fault that you're being abused, whether you're the victim or the perpetrator.

Like Wilson and Carle, Macfarlane walks away from these reversals and falsehoods and transforms into a change agent. Bullying, gaslighting, and institutional complicity are changed in her approach into empathy, honesty, and transparency. Macfarlane's book reinfuses a human element into institutions that appear to be run by faceless bureaucrats. If it is normal to sacrifice a dehumanized minority to some notion of a superior majority, when the suffering of this unhappy minority is neutralized and dismissed, and each step of the way they are faulted for suffering, we create the conditions for bullying and gaslighting to flourish. If it is normal for the majority to look the other way while leaders shirk responsibility, avoid emotional and ethical pain, wallow in their privilege and happiness, we have the grounds for bullying and gaslighting to flourish. We might even be creating the conditions for democracy to slide into dictatorship. It is critical to level the playing field. It is vital to eliminate the hierarchy and power imbalance that create a community artificially divided into a happy majority and an unhappy minority, or even a happy minority and an unhappy majority. Division is one of the greatest weapons that allows the strongman to conquer. Silencing is another.

Macfarlane's emphasis is on speaking up and reconnecting what has been divided in two: "We often try to separate the personal from the professional and the political from the academic. I have learned over and over that this is a false and disempowering dichotomy."[35] When we speak and write from a personal place that does not exclude or cover up our traumas or errors, when we draw on our professional skill set to make it meaningful for others, we create the opportunity to be authentic and empowering. The dichotomy, the split self collapses, and we stand as a united self, paving the path for others to stand with us as holistic beings in a community of equal rights.

The united self must create space for mistakes, misjudgments, and the emotional, ethical, and reputational suffering that accompanies them. Macfarlane stands bravely before her university law community of faculty and students and speaks about the repeat sexual assaults she has endured. Breaking the silence she was scripted to maintain as a victim and then as a professional brings her "a deep and lasting feeling of affirmation and relief." As she explains, "I was no longer hiding an essential part of myself."[36] In this moment, she rejects the professional hiding of the vulnerable self. She chooses to be whole, even though that includes the trauma of her past, the violation, the fear, the shame. Macfarlane's is a courageous act to be fully human, not only a professional with power, credibility, and social standing, but also a human who has suffered disempowerment, discrediting, and knows deeply what it is to have one's social standing as much at threat as one's life. She collapses the divide between the self who has power, credibility, and social standing and the self who has been abused, discredited, and socially abandoned.

Macfarlane explains that *Going Public* is written "from the perspective of both a survivor of sexual violence and a legal scholar." The split personality, which so often occurs due to trauma, transforms into a holistic author who writes a book for the rest of us that "offers an insider understanding of our flawed legal and workplace processes and the impulse to institutional protectionism."[37] Macfarlane's "institutional protectionism" is exactly what leads into institutional complicity with abuse. To remind you, in the upside-down world of normalized gaslighting, the institution protects itself, which includes protecting the abusers, while it actively revictimizes the targets. For those seeking legal and organizational culture expertise in terms of creating a workplace far safer from the lies of bullying and gaslighting, the final section of Macfarlane's *Going Public* outlines a detailed set of applicable interventions.

SPEAKING TRUTH TO POWER

Instead of being manipulated into choosing silence—offered by the apparently caring professional realm—Macfarlane chooses to go public and speak up on behalf of herself and all victims. Macfarlane understands that speaking up in a public arena is an effective way to dismantle gaslighting's insidious force. When you are being encouraged to participate in the cover-up of abuse or fraud, and you're being told the mind-bending reason that it's for the "integrity of the process," or better still to "protect" your delicate reputation, start thinking slowly. Don't fall for the apparent concern and care. If silence is one of the best weapons in the perpetrator and the institution's arsenal, then it's time to battle by articulating the truth grounded in facts.

Gaslighting flourishes behind closed doors, keeps individuals isolated, quashes dialogue and debate, frowns upon fact-checking, whips up and plays on emotional or financial insecurity. *Going Public* shines a spotlight on what's happening; brings individuals together; encourages dialogue and debate; supports statistics, research, and fact-checking; strives to replace emotional reactions with more rational responses. It debunks myths with the evidence of research.

When we consult research, leaders, managers, and HR learn that fifteen years of data show that organizations that support truth telling, that support whistle-blowers, are more productive and successful financially.[38] It makes sense. Brains that are safe are brains that can channel resources into high performance rather than threat detection. Brains that know what's true and what's false aren't anxious, aren't riddled by doubts, don't feel confused. They can be clear, creative, collaborative, and trusting.

NOTES

1. Julie Macfarlane, *Going Public: A Survivor's Journey from Grief to Action* (Toronto: Between the Lines, 2020), 2.

2. Macfarlane, *Going Public,* 5.

3. Macfarlane, *Going Public*, 91.

4. Macfarlane, *Going Public*, 36.

5. Macfarlane, *Going Public*, 25.

6. Macfarlane, *Going Public*, 150.

7. Macfarlane, *Going Public*, 18.

8. Macfarlane, *Going Public*, 145.

9. Macfarlane, *Going Public*, 71.

10. Macfarlane, *Going Public*, 19.

11. Macfarlane, *Going Public*, 31.

12. I resigned in protest from that school and went to work at another private school. I could have believed that the "retired early" strategy was unique to the school administrators that I saw firsthand covering up abuse, but in the new school where I was working, they did the same strategy with two teachers. Both were identified as luring or grooming teenage victims for sexual exploitation. I no longer work at this school either.

13. Macfarlane, *Going Public*, 31.

14. Macfarlane, *Going Public*, 31.

15. Macfarlane, *Going Public*, 26.

16. Macfarlane, *Going Public*, 32.

17. Macfarlane, *Going Public*, 116.

18. Macfarlane, *Going Public*, 5. A former student of mine who reported being groomed by an educator at a school I worked at told me what her mother asked after she was informed: "What did you do to make him act like that?" The girl was in her mid-teens. The educator, in a leadership position, was in his sixties. The police were investigating. The educator was ultimately fired, but what he did was covered up. The victim was subjected to gaslighting reversals and became confused whether she was the victim or perpetrator. She committed suicide at nineteen.

19. Macfarlane, *Going Public*, 21.

20. Macfarlane, *Going Public*, 4.

21. Bessel van der Kolk, *The Body Keeps the Score: Mind, Brain, and Body in the Transformation of Trauma* (New York: Penguin, 2015).

22. Macfarlane, *Going Public*, 4.

23. Macfarlane, *Going Public*, 4.

24. Macfarlane, *Going Public*, 4.

25. Macfarlane, *Going Public*, 103.

26. Macfarlane, *Going Public*, 141.

27. Macfarlane, *Going Public*, 103.

28. Macfarlane, *Going Public*, 103.

29. Macfarlane, *Going Public*, 23.

30. Macfarlane, *Going Public*, 62.

31. Macfarlane, *Going Public*, 62.

32. Macfarlane, *Going Public*, 65.

33. Megan Carle describes this splitting of the self while being bullied at work: "I've been curled up in a ball of nothing, / While upright, I'm first-team-all-everything-is fine, / Miss Happy-Go-Lucky." *Walk Away to Win*, 257.

34. Macfarlane, *Going Public*, x.
35. Macfarlane, *Going Public*, xi.
36. Macfarlane, *Going Public*, 71.
37. Macfarlane, *Going Public*, x–xi.
38. Stephen Stubben and Kyle Welch, "Evidence on the Use and Efficacy of Internal Whistleblowing Systems," *Journal of Accounting Research* (March 4, 2020), https://onlinelibrary.wiley.com/doi/10.1111/1475-679X.12303.

PART TWO

WHY DO WE FALL FOR LIES?

Chapter Five

Blind to Betrayal

IN PART 1 OF *THE GASLIT BRAIN*, WE FOCUSED ON THE LIES OF GASLIGHT-ing in the workplace and how they fit into a larger pattern of the lies issued in bullying and institutional complicity. We examined the lies through four case studies: my story, the Nike executive's story, the superintendent detective's story, and the law professor's story. In all four, we noted the textbook behaviors, not only of the perpetrators, but also of those in the institution who gaslight and the way in which the manipulation leads to institutional complicity. In part 2, we will look at the psychological constructs that fuel this phenomenon. We also look at the brain science to facilitate our understanding of what's happening in the brains of those who abuse, how institutions accommodate and enable them, and the way this system, constructed on falsehoods, is unhealthy and destructive.

Let's begin by looking at my story through the lens of psychological experts in the act of betrayal whether at home or in the workplace. When I witnessed the cover-up of the theater teacher's abuse, I still clung to the illusion of a mostly healthy, safe workplace for all, including the vulnerable, because I was dependent on my employment. What I learned was this dependence had made me—in the words of psychologists Dr. Jennifer Freyd and Dr. Pamela Birrell—"blind to betrayal." The transition from blindness to sight was not sudden. It took me a long time, but what I discovered in Freyd and Birrell's research supplied me with a powerful insight into how gaslighting works and how we can prevent its pernicious effects.

Freyd and Birrell explain that "coworkers may remain highly motivated not to see the injustice for fear of losing their own employment. Thus, institutional betrayal and betrayal blindness flourish."[1]

I had already put my job and career in jeopardy by speaking up about one colleague. When threatened, and with my reality distorted, I sought to stay in my position and remain part of my work community. I cherished my colleagues and was dependent on the director, leader, and the chaplain to maintain my position. Freyd and Birrell describe this accommodation: "Betrayal blindness requires this convolution, so that one can be in the dual state of simultaneously knowing and not knowing something important."[2] A border was being built within me: on one side, I was fully aware and distraught about the repeat abuse; on the other side, I was following the lies and distortion of the director, the leader, and chaplain with my eyes firmly shut. Closing your eyes to the truth of others' suffering, especially vulnerable individuals, frazzles your empathic humanity and ultimately jeopardizes your sanity.

When your confusion reaches the threshold where your brain tries to cut through the noise, haze, and chatter by taking responsibility—maybe I *am* the problem—to construct a story that makes sense of a distorted reality, then gaslighting's reversal deepens. As Freyd and Birrell explain, this is a self-protective strategy: "by remaining blind, victims or bystanders protect their place in the world, in society, and in relationship to others."[3] I can remain blind to betrayal if I take responsibility for being the problem by reporting my colleague's abuse. I might experience stressful emotions such as regret for speaking up and guilt for exposing him but maintain my place in the community. Notice that the perpetrator does not experience these emotions when abusing vulnerable targets. Notice also that the director, leader, and chaplain do not appear to suffer these negative and uncomfortable emotions while they use their positions of power, credibility, and social status to target me for speaking up while protecting and enabling abuse on their watch.

As discussed in the introduction, individuals who tell self-serving lies get comfortable with it. Their brain does not send them alerts about breaking social rules. The director, leader, and chaplain are living in their own version of reality where they decide what's "true" and make others believe and do their bidding. As Babiak and Hare learned about psycho-paths, they "experience a gamelike fascination in fooling people, getting into other people's heads and getting them to do things for them."[4] As reports piled up, my abusive colleague must have known that he was in jeopardy. The director, leader, and chaplain had granted him a second (or third, fourth, fifth, or hundredth) chance, which means he owed them a great deal, thereby increasing their power. A lot of energy must have gone into "fooling" all those who reported the abuse. The director, leader, and especially chaplain, apparently had a "gamelike fascination" with lying to me, "getting into my head," and all three could achieve the win—to make me do "their bidding": remain silent, put my blinders back on, continue to work.

Julie Macfarlane describes the dependence on an institution that creates the conditions for becoming blind to betrayal.

> *Institutions exercise control over their members because they can bestow both acceptance—successful passage through an education program for a student, promotion for an employee, or tenure for a professor; first team membership for the athlete; a leading role for an actor—or in the alternative, exclusion and rejection. Conformity to the values of the institution is essential for inclusion. The high school students who stood outside the "cult" of the abusive teacher and raised questions about his behaviour were shunned by their peers as well as for years ignored by the school board.[5]*

Macfarlane's depiction of bowing down, compromising oneself, putting on one's blinders due to the immense control held by the institution—including one seemingly as innocuous as a high school—made me feel less weak. The great danger in an institution that protects abusers is in raising questions. In the twenty-first century, that's all it takes for the community to shun you. From the brain's point of view, being shunned is akin to being given a death sentence. Evolution shaped our brains to know on a deep cellular level that we cannot live alone. We lack the sharp teeth, fur, claws, wings, hooves, talons, and fins to fight or escape. Our survival hinges on connection and community. When we are driven out of the community by daring to ask questions about abusive individuals, the reprisal of shunning is significant. Add the fundamental need to belong, the institution's added power to bestow opportunities, and you can see why we put on blinders to our own institution's betrayal.

THE RELATIONSHIP BETWEEN BULLYING AND GASLIGHTING

Lawyer Mary Inman is well-versed in the tried-and-true gaslighting response to reports of wrongdoing. When I interviewed her to draw on her expertise on how gaslighting operates in real time, she said that on the one hand, it seems to date back to medieval times and on the other hand, it is used regularly in today's corporate playbook to shut down those who speak up. What I found fascinating in her description is the way in which it compares to bullying. Inman explains that gaslighting is all about deflection. They shoot the messenger—shoot the whistle-blower—to "divert attention from the message." On a psychological level, bullying has comparable traits. You target someone to create a grand show of your own power. If you felt powerful, you would not need to degrade someone else to conjure up the illusion. Bullying is known to target those who challenge or threaten the bully's shaky sense of self. When someone triggers their low self-esteem, they respond with cruel grandiosity as a compensatory gesture. This is an established strategy to evade feelings of shame.

Inman shares that when you open the corporate playbook, you find a section on what to do if someone threatens you or challenges you. Step number one is to discredit them. Step number two is to marginalize them. Inman's whistle-blower clients are often on the receiving end of vilification and isolation. Inman explains the corporate mindset when wrongdoing is reported: "Your strategy number one if you're attacked isn't to apologize, admit wrongdoing, look inward and correct, it's to deflect." She notes that this is a shame-driven response like the one bullies use, but the institutional leaders who gaslight are doing a more sophisticated and collective manipulation. Writ small or large, individual or institutional, the goal is to reverse the terms and present the one speaking up as the one not to be trusted.

Inman articulates another way in which bullying and gaslighting share a comparable self-serving or self-protective impulse.

Companies get in a defensive crouch and their playbook says 'let's shoot the messenger, let's marginalize their voice and let's send a signal'—and this is where gaslighting comes in—to other whistle-blowers that you'd better not do this because if you do this we're going to make an example of you like this person.[6]

When the bullying individual homes in on the strong, talented, ethical targets, it sends a clear message to those without the same strengths, skills, or character to tread carefully or become the next victim. In other words, if I, the bully, can harm the greatest, I can make mincemeat of lesser beings. This may explain why often the best and brightest—as we see in our case studies in *The Gaslit Brain*—are targeted for bullying. Note how it works on the institutional level with gaslighting according to Inman's explanation. Like bullying, gaslighting sends a threatening signal. It tells those who want to speak up that they'd be better off remaining silent—and safe.

As noted, the lies of bullying are essentially that the target is not worthy and does not belong. The lies of gaslighting are essentially that targets cannot trust their own perceptions, so they cannot be trusted. This is convenient in institutional or corporate crisis because it is an effective technique to dismiss, deny, and discredit the one speaking up, who is quickly put in the position of perpetrator (regardless of track record). A sign of how seductive and manipulative gaslighting is occurs in the moment when it erases the track record and obvious questions such as: If the target is not trustworthy, why are we only seeing this now? Where is the pattern, the instances that indicate that this is, in fact, an accurate and true assessment? If you push this line of questioning one step further it leads to: Why is the target discredited when bringing very serious, unsafe misconduct forward but was always trusted previously when not alerting us to this issue? All our contemporary case studies reveal that these questions are easily swept off the table when gaslighting begins its manipulative work. As Inman notes, "Gaslighting comes in to say: 'I want you to doubt yourself. I am so sure that you're wrong that I'm going to make you doubt yourself.'" Notice that in bullying and gaslighting, the target is always wrong and at fault. The perpetrator is always the victim. That's the core reversal upon which the lies of bullying, gaslighting, and institutional complicity turn.

Inman says that the least likely of her clients to succumb to gaslighting still fell for it. She sums up the manipulation as it pertains to the least likely victim this way:

> *I literally had a woman who is a lawyer in a whistleblowing organization, she blew the whistle in a whistleblowing organization and started to doubt herself. Cause the board didn't do anything. I was like 'Noooooo . . . you're being gaslit. I have to tell you it's gaslighting!' That's how prevalent it is because she challenged the leadership of a prominent whistleblower organization and she's a lawyer and she's worked with prominent whistleblowers and I mean that's how strong it is to not resist it.*

Bullying and gaslighting require a village. If an individual with power, credibility, and social standing bullies vulnerable targets, and another powerful, credible, socially approved individual does nothing to stop it, it's natural for the targets to think that what's happening to them is OK and in fact, they may well deserve the abuse. Likewise, when leaders gaslight, and you report but the board doesn't "do anything," it's natural for the whistle-blowers to believe that they are making a mistake, blowing something out of proportion, not being a team player, and so on. When witnesses to wrongdoing look the other way, they activate a powerful reversal: the offender is fine; the victim is a problem.

GASLIGHTING REVERSALS
Jennifer Freyd refers to an abusive culture's gaslighting with the acronym DARVO: **D**eny, **A**ttack, **R**everse **V**ictim and **O**ffender.[7] The previous examples show the way in which reversal is put in motion. It's a process that requires the Offender (perpetrator) to be protected by leaders, managers, and HR while the Victims (targets) are not only sacrificed but also faulted for the abuse crisis in the workplace. In my gaslighting scenario:

- director and leader DENY that the abuse requires an intervention;
- director and leader ATTACK me for reporting; and
- director and leader REVERSE VICTIMS, including me as the reporter of the abuse, into the OFFENDER.

The actual Offender in the theater department is protected each step of the way until he's fired five years later. The other four offenders in the PE department are protected each step of the way and *not* fired. They are commended for their "professionalism."

In her work on gaslighting, Sweet puts this manipulation succinctly: "deny or occlude, then flip the script."[8] When denial does not work, then they occlude or hide or cover up what's happening. Then they reverse Offender (perpetrator) and Victim (target). What an ideal way to capture the reversal technique, the turning the tables on the victim, in which he suddenly finds himself to be the perpetrator: flip the script.

The director and the leader were such master manipulators that they added a layer of gaslighting that Freyd and Sweet haven't identified: dispatching an apparent ally, a figure such as the chaplain. He wasn't a counselor. He wasn't HR. He wasn't a lawyer. But he cloaked himself in the trappings of all three. He was in the ideal position to gather information from me (and obviously others), then funnel it to the director and leader. He played the role of caring supporter. He was dressed in the robes of the institution's moral compass. The chaplain posed as a pillar of the community who spoke as frequently about the institution's four pillars—respect, courage, honesty, service—as the leader chanted the institution's mission statement. The institution's mission statement includes the line, "We are a community shaped by the pursuit of truth." I can assure you this was a lie, but it is textbook for gaslighters. Remember, they are pros at reversal. The leader was a blatant liar who publicly labeled kids who were asking for his protection from abuse *liars*. Why did he repeat the mission statement with this line in it over and over? Because repetition is also part of the gaslighter's tool kit. As we examine in more depth in part 3, it is a simple scheme to replace sharp insight, confident questioning, critical thinking with mind-numbing repetition. It's a well-documented technique, with horrendous historical examples, to get a community to replace their knowledge of reality with what the institution tells them to believe.

Freyd and Birrell's research establishes a link between exposure to trauma, high in betrayal, and poor mental health outcomes: "symptoms of depression, anxiety, dissociation, post-traumatic stress disorder, borderline personality characteristics, and increased physical health problems, as well as an even greater risk of further victimization."[9] In *The Bullied Brain*, I supply a great deal of research that provides further evidence for the harmful impacts of bullying and betrayal specifically within the brain. We tend to think of betrayal as active, but sometimes it takes a deadlier passive form in which it makes people believe things that aren't true. Knowing the truth, but being expected to participate in a lie, was sickening on a cellular level.

In summary, betrayal is toxic to the victim and truth teller even when you're wearing blinders to the betrayal. The blinders make it far more traumatic because the victim and truth teller may end up doubting themselves: maybe I *am* the problem. If a director and a leader tell you that the perpetrator is the victim, the perpetrator (newly inserted into the victim position) will be protected, you are causing problems, a record is being kept of your behavior, you are in fact the perpetrator, then you turn the blame inward. The director and leader work together, reinforce their authority, speak from positions of power, credibility, and social standing. They operate out of a power imbalance where their version of reality wins and mine loses simply because, like a child, I am dependent on them. My childlike position is that I depend on them for my livelihood. It makes sense from a survival perspective that I would step into their hall of mirrors.

Sweet says that manipulation "works by instilling shame, which makes victims feel that the abuse is their fault."[10] The director and leader's shaming of me for repeatedly bringing their attention to the multiple reports of abuse worked like a charm. They gaslit me into believing that I was the problem. They made it clear that if I wanted to belong in the workplace, if I wanted to be a part of the community, then I needed to put my blinders back on and remain silent about the abuse. To be sure that I was complying, they sent the chaplain to check on me, make me feel heard, ensure that I felt supported without knowing that it was just another manipulation, just another betrayal.

Let's review. According to Freyd and Birrell, one way that the dependent employee "may manage betrayal" at the hands of leader employers "is to turn the blame inward." If the perpetrator is not at fault, they think *then maybe I am the problem.* Someone must be accountable if abuse is occurring and targets are reporting it, everyone is denying it, so either it's not happening and is just an illusion, or gaslighting's reversal is accepted and agreed upon: first, attack victims (receivers and reporter of abuse); then, reverse these victims with the offender. Freyd and Birrell unpack why this acceptance of and agreement with gaslighting occur on the psychological level. "Similar to being blind to the betrayal," turning the blame inward and suffering "shame" works to "protect the relationship by allowing the [dependent employee] to maintain an attachment to the abusive [workplace] by blaming him- or herself instead of the true perpetrator."[11] Freyd and Birrell apply their insights to families and speak about children and caregivers, but their research applies equally to the employee (child) and employer (caregiver) relationship. A child is dependent on caregivers even when they are abusive; likewise, an employee is dependent on employers even when they are abusive.

Gaslighting as Grooming

Perpetrators groom their targets, drawing them into a relationship that appears caring, only to reverse the terms so that caring morphs into abusing. Grooming or luring, or in the online world "catfishing," are all comparable to gaslighting in that the perpetrator seeks to convince targets that what they say and do is true while they are lying. They pretend to care to exploit. The target replaces their reality with the perpetrator's illusion. The perpetrator's agenda may be psychological (they are mentally ill, like those in the Dark Triad); the agenda might be financial (they seek to get money out of their victim investors); or it becomes reputational (an institution becomes complicit in abusive conduct or fraudulent conduct due to negligence or having benefited from the wrongdoing). Perpetrators groom higher-ups, those with power, credibility, and social standing, so that they offer protection when abuse reports start piling up.

Freyd and Birell focus on the link between grooming and gaslighting: "perpetrators often groom their victims for unawareness and denial."[12]

They document the way this behavior is used by political figures on a massive scale whereby "public memory" is "effectively blinded." Why do the victim, the institutional leaders, the populace repeatedly turn a blind eye? Freyd and Birrell explain: "Whenever a person or a group is dependent on others who have more power, it may be advantageous to remain unaware of mistreatment from the power holder(s) to preserve the status quo."[13] To be more precise, as we noted in the workplace, dependent employees put on blinders to betrayal to protect their job, preserve their career, be sure not to lose their livelihood. It's a question of survival; and when it comes to one's salary, the stakes are high. In political spheres where it's risky to call out abuse, putting on blinders to the truth may well be safer than speaking up, asking questions, confronting misinformation and lies. Freyd and Birrell pose the impossible-to-answer question this way: "What should you do when the person perpetuating the betrayal is also a person you depend on?" This double bind leads victims to remain blind to betrayal in order to survive.

Referring to Nazi Germany's Holocaust and Communist China's Tiananmen Square massacre, Freyd and Birrell emphasize that "betrayal blindness is dangerous not just to individuals but to whole societies."[14] Sweet describes the phenomenon of believing those who are betraying us: "Social theorists and writers from marginalized backgrounds have long insisted that social power works by trying to convince us that everything is normal while the conditions surrounding us are discriminatory and oppressive."[15] When this form of institutional complicity occurs in racist societies or institutions, then gaslighting more specifically becomes what academics and activists refer to as "racelighting."

In 2024, British youth were speaking out against racelighting in reference to the Grenfell fire that killed seventy-two people in 2017. Playwright Gillian Slovo writes about youth rebellion against gaslighting: "They made it clear that they would be silent no longer out there in the world, because what Grenfell has exposed about our society is that money, class, and whiteness still speak louder than the truth."[16] Like Montgomery, some young people believe the truth is worth fighting for, and in part 3 we will look at why young people's brains are more likely to rebel than older people's.

Babiak and Hare refer to political leaders such as Hitler or Stalin as comparable to "corporate puppet masters" who are more dangerous even than the classic psychopath. Here is how they operate:

> *They are adept at manipulating people—pulling the strings—from a distance, in order to get those directly under their control to abuse or bully those lower down in the organization. In essence, they use both strategies—manipulation and bullying—much like historical figures such as Stalin and Hitler, individuals who surrounded themselves with obedient followers.*[17]

The puppet master can turn just as quickly on an obedient follower as he does on a bullying target. Neither is "viewed as a real, individual person." We tend to be shocked repeatedly by the psychopathic tendency to lie, humiliate, degrade, and demean others publicly without learning the lesson that these behaviors indicate damaged brains. We don't act as if these people have serious medical problems; we perpetually assess them through an ethical lens. It doesn't make sense to hand the keys to an institution to someone who shows symptoms of heart failure. Likewise, it is even less sensible to hand the keys to an institution to someone who shows symptoms of psychopathology.

It can be very challenging to identify those in positions of power, credibility, and social standing as showing the signs of mental illness as our brains are constantly baffled by the discrepancy between the position and the person. One strategy to maintain safety and sanity is not to mix up the position with the individual. Someone might hold a position of power, credibility, and social standing, but we have endless evidence that these positions are used by some to bully and gaslight. Just because someone is a director and is backed up by an institution's leader who is given information by a double-agent chaplain does not mean he isn't covering up abuse and penalizing those who report it. Just because the leader has the most power and constantly repeats the institution's mission statement about the importance of the truth, does not mean he isn't lying about enabling abuse. Just because the director is dispatched to bully those who speak up doesn't mean you should believe the lies that you are not worthy, and you don't belong. Just because someone represents the institution's pillars, acts like a counselor, and appears to offer support like the chaplain does not mean that you should trust him.

THE RISK OF SEEING THROUGH THE ILLUSION OF GASLIGHTING

In a gaslighting workplace, it was hard to see the truth, let alone tell it. It was essentially a losing battle, and you had to be prepared for attack from multiple sides. Freyd and Birrell say that betrayal violates us. We have a powerful motivation to simply not see it. Babiak and Hare discuss blindness to betrayal in the workplace specifically. They note that "abandonment does not always lead to realization that one has been used or conned." That's how deep the blindness runs. Even those who have been pawns of the Dark Triad and finally cast aside as they're no longer valuable or have simply become boring, still sometimes cannot see it. Babiak and Hare offer an example of this type of mental breakdown: "blindness to this reality might be reflected in the perceptions of an investor who still believes in the good intentions of an exposed scamster, despite having lost his life savings."[18] Individuals who have been gaslit are ashamed that they have been conned, so they remain silent.[19] Perhaps their shame is so profound that they prefer to look the other way and simply not see the betrayal.

Through my experience of speaking up about abuse in the workplace, I learned that many people preferred the fiction issued from the offices of power, credibility, and social standing. I saw ethical, intelligent colleagues prefer to believe what made them feel safe and comfortable. Freyd and Birrell helped me understand that my colleagues knew that seeing the truth put them at risk, and as employees they were disempowered and dependent. Seeing the betrayal, speaking up about the betrayal was a risk they could not take. As Freyd and Birrell explain, the "best way to keep a secret is not to know it in the first place."[20] Ironically enough, I learned that dropping the blinders and reporting abuse made people distrust *you*, yet another reversal at work. With the perpetrator on the attack, being supported by complicit leadership, the one who reports abuse is positioned as a threatening outlier who can harm the institution itself.

The reality is that the perpetrators and leaders threaten the institution, all the more reason they need a scapegoat. The one who reports them is an obvious choice. But for all those at work who risk losing their livelihood, who associate the position of power, credibility, and social standing with the leader in it, the one who reports abuse seems to be the untrustworthy problem employee. Colleagues channel their compassion toward the poor perpetrator who has all the abuse reports about him. It's a stretch, but to keep the blinders on and believe in the leadership, dependent employees choose to believe that the abuse reports are also false. Then they don't have to keep the complicit leadership's secret because they don't know the secret. There is no secret; the reports from multiple victims are simply false.

Julie Macfarlane observes that the "final unmasking of a person who has abused their power and authority inside an institution to harass, manipulate, and exploit more vulnerable individuals is sometimes described as a shock by other members of the same institution or community."[21] But was it a shock? It's not as if colleagues want to share how they had heard rumors for years or witnessed incidents of abuse firsthand. The phrase that swirls around institutions that enable and cover up abuse—open secret—helps explain the way abuse can occur "in plain view," to use Malcolm Gladwell's phrase as he unpacks the abuse by college football coach Jerry Sandusky.[22] Macfarlane identifies this technique by institutions as a way to "compound the power of predators and abusers by hiding them 'in plain sight' through resisting or throwing obstacles in front of requests for investigation and appropriate action."[23] This technique works effectively when employees are dependent. As Freyd and Birrell attest, "most of us are in denial" as a survival strategy. Further, we are "disinclined to believe" that a person in a position of power, credibility, and social standing can also be abusive or fraudulent.[24] It does not make sense to our brains. These contradictory facts present a near-impossible story for the brain to reasonably construct. Psychologist Dr. Shawn Achor explains that in response, our brain creates counter facts.[25]

The brain generates counter facts to create a story that makes sense. The brain needs to generate alternative facts to counter the real facts when they are threatening on some level (reputation, responsibility, power base, employment, safety). For an example, with the theater teacher at my workplace, multiple individuals—faculty, parents, students—at separate times provided reports of egregious abuse. I was one among many asking the director and the leader to intervene and stop the abuse, but as they did with the other four teachers, they suppressed the multiple reports and zeroed in on me as well as targeting my son, Montgomery. This is an ideal way to control the narrative: directing questions away from the abuse and many reports; instead, focusing on one or several individuals who speak up. Here are some counter facts generated about me as the one who brought the reports to the leaders about abuse in two departments:

"She has an interpersonal problem with her colleague."

"She's crazy, incoherent, unhinged, hysterical, deranged."

"She is a problem parent; she's a helicopter parent."

"She's lying. She's trying to hijack the department."

If I had been the only complainant, these might have been plausible, but in the environment of many reports of abuse (many reports about the theater teacher, and at least thirty parents and fourteen students *in one year*), they don't make any sense. If I had a track record of these behaviors, they would make a lot more sense, but there was the opposite track record (as with Carle, Wilson, and Macfarlane). This is why track records and histories must be suppressed. These counter facts aren't very imaginative, but counter facts to cover up abuse rarely are. Those who abuse are masters at gaslighting or making others believe a made-up narrative. The lies they tell are frequently textbook.

As Rebecca Solnit describes the abuser's playbook, "You insist that anyone mentioning what you've done is insulting you, is a liar, then insist that your accuser is the abuser and you are the victim, and keep shouting it until you believe it and maybe convince others."[26] Mary Inman notes that the goal is make the whistle-blower an example. The threatening message sent in the workplace is that if you dare to speak up, you'll meet the same fate as so-and-so who blew the whistle. You will lose opportunities, promotions, your reputation, your job, your livelihood, your career, your family, your health, your life. For most, that would crush any inkling of courage to speak up about wrongdoing.

If sending a clear message by shooting the messenger doesn't work, another strategy is to drag the one speaking up into the false logic of bullying and gaslighting: mentioning the abusive conduct means that you are being insulting to the perpetrators; reporting the abusive conduct to those in a position to stop it is a betrayal of the institution (meaning that the reporter is the problem). Mentioning, let alone reporting, gets the one speaking up labeled as a "liar." The reversal takes place: accuser is the abuser. These are all counter facts to a more straightforward scenario: there's a perpetrator of abuse or fraud, multiple reports have come in from different individuals, leadership needs to make decisions about the perpetrator (not engage in an elaborate process with those who reported). There's no mind bending or reversing that needs to take place. The leader acts to address the crisis that the perpetrator has created.

As we will see in Babiak and Hare's profile of psychopaths examined in more detail next chapter, those who abuse and those who protect them—becoming complicit in the abuse—are masters of reversals and changing socially constructed "reality" with language. They use language effectively to attack and then cover it up with gaslighting. Their ability to do harm without guilt or remorse is the same ability to make others think that what they see (real facts) is something else (counter facts).

> *Psychopaths' emotional poverty—that is, their inability to feel normal human emotions and their lack of conscience—can be mistaken for three other executive skills, specifically the ability to make hard decisions, to keep their emotions in check, and to remain cool under fire.*[27]

Making an unempathic, callous, cruel decision morphs into *making hard decisions*. Not feeling any normal human emotion such as outrage and compassion at bullying morphs into *keeping their emotions in check*. Not feeling any empathy or emotion because those centers of the brain are not activating and are likely eroded morphs into *remaining cool under fire*. Language is used effectively by the Dark Triad to make a hell of heaven and a heaven of hell.

In this context, seeing how language is one of the most powerful weapons in the Dark Triad's arsenal, let's look at Solnit's description once again. "You insist that anyone mentioning what you've done is insulting you, is a liar, then insist that your accuser is the abuser and you are the victim and keep shouting it until you believe it and maybe convince others." Note here that Solnit stresses how perpetrators "insist." They don't wonder or suggest or dialogue or question. They *insist* on their version of reality, *insist* that you believe it, even when you're worried that it's an illusion. They use language to label others with damning, destructive labels such as "liar." Few insults are more serious than calling someone a "liar." The perpetrators cleverly use language to position themselves as victims who are being insulted, as they manipulate listeners into wanting to protect them. They want listeners to forget that the issue is that it's the *perpetrator* who has been reported on as abusive. Finally, the perpetrator shouts over and over until those listening are convinced. Repetition, as we examine in part 3, is a key technique in weaponizing language to gaslight. And yelling is well documented to negatively impact brain function, enhancing the gaslighters' grip on their listeners' fading reality.

Calling the ones reporting abuse "liars" is a clever reversal. Or as we saw with Wilson, it is more subtle, with the "evidence was lacking" argument, which *implies* the one reporting abuse is either a liar, too sensitive, making up allegations, and so on. Regardless, the attention shifts from the perpetrator's abuse report to the target being untrustworthy, which casts doubt on the target and makes the target into the perpetrator of wrongdoing while turning the perpetrator into a victim of falsehoods.

REBELLING AGAINST WORKPLACE LIES

When I heard Superintendent Detective Jonathan Wilson's story first-hand, I must admit, it took the wind out of my sails. I had the same reaction to reading Nike executive Megan Carle's book, the same again when reading law professor Julie Macfarlane's book and speaking with her. These are exceptional individuals. What saddened me is how much they loved their work and how dedicated they were to serving their institutions with the absolute best of their talented selves. In response, their institutions allowed and enabled the lies of bullying and gaslighting to derail them and hurt them. It's a shock to workers to discover how we can be devalued and degraded by the same workplace that has invested greatly in us and benefited extensively from our contribution. It is a betrayal that hits the employee targeted with bullying and gaslighting with a traumatic shock.

What fascinates me is that all three have rerouted their expertise, skills, and talent to shine a spotlight on their own textbook maltreatment and suffering to protect and help others. Their selfless integrity is something that not even a bullying and gaslighting culture can crush. It has incredible staying power. I am hopeful that this unquenchable drive in them brings about positive change in the workplace.

The psychopathic lies—the smear campaigns—that swirled around Wilson, Carle, and Macfarlane did not silence them. Although the Dark Triad tried to turn them into mirrors—to reflect and aggrandize the perpetrators with the help of institutional complicity—all three transformed into lighthouses, with the express purpose of not only saving future employees and institutions, but also emitting such a bright warning that leaders, managers, and HR could see the danger going forward. Institutions can choose to stay blind to betrayal and run the risk of hitting the rocks, or they can steer clear by learning from highly talented and experienced targets why the lies of bullying and gaslighting fail to create healthy, safe, high-performing workplace environments. Talent retention, profitability, productivity, succession planning, all are jeopardized when institutions succumb to the Dark Triad's smoke and mirrors.

NOTES

1. Jennifer Freyd and Pamela Birrell, *Blind to Betrayal: Why We Fool Ourselves We Aren't Being Fooled* (Hoboken, NJ: Wiley, 2013), 37.

2. Freyd and Birrell, *Blind to Betrayal*, 74.

3. Freyd and Birrell, *Blind to Betrayal*, 62.

4. Paul Babiak and Robert Hare, *Snakes in Suits: When Psychopaths Go to Work* (New York: Harper, 2006), 187.

5. Julie Macfarlane, *Going Public: A Survivor's Journey from Grief to Action* (Toronto: Between the Lines, 2020), 107.

6. All quotations from Mary Inman, unless specified, are from my interview with her.

7. Freyd and Birrell, *Blind to Betrayal*, 119.

8. Paige Sweet, "How Gaslighting Manipulates Reality: Gaslighting Isn't Just between People in a Relationship—It Involves Social Power, Too," *Scientific American*, October 1, 2022, https://www.scientificamerican.com/article/how-gaslighting-manipulates-reality/.

9. Freyd and Birrell, *Blind to Betrayal*, 58.

10. Sweet, "How Gaslighting Manipulates Reality."

11. Freyd and Birrell, *Blind to Betrayal*, 10

12. Freyd and Birrell, *Blind to Betrayal*, 93.

13. Freyd and Birrell, *Blind to Betrayal*, 95.

14. Freyd and Birrell, *Blind to Betrayal*, 112.

15. Sweet, "How Gaslighting Manipulates Reality."

16. Reference to media can be found in the references.

17. Babiak and Hare, *Snakes in Suits*, 190.

18. Babiak and Hare, *Snakes in Suits*, 137.

19. Babiak and Hare, *Snakes in Suits*, 138.

20. Freyd and Birrell, *Blind to Betrayal*, x.

21. Macfarlane, *Going Public*, 102.

22. Malcolm Gladwell, "In Plain View," *New Yorker*, September 17, 2012, https://www.newyorker.com/magazine/2012/09/24/in-plain-view.

23. Macfarlane, *Going Public*, 103.

24. Macfarlane, *Going Public*, 103.

25. Shawn Achor, *The Happiness Advantage: The Seven Principles of Positive Psychology That Fuel Success and Performance at Work* (New York: Random House, 2010), 120–21.

26. Reference to media can be found in the references.

27. Babiak and Hare, *Snakes in Suits*, 198.

CHAPTER SIX

Dr. Jekyll and Mr. Hyde

LET US NOW FOCUS ON THE ENTWINED LIES USED IN BULLYING AND gaslighting that contribute to institutional complicity. The quicker you realize that you're being lied to and understand why, the safer and saner you will be. It's hard to recognize the lies that fuel bullying, gaslighting, and institutional complicity because they hinge on a contradictory presentation: Dr. Jekyll and Mr. Hyde. A reference frequently used in media and popular culture, "Dr. Jekyll and Mr. Hyde" describes an abusive split personality. The respectable doctor and the murderous alter ego are an effective shorthand to quickly describe the dual presentation of bullies, gaslighters, and those who enable them.

In 1886, Scottish author Robert Louis Stevenson's book *The Strange Case of Dr. Jekyll and Mr. Hyde* told the story of the upstanding, moral, good doctor and his hidden urges to be callous, amoral, and violent. To cover up his murderous conduct, the doctor creates a potion that morphs him into a different figure, Mr. Hyde (note the echo of "hide"). Ultimately, his potion begins to malfunction, and he loses control of when he is the doctor and when he is the abuser. As he loses his own sense of self and consciousness, Dr. Jekyll writes a letter explaining his terrible and strange case and hoping that he—as Mr. Hyde—will commit suicide. At first, it is believed that Mr. Hyde is found dead in Dr. Jekyll's laboratory, dressed in the doctor's clothes. Then, the doctor's letter reveals that indeed he is *both* Dr. Jekyll and Mr. Hyde, respected physician and uncaring abuser.

You would never expect professional, honest, respectable Dr. Jekyll to tell a lie. You would not anticipate that he, in fact, may harm you, even destroy you. It would never occur to you that he is somehow presenting a facade, being two-faced, drawing you into a hall of mirrors, ultimately making you question your own ability to understand and reach sane conclusions. He is the pillar of society, which begs the question: Who are you? This moment of doubt may grow until you start to find yourself confused, unbalanced, struggling to think straight. And yet, the fact is, life-saving Dr. Jekyll is *also* dangerous Mr. Hyde, and you are nothing to him but in his way. He will not hesitate to cast you aside or destroy you. What's worrisome for us in the workplace is that one of the most pronounced skills of the Dark Triad is the ability to hide. Psychopaths "have a talent for hiding their true selves, so one could expect many to go unnoticed and uncounted."[1] Even more worrisome is the way in which those who uncover the Dark Triad are swiftly penalized. It is this institutional psychosis we unpack in *The Gaslit Brain*.

Dr. Jekyll and Mr. Hyde in institutional form is the caring workplace community—where an employee has put in years of devoted loyalty and hard work—that transforms into a callous workplace community as soon as the employee speaks up about bullying, abuse, or corruption. The institution, with its mission statement and pillars, vision and values, fails to properly address allegations of bullying, abuse, fraud, corruption, and so forth. Over time—due to the failure to deal effectively with these serious problems—the institution finds itself in a negligent position. Now Dr. Jekyll—symbolic of the esteemed institution—must figure out a way to manage the hidden, abusive underbelly while not exposing his or the institution's reputation. The need to hide or cover up empowers Mr. Hyde, who struts around the institution as ravenous and prey-driven as a wolf. This scenario is not unusual.

Think Hollywood higher-ups who were repeatedly complicit with the reported abuses of producer Harvey Weinstein. Think of the many figures from USA Gymnastics to the FBI who failed to halt Dr. Larry Nassar's abuse for decades. Think about the athletic director, the legal team, the assistant coach who all failed to halt the homophobic abuse being hurled at athletes by coach Mike Rice at Rutgers University. Think about the prestigious leaders of Penn State University who failed to halt the abuses by coach Jerry Sandusky and went to jail. Imagine the cardinals and bishops who have facilitated the sexual abuse of children by Catholic priests. I could go on and on, referencing well-known institutions in the past decade who have systematically covered up abuse.

Julie Macfarlane notes that there "are many reasons for a listener to resist an account that describes someone with institutional status and power as a rapist, harasser, or abuser."[2] One major reason is the split personality of Dr. Jekyll and Mr. Hyde, coupled with the experience of being targeted unjustly for bullying, then suffering the manipulative lies of gaslighting, makes no sense to the brain. Gaslighting alone is enough to scramble the brain's mission to turn endless data into a coherent narrative about reality. How can the brain produce a coherent story when gaslighting reverses relationships into a mirror image where everything's backward? The brain is baffled. As Macfarlane notes, "It's easy to see why not believing a complainant is a far easier course."[3] The brain seems to reason that if the complainant is *not* telling the truth, then the whole cognitive, emotional, ethical crisis vanishes. Far too often, the brain defaults to choosing the easy way out and deciding that the complainant is not telling the truth. In part 3, we look at ways to stop the brain from selecting this short-term path and instead, keep it on the straight and narrow path of believing the complainant that serves it and the truth far better in the long run.

In my workplace, I witnessed the cover-up firsthand. Action to protect victims was promised until it became apparent that leaders and the board had been informed at least a full year earlier and had been negligent in halting the abuse. That's when the elaborate cover-up began. That's when the institutional Mr. Hyde came out swinging. None of this is strange or surprising. Messengers who speak up in institutions to alert them to abuse or corruption or safety issues are the ones who get "shot." Recognition of the injustice of shooting the messenger goes back to ancient Greek theater, and it still applies to how we operate today. The institution is afraid of the truth and tries to maintain the illusion of duty and ethical practices at all costs. This is why Inman says whistle-blowers need "intestinal fortitude."

Recognition of a two-faced manipulator also dates to ancient times. In the New Testament, Jesus warns, "Beware of false prophets, which come to you in sheep's clothing, but inwardly they are ravening wolves" (Matthew 7:15). Dr. Jekyll presents as a false prophet. Dr. Jekyll presents as a sheep but he's a wolf (Mr. Hyde) in sheep's clothing. And note that the wolf is "ravening," namely, very hungry and hunting for prey. This description alerts us to just how dangerous and destructive these split-personality, false prophets are, whether in individual or institutional form. Abusive individuals compulsively, obsessively repeat their abuse day after day, year after year, decade after decade if not stopped.[4] Their hunger is never sated. Their predatorial nature is always on the hunt.

Luckily for us, in the past few decades psychiatric and neuroscientific experts have studied the minds and brains of these ravenous wolves in sheep's clothing. The knowledge of scientists can help us escape the clutches of Dr. Jekyll and Mr. Hyde while maintaining our sanity. There is a general awareness that the Dark Triad prey on targets, but it is less well-known that they prey just as dangerously on higher-ups.

The first step toward success is to build one-on-one relationships with important individuals in the company who will ultimately, often unwittingly, provide protection and cover for the intended plan of action. The sometimes rather elaborate charade or "psychopathic fiction" that is ultimately woven throughout the organization also fulfills the psychopath's needs for game playing, thrill seeking, and control.[5]

It requires a pretty elaborate gaslighting charade to turn heaven into hell and hell into heaven, which parallels the repeat pattern we see whereby workplaces protect those telling lies while ousting those telling the truth. Those who bully are enabled, and those who are victims transform into perpetrators. All this baffling reversal belongs to the world of psychopathic fiction from which higher-ups are not immune. In fact, they're specifically manipulated to participate. Brain science can help educate leaders, managers, and HR in institutions to better identify the Dark Triad who will groom them, make them complicit, and set their institution on a downward path toward all kinds of negative outcomes: loss of top talent, burnout, high turnover, low productivity, low morale, disengagement, profit loss, being fired or having to resign, lawsuits, fines, negative media exposure, reputational hits, jail time.

Those Who Lie with Ease

Psychopaths are alive and well in the workplace, and most of us are susceptible to them. If our case study superstars are susceptible, then we all are. Babiak and Hare describe how psychopathic individuals infect others with their falsehoods: "Victims will eventually come to doubt their own knowledge of the truth and change their own views to believe what the psychopath tells them rather than what they know to be true."[6] Let's pause for a moment. It's important to notice just how persuasive psychopaths are. They are so influential that those exposed to them may give up *their own knowledge of the truth*, which is the key to safety and sanity. If you don't know what's true or what's real, you are on a slippery slope into confusion, self-doubt, vertigo, and a degraded brain.

How far is it from the manipulative workplace to a manipulative cult? Once indoctrinated into a cult, you are in a mind that believes a spaceship is coming to take you to a higher plane, or that it's OK for someone to brand your body, or that poisoning your children and watching them suffer is acceptable. These cult followers have changed from reasonable and healthy people with *their own views* into people with dementia-riddled brains who believe *what the psychopath tells them rather than what they know to be true*. Ask yourself—do you know it's false that a spaceship is coming for you, that someone burning their message onto your body is wrong, that poisoning children is a cruel form of murder? Now imagine what has happened to your brain so that you no longer could recognize the truth of these statements and instead replaced them with a psychopath's myths.

The remarkable power of gaslighting and the reason it's a favored tool by those who seek to dominate is that it fragments, divides, confuses, and shatters victims. It scrambles their brains. What's key to understand is that the psychopaths have damaged brains as well. They were likely once victims. Their brains were eroded in key regions, and now they repeat the damage to others. It's a horrendous cycle. The brain is easily misled into trusting the institution in which it works and has served for decades. Putting in place strategies to protect ourselves from psychopaths *within* our institutions can keep us safer. Even if we're experts at seeing enemies outside, we need to apply the same brainpower to identify and be highly strategic with the enemies inside or in charge.

Psychopaths in the Next Cubicle, the Board Room, the HR Department

Remember that positions of power, credibility, and social standing do not mean that the person occupying them is safe and trustworthy. It seems melodramatic, but it's not a bad idea to ask oneself if the person is in the Dark Triad. Only the experts can give a diagnosis, but it offers us protection to be highly aware of how they operate, what's happening in their brains, just in case we're targeted for bullying and gaslighting. Ironically, our innate empathy leads us astray. We assume that because we are quick to connect with others emotionally, care about them, feel their pain, the Dark Triad also are wired this way. In fact, their brains are wired very differently. If you put a healthy brain into an fMRI scanner and show them images of people being bullied—humiliated, hurt, ignored, berated, and so on—the emotional regions of the brain would activate. In contrast, if you show these same images to a Dark Triad brain, you will not see limbic or emotional arousal. Babiak and Hare explain that the psychopath's "response seems to be more cognitive or linguistic than emotional." As if that weren't enough to worry you, they add, "their callous indifference to the plight and inner pain of others is more akin to that of a predator to its prey."[7] If you cast your mind back to our four case studies, we watched this kind of destructive relationship unfold repeatedly. It takes callous indifference to ruin another person's reputation, livelihood, career, and health.

Babiak and Hare discovered that psychopaths do *not* have a healthy reaction to the kinds of images that make most people's brains react in the emotional or limbic regions. Instead, "activation occurred in regions of the brain involved in the understanding and production of language." The fMRI studies showed that psychopaths *analyze* emotional "material in linguistic terms." Their lack of emotion is why they are understood by experts to have a "cold and empty core" that enables them to be "human predators." Rather than be brutally animalistic, they are clever and quick to do cognitive or linguistic tricks such as "*blame* their victim."[8] This combination of having brains that lack emotions and empathy, while being adept with cognition and language makes the Dark Triad very dangerous and destructive. To be influential, persuasive, charismatic, and able to make people give up their own knowledge of reality for your web of lies, you need to be intelligent and skilled at writing and speaking. You need talent in the cognitive and linguistic brain regions. Your superpower needs to include language processing. As we saw from research into telling self-serving lies, you need to practice. The more you tell lies, the easier it gets, and the more skillful you become. In *Paradise Lost*, poet John Milton gives the psychopathic cult leader Satan the gift of manipulating reality into its opposite, one of the Dark Triad's specific talents.

Remember, before Satan gaslights Eve, he rebels against God in heaven. He takes the gift of heaven from his Creator and turns it into a hell of his own making. God casts him out with the other rebel angels, and they fall into actual hell, also created by God. The angels are horrified by the loss of their blissful heavenly state as they awaken in the dark fires of their hellish future. Ever the talented cult leader, Satan in this moment articulates his great power: "The mind is its own place, and in itself can make a heaven of hell, a hell of heaven." Satan can't create anything, but he can reverse the terms using his gift with language processing. His promise to his cult followers is to turn the hell where they wallow into a "heaven." Milton has Satan attribute to the "mind" this wondrous skill, which, in fact, is the mind's pathetic, destructive manipulation. Satan says it himself: he turned God's heaven—with his mind—into a "hell." How tragic, and no amount of manipulation, lies, and bluster can bring it back. It's lost. He lost paradise and is now trying to convince his followers that it was all by design to showcase his mental prowess. Of course, they fall for it. Next on the agenda is Eve.

Abusive individuals might not all be psychopaths, but I wonder if they sidestep feelings such as empathy, guilt, and remorse because their brains are more invested in constructing "psychopathic fictions," spreading "disinformation," using strategy and language to cover up, being quick with excuses, manipulating with slippery terms and half-truths.[9] As we noted in the previous chapter, Babiak and Hare have found that psychopaths "experience a gamelike fascination in fooling people, getting into other people's heads and getting them to do things for them."[10] Their psychological explanation is chilling: "People do not exist in their mental world except as objects, targets, and obstacles."[11] As is well established, psychopaths may show early signs of cruelty to animals who also must be merely objects in their mental world. In terms of other humans, this reduction is the fundamental dehumanizing that informs all bullying from the playground to the boardroom. It can inform whole countries. It has been documented throughout history and is at work today.

Once again, let us recognize it as a full-on lie. All humans are just that. All humans have rights and belong to the human community. At play, at work, at church, in marriage, fleeing war and oppression and poverty, in a retirement home, in sports, in arts, in prison, wherever, the truth is that we are all human and all have rights. Any other explanation must be recognized as a manipulation. In part 3, we study techniques on how to win at this game. If the abuser has a playbook that helps her, we will develop our own playbook backed by brain science.

SPLIT PERSONALITY

Babiak and Hare would describe the conduct of the teachers who abused Montgomery and other students as the "macho style." "They are aggressive, bullying, and abrasive individuals, less charming and manipulative than the other types."[12] My colleagues presented as both types of psychopaths. When in Dr. Jekyll mode in front of colleagues, parents, and leaders, they were charming. When behind closed doors with students, they were in Mr. Hyde mode:

> *psychopathic bullies do not feel remorse, guilt, or empathy. They lack any insight into their own behavior and seem unwilling or unable to moderate it, even when it is to their own advantage. Not being able to understand the harm they do to themselves (let alone their victims), psychopathic bullies are particularly dangerous.*[13]

As we saw with the gift of the sexually loaded T-shirt, they could flip at times into charming their teen victims, but with an uncomfortable, manipulative twist. Whenever I saw my colleagues at meetings, presentations, discussions, and celebrations, they never used homophobic slurs. They didn't sexually harass male colleagues or use misogynistic language to humiliate or lure. I never saw them swear at anyone. They didn't get in the face of colleagues or leaders and lambaste them with humiliating rhetorical questions. They never grabbed anyone and detained them for more yelling in the face. They didn't block colleagues from opportunities they had rightly earned. They were charming.

Watching for split-personality behavior in the workplace can be a savior. When you suddenly find yourself a target of bullying, you think it's about you. Your brain is scripted to respect the position and transfer its power, credibility, and social standing to the one who occupies it. Don't make that mistake. Just remember, dictators are in control of whole countries, but it does not mean they are mentally stable, ethical, healthy, fair, have intact brains. Look beyond the position; always do a double take and look at the person. Don't listen to their promises in the future; look long and hard at their track record in the past.

Watch out for your brain's faulty logic. It analyzes the bullying and concludes that being targeted has something to do with you. Its logic is that the Dark Triad don't humiliate their favorites, their beneficiaries, those who fawn. They don't berate them, ignore them, swear at them, put them down, and therefore, something must be wrong with you. It's your fault the Dark Triad mistreat you. It's you. Your brain starts to work intensely to figure out what you're doing wrong and what about you triggers this kind of maltreatment. Stop. Instead, get your brain to record on paper each instance of maltreatment, day, time, place. That's one column. In the other column, record how the bully treats others. If you see split-personality behavior, Mr. Hyde to you and Dr. Jekyll to another, then you should be on high alert. You're dealing with the Dark Triad. The abuse has nothing to do with you, so don't waste your energy focusing on yourself. Remember, the lie at the heart of bullying conduct is that it's about you. It's not.

When the Dark Triad are exposed, their first attempt to deflect responsibility is denial. They trot out the excuse that they didn't know that what they were doing was hurtful. Don't fall for that lie. Neuroscientist Simon Baron-Cohen explains that the "psychopath *is* aware that he is hurting someone because the 'cognitive' (recognition) element of empathy is (largely) intact, even if the 'affective' element (the emotional response to someone else's feeling) is not."[14] We will do a deep dive into Baron-Cohen's research in the next chapter.

Babiak and Hare say psychopaths

can turn on the charm when it suits them, and turn it off when they want. Because of their chameleon-like ability to hide their dark side, they can quickly and easily build trusting relationships, then take advantage of them or betray them in some way.

When surveying workplaces that had bullying and abuse, Babiak and Hare found that the Dark Triad were simultaneously depicted by detractors as "underhanded, deceitful, manipulative" and by supporters as "team players and solid corporate citizens." There was a clear "split between supporters and detractors" who showed a "strong discrepancy in perception."[15] Another way to see this split is the division that occurs in bullying between the treatment of beneficiaries and targets. "It was as if these groups of coworkers were describing two people instead of one."[16] In short, Dr. Jekyll and Mr. Hyde. Listen to this description of the split personality:

Clearly, the detractors despised these individuals, and the supporters almost worshipped them. It was as if employees were describing two entirely different people. In a great number of these situations, it seemed that the psychopath could switch from warm and friendly to cold, distant, and almost hostile depending on with whom they were interacting.[17]

Our brains are always surprised by this contradiction, but they can be trained to anticipate it. In part 3, we do much needed training to take back control from psychopaths to stop being their puppets, whether they're playing us to trust and adore them or manipulating us to suffer and fear them.

Babiak and Hare explain that the "opportunistic, deceptive, and manipulative behaviors of psychopaths can be as bewildering to the victims as they are devastating."[18] What is their exact impact on victims? "Many victims become racked with self-doubt, blaming themselves for whatever has happened." It makes sense that the victims become tormented by self-doubt and blame themselves for what's happening. Their brains cannot fathom that individuals in positions of power, credibility, and social standing are also ravenous wolves. It does not make sense, and the brain's job is to make coherent stories out of endless data. Babiak and Hare note that experts refer to abusive psychopaths as "intraspecies predators." Maybe if we taught students in schools and employees in the workplace to watch out for these wolves—no matter how elaborate their sheep's clothing—they would be safer and saner.[19] They'd be less likely to doubt themselves and blame themselves for the predatorial abuse of others, others who prey on their own kind.

LEARNING TO SEE THROUGH LIES

Few of us are trained to identify lies, but we are intensively trained throughout our formative years to bow down to those in positions of power, credibility, and social standing. These childhood lessons, reinforced over and over with parents, doctors, teachers, coaches, not to mention administrators of all kinds, wire into our brains to such a degree that they are difficult to unwire when faced with someone who is not worthy of our respect, let alone our reverence and obedience. Because it isn't happening in society, we need to train ourselves how to recognize liars because that will keep us much safer and saner when dealing with the Dark Triad. We must override our impulse to believe someone in a position of power, credibility, and social standing. Do not confuse the position with the person who inhabits it.

Babiak and Hare write, "Pathological lying is a hallmark of psychopaths. They cross back and forth easily between lying and honesty during conversations because they do not have the guilty feelings the rest of us have when we try to tell a lie."[20] Remember the study we noted in the introduction. Once again, it's worth repeating the conclusions in this context. The study was about how the more a brain tells self-serving lies, the easier it gets. The brain researchers' "findings uncover a biological mechanism that supports a 'slippery slope.' What begins as small acts of dishonesty can escalate into larger transgressions." Remember, the biological mechanism they refer to is the "reduced amygdala sensitivity to dishonesty"; key is that the reduced sensitivity and increased lying occur *only* when the lies are "self-serving."

Babiak and Hare learned that psychopaths "will not only *blame* others but also create 'evidence' that others are to blame. This takes effort, but psychopaths easily integrate it into their game, seizing on opportunities to bring harm to others' careers or professional standing."

When the Cult Infects the Workplace

It's vital we learn strategies to stay safe and sane because the qualities of the Dark Triad are becoming more and more mainstream. Pulitzer Prize-winning journalist and author Chris Hedges writes, "The cult of self dominates our cultural landscape. This cult has within it the classic traits of psychopaths: superficial charm, grandiosity, and self-importance; a need for constant stimulation, a penchant for lying, deception, and manipulation, and the inability to feel remorse or guilt."[21] He identifies "armies of cultural enablers" where falsehoods takes center stage and drown out truth and authenticity.[22] This is an accurate description of my gaslighting workplace. The truth tellers were punished. Those who used charm and manipulation, interspliced with the lies of bullying and gaslighting, were protected. Legal scholar and author Amos Guiora writes that an "army of enablers" is always there when abuse flourishes in an institution: "What did the enabler do? He or she protected their 'hallowed' institution; protect the institution; enable the predator; abandon the survivor."[23] Rebecca Solnit identified that overlap between violence toward individuals (especially women) and violence toward facts and truth.

The Dark Triad are populated by skilled conmen who leave "a trail of bodies in his or her wake." The abuser plays on our fear of the harsh truth and manipulates our wishful thinking. As Babiak and Hare discover, the objective fact that psychopaths don't contribute or achieve in the workplace is "clouded by their self-serving bravado and the mystique that follows them."[24] Psychopaths at home offer a parallel to their hollow workplace contributions that help us see more clearly. Dr. Jekyll appears as a family man; in fact, it's part of a self-serving bravado, an illusion of nurture and care that is hollow. In their self-obsessed and self-aggrandizing way, the psychopaths may seek to pass on their gene pool by "the production of a large number of children with little or no emotional and physical investment in their well-being."[25] The stated goal is to have lots of children, but they find themselves exposed to the absence, ignoring, and worse, of Mr. Hyde. The illusion is a loving family. The reality is children who are abandoned.

The Dark Triad are professional at projecting an illusion of who they are. Although they find repeat victims, they also find powerful supporters. Despite year after year of abuse reports, their skill at generating "the persona of the ideal employee," at being a "pretender," makes them strangely untouchable. Although they are, in fact, a liability for the institution, putting it at risk even of lawsuits, they are protected. Babiak and Hare attribute this typical pattern to their ability to establish patrons.

> With a patron on their side, psychopaths could do almost no wrong. Powerful organizational patrons (unwittingly) protect and defend psychopaths from the criticism of others. These individuals eventually provide a strong voice in support of the psychopaths' career advancement.[26]

At Montgomery's school, as noted, one of the abusive teachers held a leadership position—built on bravado and mystique even though her team never wins any championships—which she held onto despite the abuse reports by multiple students. Since I resigned in protest, she's had further complaints and even a lawsuit trying to halt her abuse, but instead of being stopped, the institution and the regulator have kept her conduct mostly secret, and she's been granted an even greater leadership position that gives her power over even more unwitting victims who lack protection from uninformed parents. As Babiak and Hare explain, "The success of psychopathic manipulation, especially in large groups of people, depends on maintaining a cloak of secrecy about what is really going on." To "*see* the abuse they heap" on victims, the institution must avoid at all costs a "*culture* of secrecy."[27]

Armies of Enablers
Montgomery's school didn't have just one patron for the abusive teachers who were coaching, but an army of patrons. Analyzing another sport abuse crisis, Guiora describes the training conditions for American gym-

nasts prior to the conviction of Dr. Larry Nassar, who has been sentenced to prison for life. How is it possible that a doctor abused hundreds of athletes? A survivor creates the scene: "screaming coaches, humiliating training sessions, with the girls expected to be 'robotic.' All methods of training were on the table, no matter the physical and emotional consequences."[28] In the testimonies I took at Montgomery's school, they described the same maltreatment word for word. They also used the word "robotic." They were like puppets with the teachers pulling the strings. Remember Babiak and Hare's discussion of the "puppet master" who they see as one of the deadliest in the psychopathology spectrum. An abuse survivor told me that the most devastating moment for her was when she was injured and her coach dismissed her, saying she was now a "broken toy." Abusers typically threaten targets with how replaceable they are. When you don't have emotions and empathy operating healthily in your brain, then it makes perfect sense that you dehumanize and objectify targets.

I am constantly amazed by how textbook abuse is. As Guiora puts it, institutions that enable abuse "follow the same script." The good news is that if abusers and the institutions that enable them have a playbook that tells them how to manipulate and abuse and get away with it, then we can write a better playbook on ways to see through their manipulations, refuse their abuse, and hold them accountable. Echoing the despairing vision of Hedges, Guiora finds armies of enablers when it comes to abuse:

> While one army is significant, several armies are, literally, insurmountable. They come at you from different directions, they use every strategic and tactical advantage possible, they have unlimited resources, they carry the "prestige" of seemingly reputable and esteemed institutions, they represent success and power. They are arrogant; they are dismissive; they are deceitful; they are punitive.[29]

That is the most accurate description of the battle you must wage against the army of enablers in institutions that are full of bullying and gaslighting. It's easy to retreat into wishful thinking, but the *truth* is all we have that stands between us and insanity. I think it's worth fighting for.

A child of Holocaust survivors, Guiora is clear that those who follow the script and enable abuse in all its forms are reprehensible: "In deciding not to act on behalf of the person in peril, bystander and enabler alike facilitate the harm caused by the predator." He argues that both bystander and enabler have a duty to the victim, and those who fail are condemned in no uncertain terms. It is another example of how psychological abuse—unlike physical abuse—can be worse the more passive it is. The more one does *not* act, the more harm one may do.

> *The failure to positively act—to provide assistance or prevent future harm—in accordance with that duty resulted in terrible consequences to an innocent person. Why? Because the enabler and bystander made the decision to walk away, literally and figuratively. That is the essence of abandonment. Both the bystander and the enabler are of paramount importance to the predator; that understanding directly contributed to my decision to pursue this project.*[30]

Imagine a leader abdicating his duty. Now imagine a leader and others in the institution not just walking away but pouring salt into the victims' wounds—and the victims are children—as was done to Montgomery and the other students. They weren't just abandoned. They were publicly labeled as liars. Guiora notes, "The perpetrators were enabled by individuals whom the survivors similarly trusted. The theme of trust, then, is of paramount importance, for it is at the core of what was shattered by perpetrator and enabler alike."[31] Julie Macfarlane sees this shattering of one's belief system as arguably the worst phase of the abuse cycle.[32]

THE INSTITUTION TRUSTS DR. JEKYLL

It helps learning and remembering to look at individual stories, the reason that we spent time examining targets of bullying and gaslighting in part 1. Let's now look at some perpetrators of abuse to understand why institutions all too often protect them. These real-life examples of Dr. Jekyll and Mr. Hyde characters show how easily they fooled us.

A recent high-profile case of a split personality is Sam Bankman-Fried, founder and CEO of the wildly successful cryptocurrency exchange FTX. When he was indicted on eight criminal charges and in jail awaiting his trial, Caroline Ellison, former CEO of Alameda Research—which Bankman-Fried also founded—pleaded guilty. As Victoria Bekiempis and Dani Anguiano report, Ellison provided the court with a "glimpse of the inner workings of FTX and Bankman-Fried's carefully curated public persona."[33] Bankman-Fried "cultivated relationships with reporters and maintained a Twitter presence as part of his effort to present himself as a 'very smart, confident, somewhat eccentric founder.'" Cultivating relationships with influential individuals is textbook for those with split personalities who project the power, credibility, and social standing of a Dr. Jekyll while ensuring that no one finds out about Mr. Hyde. The wolf is carefully cultivating sheep's clothing. Maintaining a "presence" as a compelling Dr. Jekyll is used to cover up fraudulent and destructive tendencies of Mr. Hyde, who can ruin victims psychologically, physically, or financially.

Ellison provides another textbook component of the split personality in her description of Bankman-Fried. Like others in this psychological or neurological category, it appears that Bankman-Fried saw himself as unhampered by rules and apparently above the law. Asked in court what his philosophy was on rules, she replied that Bankman-Fried thought of himself as "a utilitarian and he believed that the ways that people try to justify rules like 'don't lie' 'don't steal,' under utilitarianism didn't work." Utilitarianism believes that actions are "right" if they benefit the majority. Another way it's expressed is that action is "right" if it promotes happiness, and the greatest happiness of the greatest number should be the guiding principle of conduct. This philosophy works for those with financial resources and power; it's not great for those without either. Bankman-Fried feels that he does not need to obey rules or laws because he is causing "happiness" to many people while fleecing millions from a minority of investors through fraud. If it benefits the majority, then it must be right according to Bankman-Fried.

The leader at Montgomery's school announced to faculty and staff that he had heard from some students who had an "unhappy" time, and now he would hear from students who had had a "happy time." Besides how remarkably offensive it was to minimize and dismiss reports by victims of abuse with this kind of language, without supplying any detail about what had been done to them, you can see a parallel with Bankman-Fried's thinking. Like the entrepreneur committing fraud, the leader's philosophy—when it came to student safety from teachers' abuse—was that the abuse was "right" if it benefited most students. If his guiding principle of conduct was the greatest happiness of the greatest number, then the fourteen students reporting abuse could rightly be ignored.

Likewise, utilitarianism would exonerate the bullying lies targeting Wilson, Carle, and Macfarlane because the majority were not targeted by them. Let's take it a step farther and say that this philosophy could have gotten Nike off the hook for the maltreatment of female employees because they were the minority. Likewise, the Met police are off the hook for maltreatment of people in marginalized groups in London because men and white people are happy. It would get the law professor off the hook at Macfarlane's university because most students were not being groomed for sexual exploitation, and only a handful were targeted. Bankman-Fried's philosophy did not work in the courtroom, and he is now in jail.

It's interesting how Caroline Ellison, once under the sway of Bankman-Fried's gaslighting, believed his justification for not following rules and laws. Ellison reports how his attitude influenced her own worldview: she found herself also lying, covering up, and ultimately, committing crimes. She, too, has been sentenced to jail. The manipulations by the Dark Triad have the power to seduce others into their illusion of reality constructed on falsehoods. Notably, at the same time Bankman-Fried is pitching utilitarianism to justify and cover up his fraud, he's careful to get others to cover up. Why would you do that if you truly believed the utility of your plan was honest, true, and fair? As Ellison states, Bankman-Fried "warned FTX employees and executives about 'not putting stuff in writing that could get us in trouble.'"

It concerns me how textbook it all is. When the four abusive teachers in my workplace were exposed by so many parents and student testimonies, part of the leadership response was to announce an official "code of conduct." If teachers don't know that psychological, physical, and sexual abuse goes against a professional code for educators and students, they shouldn't be teaching. The code of conduct the school leaders suddenly wanted to create would be not only for teachers exposed as abusive, but also for parents and students as if they had also participated in maltreatment. It was such an obvious way to dilute what the teachers had done.

Then in the style of utilitarian Bankman-Fried, parents were told if they had complaints, *not* to write them on email. Instead, they needed to report verbally: there is no paper trail when complaints are verbal. Just as at FTX, with its grand philosophy of utilitarianism, it's still best to avoid putting stuff in writing that might get you in trouble. If you're lying to others, if you're gaslighting others, the last thing you want is your words on email.

Bankman-Fried's manipulation convinced others such as Ellison that fraud was acceptable. Her initial hesitancy to commit crime was overcome by his economic philosophy that put *her* in the wrong when she adhered to laws and rules. These kinds of reversals are the cornerstone of gaslighting, as we discuss throughout. In a sense, Bankman-Fried led Ellison to believe that she was "crazy" to obey the rules when she could break them within his utilitarian framework but remember not to put anything in writing. It all looks so obvious in hindsight, but it's helpful to remember that the Dark Triad are gifted at pulling the wool over the eyes even of experts.

PERPETRATORS ARE BEYOND BELIEVABLE

Bankman-Fried's parents are leading experts in legal ethics and social fairness at Stanford University. One may fairly assume that these ethics scholars would identify their son's business dealings as at least full of risk and at worst, full of fraud. Sadly, the parents could only see Dr. Jekyll; they could not fathom that he could also be Mr. Hyde. Not only did the parents *not* recognize his allegedly shady business practices, but even after he was charged, Bankman-Fried's mother struggled to believe that her son could commit any crimes—even when she was confronted with extensive evidence, along with his colleagues who were pleading guilty and testifying against him in court, like Caroline Ellison.

Part of what seems to lead us astray with the lies of bullying, gaslighting, and institutional complicity is the belief that liars manipulate uneducated, inexperienced, or gullible people. Although that may be true, it's also true that they successfully manipulate educated, very experienced, skeptical people, people who are leaders, people who have worked hard to earn their leadership position, who know the difference between right and wrong—at least *before* the Dark Triad started manipulating them and their worldview. Many complex issues are at play, many related to how our brains operate. We will unpack that in part 3 to better understand how and why we are all so susceptible to manipulation even by those closest to us.

Sheelah Kolhatkar interviewed Bankman-Fried's mother; to repeat, his mother is a leading expert in law and ethics.[34] His mother said that "her son was incapable of dishonesty or stealing." She went on to clarify, "Sam will never speak an untruth." And finally, "It's just not in him." Most parents can relate to an overwhelming wish to protect their child and fight for his innocence, but surely she must factor in her son's eight criminal charges; his incarceration based on his conduct awaiting trial; his colleagues pleading guilty and pointing the finger at him as a fraudulent, manipulative leader; and plaintiffs who have been betrayed and lost enormous sums of money. These facts in the case carry significant weight, especially when one's life has been dedicated to being an expert in ethics and social justice. And yet, Bankman-Fried's mother sounds gaslit, cannot shake her loyalty, and shows blindness to betrayal. The case is heartbreaking on many levels.

Sam Bankman-Fried was convicted of fraud in November 2023 and is incarcerated. His prison sentence is twenty-five years.

GASLIT WIVES OF SEXUAL ABUSERS

It's heartbreaking when parents cannot face the truth that their child is a criminal. They are so dedicated to the Dr. Jekyll gaslighting, they are unable to see Mr. Hyde at work. This same dynamic occurs with sexual predators. According to Ian Simpson, the wife of Jerry Sandusky publicly stated that regardless of her husband being convicted on forty-five counts of child sex abuse against ten boys, she *still* maintains he is innocent.[35]

Likewise, as Jessica Valenti detailed, Bill Cosby's wife publicly stated that despite her husband being accused by more than twenty women of being drugged and sexually assaulted by him, she sees *him* as the "victim."[36] Of course, this claim conveys textbook gaslighting where reversals abound: the perpetrator morphs into the victim. Those who try to hold the perpetrator accountable are on a "witch hunt."

What's telling about Bill Cosby's wife is that she unwittingly describes her husband as Dr. Jekyll and Mr. Hyde. She says all she knew of him was his Dr. Jekyll side—"kind," "generous," and a "wonderful husband." As is typical in abuse, *she* was not targeted, nor did she witness her husband harming others, so she does not believe it could be true. Mrs. Cosby describes her husband's split personality perfectly: "A different man has been portrayed in the media over the last two months. It is the portrait of a man I do not know."

Bill Cosby's wife does not understand that she played the role of sheep's clothing that kept the world from knowing she was married to a wolf. She's the suit designed to stop workplaces from seeing the snake. She is the beneficiary, the defender, the normalizer who unwittingly contributes to the Dr. Jekyll construct and keeps Mr. Hyde hidden. The Dark Triad often work in pairs or small groups where they witness the others abusing targets. By not acting, he or she makes everyone, including the targets, think the abuse is normal and deserved. This role is incredibly important to confuse those who are drawn into the abuse cycle because their brains say: if abuse were happening, the other person with power, credibility, and social standing would surely stop it and protect me and other targets. When that does *not* happen, then the targets start wondering if it's their fault. They had it coming. They didn't know how to handle difficult people. They're ashamed of being targeted. They deserve it. They start saying: I was bullied because ...

The Dark Triad need cover, and ideally it can be supplied by position (that has power, credibility, social standing) or spouses, religious commitment, marching for the rights of others, social engagements in defense of the ones being harmed behind closed doors. One of Montgomery's abusive teachers was a big supporter of fundraising for a handicapped student, but behind closed doors he listened to the other teacher call the boys "fucking retards." Mike Rice was a family man, a churchgoing man, but behind closed doors he hurled homophobic slurs at college students. Harvey Weinstein was an absolute champion of women's rights, but behind closed doors he sexually abused women. Jerry Sandusky founded a home for underprivileged children, but behind closed doors he raped boys. To recognize gaslighting, you must always look beyond the sheep's clothing to the wolf, the polished words of the prophet to the corruption, the expensive suit and patterned socks to the snake. Most importantly, you must look beyond the title that confers power, credibility, and social standing to the person.

DR. JEKYLL IS THE HUSBAND; MR. HYDE IS THE RAPIST

Hugh Schofield is one of many journalists who covered the 2024 trial of a French man who drugged his wife, Gisèle Pélicot, unconscious, raped her hundreds of times, and brought other men to rape her.[37] Drugging someone unconscious is a powerful gesture of controlling and silencing. In classic Dr. Jekyll and Mr. Hyde fashion, Mrs. Pélicot had no knowledge of her husband's split personality. As we saw with Mrs. Cosby and Mrs. Sandusky, she did not know the Mr. Hyde side of her husband. When the police first showed her photographs of men raping her while unconscious, she exclaimed, "All that we had built together had gone. Our three children, seven grandchildren. We used to be an ideal couple." Her disbelief sounds like Mrs. Sandusky and Mrs. Cosby, except Mrs. Pélicot no longer believes her husband to be an upstanding, innocent Dr. Jekyll.

Mrs. Pélicot and her husband were "an ideal couple" by day, but at night her husband turned into violent, exploitative Mr. Hyde. The court tried to control the language in the trial and asked Mrs. Pélicot *not* to call what was done to her "rape." They wanted her to use the terms "sex scene." She refused. As she told the court when the judge reminded her to "respect the presumption of innocence" and use the descriptor *sex scene*, "I just think they should recognise the facts. When I think of what they have done I am overcome with disgust. They should at least have the responsibility to recognise what they did."

A victim of repeat violence, Mrs. Pélicot sounds frustrated with the court's request that she submit to further gaslighting violence against facts and truth. The court's desire to protect the delicate ears of the alleged perpetrators and ensure that they weren't exposed to a harsh word such as "rape" to describe what they're accused of is textbook gaslighting.

It focuses attention on Mrs. Pélicot harming these possibly innocent men with a factual term, rather than on the perpetrators—documented in photos and on video—who came to her home and raped her while she was unconscious.

The accused have done violence to the victim, and now they want—with the court's support—to gaslight. Rebecca Solnit calls it doing *violence* to facts and truth. However, Mrs. Pélicot turned the tables on the whole charade by ensuring that journalists had access to all the unfolding horror and the manipulations that uphold it. As reported on by Tracy Connor, Judge Rosemarie Aquilina used the same powerhouse strategy in 2018 when she gave the hundreds of victims time in her courthouse—fully open to the public and media—to tell their experience of abuse at the hands of Dr. Larry Nassar and the impact it had on their lives. Nassar complained to the court in a letter that it was too much for him.[38] The abuse didn't seem too much to him when he unleashed it on hundreds of children, but *hearing* about it overwhelmed him, and he sought mercy from the judge. He did not receive any protection from Judge Aquilina. As we have seen, Nassar behaved in the textbook way of the Dark Triad: they present themselves as victims and they reverse their victims into perpetrators.

In Mrs. Pélicot's case, the court offered her the usual protection of confidentiality as if she could *not* bear the shame if others knew what had been done to her. Like Nassar's victims, Mrs. Pélicot rejected this paternal gaslighting. "Gisèle waived her right to anonymity to shift the 'shame' back onto the accused. . . . Taking the stand on Thursday, she said she was speaking for 'every woman who's been drugged without knowing it . . . so that no woman has to suffer.'" We see this impulse again and again in victims. They speak up to protect other potential targets.

Advertised versus the Actual Self

If you want to remember this strategy, just imagine a close-up of Sam Bankman-Fried's young face on the left page of *Architectural Digest* magazine, July/August 2022. On the right is a shot of him standing amid his mission-like quote. He's dressed like a kid in Bermuda shorts, black T-shirt, and sneakers, his hair rumpled. His quote? "I'm in on crypto because I want to make the biggest global impact for good." This mighty expensive ad follows a similar two-page layout with supermodel Gisele Bündchen (famously married, at the time, to quarterback Tom Brady), who was also an FTX supporter. Her quote is, "I'm in on FTX because we share a passion for creating positive change." You can see how pairs work well together. They confirm one another's messaging. They give off the aura of nothing wrong here or we wouldn't be echoing and repeating one another's statements. But ask yourself: Why do they need to say it twice and in a mirroring way? Why doesn't Bankman-Fried offer evidence for his claim on the next page rather than bring in a supermodel? Why doesn't Bankman-Fried open his accounts, have quotes from his team, share *how* his crypto empire makes the "biggest global impact for good."

The Dark Triad are experts in mirroring; when you see it occurring, when you hear repetition, when one echoes another, when there's no evidence, when there's only prophetic language, pause. Let your inner skeptic come to the fore. Start questioning: Why is this financial entrepreneur posing as a kid? Why does he present like a mother's son? How will crypto create positive change? Why isn't there any info, just a supermodel perched on a stool?

Michael Merzenich can answer these questions from a brain perspective. When you are being presented with associations not facts—for instance, a football superstar or a supermodel—you are being encouraged to remember FTX through its associations, not its actual offering. Your brain could easily forget the crypto entrepreneur and his company FTX, but it is less likely to forget the "hook" of a football star and a supermodel. If those hooks didn't work, then the idea of doing good in the global community might be something that you don't forget. As Merzenich explains, "One of the great tricks for remembering is to associate what you're trying to remember with other things that you are not likely to forget, like numbers, or friends, or relatives, or any other such hard-to-forget 'hook.'"[39]

I can understand investing in the future, and in global impact for good, but I don't see anything in Bankman-Fried's ads that tell me what the relationship is. What good? What impact? How does crypto accomplish this? The investors who did not ask those basic questions lost millions of dollars.

As noted, Babiak and Hare inevitably find the dual persona when they take statements from workplaces about colleagues identified as abusive. Some report their colleagues' highly abusive nature, and some defend their conduct as "kind" and "generous." Babiak and Hare are told that he or she is a "wonderful" boss or colleague. This dual description is frequently the red flag of a psychopathic abuser, a split-personality Dr. Jekyll and Mr. Hyde. Bullying and abuse always have both targets and beneficiaries. The targets are the "unhappy" minority. The bystanders (who are silenced by fear or self-protection) and the beneficiaries who get rewards, gifts, opportunities, and the Dr. Jekyll side of the psychopath, form the "happy" majority. The target reports the abuse, the bystander looks the other way, and the beneficiary defends the perpetrator. It's textbook.

Sam Bankman-Fried's parents, Sandusky's wife, and Cosby's wife benefited from the Dr. Jekyll side of the convicted abuser. Their victims—whether suffering physical, sexual, or financial abuse—were initially manipulated and seduced by Dr. Jekyll but then found themselves harmed by Mr. Hyde.

GASLIT CARE FACILITIES
Let's move out of the interpersonal and financial realms into the institutional realm to see if the same vulnerabilities to lying and gaslighting present themselves. We've seen individuals in parental or marital relationships become utterly confused and brainwashed by the gaslighting done by a trusted, intimate connection, whether child or spouse. Financial fraud happens frequently, and to many intelligent and informed investors. What's surprising is that in workplaces, within institutions governed by professional relationships, the same manipulation and downfall may well occur.

Just as doctors take the Hippocratic Oath, nurses pledge in the name of Florence Nightingale, founder of modern nursing, "I will not do anything evil or malicious, and I will not knowingly give any harmful drug or assist in malpractice." The position of power over life and death, the commitment to care for vulnerable patients, those in the medical profession are living breathing versions of Dr. Jekyll, but it means there is always the terrifying—if remote—possibility it's a cover for Mr. Hyde. In

2024, a nurse was sentenced in the United States for being a serial killer of patients.[40]

As Paula Ward reports, nurse Heather Pressdee in Pennsylvania has now been sentenced to serve consecutive life sentences for killing seventeen patients and attempting to kill more.[41] Over the course of three years, she systemically killed patients in her care with deliberate insulin overdoses. Executive Deputy Attorney General Michele Kelly Walsh stated after the sentencing, "Being in the courtroom for today's proceedings, the evidence of her depravity and darkness was only outshone by the light and love of the families that she victimized." In the courtroom, Heather Pressdee's murderous cruelty was evident, but for years, dressed in her nurse's uniform, it was not.

A daughter of one of the victim's described being at the care facility the day her father died. She described her encounter with Pressdee: "I looked into the face of Satan myself the morning she killed my father." What's textbook is that Pressdee made efforts to gaslight her many victims' families so that the psychopath's fictional mask carefully covered up any association with Satan. As another daughter reported to the courtroom about her mother's murder: nurse Pressdee "had the gall to send their family flowers and a sympathy card." Is it gall or is it a textbook example of gaslighting? Pressdee is reinforcing her position as nurse with its attendant power, credibility, and social standing. She is conveying to the family her care and sense of their grief and loss while adhering to her overarching agenda to remain unidentified as a killer walking the halls of a supposedly safe, caring institution. If this family glimpsed the face of Satan behind her carefully constructed mask, the flowers and card were meant to ensure that they doubted their own perceptions and fell back on the belief that a nurse—empowered and entrusted to save lives—could not possibly destroy them.

A victim's granddaughter recounts a comparable split-personality encounter with Pressdee. The family received the call that their loved one was declining without knowing, of course, she was being systemically poisoned by her own nurse. When they rushed to her side, Pressdee "offered them chairs, tissues, and condolences." This describes the surreal meeting with the Dark Triad who don't feel guilt or remorse for their actions. They can be murdering a vulnerable person while playing the role of caring nurse for the distraught family without any internal crisis or emotional confusion. It's comparable to their ability to lie without any anxiety as the brain has become comfortable with manipulation to the point of being pathological.

Is it possible that gaslighting is so effective because it paints the picture of a reality that we want? To leave our loved ones in a care facility or a hospital, we need to believe that they are safe. To put our children in a school, we must believe that the teachers care about them and would never try to harm them or ruin their future. Belief in the systems that govern us is necessary, but perhaps it is time to be more skeptical, less trusting, use more of our critical thinking. To stay clear and sane, we need to be informed and then vigilant about what is easy and what is hard for our brain. As we will see in the following chapters, our brains can misinterpret what is happening right before our eyes. Once we understand the way our brains are susceptible to lies and manipulation, we can train ourselves to be more aware and less vulnerable.

If our brain tends to see what we want to see, is it possible that we see Dr. Jekyll more quickly and easily than we see Mr. Hyde? It's ominous that the split personality uses this weakness of our brain to her advantage. With no sense of guilt or regret, the Dark Triad are comfortable lying and offering tissues, cards, flowers, chairs, and condolences to the victims that they are scamming and hurting. They only offer these false gestures of care to cover up their murderous lack of care. The agenda they serve is to continue to have the power to do harm.

As we will learn, it's better always to be prepared for the Dark Triad. It's better to take the hard path of posing questions, scouring facts, investigating, being skeptical, getting informed on psychopathology and how it manipulates us.

The Dark Triad Infect Culture

In 2009, Hedges diagnosed the illness infecting society as "a culture of narcissism": "faith in ourselves, in a world of make-believe, is more important than reality."[42] The psychopath's gamelike fascination with winning is infectious and fuels such cultural events as the spectacle of pro wrestling. "It is all about winning. It is all about personal pain, vendettas, hedonism, and fantasies of revenge, while inflicting pain on others. It is the cult of victimhood."[43] Hedges examines how our culture has come to worship "reality" as it's fed to us from television shows: "They tell us that existence is to be centered on the practices and desires of the self rather than the common good. The ability to lie and manipulate others, the very ethic of capitalism, is held up as the highest good."[44] If lying and manipulating are championed in our culture, it's easier to understand why—in the workplace—we fall repeatedly for psychopathic abusers, why we protect them, why we enable them to harm more targets, why we penalize those who jeopardize our illusion of reality with truth telling.

In 2022, when Merriam-Webster chose "gaslighting" as the word of the year, it was clear that we have not reversed course; we've dug ourselves deeper into a culture of narcissism. Remember, narcissism—although it may have a genetic component—is seen to emerge from childhood adversity. It's not surprising that a narcissistic culture, one that has failed to halt rampant child abuse although being informed about it, will produce more and more of this kind of bullying and manipulative conduct. Narcissism begets narcissism. Abuse begets abuse. Hurt brains hurt. The cycle is well-established and documented, but it is not halted.

It's helpful to maintain your safety and sanity to know that those in the Dark Triad, including narcissists, do not see their targets as subjects. They objectify others. They position targets as objects that can be maltreated and manipulated in any way that serves the agenda. As we examine in-depth next chapter, neuroscientist Simon Baron-Cohen explains that the psychopathic brain suffers from "empathy erosion." Shuttling comfortably from brain scans to philosophy, he uses Martin Buber's famous "I and Thou" way of being that sees others as equals, as subjects, with thoughts and feelings, in contrast with the "I and it" mode of being that sees others as unequal, as objects, as not having thoughts and feelings.[45] When you see someone as a pawn in the game you are playing, it's easy to devalue them, dehumanize them, put them in the out-group. These objects serve your needs whether psychological, financial, or reputational. Like so much groundbreaking research into abuse, Buber's philosophical insights emerged through bearing witness to the Holocaust.

Although we can understand that those in the Dark Triad are mentally ill—they have brain deficits in their empathy among other neurological issues—it can be challenging to understand why *we* so easily fall for their manipulations. In part 3, we examine ways to strengthen our brains' ability to identify when what we are being told is not true.

NOTES

1. Paul Babiak and Robert Hare, *Snakes in Suits: When Psychopaths Go to Work* (New York: Harper, 2006), 177.

2. Julie Macfarlane, *Going Public: A Survivor's Journey from Grief to Action* (Toronto: Between the Lines, 2020), 30.

3. Macfarlane, *Going Public*, 31.

4. Babiak and Hare, *Snakes in Suits*, 140.

5. Babiak and Hare, *Snakes in Suits*, 121.

6. Babiak and Hare, *Snakes in Suits*, 51.

7. Babiak and Hare, *Snakes in Suits*, 184.

8. Babiak and Hare, *Snakes in Suits*, 55.

9. Babiak and Hare, *Snakes in Suits*, 48 and 129.

10. Babiak and Hare, *Snakes in Suits*, 187.

11. Babiak and Hare, *Snakes in Suits*, 46.

12. Babiak and Hare, *Snakes in Suits*, 186.

13. Babiak and Hare, *Snakes in Suits*, 188.

14. Simon Baron-Cohen, *The Science of Evil: On Empathy and the Origins of Cruelty* (New York: Basic Books, 2011), 125.

15. Babiak and Hare, *Snakes in Suits*, 136.

16. Babiak and Hare, *Snakes in Suits*, 99.

17. Babiak and Hare, *Snakes in Suits*, 137.

18. Babiak and Hare, *Snakes in Suits*, 284.

19. Babiak and Hare, *Snakes in Suits*, 93.

20. Babiak and Hare, *Snakes in Suits*, 254.

21. Chris Hedges, *Empire of Illusion: The End of Literacy and the Triumph of Spectacle* (Toronto: Random House, 2010), 33.

22. Hedges, *Empire of Illusion*, 16.

23. Adrian Horton writes about a documentary that exposes the frequency of victims reporting sexual assaults who are then charged as suspects for false reporting in a "broken system." Police are not trained to factor in trauma when taking statements and are permitted to gaslight, trick, lie to victims while doing so. The title of the documentary captures what Horton calls the "Kafka-esque nightmare" when women report rape: "Victim/Suspect." Not surprisingly, this mind-bending reversal led to suicide in a college student's case. References to media are in the references.

24. Babiak and Hare, *Snakes in Suits*, 166.

25. Babiak and Hare, *Snakes in Suits*, 48.

26. Babiak and Hare, *Snakes in Suits*, 126.

27. Babiak and Hare, *Snakes in Suits*, 168.

28. Amos Guiora, *Armies of Enablers: Survivor Stories of Complicity and Betrayal in Sexual Assaults* (Chicago: ABA Publishing, 2020), 55.

29. Guiora, *Armies of Enablers*, xxiii.

30. Guiora, *Armies of Enablers*, xviii.

31. Guiora, *Armies of Enablers*, xix.

32. Macfarlane, *Going Public*, 109. "Once the betrayal becomes obvious—in the institution's refusal to help the victim, or worse, by the protection of the predator—the emotional and psychological costs are very high. Some survivors describe this as the worst part of their entire experience. Their faith in an institution with which they closely identify is shattered."

33. References to Sam Bankman-Fried's case are from the article written by Victoria Bekiempis and Dani Anguiano unless otherwise specified. Reference to media articles is in references.

34. References to Sam Bankman-Fried's mother are from the article written by Sheelah Kolhatkar unless otherwise specified. Reference to media articles is in the references.

35. Reference to media is in the references.

36. References to Bill Cosby's wife are from the article written by Jessica Valenti unless otherwise specified. Reference to media is in the references.

37. References to Gisèle Pélicot are from the article written by Hugh Schofield. Reference to media is in the references.

38. Reference to media is in the references.

39. Michael Merzenich, *Soft-Wired: How the New Science of Brain Plasticity Can Change Your Life* (San Francisco: Parnassus Press, 2013), 91.

40. "Western Pennsylvania Nurse Sentenced to Consecutive Life Sentences after Pleading Guilty to Killing and Attempting to Kill Patients," Pennsylvania Office of Attorney General, May 2, 2024, https://www.attorneygeneral.gov/taking-action/western-pennsylvania-nurse-sentenced-to-consecutive-life-sentences-after-pleading-guilty-to-killing-and-attempting-to-kill-patients/.

41. All references to nurse Heather Pressdee are from the article written by Paula Ward unless otherwise specified. Reference to media is in the references.

42. Hedges, *Empire of Illusion*, 27.

43. Hedges, *Empire of Illusion*, 10.

44. Hedges, *Empire of Illusion*, 33.

45. Baron-Cohen, *Science of Evil*, 7–8.

CHAPTER SEVEN

The Science of Split Personalities

BEFORE WE UNDERSTAND WHY WE FALL SO EASILY FOR THE DARK TRI-ad's manipulations, we need to better understand what's happening in their brains. Dr. Jekyll and Mr. Hyde may well have a brain deficit. The neural circuits for empathy appear to be eroded. These brain circuits facilitate us being part of the human community by activating compassion, cooperation, collaboration, reciprocity, social-emotional intelligence, and loving relationships. The erosion of empathy in the brain is complex. It's worth noting that neuroscientists concur that "at least ten interconnected brain regions are involved in empathy," and likely more.[1]

How do these regions of the brain become eroded? Genetics may play a role, but the research suggests that "the majority" who suffer from empathy erosion "are victims of abuse or neglect in their childhood, the consequences of which can be long term."[2] It is tragic that we live in a society that has had this knowledge for decades and has not acted effectively to halt rampant child abuse and neglect.

We are harmed and frustrated by bullying in the workplace, but we tackle it as a downstream issue when really, if we want it to change in a significant way, we need to go upstream and change the way in which children are raised. Still, there are far better ways to manage bullying in the workplace in real time, which begins with better recognizing falsehoods and manipulation.

We will learn about how empathy operates in the brains of hurt people, people who become part of the Dark Triad of narcissism, Machiavellianism, and psychopathy. These individuals are remarkably destructive in the workplace and leave a trail of suffering in their wake. Once we better understand how empathy may have been eroded in their brains, we look at some examples of how this loss translates into the lies of bullying, gaslighting, and institutional complicity.

DOUBLE EMPATHY

To remind you, empathy is when you walk in someone else's shoes, see the world through their eyes, feel their pain. In *The Bullied Brain*, I talked about studies in empathy where individuals watched someone have their fingers pricked with a pin.[3] Those being hurt, and those watching them be hurt, were in fMRI scanners that registered their brain activation. The fascinating discovery was that the brain reaction of the one watching was almost identical to the one being pricked. The observer's brain activated the same neural networks for pain, but it was muted. Experts realize that this mirrored response is the way we survive. The person who is hurt is incapacitated. The observer "feels his pain" and has his empathy neural network light up—not enough to be incapacitated, just enough to help. These studies were measuring *affective* empathy. It's this kind of empathy, the empathy involving feelings, that is eroded in Dr. Jekyll and Mr. Hyde.

Neuroscientist Simon Baron-Cohen defines empathy as follows:

> *Empathy occurs when we suspend our single-minded focus of attention and instead adopt a double-minded focus of attention.*
> *Empathy is our ability to identify what someone else is thinking or feeling and to respond to their thoughts and feelings with an appropriate emotion.*[4]

Dr. Jekyll loses his physician's focus on his patients. He is not using a double-minded focus of attention with his "medicine"; instead, he has become single-minded in his drive to hurt others. He creates a "medicine" for himself. The potion he creates—when he could be creating healing potions for patients—morphs him into Mr. Hyde to hurt people with impunity. A doctor's mission is to heal and save others. Dr. Jekyll's impulse is to hurt and kill others. You can see the literary mastermind of Robert Louis Stevenson at work here. Mr. Hyde is Dr. Jekyll's way of eliminating his brain's empathy. The potion is symbolic of killing off or extinguishing the neural circuits for affective empathy. Dr. Jekyll ignores what someone else thinks or feels and the need to respond with an appropriate emotion. As Mr. Hyde, the doctor can cruelly ignore, disregard, trample others' thoughts and feelings. He can hurt people, even kill them, because he doesn't *feel* anything. He has no affective empathy.

In the *Divine Comedy*, Dante develops the idea of *contrapasso* or "the punishment fits the crime." Again, as a sign of Robert Louis Stevenson's literary power, note that he serves Dr. Jekyll with this kind of justice. Dr. Jekyll is so single-minded, so obsessed with his own needs and desires, that it erodes his feelings for others. He fails in the empathy exercise of being double-minded. How does his punishment fit his crime? He splits in two: his retribution is to divide into the double-minded Dr. Jekyll and Mr. Hyde. His single-minded, self-serving agenda causes him to self-destruct into the very duality he relinquished as a physician.

TRIBAL EMPATHY

Psychiatrist and empathy expert Dr. Helen Reiss discusses the way in which empathy is "tribal." She explains that evolution sculpted our brain to recognize others from elsewhere as potential threats, which is how we could prepare for an attack from a warring tribe.[5] Think Vikings and other marauders. In our multicultural world full of travel and immigration and flourishing diverse communities, this is an outdated brain reaction, but it might still unconsciously influence our reaction to and treatment of others. We need to be aware that our empathy is heightened when someone is like us and weakened when someone is not. If someone looks like you, has a similar educational background, maybe dresses the same, shares the same culture, speaks in the same way, we put them into an unconscious "in-group." If they don't, without awareness, we might put them into an "out-group." It's as if the brain registers a different tribe and does not offer as much empathy.[6]

Baron-Cohen describes how this offering and withholding of empathy can create a split personality in terms of how we treat people.

Equally important as a social factor are in-group/out-group iden-tities. As social primates we show loyalty toward the group as a survival strategy, since we are weaker alone than in the protection of the group. This can have the effect of making us prioritize our own group's interests over those of the other group, leading us to show more compassion for our own group members than those in the other group. Empathy in this context is specific to a relationship, which means the very same individual could be empathic to his or her own kin while being unempathic toward "the enemy."[7]

You can see how this plays out in family feuds or mafia families who would die for one another but not hesitate to kill those who interfere with the family's interests. Providing or withholding empathy can go beyond family to create "kin" out of similar traits while dehumanizing those who have different traits. Unconscious biases in the workplace can lead to individuals harming others without fully understanding why their empathy is compromised.

If a person is raised in a society structured on in-groups and out-groups, offering or withdrawing empathy can become dangerously divisive, unfair, lead to harm, cause sociopathy. I define sociopathy and distinguish it from psychopathy as a mental deficit caused by society, by culture, by training. If you are raised in a racist society, it's likely you'll grow up and have your brain wired to believe that other races are not the same as yours, and you put them into the "out-group." They do not receive equal rights, and they do not get your empathy. Likewise, if you're raised in a misogynistic society, it's likely you'll grow up and have your brain wired to believe that women are not equal to men. They do not have the same rights. We will examine these forms of social maltreatment as gaslighting examples in the next chapter.

Any time you are encouraged to put others in the out-group, through gossip or public humiliation, or subtle disparaging remarks or comments about their differences, you should be on high alert. If someone tries to connect with you based on your similarities, who makes you feel like you're worthy of the in-group and others are not, you should be wary. These manipulations fuel bullying and gaslighting. As soon as you're in a dynamic where some get privileges and others are targeted—and the justi-fications can be trained in you already by society but should still ring alarm bells—you are in an unhealthy workplace. In these kinds of environments, the privilege and connection of being in the in-group can be used against you or to benefit you at the expense of others. Your special opportunities and sense of belonging can be used to make you behave in ways that go against your ethics and your affective empathy. When this division is normalized—and meritocracy, equity, diversity, and inclusion are dis-missed, dismantled, seen as weak—you're in unhealthy territory. Your impulses to survive and show loyalty are exactly what the institution, com-plicit in bullying and gaslighting behaviors, will manipulate. Economic lines historically are drawn to privilege the elites at the expense of others. We would not need unions if those with wealth treated those who work for them fairly and humanely. The only difference in this case between in- and out-group is simply money: haves and have-nots, with those who *have* lacking basic human empathy for those who have not.

WHEN EMPATHY DOESN'T FALTER BUT ERODES

All of us have moments where our empathy circuit collapses, when we yell at our kids, when we are infuriated and swear, when we mock our spouses in a fight, when we say something mean. In the healthy brain, this is a transient moment. When your empathy circuit comes back on, you feel embarrassed, saddened, guilty, ashamed, apologetic. These feel-ings cause you to act and strive to make amends, try harder next time, articulate why you lost your cool (your empathy). You feel responsible. Not so for those in the Dark Triad. They suffer from *"permanent* under-activity of the empathy circuit."[8] Their disordered brains explain why they risk everything to compulsively abuse in the same way year after year.

Think about the high-profile cases you know where the individual had a fabulous job, great family, impressive career, and yet, behind closed doors they could not stop themselves from maltreating others. When they're exposed, sometimes, when the institutional complicity fails to protect and enable them, they lose everything. Sometimes they end up in jail. Those who abuse, and a pattern is identified, do not have transient moments when their empathy collapses. For those in the Dark Triad "the empathy system may be permanently down."[9] This is why borderline personality disorder, Machiavellianism, narcissism, and psychopathology are seen by experts as "disorders."[10] They do not have brains that can self-regulate. They have brains that are dysregulated. They are mentally ill in a serious and dangerous way, but their victims are sent to mental health professionals, whereas they are more likely to just keep infecting others.

The Dark Triad lack affective empathy, which is why they don't feel their victims' pain. As we saw in the previous chapter, Babiak and Hare's research shows that the Dark Triad don't feel guilt or remorse or regret. It's as though their affective empathy is simply switched off. They have a gamelike engagement; beneficiaries and targets appear to them as pawns, objects, playthings. Their single-minded focus sees others dehumanized. Baron-Cohen unpacks "evil" acts and explains that whether they are "physical unempathic acts" such as violence, torture, rape, or "nonphysical unempathic acts" such as "deception, mockery, verbal abuse," they can be understood as moments when the "empathy circuit goes down." In the Dark Triad, what makes them dangerous and destructive is that their unempathic acts occur over and over, year after year, decade after decade. These are *not* crimes of passion. They are *not* mistakes. They are the unempathic acts of a dysregulated brain.[11] When you are striving to cut through the lies of bullying, gaslighting, and institutional complicity, it's key to look for patterns and repetition.

Imagine an employee who comes to a higher-up on a scorching day at work and says they're desperately dehydrated and need water. Pay attention. Does the higher-up say yes or no? If the higher-up's impulse is to get the person water, sit her down, and give it to her, you are witnessing someone tap into their affective empathy. How often does this happen? Is it only for some workers or does this healthy human response happen for *all* workers? If instead you witness the higher up say "no" to the dehydrated person, followed by justifications such as, "You need to finish your shift," "you don't have time," "tough it out," "you're fine, stop complaining,", then you might be seeing a deficit in affective empathy. Important for leaders, managers, and HR to understand, brain deficits can be repaired and rehabilitated, but if you enable them, they will only get worse.[12]

I found it hard to understand how Dr. Jekyll could have caring, nurturing, respectful relationships with some people if his affective empathy was eroded. His lack of feeling explains his cruel and destructive acts as Mr. Hyde, but how can he light up his neural networks for affective empathy when he's acting as the good doctor? Let's recall some of our examples from the previous chapter: how does entrepreneur Sam Bankman-Fried scam investors and convince his parents he's incapable of lying? How does nurse Heather Pressdee kill a vulnerable individual and then comfort the devastated family? How does Bill Cosby drug and sexually assault a woman and still be a caring husband? How does Mike Rice hurl homophobic slurs at players and then go to church with his wife and sons? The split personality is confusing and baffles the brain.

The Dark Triad are often popular. They're often intelligent and charismatic. They build followings like a cult leader or a prophet. They have staunch, loyal defenders, as we saw in Babiak and Hare's research. Half of their colleagues "almost worshipped" them while the other half "despised" them. The answer to this perplexing presentation lies in the brain. Dr. Jekyll and Mr. Hyde have eroded *affective* empathy, but they have intact *cognitive* empathy, which makes them good at gaslighting. Remember, affective pertains to feelings; cognitive pertains to thinking.

Cognitive empathy enables you to read others like a book. You can identify their strengths, weaknesses, hopes, and dreams. You can see what pains them and what empowers them. You can decode what makes them who they are. It's just that you don't attach any emotion to this analysis of others. You read them like an X-ray. You don't feel their pain.

The Dark Triad are deadly because they harness their cognitive empathy to cover up their missing feelings and their eroded affective empathy. They are skilled at pretending to care when they don't. They use their cognitive empathy to figure out what someone is thinking, feeling, and intending, not to help them or connect with them but instead, to play them. The game is domination, self-serving manipulation, self-promotion, and they want to win. Baron-Cohen notes that because psychopaths "often deceive others" it "suggests that their cognitive empathy is frequently intact."[13]

COGNITIVE EMPATHY

Cognitive empathy helps you imagine what makes someone tick, but you have no feelings for them, just like you would have no feelings for a clock. Others are mere objects or mechanisms to you. Cognitive empathy allows an individual to be strategic, plan ahead, act on insights to seduce or destroy another person because he is objectified and dehumanized. Cognitive empathy allows the Dark Triad to sleep at night because their feelings and emotions are not active. They don't *feel* guilty, or suffer remorse, or any kind of anguish. Why? Because they lack affective empathy. It's eroded, usually from their own past trauma and suffering.

Cognitive empathy allows the split personality to turn on and off the appearance of caring and concern: they present with higher-ups and colleagues in public as a caring, upstanding citizen; at the same time, they present behind closed doors as a harmful abuser. Even children or youths who bully usually are adept at covering up their harm when adults are present. Adults who bully and abuse can put on a show of affective empathy for their beneficiaries, which they just as handily turn off for their targets. Remember, the beneficiaries play an important role in the cover-up. You are far less likely to think a teacher is abusing teenage boys behind closed doors when he is a caring husband and father. Likewise, why doubt family man Cosby with his devoted wife, or founder of a charity for poor kids Sandusky with his equally devoted wife? The beneficiary, the normalizer, the sheep's clothing are the roles required in the Dark Triad's game. We tend to focus on targets but imagine the way the whole community is drawn into the deadly game of those who bully and gaslight.

The pedophile is adept at grooming parents, colleagues, and targets with his skills at cognitive empathy, but his lack of affective empathy allows him to lure and sexually exploit children. All those who bully have this skill. The emotionally abusive manager presents to higher-ups as a gracious, warm, charismatic colleague but has no problem psychologically and verbally ruining specific targets who work under her. Physically abusive spouses present at work with charm, wit, and respect, but at home they physically harm or kill their partners and children. Even the neighbors are shocked because he seemed like such a nice man. The pillar of the community (whether teacher, coach, director, chaplain, leader, board), with their power, credibility, and social standing, could not possibly be lying, bullying, gaslighting, and colluding to cover up abuses through institutional complicity. It's just impossible says the brain. It doesn't make sense.

The Dark Triad do not turn their empathy on and off. Their affective empathy is off; their cognitive empathy is on. The lack of feeling coupled with the strategic impulse to win, manifest power, never be vulnerable, results in evil, or to use Baron-Cohen's more scientific term, "empathy erosion." Institutions mistakenly give these individuals the benefit of the doubt; they give them second chances. As their maltreatment intensifies, they discover that they did not learn from the threats issued, the courses in anger management, or boundaries insisted upon. The institution encourages the Dark Triad to become even more unwell by allowing them to continue. If the institution really wants to help the Dark Triad, they are more likely to rehabilitate with time off and intensive intervention. Their mental illness is far more likely to be recovered and repaired if it was treated like an addiction issue. In many ways it parallels addiction, but it is much more contagious.

The Dark Triad compulsively hurt people, manipulate people, exploit people, and get a psychological boost from it. They cannot stop themselves and need help. What's worrisome is that the employee addicted to a substance is not infectious, whereas the Dark Triad, addicted to maltreatment and manipulation, are. The defining feature of Dr. Jekyll and Mr. Hyde is manipulative cruelty, which can infect others. Leaders, managers, and HR who believe they are immune from the Dark Triad have fallen for their lies. No one in the institution is immune.

THE SCIENCE OF EVIL

Baron-Cohen paints a chilling picture of the psychopathic brain. Like Dr. Jekyll and Mr. Hyde, the Dark Triad have become divided, their affective empathy eroded. Baron-Cohen's Dark Triad of empathy erosion or malfunctioning include those with borderline personality disorder rather than Machiavellians. Regardless, along with narcissists and psychopaths, all suffer from empathy erosion or malfunctioning. Baron-Cohen positions Machiavellians as demonstrating a milder form of psychopathology. He cites colleagues who describe them as "individuals who use others for their own self-promotion. They lie to get what they want."[14]

In the workplace, these are the higher-ups or colleagues who steal your ideas and present them as their own. They spread gossip about you or initiate a smear campaign to cast doubt upon your commitment or character. They wear the mask of a friend to find out your vulnerabilities and then they use them against you. Like others in the Dark Triad's game, you are just a pawn, and they want to win. If it means sacrificing you, no problem. They don't feel anything.

Notably, those with borderline are not always abusive. They can act in a caring, empathic, loving way (Dr. Jekyll), but in moments when they are stressed or overwhelmed or feel threatened or disrespected, then Mr. Hyde comes into play.[15] This dual presentation, a complete contradiction in terms, makes them difficult to identify as an individual and on an institutional level. In an investigation or in a courtroom, individuals defend the Dr. Jekyll personality and truly cannot believe that he could ever act like Mr. Hyde. The defender has never seen Mr. Hyde and cannot fathom that the respectable, caring doctor could ever conduct himself in an immoral, cruel way. This reveals our brains' difficulty in identifying one individual as having two different selves in complete contradiction. We saw this articulated poignantly by Bill Cosby and Jerry Sandusky's wives and Sam Bankman-Fried's mother.

Baron-Cohen stresses that the link between "borderline personality disorder" (Dr. Jekyll and Mr. Hyde) and childhood abuse and neglect is very strong. He describes the case study of "Carol," whose mother showed no physical affection and used constant put-downs, including criticizing her daughter in public. While the mother was abusive to Carol, she "overtly favored Carol's younger sister."[16] The lies of bullying at home parallel the lies of bullying in the workplace. Through bullying, the mother tells Carol lies. The lies are that Carol does not belong, is unworthy, is deserving of humiliation and emotional neglect. The lies are that Carol's sister *does* belong, is worthy, and is deserving of overt care. Carol is put into the role of target, and her sister is put into the role of bystander/beneficiary. The truth is that both children have equal rights, and both deserve their mother's nurture. But bullying sets in motion the lie that targets do not have rights, are objects, are in the out-group, are dehumanized, while bystander/beneficiaries do have rights, are subjects, are in the in-group, are human. The beneficiaries are the happy majority, and the targets are the easily dismissible, unhappy minority. The truth is that both groups manipulated by an abusive individual are objectified.

This dual treatment—respect and care for one versus disrespect and cruelty for another—can be as simple as children on the playground, a mother to her children, or as complex as a racist or misogynistic nation. The same damaged brains are at work. It's recognizable and understandable in interpersonal relationships whether parent to child, peer to peer, husband to wife, and so on. Where it becomes deeply concerning is when the damage to brains—the empathy erosion—occurs on the institutional or national level. We have therapy and counseling for individuals, and we tackle mental illness one-on-one, or in small group therapy, but how do we address it when the illness has spread through an institution or a nation?

TRAPPED IN THE ABUSE CYCLE
The bullying dynamic isn't new. It's as old at least as Cinderella. The "evil" stepmother—who seems an awful lot like Dr. Jekyll and Mr. Hyde—treats her own daughters with overt care, keeping them from menial tasks that would block them from opportunities. They are on the receiving end of Dr. Jekyll. In contrast, her stepdaughter, Cinderella, receives the "evil" of Mr. Hyde, who blocks her from opportunities and keeps her busy at tasks that hold her back. Like Baron-Cohen's patient Carol, who suffers from borderline personality disorder—and he links it to her abusive upbringing—the stepsisters who witness and benefit from their mother's cruelty are also callous and cruel in their maltreatment of Cinderella. They are the "evil" stepsisters who mirror their mother's conduct. Empathy erosion is infectious. Children most often are infected at home, school, sports, arts, clubs, churches, and then spread the illness in the workplace when they grow up. If we sidestep the moral language and switch it for medical language, the stepmother has what Baron-Cohen diagnoses as "empathy erosion" in the brain, and she infects her daughters with it; for all we know, Cinderella becomes someone who suffers from borderline personality disorder in her marriage to the prince, the parenting of her own kids, and in the workplace.

Individuals in the workplace who behave in destructive ways are understood by scientists to have "an untreated form of childhood post-traumatic stress disorder," but this is not addressed as a public health issue.[17] It's addressed in outdated moral ways that allow mentally ill people to do incredible harm and their hapless victims to pile up. Even more frustrating and sad is that those who are suffering from borderline personality disorder could get help, could get better, could stop hurting people, but this is not widely known and rarely acted on.[18] If you're an alcoholic at work, you get help *away* from the workplace. If you're abusive, you are protected, and the abuse is covered up. You get a promotion, or you get fired, but you don't get a mental health intervention and medical help.

Borderline personality disorder becomes more deadly when the focus is on those with psychopathology. Like victims who feel trapped in abuse scenarios at home or work develop "learned helplessness" or the "perception of inescapability," Baron-Cohen describes those who are trapped by their mental illness. In his Dark Triad of borderline, psychopathology, and narcissism, he refers to them as "imprisoned in their own self-focus" and explains that their empathy cannot recover. This is exactly what happens to Dr. Jekyll. He stops being able to return to himself as the doctor and becomes imprisoned as Mr. Hyde. Baron-Cohen describes the brains of the Dark Triad as stuck on "self-focus" with the inability to activate their affective empathy and share feeling with others "as if a chip in their neural computer were missing." As happens with Dr. Jekyll, when lack of empathy endures and becomes a "stable trait," then the individual's brain may no longer be "rescuable."[19] The Dark Triad's lack of feelings for others remains stable and permanent while at the same time they appear dynamically strategic and highly manipulative.

Baron-Cohen's research shows that psychopaths share outbursts with borderlines such as a "hair-trigger violent reaction to the smallest thing," but more concerning is their "willingness to do *whatever it takes* to satisfy their desires." Dr. Jekyll is in the camp of the psychopaths, not the borderlines. Psychopaths' harm can "take the form of cold, calculated cruelty," and it's not threat or stress that triggers this response. Instead, it is "a need to dominate, to get what one wants," and this exertion of power, this impulse to put down a target, requires "a complete detachment from another person's feelings" and even "some pleasure at seeing someone else suffer."[20] It is this sadistic quality that draws the psychopath to do the same behaviors over and over, just switching up the victim. It is why they are called "intraspecies predators."

Psychopathic individuals put into brain scanners show more "activity in both the amygdala and the reward circuit" when they are shown films that have "deliberate infliction of pain on another person." To remind you, the amygdala is involved in identifying threats. When an individual's brain has reached the point of psychopathology, the overlap is abnormal between sensing threat and feeling enjoyment at another's suffering.[21] Baron-Cohen discusses persuasive research that shows "the amygdala is not working normally." In neuroimaging studies, researchers find that psychopaths' amygdala is muted even under stressful conditions.[22] The alert is muted. It's comparable to the research where they found those who tell self-serving lies have less and less amygdala alerts to the wrongness of what they are doing. This makes it easier to lie. Baron-Cohen shares James Blair's research into how we inhibit impulses to be violent (whether psychologically or physically). It documented the way we are highly attuned to the distress of others. Like other animal species, we have an automatic impulse to reduce the distress of others. We are wired to respond to a sad expression or a voice that conveys being hurt. Your heart beats faster, you begin to sweat, and your brain inhibits your aggressive behavior as a result. In contrast, psychopaths have an "underactive" inhibitive response.[23] They aren't stopped by amygdala alerts, just like they aren't stopped from lying. If you whimper or cry, your dog will halt all action to figure out if you are OK. This mammalian response is missing in psychopaths.

When human mammals no longer interact in person, when their wiring is turned off because they are acting online, when they cannot register the pain they cause, it's not healthy for brains. Technology's intervention in how we interact with one another is not the focus of this book, but it's worth noting at this juncture that it has the capacity to turn us all into beings with eroded empathy. Likewise, artificial intelligence is wonderful for cognitive tasks, but it's important to also note that it mimics the psychopathic brain. It lacks affective empathy. Even more concerning, it can put on the facade or mask of affective empathy, but that's exactly what the psychopath does. The child luring, the honeymoon phase of domestic abuse, the interview and hiring process cannot occur without a skilled portrayal of emotional connection, care, and sophistication. AI can be as intelligent as can be in the cognitive sphere, but it does *not* have affective empathy. It does *not* experience emotions. It does *not* register the harm done to others or the pain they suffer. AI parallels the brains of psychopaths.

The four teachers at Montgomery's school that students reported on as high in cognition and low in affective empathy appear to have a "need" they are trying to satisfy, and they appear to get "pleasure" from making targets suffer. How do we know? Because—as shown in the students' testimonies from one year alone that included second year university, first year university, grade 12s, grade 11s, and grade 10s—they can't resist doing it year after year. It's a pattern—satisfying the same gnawing need to dominate and humiliate; drawing the same pleasure from watching those over whom you have power suffer. Why else would you do the same acts and say the same words with a revolving door of victims? This pattern isn't unusual. It's textbook. Look at any recent, major abuse case, and you'll see the identical repeat behavior.

Baron-Cohen's research provides insight into the compulsion that drives highly successful people such as producer Harvey Weinstein, Dr. Larry Nassar, Coach Mike Rice to repeat their abuse over and over. They're not in control of it. They're smart, talented, skilled, but something is missing that leads them to harm others behind closed doors. They are acting with brains that have deficits—specifically, eroded empathy. From a medical point of view, they have dysregulated brains. Diabetics cannot regulate their insulin. Persons with blood cancer cannot regulate the white blood cells in their bone marrow. Persons with psychopathology cannot regulate their brain.

This medical perspective is not meant to remove accountability. It's meant to increase it. People who are ill and infectious need to get better and follow protocols so that they don't infect others. Psychopaths should be quarantined because they make others ill. They can infect whole institutions and nations. Humanity would become much healthier if we treated harm being done to brains that makes them dysregulated as a public health crisis. A quick glance at how humanity is faring in the twenty-first century suggests this is an urgent public health crisis.

Since the 1940s when psychologists were identifying psychopaths who are adept at wearing the "mask of sanity," experts have recognized how they rarely cross the line with physical aggression or break the law. As Babiak, Hare, and Baron-Cohen warn, they may be the snakes in suits we encounter in the workplace.[24] Attachment expert John Bowlby published a study of juvenile delinquent thieves in 1944 that was the foundation of his influential attachment theory. The juveniles in the criminal justice system who were rejected by their parents were described by Bowlby as becoming "affectionless psychopaths." Baron-Cohen stresses that not only were they emotionally dysregulated, but they were also lacking a moral compass.[25] Our affective empathy fuels our morality. AI is a genius at cognitive tasks, but it is amoral because it doesn't have affective empathy.

In the 1990s, the Adverse Childhood Experiences (ACE) Study documented the correlation between rejection and abuse in childhood and midlife chronic disease and shortened lifespan.[26] Since then, experts have added countless studies that document the significant harm to children from parental rejection and abuse. Parental figures who reject children can lead to "a child growing up to become violent or a psychopath."[27]

Considering that children begin spending more time per day with other adults—in loco parentis—such as teachers and coaches, we need to factor in the impact of these relationships as well. If we want children to grow up and enter the workplace healthy, mentally healthy, with healthy brains and a moral compass, then we need to stop rampant child abuse and rejection. What do children need? According to experts, it's pretty simple. They need "deep, trusting relationships" with the adults in their world.[28] Children who live in a home where the parents abuse or reject them, then are abused or rejected by a teacher or coach, are like athletes having repeat concussions without time to repair the brain between them. It's hardly surprising that the brain becomes "evil" or suffers from "empathy erosion."

Workplace bullying, gaslighting, and institutional complicity usually come as a shock. It did to me. We are far better off if we put abuse and brain science on the agenda. We need to train leaders, managers, HR, and all our colleagues that the Dark Triad are a threat. From onboarding until exit interviews, it needs to be part of organizational culture. If we have concerns about the Dark Triad in the workplace, we need to change how children are being raised, how parents are educated, how caregivers are healed before they infect children with abuse from *their* formative years. It's as if society is trapped on a psychotic merry-go-round. Abuse begets abuse; hurt brains hurt; the workplace suffers from bullying, gaslighting, and institutional complicity; psychopaths far too often run the show. When will we stop the turning of the wheel? We have the knowledge.[29] This knowledge empowers the workplace to choose a healthier path.

WHEN CHILDHOOD ABUSE INFECTS THE WORKPLACE

The research shows that although the damage to the brain may occur during childhood, the employee might not manifest it until much later. Baron-Cohen says the almost irreversible damage from childhood is "not always evident" until midlife when it can come hurtling back "like a lead boomerang" that hits the individual "in the back of the head." Baron-Cohen notes that "environmental triggers" like becoming a parent can reactive the brain damage from childhood neglect and abuse.[30] During the hiring process and while they are starting out, they show no signs of mental illness, no signs of bullying and manipulating, but as they gain power in their positions, these destructive behaviors emerge. In "midlife" means these individuals may well be in positions of power, with accompanying credibility and social standing. Their position confers respectability, obedience, and a no-questions-asked response to their conduct. If they have been hit with the boomerang of empathy erosion, targets, bystanders, and the institution as a whole will suffer brutally.

I spent extended time in *The Bullied Brain* examining obedience via the famous Stanley Milgram experiments. Other research into obedience is highlighted by Baron-Cohen. It can lead to "the banality of evil," to "conformity," and to the abrupt erosion or malfunctioning of empathy when given power as witnessed in the "prison experiment."[31] These social psychological experiments demonstrate that "institutional culture" conveyed by "pressure from others" has the ability to dampen or even shut off the natural empathic response.[32] You can imagine how trapped an individual may feel: one part of her brain wants to belong to the group, be part of the culture, stay safe and survive; another part of her brain does not want this belonging to be contingent on hurting those pushed into an "out-group." Making the brutally hard choice to stay in the institution and compromise one's empathy or leave the institution and keep one's empathy intact is the choice facing whistle-blowers on abuses. Most opt to stay with those in power who rule the institution. A few walk away from the institution, with all the pain and risk that come from such a courageous move. Still, they preserve their empathy.

As Baron-Cohen notes, different studies that reach similar conclusions come together to support Reiss's research, which shows that power and empathy are in an inverse relationship.[33] In other words, the more power you have, the less empathy you feel with the suffering of others. In fact, your empathy may be eroded permanently, leading you to do "evil" without a twinge of guilt or anguish, just like you can tell lies without your brain alerting you anymore.

Baron-Cohen asserts that "empathy itself is the *most valuable resource in our world*."[34] He cannot fathom how it is not on the agenda in education, business, or politics.[35] Leaders, managers, and HR who make empathy a priority—getting their community educated, proactive, informed, and encouraged to identify empathy erosion—will create much safer, healthier, and high-performing cultures. Not only will those imprisoned in the Dark Triad stand out in ways that expose and halt their infectious conduct, but all employees will learn to harness their neuroplasticity to make empathy a priority in how they interact with one another and with all clients and stakeholders.

WORKPLACES CAN CREATE CULTURES OF EMPATHY
What kind of workplace culture makes it difficult or impossible to create the conditions for the lies of bullying, gaslighting, and institutional complicity? Workplaces that privilege and prioritize truth telling and empathy for all, not just for beneficiaries or the in-group, can create a foundation that turns normalized bullying into collaboration; gaslighting into safe exchanges that are honest, challenging, and vulnerable; and institutional

complicity into transparent leadership. From a brain perspective, the key is strengthening empathy, not just cognitive empathy, but also affective empathy. The goal is to train individuals—especially leaders, managers, and HR—to know the value of working with cognition and language, alongside the value of working with healthy emotion, conveyed through nuanced language as we discuss in detail in chapter 9.

Baron-Cohen examines the ways that empathy can be eroded, which can be used to draw a blueprint for fostering empathy. He explains: "If you feel threatened, it is hard to also feel empathy." Individuals, such as those in the Dark Triad, who have a "history of insecure attachment" or a "history of abuse" may find that their empathy shuts down when they feel under threat. Baron-Cohen notes that when an individual is stressed, it can "impede any capacity for empathy."[36] Workplace culture that strives to lower stress levels and encourage practices such as aerobic exercise, mindfulness, and coregulation is less likely to struggle with empathy reduction. Those in the Dark Triad may be hypervigilant from a traumatic upbringing that may compound their eroded empathy and potential bullying and gaslighting conduct. A workplace that proactively strives to create an environment where affective empathy is foregrounded as a necessary, sought-after quality may reduce the sense of threat that can trigger high stress levels and a resulting reduction in empathy.

Leaders, managers, and HR benefit from discerning between stress in the moment that results in abrasive bullying behaviors and chronic stress from the past that results in abusive bullying behaviors. "Boss Whisperer" Dr. Laura Crawshaw is an expert in dealing with managers who become stressed out, feel threatened, and lash out at their teams. These are abrasive bullies who respond very well to the kind of coaching and rehabilitation at which Crawshaw excels.[37] Baron-Cohen discusses our "fight-or-flight self-defense system" and the way in which activation occurs in a part of the amygdala. For some, this activation can make it become "overreactive."[38] Stress has a way of taking an abrasive manager's reactions higher and higher until she becomes highly aggressive and blatantly bullies a target or the whole team.

A small threat usually leads an animal to freeze in order to avoid getting any closer to the threat and to take stock of what to do next. Freezing can also minimize an attack if the aggressor is responsive to your movement or is looking for a sign that you are submissive. If the threat gets a bit closer, this typically leads to "escape" behavior. A bigger and closer threat, where escape is not an option typically leads an animal to show reactive aggression.[39]

Crawshaw teaches managers who suffer from reactive aggression to recognize their assessment of threat before it gets out of control. She effectively walks them through the self-defense system that naturally is part of us and can go into hyperdrive when we feel that we are going to fail, our team is letting us down, a crisis at work is on the horizon. The reactive aggression is activated by fear, specifically a fear of failure and a fear of being seen as incompetent. These abrasive bullies who are put through Crawshaw's method rehabilitate and learn to manage their feelings of threat and fear. They learn to replace an out-of-control impulse that results in reactive aggression with a much more intentional response that draws on stress reduction, empathy, and team building to get the job done. Fight, flight, freeze, and fawn are well-established reactions to stress. Those in the Dark Triad have another reaction, which is fabricate. They lie to create scenarios whereby they won't be exposed to stress beyond their control. They are the stress makers, the puppet masters who create and control stress, those who control the game to win.

The Dark Triad are *not* made up of abrasive managers with anger issues.[40] This is why the idea of sending them to a "boundaries" course or an "anger management" course is unlikely to work. These individuals are not triggered by threat and stress in the moment. Remember, their affective empathy is turned off *permanently.* They are more likely to be individuals who were exposed to chronic stress from abuse and neglect in childhood that results in abusive bullying and gaslighting. As Gabor Maté argues, they are much more likely to be those who espouse fascist ideals of the superior strongman and scan their environment for an enemy to put in the out-group. Their self-concept of being winners hinges on categorizing others as losers. Their insecure caregiver attachments in the past deprived them of the psychological oxygen to flourish in healthy, present-day relationships at work. They divide and conquer and are divided—oftentimes into a Dr. Jekyll and Mr. Hyde presentation. They create the stress; they use threat as a weapon; they do not freeze and become submissive or escape when under pressure. They are the predator that causes the fight, freeze, and flight in others. Their response is to fawn over higher-ups, groom them with self-serving lies, seek their vulnerabilities, establish bonds so that when abuse reports come in, the leader is confused and conflicted. Their response is to *fabricate* generating the self-serving lies of bullying and gaslighting. When their brains are scanned, as documented in Baron-Cohen's research, you find neurological abnormalities.

Baron-Cohen's description of a brain that is stressed and moving toward reactive aggression elucidates the challenges of dealing with abusive bullying in the workplace. He describes a kind of seesaw activity between the amygdala (threat detection) and the frontal cortex (self-regulation). These regions in the brain—like all regions in the brain—are part of a vastly more complex and inseparable network, but for the sake of us laymen seeking to apply neuroscience insights into our work lives, this depiction of the two regions interacting more simply is helpful. Baron-Cohen explains that when the threat detection (amygdala) is overreactive and the inhibition or "brakes" (frontal cortex) is underactive, abrasive outbursts or reactive aggression can occur.[41] Now, what is disturbing about the Dark Triad is to see how this brain system is harnessed in a self-serving way to fabricate lies and manipulate others.

The narcissist, Machiavellian, and psychopath are identified by their use of self-regulation and inhibition (prefrontal cortex) when needed. They intentionally present as Dr. Jekyll. They harness the prefrontal cortex to cover up the overreactive conduct (amygdala) that they unleash on targets as Mr. Hyde. They are *not* being overwhelmed by stress and threat. They are using cognition and language to create a self-serving persona who acts as a cover to give free rein to a destructive inner force. To fabricate, to effectively lie requires the cognition and language of the prefrontal cortex. To effectively harm someone requires empathy erosion coupled with reactive aggression set in motion by the amygdala. In short, self-regulation and inhibition usually are the brakes we lean on to stop ourselves from losing it and hurting someone—and they are used in reverse by abusive bullies. These mechanisms are used to cover up reactive aggression until it can be unleashed behind closed doors on targets. The abuser's foot comes off the brake only when it's safe to maintain one's reputation as Dr. Jekyll with his power, credibility, and social standing. He's the last person you'd ever think would repeatedly take his foot off the brake and run roughshod—for no reason, no stress, no threat—over innocent others. Baron-Cohen stresses that the amygdala and frontal cortex are key regions in the empathy circuit, and they can suffer from abnormalities. The Dark Triad have brains that suffer from abnormalities.

Cultural Sanctions

Baron-Cohen examines the way "social factors such as cultural sanctions" can erode our innately wired empathy. "If your culture is telling you it is acceptable to beat your servant or your horse or to burn those suspected of witchcraft, this too, can erode your empathy." Leaders, managers, and HR can reverse this erosion by establishing social factors and cultural sanctions in the workplace that increase affective empathy. If it is acceptable to respond to employee challenges, worries, errors, or even failures with empathy and compassion, this can strengthen affective empathy at work.

Baron-Cohen focuses next on "ideological factors, such as beliefs" and provides an example of a belief-system whereby an individual's empathy is extinguished for those in an out-group—namely, a group that does not align with his belief system. Baron-Cohen offers the example of capitalism as "the source of all evil" and the response being a bomb that kills "innocent victims of your terrorism."[42] Less dramatic and deadly versions of this kind of thinking manifest in the workplace as having no empathy for the targets of your bullying and gaslighting. If your belief system places them—for whatever conjured up reason—into the "out-group," then you can degrade, demean, and dehumanize them in the workplace without any emotional suffering on your part. Hurting others, ruining their career, shaming them, maltreating them, threatening their livelihood, blocking them from opportunities—and not feeling guilt, remorse, anxiety—signals empathy erosion. For leaders, managers, and

HR, this dynamic is where cultural sanctions are vitally important. If it is socially acceptable to bully and gaslight others in the workplace, in fact it's enabled by institutional complicity, then talent is lost, rot develops, and a breakdown of trust ensues. It is critically important to know that like other skills, empathy can be taught. As Riess stresses, "Empathy training is the key transformative education."[43]

Empathy can transform even workplaces entrenched in these normalized ways of malfunctioning. Baron-Cohen asserts that empathy "is a universal solvent. Any problem immersed in empathy becomes soluble."[44] In other words, if your workplace is blocked by seemingly established abusive and manipulative practices, empathy can be a change agent. If the problems of your workplace appear to be irreconcilable conflicts, disputes, and deadlocks, empathy can solve them. Baron-Cohen reminds us that unlike costly interventions, empathy—wired into the human brain from gestation—is free. Merzenich's decades of research have shown that if neural networks have been eroded in the brain, they can be strengthened back to organic health. In chapter 9, we study Merzenich's brain training in detail. We can hope that with training, stress reduction, shift in cultural sanctions, and a dedicated adherence to the truth over the lies of bullying, gaslighting, and institutional complicity, we can see a resurgence of affective empathy, and with it, holistic brain health.

NOTES

1. Simon Baron-Cohen, *The Science of Evil: On Empathy and the Origins of Cruelty* (New York: Basic Books, 2011), 30.

2. Baron-Cohen, *Science of Evil*, xiii. Throughout his book, Baron-Cohen looks at genetics as part of a complex interplay of factors affecting empathy, along with corrosive emotional states, physical factors such as fatigue or hunger, and neurological conditions.

3. Jennifer Fraser, *The Bullied Brain: Heal Your Scars and Restore Your Health* (Lanham, MD: Prometheus, 2022), 163–64.

4. Baron-Cohen, *Science of Evil*, 18.

5. Helen Riess, *The Empathy Effect: Seven Neuroscience-Based Keys for Transforming the Way We Live, Love, Work, and Connect across Differences* (Boulder, CO: Sounds True, 2018), 33.

6. Riess, *Empathy* Effect, 61–71.

7. Baron-Cohen, *Science of Evil*, 173.

8. Baron-Cohen, *Science of Evil*, 9.

9. Baron-Cohen, *Science of Evil*, 178.

10. Baron-Cohen, *Science of Evil*, 97.

11. Baron-Cohen, *Science of Evil*, 178.

12. Baron-Cohen, *Science of Evil*, xiii–xiv.

13. Baron-Cohen, *Science of Evil*, 79.

14. Baron-Cohen, *Science of Evil*, 70.

15. Laura Crawshaw, *Grow Your Spine and Manage Abrasive Leadership Behavior: A Guide for Those Who Manage Bosses Who Bully* (New York: Executive Insight Press, 2023). Known as the "boss whisperer," Dr. Laura Crawshaw is very successful in coaching individuals who resort to an aggressive "fight" or bullying mode. She has an effective method to train them how to cope with stress in ways that are less panicky and defensive, calmer and more productive.

16. Baron-Cohen, *Science of Evil*, 55.

17. Baron-Cohen, *Science of Evil*, 55.

18. As Baron-Cohen writes in *The Science of Evil*, 67, "I do want to draw attention to what happens to their empathy circuit when they are having a crisis, and I want to show how they lose sight of the other person as someone with feelings. This new view has direct treatment implications: help the person with their empathy. This approach (called 'mentalization-based therapy,' or MBT, developed at University College London by clinicians Peter Fonagy and Anthony Bateman) is already showing potential benefits."

19. Baron-Cohen, *Science of Evil*, 20.

20. Baron-Cohen, *Science of Evil*, 68.

21. Baron-Cohen, *Science of Evil*, 87.

22. Baron-Cohen, *Science of Evil*, 87.

23. Baron-Cohen, *Science of Evil*, 89–90.

24. Baron-Cohen, *Science of Evil*, 73.

25. Baron-Cohen, *Science of Evil*, 74–75.

26. Fraser, *The Bullied Brain*, 87–104.

27. Baron-Cohen, *Science of Evil*, 73.

28. Baron-Cohen, *Science of Evil*, 76.

29. Henry Harlow's study of maternal deprivation was shared with American psychologists in 1958. As Baron-Cohen reports in *The Science of Evil*, 76, "This animal model—although ethically questionable—has taught us a lot about how in social primates (whether humans or monkeys) a difficult attachment relationship increases the risk not only of a monkey developing aggression, mistakenly interpreting friendly approaches as aggressive, but also of a child growing up to become a parent who is harsh and abusive." We have this knowledge, which has been confirmed endlessly since 1958.

30. Baron-Cohen, *Science of Evil*, 154.

31. Baron-Cohen, *Science of Evil*, 168.

32. Baron-Cohen, *Science of Evil*, 172.

33. Riess, *Empathy Effect*, 25.

34. Baron-Cohen, *Science of Evil*, 157.

35. Baron-Cohen, *Science of Evil*, 191.

36. Baron-Cohen, *Science of Evil*, 172.

37. Crawshaw, *Grow Your Spine and Manage Abrasive Leadership Behavior*.

38. Baron-Cohen, *Science of Evil*, 88.

39. Baron-Cohen, *Science of Evil*, 88.

40. Jennifer Fraser, "Is Your Bully Abusive or Just Abrasive?" *Psychology Today*, May 8, 2023, https://www.psychologytoday.com/intl/blog/the-bullied-brain/202305/is-your-bully-abusive-or-just-abrasive.

41. Baron-Cohen, *Science of Evil*, 89.

42. Baron-Cohen, *Science of Evil*, 172.

43. Riess, *Empathy Effect*, 71.

44. Baron-Cohen, *Science of Evil*, 194.

CHAPTER EIGHT

Whistle-Blower Antidote

ALTHOUGH SPEAKING UP ABOUT WRONGDOING IN THE WORKPLACE CAN be psychologically healthy and restorative, to truly understand the lies of bullying, gaslighting, and institutional complicity, we need to examine how speaking up far too often results in silencing. Just because we focus here on case studies of those who recovered does not mean that the present-day workplace tendency to silence targets or even observers of wrongdoing is without psychological risk and danger. By celebrating the recovery of targets such as Montgomery, Wilson, Carle, and Macfarlane, it does not mean that the harm meted out to them was without serious risk. For every target who succeeds in recovering organic brain health, uncounted others don't.

Mary Inman—the most knowledgeable professional I know on the subject of gaslighting, who constantly has to see through it, who watches the dirty work it can do to courageous individuals—believes that the impulse to lie and cover up is hardwired into us, but she also believes we can be change agents. Just because a belief system is entrenched does not mean, with our neuroplastic brains, that we can't intentionally establish a better way going forward.

Inman is one of the authors of the following article on the normalized, institutional harm meted out to whistle-blowers. When you read the description of a whistle-blower who alerted his company to safety issues, it's striking how it mirrors the attempts by Montgomery and his peers, as well as Carle, Wilson, and Macfarlane, to recognize and report "safety issues." Although the whistle-blower in the article raised issues around construction safety, his maltreatment for speaking up—by his institution—is all too familiar.

> *Barnett has been described by many who knew him as a "brave, honest man of the highest integrity." This describes most whistleblowers. We know because we have worked with hundreds of them—people who have come forward about unsafe practices in workplaces, theft from public funds, and threats to public safety. We have seen brave and honest people fired, gagged by NDAs, isolated from former colleagues, harassed, their lives and careers left in ruins. And sometimes, they end up dead.[1]*

Barnett committed the institutional crime of telling the truth, speaking up about production quality and safety issues that could have saved Boeing a great deal of negative reputational damage and an enormous amount of money, not to mention the lives of flight passengers. He was badly treated by Boeing and in 2024—after seven years of public gaslighting and vilification—he couldn't take it anymore and apparently shot himself.

The three employees in our case studies are brave, honest, and of the highest integrity. Yet like Barnett, their reward was to be vilified, gaslit, isolated from former colleagues, and have their lives and careers left in ruins. Even a teenager such as Montgomery was subjected to this horrendous maltreatment for speaking up. No amount of regaining power, recovering health, fighting back can return to them their lost communities, finances, and careers. Inman and her colleagues detail the seriousness of the irreparable harm.

> *Another study found approximately 85 percent of whistleblowers "suffer from severe to very severe anxiety, depression . . . distrust . . . agoraphobia and/or sleeping problems." Research suggests 69 percent of whistleblowers suffered declining physical health, and 66 percent endure severe financial decline. This has to change, and if companies won't change, lawmakers need to step in and do it for them.*

The battle of those who speak up like Montgomery, Wilson, Carle, and Macfarlane to regain health and clarity cannot fully rebuild what was done to them. It's important for all of us to remember that although speaking up is challenging, it does not always have to result in self-sacrifice as institutions would have you believe. It can also result—as my case studies document in *The Gaslit Brain*—in self-determination. As Inman notes, over the decades she has had "many clients who leave the whistleblower experience *not* dead, not fully scarred, but empowered."[2] The worst scenario is what happened to Montgomery: not only was the institution trying to silence whistle-blowers, but so was the regulator. When government regulators tell bullying and gaslighting lies, it's almost impossible to stop rampant abuse. When government regulators support institutional complicity, it's a challenge to protect victims, let alone whistle-blowers. We have an epidemic of bullying because we do not prevent its transmission.

Boeing offers another example of a workplace culture whereby bullying, gaslighting, and institutional complicity were enabled and flourished. These lies specifically target those who speak up. That said, the world is watching the negative impacts on Boeing for covering up its weakness and carelessness. Boeing's significant loss in reputation indicates once again how short-term solutions, which drive out those who speak up and protect those who perpetuate an abusive or unsafe culture, in the long run do not maintain a safe, productive, profitable corporation.

The NDA is a symbol of destructive workplace culture. Along with Zelda Perkins—Harvey Weinstein's former assistant who blew the whistle on his misconduct and took the remarkably brave step of breaking her NDA to do it—law professor Julie Macfarlane is gathering support via their not-for-profit Can't Buy My Silence to bring about positive change in the workplace. Perkins and Macfarlane are working together to disallow NDAs when they are used to "gag" victims or whistle-blowers from reporting workplace abuses.

Inman's depiction of whistle-blowers' maltreatment speaks volumes about today's workplace and its concerning comfortability with issuing falsehoods. As we have seen throughout, perpetrators almost seem to work *with* leaders, managers, and HR with the "team" using a "playbook" to revictimize victims, ensure that perpetrators are protected and a cover-up silences reports of abuse or safety concerns—business as usual.

Inman and colleagues think we're at a breaking point where it's time for companies to "change their playbook." They don't mince words after Barnett's suicide: "As whistle-blowers struggle to bring important information to light, the corporations know exactly what playbook to deploy. Whistleblower crisis management is engaged before the employee even knows what is happening." Lawyers who've fought many cases on behalf of whistle-blowers are accustomed to coming face-to-face with the playbook. They've seen it used on whistle-blower clients who are positioned as the problem, not the first step toward a solution. It's backward on so many levels. Those who speak up are the institution's allies but are treated like traitors. These are brain malfunctions that we strive to identify and correct in part 3. In the article on Barnett, Inman and her colleagues stress the harm done to whistle-blowers as if they are the enemy.

> In the whistleblower cases we've seen, gaslighting and harassment was nearly universal. A 2018 study noted "although whistleblowers suffer reprisals, they are traumatized by the emotional manipulation many employers routinely use to discredit and punish employees who report misconduct."

Employers' emotional manipulation often takes the form of bullying (you are not worthy; you do not belong) and gaslighting (you do not understand what happened; your perceptions are off; you are not trustworthy; you can't even trust yourself). We saw these lies used against Montgomery and me. Wilson, Carle, and Macfarlane reported their use as well. It is traumatic to do the right thing, only to find yourself discredited and punished as a result. It's destabilizing. The brain struggles to construct a meaningful, coherent narrative when data is distorted by "gaslighting and harassment." This distortion isn't coming from outside, from enemy organizations, or cutthroat competitors. No. It's coming from the inside, from one's community, from the once-trusted institution populated by known leaders, managers, and HR.

We teach children to beware of the harm done by strangers, but statistics show that the harm is far more likely to come from an adult the child knows. We struggle to teach children this uncomfortable truth. Likewise, we don't train nearly enough about the risk of harm from those known to the target in the workplace. And we certainly do not train employees how to cope with reprisals, not only from perpetrators but also quite possibly from panicky leaders, managers, and HR when they use the playbook to shut down organizational risk. The playbook doesn't do the institution any favors. It only kicks the can down the road, creating far more risk. Wilson, Carle, and Macfarlane, Montgomery, and I were all revictimized, but none of us was ever alerted that it might occur or how to navigate through it without self-destructing.

If that sounds melodramatic, let's review one more time what happened to privileged, healthy, committed, excelling individuals after they reported the lies of bullying and gaslighting: Boeing whistle-blower Barnett committed suicide; Montgomery suffered severe depression, anxiety, and panic attacks; I had ulcers all over my esophagus; Carle put her family at risk; Wilson suffered from suicidal ideation; Macfarlane has cancer. And we are—except for Barnett—the lucky ones, the survivors. One hates to think of those without the privilege of whiteness and education who protect themselves by suffering their maltreatment in silence. Whistle-blowers lose their work community, their livelihood, their career, their ability to get another job because their reputation is smeared. Oftentimes they lose their houses, and sometimes their marriages and families.

Although institutions and corporations have a "playbook" for dealing with whistle-blowers who report abuses whether of safety regulations in planes (Boeing) or cars (Hyundai), or social media dangers to kids (Facebook) or to individuals such as those in our case studies who reported bullying and gaslighting "misconduct," Inman and company point out that the reporters have no playbook. If you speak up internally or take it another level up and choose the whistle-blower path, there is no "master class." Those who speak up do it to protect others. As we saw in all the case studies, the one reporting rarely if ever gets legal advice until the institution does a terrifying transformation from being Dr. Jekyll into Mr. Hyde.

The institutional messaging has only ever spoken in the voice of Dr. Jekyll. Wilson was told, before he was betrayed, that his workplace did not tolerate bullying. But when he was alone in Ball's office, she began bullying him in response to a bullying complaint. If that makes your head spin, it's designed to do exactly that. The playbook advises leaders, managers, and HR not to learn about the harm being done; instead, deny, dismiss, discredit, and then flip the script. Inman and her colleagues identify the textbook reversal where the perpetrator and the victim switch places. She asks a critical question: "How do we better ensure that bad actors pay the price for a whistle blown—not the whistleblower?" Other ways we can ask this question: "How do we better ensure that bullying and gaslighting actors pay the price for the victims' reporting—not the victims?"

ESTABLISHING A NEW COMMUNITY

Rather than anguish endlessly over the pain of being ostracized, Montgomery set his sights on belonging to a new community, one that wasn't built on lies, one he could respect. That is exactly what he found at the University of Oregon. I have created a new community that includes the likes of Wilson, Carle, Macfarlane, and Inman. We share a mission to shine a spotlight on the lies of bullying, gaslighting, and institutional complicity because we believe healthy change, long overdue, is possible.

Inman spends a great deal of time preparing her clients to take the incredibly difficult path of the whistle-blower with "eyes wide open." She has them read books on gaslighting and institutional complicity. She makes them watch challenging films about how risky and dangerous whistle-blowing can be. She insists that the whistle-blower do a serious search for skeletons in the closet and ensure that she has buy-in from their family who will also likely get dragged through the mud to shoot the messenger and deflect from the message. One of the key prescriptions Inman provides her clients is the challenging task of building a new community.

The prescription I give them is: you need to start and create a whole new friend base, I'm so sorry to tell you this, but your prescription is you've lost your community, and we all know the recipe for a fulfilling life is connectedness, you've lost connections and we have to find ways to connect you. Often connecting them to other whistleblowers is the first piece, but having another plan that is outside your whistleblower story so that you can evolve because the other thing is—wonderful woman at Yale and she said "whistleblowers get frozen in carbonate like Hans Solo in their whistleblowing moment and they don't evolve."

It's well-established in brain science that connection is as vital to health and development as shelter and food. It cannot be underestimated. Inman's other key piece of advice rests on the concept of "new," which reminds those who report abuse or become whistle-blowers to move on from the labels that bullying and gaslighting apply. As neuroscientist Rick Hanson has said with great impact—the brain is like Velcro for bad things and Teflon for good things. If you've been harmed and labeled and vilified, you'll find it hard to tear away those repeat insults. It takes work, but it's worth it. Your new community can be constructed on other qualities you possess beyond your integrity, courage to speak up, and resilience in surviving the attacks from those you have exposed.

RESEARCH ON WHISTLE-BLOWING

Whistle-blowers often find themselves driven out of the institution for "committing the truth," but what does the research say about their contribution. Are they really saboteurs? Do they put the institution at risk and need to be scapegoated to silence others?

In an article for *Harvard Business Review*, Dr. Kyle Welch and Dr. Stephen Stubben wrote in 2020 that we are entering into a "golden age" of whistle-blowing, not because there are more crimes to report but because business leaders, managers, and HR are creating environments where whistle-blowers are safe, valued, and their information is properly investigated and acted upon when required.[3] In stark contrast to workplaces where whistle-blowers are retaliated against, institutions that welcome internal reports about abuses have more "positive attributes" and are "more profitable and have better governance practices." Fifteen years of anonymized data reveal that institutions "with a robust whistle-blower and reporting system had greater profitability and workforce productivity." Moreover, they had fewer lawsuits and fewer whistle-blower reports to regulatory agencies and other authorities. Let that sink in: if you want to increase profitability and productivity in your workplace, then you need to treat whistle-blowers as allies, not as enemies.

Welch and Stubben learned that firsthand reports might seem more trustworthy than secondhand reports, but the reverse is true. Noting that it seems counterintuitive, the research revealed that a firsthand report may express a personal grievance or frustration, whereas a secondhand report tends to be more objective and takes more of the whistle-blower role, communicating to higher-ups that something is wrong, and the institution itself could be at risk. They stress that firsthand reports are key in the investigation, but that companies suffer serious consequences by failing to invest resources into fully investigating the information in secondhand reports. The research also shows that individuals may not offer a great deal of detail at first, but if they receive a trustworthy response, they tend to share more of what they know or suspect. A red flag that gaslighting was occurring in my workplace was the leader dismissing secondhand reports from parents as suspect. He required firsthand reports from student victims. When he received those reports, he dismissed them as well. That was the first clear sign that the playbook on silencing reports of wrongdoing was being deployed.

If abusive and fraudulent individuals have groomed higher-ups, presented themselves as the "pillars of the community," put on the facade of dedication as the textbook cover-up for harmful acts, they can assume that when a whistle-blower reports them, that's who will be penalized. However, when workplace cultures make it safe for concerns, complaints, reports of abuses or fraudulent activity to be shared with leaders, managers, and HR, the whole environment shifts because wrongdoers become the ones at risk. Suddenly, no playbook protects and enables the wrongdoer. That is a massive deterrent and culture game changer. In a psychologically safe workplace—one that welcomes reports of wrongdoing and takes care of the whistle-blower—the wrongdoer should worry about exposure and consequences. This culture shift enhances not only the health of the work community, but also as shown in research, improves the bottom line. Profitability and productivity—as documented in a massive dataset—go hand in hand with a truth-telling culture, not a lying one.

What if We Tried Listening?

How do we halt the playbook default, as examined previously, to what psychologist Jennifer Freyd refers to as DARVO—namely Deny, Attack, Reverse Victim and Offender? What would happen if the playbook told us to default to RISE—namely Record reports, Issue surveys, See Patterns, and Establish safety? RISE can apply to production and safety issues in construction as effectively as it applies to bullying, harassment, and abrasive or abusive conduct among employees.

Record reports
Issue surveys
See patterns
Establish safety

The mission of RISE, unlike DARVO, is not "shoot the messenger." The mission of RISE is to gather as much information as possible that can reveal concerning, risk-filled, dangerous patterns happening beneath the radar of leadership, management, and HR.

Record Reports

Keeping reports is vital to institutional health. When leaders, managers, and HR erase reports of wrongdoing, the institution is at risk. The concept of keeping reports parallels the critical information gleaned from employee track records. One of the most serious harms done in institutional complicity is to erase the track record of those who report. It should be one of the most important components in whistle-blower scenarios, but as we saw with Carle, Wilson, and Macfarlane, their years of exceptional work were not factored into their being maltreated or their being mistrusted when they reported. If anything, as soon as they spoke up, their track records vanished. Likewise with Montgomery; as soon as he spoke up, he was positioned publicly as telling "nasty lies" with no track record of behavior that would ever indicate that as a possibility. None. The same with me. As someone who was not targeted but was bringing forth secondhand information that was vitally important not only to the victims but also to the institution, I was treated as a problem employee. Strange, because I had no track record of any wrongdoing in years at the school, except for speaking up about the drama teacher's abuses.

You can see the pattern. The institutional playbook says "shoot the messenger" is the way to keep safe; the messenger is punished for telling the truth while telling lies is normalized and rewarded. The irony is, the leader used me because I was seen as so trustworthy by students and parents that they told me the truth about what had been happening, even though it was painful, and even though it was riddled with shame and misery. Then the leader lied publicly in letters to the community, saying I had acted on my own. Classic reversal. The liar calls the truth teller a liar.

Institutions that keep excellent, thorough records—not only of reports of wrongdoing, but also performance reviews of their employees—will be well-informed to throw out the playbook and instead identify patterns. If the employees speaking up have no reports of wrongdoing, why would you treat them like an enemy of the institution? If the employee with a report of wrongdoing has multiple reports in the past and present, you have the pattern exposed that puts the institution at risk and can act to mitigate it. Why would you use this new playbook? Because research shows that it increases your productivity and profitability, not to mention retains talent who have a track record of excellent performance.

ISSUE SURVEYS

Remember, Babiak and Hare survey employees to see whether they have a split personality at work. If the responses from one group indicate a respectful, caring, wonderful manager but responses from another detail a humiliating, harmful, horrendous manager, the experts are made aware they could well have uncovered the Dark Triad. As noted, they say these survey responses read as if they are describing two completely different people. Of course, this is the red flag of Dr. Jekyll and Mr. Hyde. And note that Dr. Jekyll's self-regulation, his control, his cognitive calm is exactly what allows him to cover up his destructive alter ego until he is under the cover of darkness or behind closed doors.

As discussed, the "boss whisperer" Laura Crawshaw sends out workplace surveys so that she can confront the abrasive manager with how his unstable treatment—highly abrasive or bullying at times—is experienced by colleagues and thereby help him on the path to healthy rehabilitation. These surveys do not reveal a potentially borderline personality or psychopath; in contrast, they show an individual who is intelligent and hardworking but loses his temper when feeling under threat. This manager is fine until very stressed, then succumbs to a bullying "fight" mode to cope. It's not hidden. It's a flare-up. It's not covered up with a facade; it's a symptom of the sympathetic stress response. This manager needs to learn strategies to stay calm, keep his cool, not resort to angry defensive outbursts when feeling exposed to scrutiny and pressure. Unlike the Dark Triad, who are in denial, they respond to rehabilitation.

As discussed, the key intervention at Nike that brought about positive change was a survey internally organized by the women victims of male executives who manifested the traits of the Dark Triad. When the CEO received the survey responses that detailed for him what was happening behind closed doors, he fired those responsible. Nike did not collapse. It continues to be an incredibly successful company, and its head offices are no longer rife with misogyny, sexism, and sexual harassment. It is possible to hold perpetrators accountable and *not* set in motion gaslighting's reversal.

Instead of silencing the one speaking up, RISE amplifies the voice to figure out whether this is a one-off crisis or a larger pattern leading the institution into dangerous waters. Safety on the production line, in the accounting books, and in terms of interpersonal safety cannot be established when leadership, management, and HR do not have the necessary information, as challenging as that information might be.

As discussed in Wilson's case, Ball did *not* issue a survey. She went straight to the two perpetrators who were targeting him with bullying and gaslighting lies. If you report two bullies who are lying, it makes no sense for your manager to confer with them to find the truth. Of course, the two bullies denied their wrongdoing (the D of DARVO). Ball then attacked Wilson (the A of DARVO), and her technique was also gaslighting. Next thing you know, as is textbook, Wilson must be driven out as a trumped-up offender (the O of DARVO) who is in reverse position with who he truly is—a victim (the V of DARVO). This reversal is mind-bending because Ball makes it happen in a moment, and that is all it takes to erase a stellar track record of almost thirty years. How is that possible in the workplace? Ball's lack of surveying, and her corrupt control of the narrative conveniently prop up her position, meaning that the two bullies can continue to disseminate falsehoods, ruin careers, break the trust between the police and Londoners, and perhaps even break trust in the police among the whole nation according to Baroness Casey. Note that Casey did not speak only to the two bullies who were telling lies to Wilson and about Wilson—in other words not the best source for truthful information—but surveyed all kinds of police in the force and all kinds of citizens for a year to gather data.

SEE PATTERNS

Those who abuse don't do it only once. It's compulsive and repeated. It forms an obvious pattern. It results in reports from multiple targets, victims, and bystanders. It is revealed from multiple perspectives and sources. This fact is exactly why surveys are vital to institutional health, but only if they are anonymous and the information is acted upon. Anonymity stops the perpetrator from retaliation and reprisal. If the institution normalizes complicity with lack of safety, fraudulent acts, abusive conduct, then it will lash out like the leader did at me when I suggested that he gather information with a survey. "Don't tell me how to do my job" really meant: I condone the abuse. I've known about it for years. I have many reports. I didn't act in the past, and so I cannot act now. If abuse is discovered, then I am negligent. But of course, he can't say this in an institution that uses the playbook to drive out the whistle-blower and protect the wrongdoing.

Remember, in my workplace, the board asked me to have parents write to him about their children's experiences with the teachers who had been reported as abusive. I received many reports from parents, not only of abuse, but of the measures they had taken to demand that the teachers stop. They were shocking. I did not know these parents and I certainly did not know that they were actively reporting and trying to stop the abuse to which my son was being subjected daily. These parents comprised but a one-year record. Now, do you think the abusive teachers only abused this one year? If that's the case, why? What was it about this year that turned them from healthy, safe teachers into abusive ones? Doesn't it make far more sense that we had a snapshot of a perpetual cycle of abuse?

The leader told me that he had no previous records of abusive conduct. That was odd, because from my first year of teaching at the school I heard about the open secret of the older teacher's abuse and how students dropped their sport to avoid him. The leader's energy went to a cover-up, as we have seen at so many other institutions where child abuse flourishes. Whether it was years of the drama teacher's abuse or PE teachers' abuse, he was going to cover it up and thereby enable it until it hit the crisis point: the drama teacher was fired, and the PE teachers put the school and the government regulator on the front page of national news and investigative TV that specializes in exposing wrongdoing.

ESTABLISH SAFETY

To be safe at work is a basic human right. If an institution, if a workplace cannot demonstrate that it is safe, it should be shut down until it can. Institutions that do not meet fire code requirements are shut down until further notice. Restaurants that cannot guarantee the safety of their environment and food production are shut down until further notice. Institutions that cover up toxic environments, safety threats, fraud that costs targets their livelihoods, life savings, health, mental health, careers, and reputations should be shut down until further notice. The kind of fire safety regulations we normalize need to become normal professional assessments done at least twice a year by mental health professionals and insurers for workplaces where speaking up about wrongdoing is a crime and doing wrong is covered up, protected, and enabled. We don't enable arsonists. We don't enable tainted food. Why do we enable those in our institutions who blow people up, poison others, and burn down the place?

DIVISION BECOMES UNITY

Remember, those who deal in the lies of bullying and gaslighting succeed through the tried-and-true method of divide and conquer. They manifest their power and control by deciding who is in the in-group and who is in the out-group, dismantling the truth and the fact that we all have rights, we all belong, we're all in this together. They invoke a new world order—a mirror that reflects back to them their privileged status and power—where they decide who to benefit and who to harm. We don't have to scurry around trying to curry favor with them, selling out our beliefs, principles, and most importantly our affective empathy; we can resist. One of the best ways to prevent division and resist duality—the splitting apart that can turn our brains into the psychopathic version that is Dr. Jekyll and Mr. Hyde—is to always protect our commitment to the truth that we are all worthy and we all belong. As a foundation in the workplace, this approach can act as a solid defense against the manipulations that lead to all forms of corruption and complicity.

Inman and her coauthors, whose legal work is to protect whistleblowers, convey in no uncertain terms that failure to change our approach does not bode well for a safe or healthy future.

> *Corporations and billionaires are becoming more and more adept at hiding their nefarious doings while government regulations lag. Too often, only the insider can flag a problem that will cause real-world harm—like a plane crash. Yet, we leave these individuals to face down the powerful on their own, navigating a minefield of legal and personal risk.*

"Adept at hiding nefarious doings" is the modus operandi of Dr. Jekyll and his counterpart, Mr. Hyde. We have studied the playbook of *hiding* Mr. Hyde and how it wreaks havoc with victims and with the careers and lives of those who report. Institutions that choose to cover up in the short term put themselves at risk in the future. Allowing Mr. Hyde to target and harm employees behind closed doors does not produce safe, healthy, high-performing brains. It leads to brains that are anxious, scanning for threat, unsure, not as productive, and profitability drops. With all these negatives, a switch from DARVO to RISE makes sense. But first let's learn ways to help our brains move from a fearful, panicky, knee-jerk response to abuse reports and develop neuroscience-informed techniques to be more knowledgeable, more articulate, and more intentional in our responses to challenging information that threatens us. Let's learn techniques to avoid being groomed by those in the Dark Triad so that when we receive reports about their misconduct, we can respond in safe, healthy, and fair ways.

Inman, representing whistle-blowers since 1998, reinforces what we have experienced and what we suspected: all industries—whether it's health care, tech, the government—they all use the same playbook. Here's where Inman takes it up a level: "it begs the question—if that's our universal response, it's got to mean we're hardwired for it." She then adds, "I often think it's a tribal response." In part 3, we examine the brain science that reinforces Inman's insight.

Inman's insight is good news for us in *The Gaslit Brain* because we are about to embark on ways to harness our soft-wiring (an adaptive response) to change our hard-wiring (our evolutionary response). In other words, our brain's neuroplasticity gives us the opportunity to lay down neural networks that lead to different ways of handling our hardwiring to survive. In the same way that we can override our tribal response to throw a spear at someone we haven't seen before, someone clearly from a different tribe, we can also learn to shut down our tribal response to attack messengers who bring us really bad news about what's happening in the tribe.

In the twenty-first century, we are well aware that we can have a much closer kinship with individuals who appear physically to be from other tribes but share with us beliefs about proper conduct, hopes for the future, dreams of creativity and innovation, humor about life's ridiculousness, ethics around caring for all, and so on. Likewise, in the twenty-first century, we can learn to handle individuals who speak up about wrongdoing as allies who are courageous enough to speak truth to power about the institution rather than look the other way in a gesture of self-protection.

Inman explains how she has witnessed over decades this hardwired response to shoot the messenger in ways that help us understand, maybe even feel some empathy, for institutional protectionism.

Evolutionarily wise, Darwinian, you weren't necessarily supposed to doubt your leader when he said there was a Tyrannosaurus Rex coming. You weren't supposed to say "are you sure about that?" We're all supposed to follow the leader. . . . I don't know what it is about, but it's just so strong that every culture around the globe has a different derogatory term for a whistleblower.

Considering just how much whistle-blowers get a bad rap, and are made to suffer, I asked Inman what drew her to representing them in her law practice. Her response is multilayered and vital for our contemporary society, and the concerning direction we are being pulled via technology.

I often say whistleblowers are like the Fifth Estate. We talk about the Fourth Estate being journalism and I really increasingly believe whistleblowers are the Fifth Estate as media has been marginalized. We doubt everybody's facts. And I believe in a very American, David and Goliath way, that the little person matters as in the Margaret Mead quote about 'how all it takes is one person to change the world.' I really do believe that sunlight is the best disinfectant and I'm fascinated with these people that have the intestinal fortitude to speak out against all odds.

You have heard the stories of Montgomery, Carle, Wilson, and Macfarlane, individuals who have "intestinal fortitude." They were dedicated to shining "sunlight" as a disinfectant into some very dark corners. Especially in Montgomery's case, along with his teenage peers, they were Davids, well-aware that they were speaking up about their institution's Goliaths. In Carle, Wilson, and Macfarlane's case—they had the power and stature of Goliaths—which makes it more shocking to be treated as deniable, dismissible, and most of all, discredited. That response is almost impossible to anticipate because it is so counterintuitive. When you are diminished by the lies of bullying, it reduces your sense of selfhood to that of a David. You have been beaten down or "broken," to use Jonathan Wilson's term. And yet, those who resist all share that spark. It's a teenager like Montgomery daily having this mantra: "I won't let them break me."

Wilson, Carle, and Macfarlane are some of the least broken people I've ever had the pleasure to learn from. They have street smarts from fighting their institution in real time, not reading about it in a book. They have the insights that come through extreme pain when one's sense of selfhood is violated and misrepresented. And they are committed to being what Margaret Mead identified in humanity—the single individual who sets out to change the world. The single person becomes a colossal force when in the twenty-first century, they stand up and question the leader, manager, and HR's hardwiring to shoot the messenger and become complicit with wrongdoing.

In the present-day cloud of disinformation under which we are all suffer, those who have handed over their affective empathy in a Satanic bargain to have insane amounts of power and money can lie more and more easily. They can use social media platforms as disseminators of falsehoods, apparently with impunity. As Inman says, government regulation is dragging its feet, seems to lack urgency or a will to act. When the lies of bullying and gaslighting result in fines and jail time, we will see a great reduction in institutional complicity and a great increase in productivity and profitability for all, not just for those who have bargained with the devil. Selling out one's fellow humans is tragic; selling out the planet tells us that affective empathy has been truly eroded. We can watch this crisis unfold, or we can speak up. Everyone now must find his intestinal fortitude, or we will simply fling ourselves and nature itself, like lemmings, over the cliff. As this concerning future looms, in part 3 brain scientists will talk about how it is time to chart a different course. Knowing how to work *with* our brains, not against them, shines an empowering light.

Inman talks about how she fell in love with fighting for the rights of whistle-blowers. She says the impulse comes from a deep sense of empathy, which leads her to be with them in their struggle to battle the institutional and corporate Goliaths they encounter, armed only with the slingshot of truth telling. Inman is the allegorical figure for affective empathy. Listen to her understanding of what speaking up is about. As an American lawyer, she reveals the role whistle-blowing plays in her country; and I must admit, as a Canadian, with some of the weakest protections for whistle-blowers in the world, I am envious.

I loved the idea that whistleblowing as a concept began with the Revolutionary War, I loved that it's a concept we borrowed from English common law. I love the idea, it's a very American ideal especially under the false claims act an individual can stand in the shoes of the government and launch a case to protect the government's interest. No other country in the world let's that happen. I also love the bi-partisan nature of it that it's actually the kind of thing that no one can be pro-fraud so it's one of the rare places where both sides of the aisle Democrats and Republicans get behind it. I mean the biggest champion of whistleblowers is Senator Chuck Grassley of Iowa. I mean they don't get more Republican than that.

Whistle-blower protection was signed into law in 1778 in the United States because ten officers refused to look the other way when one of their naval officers was torturing British prisoners of war. Congressional politicians not only supported them but built in a provision for legal costs the whistle-blower might have to bear in the future. This impulse to listen to and care for those who have the ethics and courage to report wrongdoings and harm to others suggests that our hardwiring, our tribal response to shoot the messenger, can completely shift.

It must have been terrible for leadership to receive the information that an officer empowered and entrusted to protect and fight honorably was doing terrible harm that tarnished his position and his profession's reputation. Still, the whistle-blowers were listened to. As Inman says, America has become a nation that still legally honors individuals who speak up to the government to stand with it to protect its interests. Note, the tribal response to shoot the messenger was overridden by a newer adaptation. We can change our brains. We can oust the old playbook and write a new one. Across the political divide, perhaps nothing is more deeply American—in its era of articulating what kind of nation it aspired to be—than to stand as one in refusing cruelty, lies, and cover-ups. Whistle-blower protection dismantles the fraudulent, self-serving lies of bullying, gaslighting, and institutional complicity.

I am privileged to be on the board of the Whistleblowing Research Society of Canada. Inman is on the advisory board. Under the staunch and informed leadership of Pamela Forward, we hope to bring this defining American affective empathy, courage, and truth telling to Canada. To date, the battle has been uphill. What Inman feels, understands, and articulates is that we are stronger together. We cannot afford to fall for the psychopath's bullying and gaslighting lies that set the stage for divide and conquer.

NOTES

1. References to media are in the references.
2. Unless specified, all quotes from Mary Inman are from my interview with her.
3. Stephen Stubben and Karl Welch in *Harvard Business Review*. References to media are in the references.

Part Three
Six Proven Ways to See the Truth

CHAPTER NINE

Replace Static with Clarity

Proven Way #1: Strengthen Exteroception

IN PART 1, WE LEARNED FROM CASE STUDIES ABOUT THE LIES OF BULLY-
ing, gaslighting, and institutional complicity and how they impact individuals in the workplace. These stories formed a critical foundation for
the rest of *The Gaslit Brain* because our brains learn from stories much
more effectively than they do from statistics. Our key takeaways from
the four case studies were that everyone—including privileged, highly
educated, talented individuals—is at risk for bullying and gaslighting.
We discovered that bullying at work follows a textbook pattern regardless
of whether it's at an international boarding school, a top-level corporation, an elite police force, or the faculty of law at a university. It follows
a frankly tiresome pattern, whether it's in Canada, the United States,
or the United Kingdom. One of the driving forces behind this book is
to identify this pattern in the workplace and prevent it. Why do we let
it ruin individuals and talent? Why do we let it destroy livelihoods and
careers? Why do we invest in leaders at work, only to let them exit with
all their knowledge and skill because we fail to hold bullies and gaslighters accountable? Why do we drive integrity out of our workplaces and
protect those who harm others and lie about it?

In part 2, we examined the psychology of being blind to betrayal. We
learned about psychopathic brains in the workplace and how they present
as a dual personality like Dr. Jekyll and Mr. Hyde. We ended on how
truth tellers and especially whistle-blowers are an antidote to the lying

and manipulating of the Dark Triad, even though they are frequently penalized and badly harmed in the workplace. We discovered that our society has slipped into normalizing lies, absorbs disinformation as if it's factual, and has lost the battle of the war on truth without being aware of the significant damage this may do to brain health and stability.

In part 3, we will learn that the key barrier between sanity and insanity for us as individuals and an international community is, in fact, the truth. It is our most precious commodity. It needs to be protected by the most stringent laws. This is not my opinion. It is an argument grounded in established neuroscience. Our brains remain healthy when we can discern between truth and lies. When that capacity is lost, we are all at serious risk.

WE CAN CHANGE OUR BRAINS

Before we learn from neuroscientists about how our lack of knowledge about our brains can create workplace dynamics that protect those who lie and oust those who tell the truth, we need to be inspired and empowered about our brain's capacity to change. *The Gaslit Brain* would be a very depressing book if we were doomed to see the brutal injustice detailed in the case studies simply repeated. In this first chapter of part 3, we learn that the opposite is true.

Neuroplasticity means that we can replace the limiting cognitive habits of outdated workplaces and rewire our brains with proven habits that increase productivity and profitability. Once we understand our brain's innate ability to change, we can discover step-by-step the other proven ways to become adept at recognizing the self-serving lies of bullying and gaslighting. We can learn a new way that avoids institutional complicity and instead, sees our truth tellers as trusted allies and those who tell lies as serious threats.

The first proven way to strengthen our brains and make them ready to do battle against the lies of bullying, gaslighting, and institutional complicity focuses on exteroception, the process by which our brain perceives the environment through the senses. Exteroception refers to our five senses that help us become aware, process, and adapt to stimuli outside of the body. When we exercise and train these fundamental brain processes, it influences higher-level thinking. Drawing on the work of neuroscientist Michael Merzenich, we learn about an accessible daily program and practice that can keep us safer and saner.

If you had to go into the ring and box against those issuing the lies of bullying, gaslighting, and institutional complicity, you'd want to get into the best physical shape possible. You'd want to minimize the harmfulness of the blows they would rain upon you. Considering that we work in a world suffering from a bullying epidemic that has an "army of enablers," you might even want to keep training after the big fight to keep your resilience and readiness for the next time. You'd want to stay in peak form. Unfortunately, being in top physical form won't help you triumph over the lies of bullying and gaslighting. It won't keep you safe when you are inexorably drawn into the betrayal of institutional complicity. Being in top neurological form is what you need. You need to *train* your brain to prevent bullying and gaslighting, to defend yourself if they happen, and to become resilient against those who tell self-serving, harmful lies. Is it possible to do this training? As Merzenich, winner of the 2016 Kavli Prize for Neuroscience, would reply, "Absolutely."

EXTEROCEPTION

A clear, sharp representation of reality starts with the senses. Your ears, eyes, and other sensory organs constantly send information to your brain. Your brain uses this sensory data to construct your experiences and memories, from the intense—landing a big client, solving a challenging problem, earning a promotion—to the ordinary—working through your to-do list, participating in meetings, writing reports. The more sharply and clearly your brain registers this information, the better you can respond to it and store it so that you can remember it and use it later.

It's important that your brain effectively processes all the sensory details of what you see or hear. A cloudy or static-filled version of those details results in most of the errors and confusion that can limit you, and it's difficult even to know what you're missing. Imagine the sense of distraction and disruption in a brain afflicted by the lies of bullying and gaslighting. Your brain misses lots of details, which causes it to slow down quite a lot, because it is trying hard not to make mistakes but is struggling because it's unsure and overwhelmed. Most importantly, if your brain is cloudy and imprecise in its most elemental operations, all its higher operations in thinking and acting will suffer. You can practice higher-level cognition, but it just can't improve very much if you are depending on fuzzy or incomplete sensory data.

Improving your brain's sharp representation of the details of what you see, hear, and feel is a key step in improving your overall brain function and your brain's ability to create a sharp representation of reality. When you focus on strengthening your brain's exteroception—namely, increasing the quantity of sensory data the brain absorbs while improving the quality with which the brain processes and records this data—then this foundation strengthens all the higher functions of your brain that depend on this information.

CLOUDING YOUR BRAIN'S SHARP REALITY

Bullying and gaslighting target your brain. As we learned in part 1 and part 2, perpetrators use tried-and-true techniques to scramble your brain's ability to think properly and keep you safe. They replace the clarity you're used to with a kind of static, made up of repetitions, deflections, reversals, manipulations, and lies. Merzenich's lifetime of research—that significantly changed how scientists understood the brain—is designed to replace static with clarity. It is designed to take fuzzy confusion and return it to sharp focus.

Most of us know the basic facts and vocabulary of physical fitness. We've seen the movies where the fighter runs on the beach early in the morning, goes to the gym and lifts weights, practices his footwork over and over, and then spars with a trainer in the ring, dodging and landing blows. Most of us don't know the basic facts and vocabulary of brain fitness, but it follows the same principles. Being physically fit may help with bullying and gaslighting because aerobic exercise is very good for your brain, but targeted brain training is far more effective. Merzenich and an international team of colleagues have designed brain training that more specifically makes you a formidable mental fighter.

Let us enter the lab where Merzenich and brain scientists who specialize in neuroplasticity work. Let's learn from them about how to harness the innate power of our brains to push back against manipulative harm such as bullying and gaslighting to stay clear on what's true and what's false.

> *Our plastic brains provide us with the capability of operating with greater clarity, power, reliability, efficiency, remembering, and understanding tomorrow, as compared to today. Believe me—and take it to heart—that it is in your general best interest to understand how that can be achieved.*[1]

Suppose someone tells you or acts as if you are unworthy and you don't belong, says *you* are the problem, strikes a blow at your accustomed sense of clarity built by hard work, dedication, intelligence, and integrity. You suddenly find yourself inefficient, distracted, focused on trying to figure out what you've done wrong, why you're being targeted. You struggle to remember and understand as they widen the circle, erase your track record, and cast you out as dismissible and irrelevant—perhaps even with a cloud of false echoes around your supposed wrongdoing or failure so that they can justify their blatant maltreatment. It's then that you need to know what has happened to your once healthy brain and how to restore its power. Better still, when you know about the lies of bullying and gaslighting, you can prevent their harm by training your brain to be in tip-top fighting form to prevent bullies and gaslighters from knocking you out in the first place.

BRAIN PLASTICITY REVOLUTION
When I wrote *The Bullied Brain* and sent it to Merzenich, he commended me for becoming a "general" in the battle to get our society to understand that we are in the throes of a scientific revolution that can benefit everyone's health, happiness, and high performance. Much to my delight, he referred to me as "Sir" in acknowledgment of the rank he bestowed upon me in advancing the neuroplasticity mission. I took this compliment to heart because I'm an educator who wants more than anything to get the brain science into the hands of those who need it. And we *all* need it, but we especially need it when our brains have been filled with the static

of normalized lies. Having been in the trenches for years trying to find answers to the harm I witnessed and experienced, with most of my workplace acting as though what was done to Montgomery and other students was normal, led me to Merzenich's research. Although the journey was arduous and painful, it was worth it.

Once the invisible world of the brain has been revealed to you through the research of the world's greatest scientists such as Merzenich, your world vision changes significantly. My biggest takeaway—that applies powerfully to those who have been targets—is that your brain has a "remarkable built-in ability to strengthen and grow the person you are, at any age."[2] It doesn't matter *when* you were lied to, when you were attacked and maltreated. It can happen in childhood, as with Montgomery. It can happen at the peak of an illustrious career; think Carle, Wilson, and Macfarlane, or mid-career as it did to me. It doesn't matter. You can set in motion repair and recovery. You can come back even stronger from the injustice. As Merzenich writes, "every human has the built-in power to improve, to change for the better, to significantly restore and often to recover. Tomorrow, that person you see in the mirror can be a stronger, more capable, livelier, more powerfully centered, and still-growing person."[3] When you recall that Carle could no longer even see herself in the mirror after being turned into a ghost at Nike, neuroplasticity is incredibly hopeful. Not only can Carle return once again to her empowered self, but she can become even stronger than before.

You can oust the brain fog of static from self-serving lies and once again be sharp and focused. Just as if they beat you up physically, your body—with the right care and informed rehabilitation—has the built-in capacity to recover and even get stronger; so, too, does your brain. Your brain is designed to repair and recover. It is organic. What has withered—deprived of the needed water, nutrients, and sunlight—can *grow* back to health. Merzenich has studied the brains of individuals who have been traumatized, like those of us who were targeted, but in his lab he and his team also researched the impact of brain training on individuals who had to have one brain hemisphere removed or suffered substantial physical damage to their brain in an accident. Even these severely physically impacted brains benefited and responded positively to brain training.

Decades of research led Merzenich to discover that we "are in the early stages of a Brain Plasticity Revolution. That revolution begins with a clearer understanding that the brain's machinery is being continuously rewired and functionally revised, substantially under your control, throughout the course of your natural life."[4] This revolution is why scientists call Merzenich the "father of neuroplasticity." Neuroplasticity means you can change your brain by what you practice. The best part for those of us who feel as if—due to workplace bullying—we lost control of our careers, our livelihoods, our mental health and health, is that brain-training and the recovery it brings is "substantially under your control." In other words, this approach has two benefits: not only do you train your brain back to normal organic health, but you also regain a sense of agency. You get back your power.

WOUNDS TO THE BRAIN FROM LYING AREN'T RECOGNIZED

That said, we are still in the early stages of the brain plasticity revolution. Not only are most of us uninformed about how to prevent harm to our brains, how to protect them from lies, how to understand the physical harm that can occur from bullying and gaslighting, and how to get them better, but we are also employed in workplaces that don't know how important it is, and thus, don't create psychologically safe conditions for our brains. Laws protect our bodies at work, but we do not have effective laws to keep our brains safe. We lack the laws required to protect brain and body from the serious harm done by myriad behaviors that do not touch us physically.

Our laws are out of synch with at least two decades of extensive, peer-reviewed, replicated, consensus-built science. If science informed our workplaces, we would have leaders, managers, and HR, and an entire workforce well-trained to understand the harm to the brain from all forms of bullying, gaslighting, and institutional complicity. In contrast, far too many workplaces operate on an outdated model that at best doesn't know, and at worst doesn't care. Status quo has so effectively wired our brains in the outdated model that a new way of thinking and understanding seems like far too much work. We keep talking about the bullying epidemic, but we don't want to learn about the well-established remedies.

As our case studies reveal, we are in a society that does not train us effectively how to recognize the lies of bullying and gaslighting. We are not made aware that our cherished institutions may well turn on us, regardless of the quality of our work and contribution over the years, and throw us under the bus, while protecting those who have done serious harm. Top-tier employees such as Carle did not even recognize her maltreatment as textbook "bullying." Top-tier employees such as Wilson did not even know the term "gaslighting" or the way this insidious manipulation could be deployed. Top tier—national award-winning—employees such as Macfarlane could not even have imagined that her colleagues in the university's faculty of law would send a sexually manipulative colleague on to another university where he could prey on unsuspecting victims carefully protected and enabled by an NDA.

What's deeply concerning to me and not recognized by our society as evidenced in our laws, when you use bullying, gaslighting, and institutional complicity to target someone or whole populaces, the harm you do is invisible. It appears in the form of a brain that isn't working properly, but that is seen as the fault or responsibility of the target. Even worse, those targeted are rarely informed that there are ways to train their brains back to normal health, even after they have been repeatedly attacked and infected in a workplace that enables and is complicit in bullying and gaslighting.

It's time to tune out the static far too many of us endure and listen to Merzenich, whose goal is "to help you understand the true nature of the plastic brain, on the path to understanding how the science of neuroplasticity explains both the origin of the person you are, and the better, stronger person that you could be."[5] Our brains are vulnerable to bullying and gaslighting because they are what Merzenich calls "soft-wired," and that wiring can change based on environment and interactions. Many of us have no idea that neural networks and brain architecture are physically and functionally impacted by the way in which we are treated, not just as children, but also as adults. We tend to believe our brains are hardwired and impervious to verbal or social harm. It is worth repeating: although so many still believe that being ignored, ostracized, mocked, belittled, publicly humiliated, laughed at, put down, demeaned, degraded, threatened, betrayed and so on only hurts our psychological makeup and our emotional landscape, it is actually *physically* damaging our brain architecture and function.

Often perpetrators are masters at infusing emotion into interactions. Whether it's love bombing or yelling, shaming by ignoring or ostracizing, using humiliating slurs or lying to your face, they associate themselves and their messaging "under emotionally charged circumstances."[6] This is a surefire way to leave an indelible imprint on someone's brain. It increases the power of the one bullying and gaslighting as the sense of being seen and loved, or experiencing feelings of anxiety or sense of threat, or being overwhelmed by shame or confusion all activate the brain's plasticity. Merzenich describes how it works:

> *The neurotransmitters that accompany those strong positive and negative emotions are the self-same modulators of brain plasticity. When they're switched "on," as in these greatest triumphs or disasters in our lives, plasticity is powerful, and we almost never forget. Our memories are thereby strongly nuanced by our brain's own determination about just how important every event is to us.*[7]

When you understand what's happening in the brain, it explains why targets of bullying and gaslighting often suffer from rumination. Their brain circles around and around the traumatizing memories. The emotionally charged moments when you're being lied to become all-encompassing and drown out other memories and experiences that lack the same traumatic force. Each time you ruminate, you reinforce the maltreatment; it wires more intensively into your brain. You can imagine how easy it is to remember one's own memories and perceptions when being overwhelmed by the emotional onslaught favored by those who bully and gaslight. What is reasonable and measured pales in comparison to these emotionally charged exchanges that take over in the brain. Perhaps this is why even psychiatric experts are drawn to doubt their own memories, emotions, and perceptions when faced with the Dark Triad.

Workplace Laws Are Catching Up to Brain Science

A 2024 opinion piece in *The Boston Globe* quotes lawyer David Yamada as he presented before the Massachusetts Senate, where he argued that the harm done by psychological abuse cannot be measured and, therefore, cannot be the responsibility of the institution. He stated that psychological abuse was about mind-sets and integrity and thus could not be assessed in the same way as physical harm. I also presented to the Massachusetts Senate but argued that, in fact, the institution is responsible when employees are hurt at work and the damage is not visible to the naked eye. A broken bone isn't visible to the naked eye either, but noninvasive technology (the X-ray) exposes it. A neurological scar isn't visible to the naked eye, but noninvasive technology (brain imaging) exposes it. Why does one have legal protection and not the other?

Writing to the editor of the *Boston Globe*, I put forth the science-informed view that indeed, measurement can be done. Harm is *not* an issue of integrity or mind-set. It is still not widely known that these kinds of cruel behaviors can do physical damage to the brain and body, and it *is* visible and measurable on brain scans and biomarker, blood pressure, and heart-rate tests. Here is my letter written on January 16, 2024, and published in the *Boston Globe*, which shows the way in which lawmakers are paying attention to the brain science. The headline the editor created for the letter conveys this potential legal shift: "Cruelty of Workplace Bullying Grabs the Attention of Mass. Lawmakers."

> Damage to the brain must be prevented, just as you would see to a broken bone. I write in response to Tanzina Vega's excellent op-ed "The psychological abuse of workplace bullying" (Opinion, Jan. 8). In October 2023, I was one of the individuals who provided testimony to the Massachusetts Joint Committee on Labor and Workforce Development, which is considering legislation focused on protecting employees. I respectfully question the assessment by David Yamada, a law professor and the author of one of two bills before the Legislature, that trying to establish psychological safety in the workplace is akin to "trying to mandate a state of mind, which is often less about the law and more about the integrity of people in the workplace."

If we have laws that protect the body from abusive, harmful acts in the workplace, why do we not have laws that protect the brain from such acts? Can you imagine being an employee of a workplace where, when your arm is broken by a manager, you are told that there is no law that protects you? Where, in fact, you are more likely to be fired for reporting the broken bone? Can you imagine being told that there is no law because it's an issue of integrity that led your manager to harm you in this way? As I showcase in my book "The Bullied Brain," there are at least 20 years of extensive, peer-reviewed, replicated research that documents physical harm to the brain from all forms of bullying, harassment, and abuse. This damage is visible on brain scans. All forms of bullying and abuse have the capacity to leave neurological scars and dismantle brain architecture.[8]

Our brains are impacted by their environment and by those who populate it, just like our internal bodily systems are. Living in a society that does not legally acknowledge the potentially horrific harm to an individual bullied in forms that don't touch the body makes it unlikely that you are aware and informed about how to get your mental strength back and return your brain to normal health no matter how horrendous your maltreatment. Merzenich informs you in no uncertain terms:

You have powers of re-strengthening, recovery, and re-normalization, even when your brain has suffered large-scale distortions that accompany developmental or psychiatric disorders, and even when it has been physically damaged in any one of the innumerable ways that can befall you in your life.[9]

Those exposed at work to bullying and gaslighting frequently develop "psychiatric disorders" such as anxiety, depression, substance abuse, and self-harm, so it's vitally important that they are well-informed of the power in their brain that can set them on a healing journey. There isn't a pill or course of medicine that can make you better after being exposed to the harms of bullying, gaslighting, and institutional complicity, but a rebab program with brain training is a key component for recovery.

Brain training's capacity to recover neurological strength and clarity speaks powerfully to the trauma victims have suffered in abusive workplaces. Being psychologically unsafe day in and day out at work can take a terrible toll on your neurological (brain) health and physiological health (brain and body as linked through the nervous system). Working with a mental health professional is effective in diagnosing and articulating what you've been through, providing the accurate language so that you can understand the impact, and developing a way to recover and regain your mental and physical health. Supporting this psychological recovery is Merzenich's brain-training program. It's like going to the gym for half an hour a day and doing a workout. It's just that the repetitions aren't targeting a group of muscles and strengthening them, the reps are targeting brain "muscles" such as focus, working memory, processing speed, navigation, social-emotional cues, and so on.

Merzenich and his team saw demonstrated in the lab that this rehab approach can be "employed therapeutically to empower under-functioning brains."[10] Students bullied in educational institutions may struggle with academics and see a drop in their marks; employees targeted in the workplace may struggle to concentrate, focus, remember, accomplish tasks in their usual speedy way, navigate the office, which suddenly feels more like a minefield, and socially-emotionally read the room. When we understand that most forms of bullying, gaslighting, and institutional complicity target the brain, these kinds of brain dysfunctions are not surprising.

In the lab, Merzenich and his colleagues added "noise" either into the environment or directly into "the processes in the brain." They witnessed how the noise affected "a negative change in the sharpness of the brain activities that represent 'what's happening,'" namely exteroception.

When the brain struggles to resolve what it senses, hears, sees or feels because its machinery is plagued by background "chatter," the processes of memory, thought, and movement control deteriorate. Buzzy brains must take longer to get the answer right. When that "noise" is present, the signals from the eyes, ears, and body are fuzzy and indistinct, so more concentration and more time is required to determine "what's happening."[11]

From a brain perspective, the distractions, deflections, denials, dismissals—and, most of all, the lies and reversals—of bullying and gaslighting produce "noise" and "chatter." All too often, targets develop "buzzy brains" that struggle to answer the question. They lose productivity and efficiency. They may come to believe that their poor performance is their fault. The extra concentration and time required to do even basic brain processes that they used to do with ease, may make them exhausted and unbalanced.

Targets may feel psychiatrically impaired through bouts of anxiety, depression, poor health, self-harm, and turn to self-medicating. Again, this is not surprising. What is surprising, empowering, and exciting is that along with the specialized approach of mental health experts, Merzenich and his team's brain training has the well-documented capacity to "drive neurologically or psychiatrically impaired or dysfunctional brains in strongly corrective directions through training."[12] This monumental discovery is why their brain-training program—*BrainHQ*—is designed for the masses and is available to anyone with a device and Wi-Fi. It costs about as much as a couple of coffees a month. It's far cheaper and more accessible than any gym. Its personal trainer "Daily Sparks" is a fraction of the price of a physical personal trainer.

Merzenich's mission is for everyone to know that they can have a stronger, faster, more focused brain by putting in thirty minutes a day for sixty days if they need to get back to a healthy brain baseline. They can continue indefinitely like professional athletes—such as quarterback Tom Brady and striker Harry Kane—who want to keep their brain in top competitive form. They can continue indefinitely like personnel in the US armed forces who want to stay sharp during active duty and recover more effectively from possible PTSD. They can continue indefinitely like older people who want to avoid as much as possible the ravages of aging brains.

How Does Brain Training Silence the Static of Bullying and Gaslighting's Lies?

I have taken four specific ways that brain training tackles the noisy disruptions to the brain from self-serving lies in the workplace designed to disrupt your work, interfere with your ability to hear colleagues accurately, mess up your concentration as you struggle to identify the constant buzz, and replace your clarity with confusion. The list of positive impacts of brain training is longer, but for our focus, these are the four key improvements. Whereas bullying and gaslighting lies are designed to throw you off your game, Merzenich's brain training is designed to get you right back into the game—stronger, sharper, and more resilient.

Check out the following four brain changes that can silence the static of self-serving lies when you do your reps in the brain gym.

- We can systemically increase (if necessary, recover) the accuracy with which the brain represents the information it receives.[13]
- We can significantly improve the capacity for our brain to enduringly remember what we see, hear, feel, or learn.[14]
- We can speed up the operations of the brain in all systems in all kinds of ways that improve the sharpness and completeness of how our brains represent and record information.[15]
- We now know that the brain machinery responsible for remembering, learning, and suppressing distractors can be substantially rejuvenated by training.[16]

The lies of bullying and gaslighting try to convince your brain that it is *not* representing information correctly or accurately. Your brain registers dimming gaslights and noises in the attic. The self-serving lie you're told is that there is *no* dimming and there are *no* sounds. In the workplace, you may notice maltreatment, injustice, manipulation. The self-serving lie you're told is that you're "too sensitive," or imagining things, or just don't understand that this kind of conduct is to motivate, discipline, and prepare a workforce to cope with a tough world of competition. Homing in on this kind of confusion and self-doubt, targeted step number one of Merzenich's brain training "can systemically increase (if necessary, recover) the accuracy with which the brain represents the information it receives."

Bullying and gaslighting lies try to make you doubt your own perceptions and your own memory. You raise an issue, and the response is denial. "What are you talking about? That never happened." You report that you are being bullied and told lies about what your colleagues are saying about you and the response is attack. "I've consulted with those who you report as lying and manipulating. They deny this behavior (and are fully trusted while you with your perfect track record of trustworthiness with the most sensitive information, are not). It would appear *you* are the problem." You speak the truth to a university about to hire a serial predator who has been fired from your workplace, and the predator launches a defamation lawsuit against you. Abruptly, reversal occurs between victim (you) and offender (serial predator). Targeted step number two of Merzenich's brain training "can significantly improve the capacity for our brain to enduringly remember what we see, hear, feel or learn." If you are in a workplace where institutional complicity enables and covers up bullying and abuse, having a watertight memory that records your perceptions and memories will be an asset.

Bullying and gaslighting slow down the brain across all systems as it is fed false and threatening information. The brain's job is to create sharp and complete representations of information, but if the static of bullying and gaslighting dials up, dullness and incomplete information occurs. The bullying lies are that you are unworthy and don't belong. Gaslighting lies reinforce these falsehoods, but your brain is no longer providing you with sharp and complete information. Doubt creeps in; maybe you aren't worthy. Maybe you don't belong. Everyone else is thinking fast, and you feel trapped in a brain fog going slowly. You're mentally stumbling and can't see a clear future for yourself.

Targeted step number three of Merzenich's brain training "can speed up the operations of the brain in all systems in all kinds of ways that improve the sharpness and completeness of how our brains represent and record information." If those bullying and gaslighting were targeting your body, slowing it down, making it stumble and fall, you'd benefit from running, going to the gym, working with a trainer. Likewise, when they target your brain, you'll benefit from increasing your processing speed, doing reps in the brain gym to strengthen your mental operations, and working with a mental health professional. Their goal—to make you disbelieve in yourself—needs to be responded to with training and guidance that gets your brain back up to speed.

The overarching goal of those who bully and gaslight is to make you so confused, so full of self-doubt, so slow and sluggish that your brain can't answer the question. Remember, Merzenich informs us that when the brain cannot make sense of reality, cannot decode the onslaught of external and internal data, cannot narrate a coherent story out of the data—when your brain can't answer the question—it degrades all systems. It can slow down a brain to such a debilitating degree that the individual feels like he's suffered a concussion, or worse, is in early stages of dementia. Instead of problem solving, being creative or analytical, collaborating with colleagues, the brain is aware that it's under threat, it tries to figure out what's going on, it's destabilized by distractors and can no longer focus. Targeted step number four of Merzenich's brain training tackles all this noise and haze. As Merzenich shares, "We now know that the brain machinery responsible for remembering, learning, and suppressing distractors can be substantially rejuvenated by training." Being in a toxic workplace can take years off your brain and your life, but brain training can rejuvenate them.

BRAINS ARE VULNERABLE TO LIES

Merzenich stresses that our brains are vulnerable to lies. He is *not* referring to the 1944 American psychological thriller *Gaslight* in which the manipulative husband is trying to make his wife believe she is insane by lying to her about her own perceptions. But his explanation about how brains can be degraded sounds a lot like the movie:

> *Adding a "continuous hissing noise" "in the background as you are listening—or degrading the clarity of your vision by simply turning the lights down low—results in an immediate decline in your ability to remember what you've just heard or seen. In an older brain, that "noise" is growing from the inside, since the way the brain encodes what you hear becomes less precise—fuzzier—over time. You don't actually hear this growing, internal chatter; it lives in the machinery itself. Still, that growing internal "noise" has exactly the same effect for degrading your ability to record sights and sounds as would turning on that hissing radio or dimming down the lights.*[17]

What does the husband do in *Gaslight*? Dims the lights, literally and figuratively, and denies any changes when his wife notices them. The husband's noises in the attic, which he denies are happening, result in his wife undergoing "an immediate decline" in her ability to remember or trust what she hears or sees. She becomes so full of self-doubt that when he tells her she's been stealing things, she believes him. As noted, this is not surprising when engaged with a psychopath. They can manipulate psychiatric experts, let alone a trusting wife. It's uncanny that a 1944 movie would anticipate in such close alignment what is discovered half a century later in advanced neuroscientific research.

Merzenich's repetition of "hissing" to describe the subtle, hard-to-notice, slowly but surely destabilizing sound—the sound a snake makes—evokes Satan in the Garden of Eden, as well as psychologists Babiak and Hare's *Snakes in Suits*, the psychological study of the deadly impact of psychopaths. Although Merzenich's way of describing a brain being dismantled by hissing static and hazy out-of-focus lighting reminds us of *Gaslight* and the mentally destabilizing force of gaslighting in the workplace done by the Dark Triad, do not lose hope. Merzenich calls this dismantling of the brain "negative learning," an apt way to describe the force of bullying and gaslighting's lies on the brain.[18] It makes brains very unwell. It poisons them with negative learning. Merzenich's brain training is the antidote to the venom.

Brain training replaces the "infernal hiss" with brain exercises, positive learning, focus, and clarity. "Every moment of learning provides a moment of opportunity for the brain to stabilize—and reduce the disruptive power of—potentially interfering backgrounds or 'noise.'" Merzenich explains that as you do your reps in the brain gym, which strengthens your brain's connections as you master desired skills, "the same machinery takes the next moment in time to weaken other connections."[19] Your goal is to weaken the connections of negative learning that destabilize you with the lies about not being worthy, not belonging, and not trusting your own perceptions and relationships. As you weaken the toxic lies, you strengthen your brain's exteroception.

Positive and negative plasticity work in concert. Positive plastic brain changes work to create a brighter and sharper picture of what's happening. At the same time, negative plastic brain changes are erasing a little of that irrelevant and interfering haze or noise that frustrate the construction and recording of a clear picture.[20]

Gaslighting lies may subject you to reversals—you can't tell what's up and what's down, who's safe and who's treacherous, who to trust and who is lying, who is a sheep and who is a wolf. So, you may suffer from vertigo. The dizziness results from a brain that cannot answer the question. When institutional complicity suddenly erases your track record and switches you from the victim to the offender, it's extremely difficult to keep your mental balance. When you commit to brain training, you are not only wiring in healthy neurological skills, but you are *unwiring* the self-destructive wiring done to you in a toxic workplace environment.

Let's end off with Merzenich's rousing encouragement to prevent succumbing to noisy, hazy, or outright false constructions of reality by keeping exteroception fit and finely tuned in our brains. It's up to each of us to "grow these precious neurological resources," these roots that fuel sophisticated cognitive functioning. We need to take active hearing, seeing, and feeling and make them work hard to "refocus and reintensify" their reading of the environment. In day-to-day life, as in the targeted brain training of *BrainHQ*, we need to choose "behaviors that are demanding on every level of perception and cognition." At all costs we must avoid the tendency to master our workplace lives to the point where we do them on autopilot; letting down the neurological guard can open us up to the highly destructive impact of bullying and gaslighting lies. Shield your brain by keeping it in top fighting form even when things seem calm and peaceful at work. Merzenich advises us to address "details of sensation and perception through complex levels of reasoning and planning."[21] Don't assume you're in a safe place. First and foremost, don't believe that your colleagues and leaders are ethical, so you can always trust them. Don't think that your track record protects you. Don't take a sense of security from the belief that others always tell the truth. Sadly, it's simply not an accurate assessment of reality, much as your brain has had all these experiences and predicts that they will continue. It's almost impossible to prepare for the Dark Triad. They are in disguise.

NOTES

1. Michael Merzenich, *Soft-Wired: How the New Science of Brain Plasticity Can Change Your Life* (San Francisco: Parnassus Press, 2013), 7.

2. Merzenich, *Soft-Wired*, 2.

3. Merzenich, *Soft-Wired*, 80.

4. Merzenich, *Soft-Wired*, 2.

5. Merzenich, *Soft-Wired*, 3.

6. Merzenich, *Soft-Wired*, 75.

7. Merzenich, *Soft-Wired*, 91.

8. Jennifer Fraser, "Cruelty of Workplace Bullying Grabs the Attention of Mass. Lawmakers," *Boston Globe*, January 16, 2024, https://www.bostonglobe.com/2024/01/16/opinion/letters-to-the-editor-workplace-bullying/.

9. Merzenich, *Soft-Wired*, 5.

10. Merzenich, *Soft-Wired*, 22.

11. Merzenich, *Soft-Wired*, 153.

12. Merzenich, *Soft-Wired*, 22.

13. Merzenich, *Soft-Wired*, 189.

14. Merzenich, *Soft-Wired*, 189.

15. Merzenich, *Soft-Wired*, 189.

16. Merzenich, *Soft-Wired*, 192.

17. Merzenich, *Soft-Wired*, 115.

18. Merzenich, *Soft-Wired*, 118.

19. Merzenich, *Soft-Wired*, 57.

20. Merzenich, *Soft-Wired*, 58.

21. Merzenich, *Soft-Wired*, 209–10.

CHAPTER TEN

Outsmart Manipulators with Emotion Concepts

Proven Way #2: Nuance Interoception

THE SECOND PROVEN WAY TO STRENGTHEN OUR BRAINS AND MAKE them ready to do battle against the lies of bullying, gaslighting, and institutional complicity focuses on interoception, the process by which perceptions from inside your body—such as changes in temperature, tension, or pain—reach your brain. These bodily sensations give your brain feedback about whether you are hungry or full, thirsty or worried, flush with excitement or running a temperature, sharp or sleepy. The way you interpret your internal world of sensations is significantly influenced by your culture, yet it feels automatic as if it arises from you. Knowing that it's shaped by culture provides us with opportunities to reinterpret, rethink our emotional reading of the world and our interactions, and specifically for us, become better attuned to manipulation. Drawing on the work of neuroscientist Dr. Lisa Feldman Barrett, we can become more conscious and intentional about the way we construct emotional responses to our external and internal world that can keep us safer and saner.

As we learned in the last chapter from Michael Merzenich, with his focus on exteroception, Barrett reminds us that "every waking moment, you're faced with ambiguous, noisy information from your eyes, ears, nose, and other sensory organs." She refers to your brain's effort to organize this data as a "hypothesis" that uses "past experiences" to construct a "simulation" so that you can "impose meaning on the noise, selecting what's relevant and ignoring the rest."[1]

As noted, the lies of bullying and gaslighting interrupt your brain's ability to construct meaning and sort out what's relevant. Those who use bullying and gaslighting lies are masters at making us focus on what's irrelevant and leading us to ignore what matters. Our brains get confused as their goal is to "impose meaning," and falsehoods scramble meaning. Your brain wants to construct simulations to understand what's happening in the world but struggles to produce a coherent narrative when exposed to manipulation.

Barrett notes that although our brains strive to give meaning to external sensations from the environment (exteroception), they simultaneously "uses concepts to give meaning to internal sensations" (interoception). Imagine if your stomach ached. Your brain might construct "an instance of hunger, nausea, or mistrust."[2] Notice that your brain has all these options because it has learned them from culture. Your brain has been taught that the internal sensation of discomfort in your gut is quite possibly a signal that you need food, you are going to vomit, or you are in danger from an untrustworthy person. Barrett's approach is to ensure that you learn how to manage your hypotheses and simulations so that vital information from your internal system—your gut instinct in this case—is alerting you to risk and danger, not being dismissed as hunger or nausea.

Barrett's research contributes to what she terms the "theory of constructed emotion":

> *Emotions are not reactions to the world. You are not a passive receiver of sensory input but an active constructor of your emotions. From sensory input and past experience, your brain constructs meaning and prescribes action. If you didn't have concepts that represent your past experience, all your sensory inputs would just be noise.*[3]

Just as Merzenich emphasizes our brain's way of cocreating reality with sensory data, Barrett concurs with a focus on how we construct emotion. Whether taking in data from environmental sensations (exteroception) or internal sensations (interoception), to turn noise into meaning, we depend on experience as well as culturally taught concepts. Barrett explains that our emotions are *not* within us waiting to be revealed. In contrast, we "construct our own emotional experiences, and our perceptions of others' emotional experiences, on the spot."[4] Becoming more conscious of and intentional about the way our brain constructs emotion strengthens our ability to resist emotional manipulation at the hands of the Dark Triad.

Let's look at an example of how we construct emotion based on our cultural experiences. Our culture may have trained us to be excited by, thankful for, and trusting of gifts both big and small. We receive a gift, and our brain provides three emotional simulations to choose from: excitement, gratitude, trust. We could blend these hypotheses to make meaning as we receive a gift. Our brain came up with these specific simulations as they occurred in the past and were effective responses in our culture. Notice that our emotional constructs of excitement, gratitude, and trust parallel emotional constructs we assume in the gift giver, such as thoughtfulness, generosity, and ethicality.

It gets challenging when an individual who is bullying or gaslighting uses this cultural knowledge to get us to *feel* (or decide to construct emotion concepts of) trust, gratitude, and excitement. What if the gift is *not* authentic, not a gift at all, but a trick to exploit us and bring about ruin?

In Homer's epic poem the *Iliad*, the Greeks lay siege to Troy for ten years. Then, the Greek warriors appear to give up. The fleet sets sail, leaving smoke trailing from their empty camp. One Greek fighter, Sinon, is still at the camp when the Trojans arrive to investigate, and with him is an enormous wooden horse. Sinon tells the Trojans that the Greeks were going to sacrifice him to ensure a safe journey home, but he escaped. When the Trojans ask about the huge horse, Sinon says that the Greeks offered it to the goddess Athena to guarantee a safe journey home. The horse is meant to atone for the Greeks' ruin of Athena's temple. In response to the gift of the wooden horse, the Trojans simulate excitement, gratitude, and trust.

Sinon provokes one more simulation prized by those who bully and gaslight. He plays the fear card. We rarely make wise decisions when our brains are overwhelmed by fear. And notice, like Satan, he links the fear-inducing threat of loss to a gift of power if, indeed, the Trojans follow his advice. He tells them that if they destroy the wooden horse, it will mark the end of Troy (fear). But if they bring it within the walls, into the city, then the Trojans can conquer other lands and peoples (power). All the emotion concepts generated by the "gift" of the horse and the words of Sinon lead the Trojans to decide to bring the horse into the city walls that have kept the Greeks safely out for a decade to protect their city.

In the night, Sinon lights beacons informing the Greeks—who have been in hiding—that the horse is now behind the city walls, they can return and destroy Troy. In the middle of the night, after celebrating, the Trojans awaken to find Greek warriors pouring out of the wooden horse. The Greeks slaughter almost all Trojans, open the city gates to the rest of the army, and raze the city.

Sinon is a textbook gaslighter. He plays on the Trojans' vulnerabilities. Their temple to Athena was desecrated. They've been in a war of attrition, trapped behind city walls for ten years. The Trojans appear to forget that Sinon is the offender. Unaware of the reversal underway, they bond with him as he presents himself as a victim, like them, of the merciless Greeks who were going to sacrifice him. The connection and mirroring build trust with the Trojans. He uses the cultural concept of "gift" to further manipulate them into creating the emotion concept of safety when they are in great peril. In short, Sinon presents like Dr. Jekyll but carefully covers up Mr. Hyde. The Trojans are blind to the betrayal unfolding right before their eyes, and they enable it. In the night, when the Trojans are asleep—symbolically, at their most vulnerable—Mr. Hyde, in the form of murderous Greek warriors, is unleashed from the horse's belly.

We might have become fascinated in 2022 with gaslighting, but it's an ancient phenomenon. Barrett explains that it is due to our brains and the way they function:

> *In a sense, your brain is wired for delusion: through continual prediction, you experience a world of your own creation that is held in check by the sensory world. Once your predictions are correct enough, they not only create your perception and action but also explain the meaning of your sensations. This is your brain's default mode.*[5]

We tend to think that those who fall for the lies of bullying and gaslighting are somehow not being smart or are being gullible. Brain science doesn't back that up. All of us have brains that depend on predicting what will happen next. The only way we can predict is by shuffling through (at lightning speed) the file folder of our experiences. Our culture, society, and upbringing shape our past and, therefore, also our predictions. We create our own reality. We think we perceive the world and act on it, but as Barrett clarifies, in fact, we *create* the world we see and act within that construct.

Merzenich puts it this way: "Your world is a brain world. It made it up. Fortunately for you, your brain calibrated its construct of the 'real world' so that this grandest of fictions makes sense. Sort of."[6] In other words, "reality" is a dialogue between our brains and the world. This insight from neuroscientists is incredibly exciting because it means that we are not passive viewers and listeners. No. We are cocreators with our reality, a collaboration that gives us the opportunity to better protect the world we create from those who'd like to take it away. If we know that our brains are wired for delusion, then we need to focus on more intentional, thoughtful, cautious predictions.

Eve believed Satan's predictions. He was skilled at providing a world-view that closely matched her desires, and she threw caution to the wind. The Trojans believed Sinon's predictions. He, too, was skilled at providing a worldview that closely matched their hopes and emotions, and they threw caution to the wind. It ended badly for Eve and for the Trojans, but they did not have the benefit of brain insights from experts.

CHOOSING TO WALK AWAY

Barrett's theory of constructed emotion is incredibly empowering in that it provides us with choice. We saw with Merzenich that we can train our brains to be far stronger at exteroception, and Barrett teaches us how to train our brains to be far more intentional in how we respond to outside *and* inside data (interoception).

If we apply Barrett's knowledge of constructed emotion, we could train individuals to be wary of gifts. As is well established, the Dark Triad uses "love bombing," and the phrase itself exposes the lie. The last thing you expect to blow you up and explode your life is "love." Those who bully and gaslight act as if they're inviting you to a meeting, but it's what Wilson exposes as an "ambush meeting." Again, the two terms expose the manipulation. Carle attended the meeting where she was supposed to be recognized in her new position as VP; instead, she was ignored and humiliated. Macfarlane tells the truth about a predatory former colleague and discovers that her institution will not protect her legally from his retaliatory attack. These invitations, gifts, expectations, gestures of connection are used by manipulators to draw you in only to harm you. You let down your guard because your brain generates incorrect simulations. You predict fairness, ethics, connection but receive injustice, corruption, and ostracizing. It's a traumatic shock on a brain level because your brain is wired to make a prediction, pursue the hypothesis, make an accurate response, and instead of a coherent story unfolding, it encounters lies, manipulations, and reversals. As Merzenich's decades of research teach us, and we learned from last chapter, the brain that cannot answer the question becomes quickly overwhelmed by noise, haze, and chatter.

Imagine the noise in the brain of a teenager witnessing adult leaders, the rule makers and the arbiters of proper conduct, *lie* and revictimize kids asking for protection from abuse. Montgomery and the other students who spoke up had to survive the destruction of the reality they had been scripted to believe since childhood. This collapse can lead to self-destruction or self-determination. Montgomery chose the latter. We can walk away from spectacles that try to pass themselves off as authentic when they're constructed of self-serving lies. I'd far rather be in a community with the likes of Carle, Wilson, and Macfarlane, who also walked away. They chose truth over corruption.

Walking Away Takes Energy

Throughout *The Gaslit Brain*, we have examined how the self-serving lies of bullying, gaslighting, and institutional complicity put our very survival at risk. Those who speak up and walk away—the whistle-blowers in our workplaces—suffer in extreme ways ranging from losing their colleagues, being thrown off their career path, suffering serious financial losses, with all those negatives contributing to trauma that impacts health and mental health. From a brain perspective, the dangers associated with speaking up are compounded by the confusion of being penalized for doing the right thing. The brains of whistle-blowers are wired by culture, society, and upbringing to choose integrity over corruption, safety for all over cutting corners, being empathic not abusive, telling the truth, not lying. These brains predict that their courageous honesty is sought after in the workplace and needed in the institution. It is a traumatic shock to the brain when its predictions are completely wrong, as occurs in these crises of bullying and gaslighting.

Barrett explains: "Your brain is always predicting, and its most important mission is predicting your body's energy needs, so you can stay alive and well."[7] Just imagine the brain's colossal failure when it predicts the energy needs required for you to survive an intensive attack from those you assessed incorrectly as ethical, empathic colleagues. The brain struggles to predict the body's energy needs when faced with the lies of bullying, gaslighting, and institutional complicity because they don't make sense from past wiring or present-day data.

Barrett describes the way our brains respond to danger that exposes how completely baffling it is to the brain—as it's managing the body's energy needs—to survive the threat from one's own colleagues.

> To escape from a poisonous snake, your heart pumps blood faster through dilated blood vessels to rush glucose to your muscles, which increases your heart rate and changes your blood pressure. Your brain represents the sensations that result from this inner motion; this representation, you may remember, is called interoception.[8]

These bodily reactions represent withdrawals from "body-budgeting regions" that the brain keeps careful track of as it's balancing resources to "keep you alive and flourishing, using past experience as a guide."[9] But the brain makes prediction errors when the snake is not slithering along the ground. Instead, it's a snake in a suit. The body draws on enormous resources that could help you fight the snake, or take flight from the danger, or freeze so it doesn't notice you, but none of these intensely physical reactions match up with the Dark Triad. This imbalance is why the lies of bullying and gaslighting can do such significant damage to your cardiovascular health because your brain is demanding resources that aren't needed. The Dark Triad are very dangerous, but you need to outsmart them, not respond physically. Their weapons are language and cognition, and Barrett's expertise in constructed emotion can help us fight them on that level.

Here's the key: We need to *predict* what they are going to do, and as we've already learned, the brain is all about predictions. The key is that our experience does not help us with the Dark Triad. In fact, it is far more likely to put us in jeopardy. We have had so many experiences of truth telling with colleagues, we do not predict lies. We have lived through myriad encounters with colleagues who are ethical and empathic, so we do not predict bullying and sabotage. We have worked closely with HR throughout our career in a trusted way, so our brain does not expect them to have become the institution's "black ops." As you can see, when it comes to prediction and emotion concepts, we need to train our brain to develop a double system. One prediction is for Dr. Jekyll; the other, for Mr. Hyde.

Paying Attention to Affect

How do you feel right now, on a simple or basic level? You might feel interested or bored, maybe you're a little cranky or calm. You could feel tired or energetic. These are what's called "affect," which scientists link to two features: valence and arousal. Stay with me in learning this vocabulary because if we can identify our affect, name it for what it is, not misinterpret it as coming from the outside world, then we are moving in the right direction to better recognize lies.

OK, first, affect has the feature of valence, which tells you whether you feel pleasant or unpleasant. It's pleasing to feel energetic and interested, but the valence of feeling tired and bored is unpleasant. When a sensation arises in you, ask the question: What's the valence? Do I feel pleasant or unpleasant? The second feature of affect is what's called arousal, and it's when you feel calm or activated.[10] Here's why this matters, and this vocabulary is useful: We live in a culture that tells us, seeing is believing. But neuroscientists now know it's the opposite: believing is seeing. Remember:

your brain creates reality. What you believe is what you see. What you believe (based on your past scripted by culture) predicts what you will see.[11] If you believe women are inferior, merely objects to be manipulated or exploited, that is how you *see* women and it impacts how you treat them. If you believe your religion is superior and put those who worship different gods into an out-group, that is the reality that you *see.*

Barrett provides powerful examples in research: Judges deny parole *before*, not after lunch.[12] A judge is considered one of the most thoughtful, rational, bound by law kind of professionals. If she can change her decision-making based on the information she's getting from her body, then the rest of us are also susceptible to interoception. Imagine the judges' affect before lunch. The valence: they feel unpleasant (hungry, low energy). The arousal: they feel agitated (hungry, uncomfortable). What happens? Their judgment of the "evidence" they *see* (out in the world) is affected by their beliefs fueled by sensations, their valence and arousal (inside their bodies).

Here's another research study Barrett discusses: interviewers rate applicants more negatively when it's raining.[13] Once again, interviewers are primed to weigh the pros and cons of applicants, making informed and judicious decisions about who is the best fit for the position. They are not in positions that we associate with being influenced by outside forces. All it takes to change their assessment is rain. Imagine their affect. The valence: they feel unpleasant (dampness, darkness). The arousal: they feel sluggish (cold, withdrawn). Interviewers probably have no concept that the weather impacts how they *see* the "reality" of job applicants before them. Just like the judges would be surprised, perhaps shocked, to learn that their levels of hunger could change an inmate's parole opportunities, *not* the inmate's conduct or track record. The inmate's "reality" is less real than the judge's sensation of hunger.

Imagine the affect that comes from culture and society for certain groups who believe that women are "asking for it" when raped. They believe it's the woman's fault, so that's what they *see.* Their "reality" is what they believe.[14] If you are a judge who believes in and uses the language of "Eve-teasing," then you *see* a rape victim as a perpetrator. For those who have been or may be exposed to the lies of bullying, gaslighting, and institutional complicity, affect is a sensation worth listening to. As Barrett puts it, "Anytime you have an intuition that an investment is risky or profitable, or a gut feeling that someone is trustworthy or an asshole, that's also affect."[15] Essentially, what we need to learn is how to become more aware of our affect and how it impacts our cocreation of "reality."

Just because affect tells you that someone has a pleasant way of talking and behaving (Dr. Jekyll), do not rule out that this same person might also have an unpleasant way of talking and behaving (Mr. Hyde). You need to have a sense of double valence. Just because someone makes you feel calm and at ease when with them (Dr. Jekyll) does not mean that they can't suddenly morph into someone with whom you feel agitated and ill at ease (Mr. Hyde). You need to have a sense of double arousal. Only in this preventative way can you tune into your affect to better create a complex, unpredictable "reality" at work.

Research documents how a police officer, under stress, can absolutely *see* a gun pointed at him when it's a phone.[16] Why? Because a gun has been pointed at him before, likely more than once. His brain is making a smart—especially considering that it's life and death—prediction. I'm not trying to minimize the tragedy of this kind of error, but it is a clear example of "the brain sees what the brain believes." It's how the brain makes sense of the "noise" of an environment bombarding it with data. When that decision must be made in a split second, the brain training of exteroception can strengthen a sharp, accurate representation keeping us all safer.

If your brain makes errors (sees a gun)—due to cultural and societal training, along with experience—when there is *no gun*, then you can't simply follow its predictions about "reality."[17] You need to listen to your "body-budgeting regions," which we name with "emotion concepts," at the same time as you need to use cognition and language to proceed with doubt and caution. If you want to prevent being manipulated, then you need to take measures for its possibility. You need to put guardrails on even when your experience tells you that the situation is safe and trustworthy. Many people make poor investments and believe that someone is trustworthy when they turn out to be—in Barrett's terms—an "asshole."

At this juncture, we can more easily understand why Montgomery as a teenager was in a better position to see the Dark Triad than we were as adults. Although Carle, Wilson, Macfarlane, and I all had had experiences with harmful people, they were far less often than the many, many positive experiences with leaders, colleagues, and HR over the decades. In a sense, we grew accustomed to a "reality" in which the people we worked with were supporters, not detractors; mentors, not bullies; trustworthy, not corrupt. Our brains were wired with the delusion that everyone we worked with was an ally, not a saboteur. We let down our guard over the decades and suddenly coming face-to-face with the lies of bullying, gaslighting, and institutional complicity, we were hit with a traumatic shock. Our brains' ability to predict correctly collapsed.

In contrast, Montgomery was exposed to one of the abusive teachers as early as fourteen, and he reported then and there that he didn't want to be around him. This teacher wasn't coaching his team yet but would do drop-in sessions. Montgomery said he couldn't stand his "disgust," combined with the teacher's screaming and yelling during games. Montgomery was able to escape him at fourteen, but the following year he had the choice of giving up the sport he loved or putting up with this teacher. Luckily, another teacher who coached with him was not abusive, which worked to keep the abuser in check.

The next year, the two teachers who coached were *both* abusive as described previously. There were no longer any checks and balances, just relentless abuse. But think about it: Montgomery's brain predicts abusive coaching. It was *not* caught off guard by many experiences of trustworthy, ethical, respectful "managers" and "leaders." He was primed in many ways for the Dark Triad because he'd seen it in action year after year. It's still amazing that he and the other students had the courage to name it and report it in detail. According to Barrett, language is the key to being aware of and attuned to one's emotion concepts and their accurate reading of "reality."

LANGUAGE TO THE RESCUE

Barrett's decades of research show that the more vocabulary we have to express our brain-body dialogue that creates our reality, the better. Our workplaces would vastly improve with "the neural advantages of high emotional granularity." In other words, it's advantageous for humans to have lots of detailed vocabulary to share with one another as we collectively cocreate our "reality." The goal is to construct "more precise emotional experiences."[18] The less precise our emotions, the less ability we have to express their nuanced meaning, the less we understand ourselves and one another. Our culture has taught us to think that we *feel* an emotion and then apply a word to it. Barrett explains that we cannot feel until we have an emotion concept for the feeling. We have seen in our case studies the brutal truth of this brain insight.

Carle did not know that she was being bullied until her counselor gave her the word. She knew that she felt incredibly sick and desperate. Her interoception was giving her messages that she was at risk to the point where her family was at risk. Suppose we asked, before the counselor named it, how do you feel about what happened at work? She might have talked about stress or having a breakdown or struggling to excel as she had for twenty-plus years at her job. She had intense physical sensations, but without the emotion concepts "targeted, victimized, degraded, demeaned, dehumanized by bullying" she could not see the "reality" of her maltreatment. The sickness was *not* within her, nor was it being generated from her own body. It was a toxicity, like poisonous air, that she had been breathing at work. Her interoception completely transformed its messaging. So, what if we asked her the question now, how do you feel about what happened at work? She may say, "I was bullied. I was humiliated and harmed. I had my sense of selfhood so brutally eroded that I could no longer recognize myself in the mirror." It's the same bodily sensations with completely different emotion concepts conveyed with different words.

Wilson did not know he was being gaslit by his leaders until he learned the vocabulary and then was able to *feel* this betrayal. Initially, if asked how he felt about what happened at work, he may have said, "I am dealing with difficult people. I feel crazy. I feel suicidal ideation." But when he learned the detailed, highly specific term "gaslighting," it changed his "reality." His interoception completely transformed its messaging. So, if we asked him again how he felt about what happened at work, he would say, "I feel deceived. I feel falsely accused. I feel infuriated.

I feel betrayed." Again, it's the same bodily sensations with completely different emotion concepts conveyed with different words.

Macfarlane's interoception led her to be beaten each night with the culturally wired messaging that she deserved it. Her mother said she provoked it, and a book said she sought it out. When she escaped, when she had a daughter, when she was a mother, she found different words to create her reality. She gave her three daughters as much detailed vocabulary as she could so they would know the dangers they may face and to report it accurately if it happened. Her daughters likely would suffer similar bodily messages if being abused, but their emotion concepts—taught to them by their mother—would allow them to replace a sense of guilt and shame with "feelings" of outrage and belonging. The language, not the physical sensations, is what radically changes "reality." Again, it's the same bodily sensations with completely different emotion concepts conveyed with different words.

We have been taught that if someone gives us a gift, we naturally *feel* the emotion of gratitude. We have been taught this lesson and need to unlearn it, especially when exposed to self-serving lies. Barrett's research shows that we can choose our emotional response, and we will choose much more insightfully and accurately when we have detailed language, granular "emotion concepts," to do it. We receive a gift and our experience—informed by what we have learned in our culture—has trained our brain to predict that "thankfulness" is the correct "feeling." We saw with the Trojan horse that receiving the gift of the horse, drawing on experience and cultural training, being manipulated by Sinon meant that choosing the response "thankful" was a fatal brain mistake. With the right training, the Trojans' brains could have considered the prediction "thankful," but also—with knowledge of self-serving lies and gaslighting's reversals—could have selected "alarming." The physical surprise of the gift might have given the brain and body a pleasant valence and an excited sense of arousal, but we can learn that these interoceptive messages carry lots of detailed possibilities when we have "high emotional granularity." The gift of the Trojan Horse, offered by enemies, should also give the brain and body an unpleasant valence and an activated arousal, both signaling threat.

When You See a Snake

Barrett uses the sighting of a snake to further explain how we construct our reality. A woman sees a snake, and her brain selects the emotion concept "fear" because she has seen a TV show about how poisonous they are. A boy sees the same snake, and his brain selects the emotion concept "excitement" as he has been hoping for a pet snake. Finally, a dad sees the same snake, and his brain selects the emotion concept "irritation" because his son has been nagging him for a pet snake.[19] Again, it's the same reality, but different emotion concepts construct different realities. Barrett explains: "Words (like fear, excitement, irritation) allowed your brain to go beyond the physical regularities that you learned, to invent part of your world, in a collective with other brains."[20] These brains could share their diverse emotion concepts because they had shared vocabulary.

Barrett says it's tiring for your brain when you have one word that covers all kinds of nuanced emotion concepts that lead you to different actions. For instance, if your manager yells at you in your face, you may use the word "anger" to describe how you react, but your anger may take many different forms. You might feel an angry frustration that leads to the action: walk away. You might feel fury that makes you freeze in place. You might be overcome with rage and knock over a chair or slam the door. Barrett says "your brain selects a *winning instance* of 'anger' that best fits your goal in this specific situation. The winning instance determines how you behave and what you experience. This process is categorization."[21] If you had three nuanced emotion concepts with words to match— frustrated, paralyzed, violent—to convey your "anger," your brain would *not* have to categorize and could save some resources in your body budget.[22] Further, you're more in control of how you respond and act in various interactions when you have a richer vocabulary, thus a choice of behaviors.

We can combine the brain training of Merzenich with the control network Barrett draws our attention to in her theory of constructed emotion. Ensuring that our exteroception is top-notch, fit, operating at full potential, constantly being exercised can make an enormous difference for our brain health and higher-level cognitive functioning. It provides us with clarity and distraction-free focus from noise and chatter. If we combine this with Barrett's insights into training our interoception, the combination provides a neurological advantage. Knowing that we may come face-to-face with the lies of bullying, gaslighting, and institutional complicity, having a competitive advantage in how our brain creates our reality could help us stay safe and sane. Barrett takes us through the brain's process as it predicts a response such as anger and the next steps to take.

> *Each time you categorize with concepts, your brain creates many competing predictions while being bombarded by sensory input. Which predictions should be the winners? Which sensory input is important, and which is just noise? Your brain has a network to help resolve these uncertainties, known as your control network. This is the same network that transforms an infant's "lantern" of attention into the adult "spotlight" you have now.*[23]

If someone yells in your face, it is reasonable to assume she has lost control of her *control network*. She is *not* choosing a winning prediction. She has succumbed to sensory noise and is making a lot of it. She has collapsed back to an infant's lantern of attention pulled in all directions without the required development needed to concentrate her attention in deciding what's important. Mirroring her out-of-control behavior with your own, which you may have learned at home or in school or on TV, is reactive and might not provide you with the longer-term outcomes you seek. A whole series of steps described here can change how you feel and then respond.

Start with how you categorize with concepts. Your culture has given you "anger" as the emotion concept appropriate to someone yelling in your face. But you could categorize with "sympathy." Though you're being bombarded with high-level sensory input, you could select as your winning prediction "sympathy for someone out of control." The noise of her yelling becomes just that, and you draw on your control network to shine the adult spotlight on her dysregulated conduct, which leads you to act as follows.

Acknowledge her anger with respect. Advise her to calm down. Call in support or security if needed. Report the incident in writing to the appropriate individuals. Note the importance of having nuanced vocabulary to construct your response. If you only had "anger," it would be far more difficult to be intentional about your response. Imagine how you have used far fewer resources in your body budget with the winning prediction "sympathy," rather than the automatic, culturally wired prediction "anger" that often leads to the stress responses of fight, flight, freeze, and fawn.

Are We Blind to Betrayal or Did We Simply Not Learn the Concept?

Barrett uses the old conundrum "If a tree falls in the forest and no one is present to hear it, does it make a sound?" to teach us further about how our brain constructs reality. The lesson is useful when we strive to understand why we are susceptible to lies and manipulation.

> *For this, the brain needs the concept of "Tree" and what trees can do, such as fall in a forest. This concept can come from prior experience with trees, or from learning about trees in a book, or from another person's description. Without the concept, there is no crashing timber, only the meaningless noise of experiential blindness.*[24]

Let's rewrite this in terms of the concepts of bullying, gaslighting, and institutional betrayal.

Our brains need these concepts and what they can do such as demean, objectify, and discard unjustly. These concepts can come from experience with bullying, gaslighting, and institutional betrayal or from learning about them in books or from others. How many of us have been taught about them, how they work, what to watch out for, what to do in response that is effective and protects us? If we were trained to know about the Dark Triad, how bullying is one of their most subtle and devastating tools, we'd be better prepared for the onslaught and less likely to fault ourselves. If we were trained in our culture what gaslighting was, it wouldn't have been looked up so many times that it became the Merriam-Webster word for 2022. If we were taught that the same institution that hired us, invested in us, cared about us, honored us for our work ethic, exceptional skills, and dedication would abruptly turn on us and drive us out, we'd suffer less trauma and be clearer on protecting our rights.

Unfortunately, as Barrett explains, without these concepts, we have no crashing timber, only the meaningless noise of experiential blindness. This description of the brain's inability to answer the question, "What is the sound of bullying, gaslighting, and institutional complicity?," offers another way to understand why we are blind to betrayal. It's not just that we are dependent at work on our relationship to our employer, like a child on a parent, but we are neurologically blind. Our brain can't *see* what we don't believe. Because we don't believe that Dr. Jekyll could possibly also be Mr. Hyde, we can't see our own demise as it happens. We are taught to believe that if someone is in a position of power, credibility, and social standing, then he must be trustworthy. He does not bully. He does not gaslight. He cannot transform you from a victim into an offender. He cannot possibly receive protection from your institution after wrongdoing such as assault, fraud, lying, and manipulating. All this construct is so unbelievable that you cannot *see* it. Your brain is bombarded each step of the way by meaningless noise that you cannot put into any kind of coherent narrative. You can't answer the question. I will never forget what Merzenich told me: the brain's response to this crisis is to degrade all systems.

You lose your balance, suffer vertigo, have serious health issues, can't concentrate, struggle to remember, cannot produce. You withdraw, self-medicate, ruminate, stop trusting your own perceptions, feel crazy, suffer anxiety, go into depression, have panic attacks, contemplate suicide. So much of this unjust misery could be avoided by training, by developing a rich vocabulary of emotion concepts that don't ignore the lies and manipulations. If we were educated in our culture to know exactly what concepts and actions to apply to these destructive behaviors, our brains would not need to degrade all systems because our brains would be able to make sense of the meaningless noise being sent our way. Instead, all too often, we get pulled into the perpetrator's "reality"—a narrative positioning us as the villain who must be ostracized.

Just think of brilliant Carle, Wilson, and Macfarlane, and how different their suffering of maltreatment would have been if immediately they had had an array of nuanced emotion concepts to address the bullying, gaslighting, and institutional complicity. It certainly would have saved me. Believing that all this manipulation could occur in the workplace would have made them and me safer and saner. Montgomery was young enough to see through the position of Dr. Jekyll and name Mr. Hyde. As he put it, "They're freaks." But when he spoke to a journalist, he also said that at times he thought, "Maybe I am a pussy." You can see his brain fighting against his abusers and their violence toward facts and truth. It's amazing that he retained clarity when the government regulators—infused with power, credibility, and social standing—reinforced the abusers' maltreatment and lies by applying blatantly corrupt practices.

BABY FOOD

To give you a sense of just how challenging it is for the brain to override the trappings of a position of power, credibility, and social standing and see through them to how the individual behaves, one of Barrett's experiments stands out for its simplicity. While our brain is busy generating predictions from our past and from the way we were wired by culture, we believe that "sensory inputs from the outside world" hold us in check. This is exactly why there is a great flurry of fact-checking these days during our era of proliferating disinformation. We believe that when someone is confronted with facts, she will know what is true and what is not. Barrett's simple but memorable experiment shows that this isn't how the brain works. The brain is much more likely to ignore sensory inputs when it is being influenced by positions of power, credibility, and social standing.

Imagine that you take the lids off jars of baby food. Your sense of smell tells you it is baby food. But Barrett took this same baby food and put it in a different position: on a baby's diaper. When participants were confronted with the food in the diaper, their brain ignored the sensory input of the scent of food, and they believed it was excrement.[25] It grossed them out. No amount of fact-checking or sensory input could bypass their belief that the "reality" was baby poo.[26]

Barrett's simple experiment has undergone endless diverse variations over the decades in her lab that shows again and again: we construct reality out of what we believe, *not* what we see. Believing is seeing. All it takes is a change in position for us to decide one person is trustworthy whereas we doubt another. A person in a position of power, credibility, and social standing can tell a self-serving lie, for instance, about how big an audience attended their event. Fact-checking reveals that the size of the crowd has been greatly exaggerated. Regardless of the facts, brains that privilege the individual's position *ignore* the sensory inputs (visible evidence that the crowd is far smaller than claimed). When you find yourself swayed by someone's prestige, influence, wealth, power, credentials, authority, do a quick mental check: What's his position—jar or diaper—and how does that change what you believe and what you *see* and smell?

Our culture wires us to *see* the position and ignore the person in it. We are wired to see Dr. Jekyll—the priest, the Anglican minister, the teacher, the producer, the TV star, the coach, the government regulator, the doctor, the politician, the billionaire, the tech entrepreneur, the professor, the romantic partner—*not* the human being who occupies the position. Regardless of the position's power, credibility, and social standing, the one who occupies it may well be lying and harmful. Even when the lies are exposed by fact-checking or evidence, we choose our belief about the world over what we *see*. As we saw with Mrs. Cosby, Mrs. Sandusky, the mother of Sam Bankman-Fried, families who trusted nurse Pressdee, our belief about reality is far more powerful than the facts. In short, our beliefs construct what we believe is reality. This neurological process is why we believe that baby food is baby poo. All we see is the position, namely, the diaper. Our belief system about diapers takes over and ignores even the plain facts that our senses supply.

Our culture does not teach us how to have a healthy brain foundation, but Merzenich does. Our culture does not teach us how to design a shelter for ourselves at work to keep us safe from bullying, gaslighting, and institutional complicity, but with Barrett's insights, we're building one now. Psychological research is supporting us in constructing a social-emotional "reality" where lies are seen as harmful, and the truth is privileged—even if it's tough or painful or shocking. Shelter for us means that no one is left out in the cold because we know that the essential lie at the heart of bullying is that some are not worthy, some do not belong. When we have workplaces where this lie is immediately exposed, we can become collectively trustworthy, safe, and sane.

In the next chapter, we'll look at the ways leaders, managers, and HR can work with employees to construct a community culture that *unwires* our normalization of bullying, *unwires* the manipulation that occurs through gaslighting, and *unwires* the default pattern of believing that the winning prediction for the institution is to cover up wrongdoing and silence victims. A quick glance at Boeing provides a lesson for all workplaces.

NOTES

1. Lisa Feldman Barrett, *How Emotions Are Made: The Secret Life of the Brain* (New York: Houghton Mifflin Harcourt, 2017), 27.
2. Barrett, *How Emotions Are Made*, 30.
3. Barrett, *How Emotions Are Made*, 31.
4. Barrett, *How Emotions Are Made*, 40
5. Barrett, *How Emotions Are Made*, 65–66.
6. Michael Merzenich. *Soft-Wired: How the New Science of Brain Plasticity Can Change Your Life* (San Francisco: Parnassus Press, 2013), 81.
7. Barrett, *How Emotions Are Made*, 66.
8. Barrett, *How Emotions Are Made*, 66.
9. Barrett, *How Emotions Are Made*, 69.
10. Barrett, *How Emotions Are Made*, 72.
11. Barrett, *How Emotions Are Made*, 76–78.
12. Barrett, *How Emotions Are Made*, 75.
13. Barrett, *How Emotions Are Made*, 75.
14. Barrett, *How Emotions Are Made*, 75.
15. Barrett, *How Emotions Are Made*, 72.
16. Barrett, *How Emotions Are Made*, 76.
17. Barrett, *How Emotions Are Made*, 76.
18. Barrett, *How Emotions Are Made*, 121.
19. Barrett, *How Emotions Are Made*, 109.
20. Barrett, *How Emotions Are Made*, 110.
21. Barrett, *How Emotions Are Made*, 112–13.
22. Barrett, *How Emotions Are Made*, 121.
23. Barrett, *How Emotions Are Made*, 122.
24. Barrett, *How Emotions Are Made*, 129.
25. Barrett, *How Emotions Are Made*, 64.
26. Tali Sharot and Cass Sunstein discuss this brain function, which we will study in greater depth in chapter 13. "How you value and perceive objects, concepts, and events, and even whether you notice them at all, depends on context. Values and perceptions depend on which other objects or events you experience at the same time and which you have experienced in the past." *Look Again: The Power of Noticing What Was Always There* (London: Bridgeport Press, 2024), 236.

CHAPTER ELEVEN

Establish Brain Safety for High Performance

Proven Way #3: Connect Neuroception

THE THIRD PROVEN WAY TO STRENGTHEN OUR BRAINS AND MAKE THEM ready to do battle against the lies of bullying, gaslighting, and institutional complicity focuses on neuroception. Merzenich's brain training strengthens our powers of exteroception, which then improves higher-level cognitive functions. Barrett's theory of constructed emotion teaches us how to understand our powers of interoception to create a more nuanced and intentional interaction with one another and the world.

Dr. Stephen Porges has coined the term "neuroception" to describe our nervous system's strategies for figuring out whether someone is safe, dangerous, or life-threatening. We have seen just how overwhelming and challenging it is for our brains to identify, let alone protect us from the lies of bullying, gaslighting, and institutional complicity. Learning more about the way our neural circuits strive to identify threat, risk, and danger is another critically important step toward establishing safety and sanity at work.

Coauthors Stephen and Seth Porges note that destabilizing someone, so they feel at risk, as if they're in jeopardy, as if aggressive yelling at them and grabbing them means you might strike them, makes the target and witnesses ripe for manipulation. Making someone feel as if they don't matter, aren't seen, aren't heard—in short, making them feel unsafe—is likewise an excellent foundation for manipulation.

When we feel unsafe, our very senses change. Things taste, look, smell, and sound different. Experiences we once loved lose their luster. Our ability to live, learn, and think critically evaporates in favor of an immediate need for survival. We become easy to manipulate and susceptible to following the direction of our most craven and cynical peers.[1]

It's a red flag that you are being manipulated when someone says that you are at risk, unsafe, under threat. It isn't only their words; they might be making you feel this way by their actions: yelling in your face, berating you, threatening you, expressing intense anger. They might be making you feel unsafe by privately or publicly positioning you as unworthy and not belonging. These are textbook ways to make brains panic. When your brain is anxious, destabilized, and feels unsafe, your "ability to live, learn, and think critically evaporates." Now you are in the ideal position to believe lies and succumb to manipulation. People assume lack of education or ignorance is why people believe lies. They don't look necessarily at the conditions people are in, such as feeling unsafe. People can feel unsafe not just physically, but financially. Their reputation may be at risk. Livelihood depends not just on physical integrity, but also the ability to put food on the table and a roof over one's head, not to mention caring for one's family. As we have seen throughout history, and still today, food scarcity or very high prices for groceries can make a whole populace feel so unsafe that they become easy to manipulate.

Montgomery—like many dedicated athletes who are abused—associated what he once loved, his favorite sport, with being repeatedly harmed. Basketball lost its luster. As he reported to national media, the teachers took away "[his] passion." Stephen Porges's research shows that this is a textbook response to repeated instances of trauma designed to make him and the other athletes feel "unsafe." In Montgomery's case it did not work. He did not become "susceptible to following the direction" of the most cowardly or "craven" educators. In fact, what he discovered was that he had "courage when other people didn't," as he told a college recruiter who asked him what he learned in his senior years of high school. But he had to sacrifice playing the sport he loved.

Carle's first moment of being bullied occurred in what should have been a celebration of her new position and introduction to the team. Instead, the carpet was pulled out from under her. It was a subtle public erasure of her value. She wasn't worthy of being introduced. The messaging was essentially that she wasn't there. She believed that she had been promoted to a remarkable position of importance, but the lack of introduction insinuated that her perceptions were wrong. The war of attrition to remove her confidence, confuse her belief system, erode her self-trust, humiliate her had just begun. Making Carle feel unsafe was an ideal way to block her high-level critical-thinking skills: it made her susceptible to manipulation.

Wilson's first moment of being bullied occurred when he was told that colleagues were upset and offended by his conduct. His perceptions of his interactions in the past and in the present did not correspond with this falsehood, which led him to confusion and self-doubt. He felt "mortified," but they rendered him powerless to rectify the situation by withholding any details. Of course, no details existed because it was a complete fabrication designed to make him feel unsafe. The larger agenda was to destabilize Wilson's confidence and critical thinking, to make him susceptible to manipulation.

Macfarlane's first moment of being bullied by her institution was in their withholding of information. Their cover-up of the process around removing an abusive colleague to protect students lacked transparency and created confusion. They covered up the use of an NDA to pass this abusive professor on to unsuspecting victims in another university. This abject failure in their duty to all students must have been uncomfortable for them, so they did not inform involved professors such as Macfarlane. When she spoke the truth about the abuser, he filed a defamation lawsuit against her. The colleagues who signed the NDA did not support her or protect her. All these behaviors convey the essential bullying lies: you are unworthy (of knowing what we're doing, why we're doing it, how it impacts vulnerable others) and you do not belong (by telling the truth while we covered up, you no longer are in our community, you are the offender who has put us at risk, we do not support you). Needless to say, Macfarlane was made to feel unsafe. The colleague preying on students used gaslighting to turn Macfarlane into the offender, which positioned him as the victim. This reversal was made possible by the law department's NDA. Although he lost his lawsuit against her, imagine the trauma she endured.

Making others feel unsafe may stem from one's own sense of being at risk or under threat. It is the abuse cycle. The Dark Triad almost always come into being from abuse and neglect.[2] The Porgeses describe their suffering: "When we don't (or perhaps never) feel safe, our sense of self-preservation trumps all else, and selfish, desperate, and aggressive behaviors are all but inevitable for most people."[3] We can allow these individuals to take power or we can recognize that they suffer from a contagious illness and need to be kept away from others until they can be healed. If an individual suffers from the pathology of telling repeat lies, it is unsafe and unhealthy to put them in positions of power, credibility, and social standing when we are aware that they will use their position to confuse the brains of those exposed to their lies. The Porgeses believe that recovery is possible for those who suffer from the pathology of lying and manipulating, but that requires us to change how we handle the epidemic of bullying, gaslighting, and institutional complicity. If we want recovery, we need to recognize it as an infectious disease putting the institution as a whole at risk.

Socialized to Believe

Stephen Porges's research unpacks our socialization to believe that when we freeze, the passivity of the response casts doubt on the victims. If the victims do not fight or take flight, we question whether they were truly unsafe and truly traumatized. We have returned to what we learned from Lisa Feldman Barrett: culture wires the way we construct reality. Stephen Porges concurs: "We are taught to assume that people who are threatened will naturally run or fight" and, therefore, we do not believe in the freeze response. We cannot *see* it without the belief that it is a sympathetic stress response that is just as automatic as fight or flight.

Because we assume that the inevitable response to a threat is to run or fight, assault victims who fail to respond this way are often doubted by judges, juries, legal systems, peers and a press that assumes dire circumstances such as physical assault must logically be met with signs of struggle.[4]

When we have a cultural lens that tells us fight and flight are proper responses, and dissociating or freezing are not, the impacts lead to injustice. Stephen Porges notes that the automatic freeze response can be misinterpreted because people are "socialized to believe that inaction or silence can be construed as consent."[5] We learned from Barrett just how much being "socialized to believe" informs what we think is "reality." It's very difficult to realize that the way we *see* the world is wired by our society and is, therefore, a "construct" or concept about the world.

Remember the obvious example: due to our societal training, which is concerned with the health risks of excrement, baby food becomes poo when it's *positioned* in a diaper. Likewise, an Anglican minister is a godly man and completely safe when he is *positioned* in religious robes. Our brain does not believe the baby food is safe, just like it does not believe the minister is dangerous. But our brains are wrong. They depend on the social construct, which makes it hard for them to *see* reality and allows them to be easily victimized by the Dark Triad.

As neuroeconomist Daniel Kahneman explains, "Your moral feelings are attached to frames, to descriptions of reality rather than to reality itself."[6] If victims did not fight or take flight, then the abuse wasn't that bad, or they were participants in their own harm. This projection of a moral frame onto "reality" discounts the freeze response, which is the brain being wrong again. It's well-established in science that a trauma response—a survival response—is to become paralyzed and silenced as if one is playing dead. When we lean on our "descriptions of reality" rather than facts and truth, we are led astray. We think baby food is poo, Anglican ministers are always safe, and victims who are paralyzed by trauma are complicit.

In Macfarlane's lawsuit against the Anglican Church—who allowed a shocking number of ministers to sexually abuse children—the church's lawyers tried to say that as a child Macfarlane did not find the sexual abuse "unwelcome." Were there no signs of struggle or escape? Freeze was not possible, so if she did not fight or run, then as a child she was complicit. When brains are trained to *see* the world and one another in a certain way, they struggle to recognize that they have mistaken a construct for reality. Barrett refers to this kind of "reality" as socially constructed. Let's look at an instance of social reality that we conjure up together creating the social world we live in. It leads to one of the ways the Dark Triad manipulate us.

One example of the social world is money[7]—pieces of metal or paper that we agree have certain values. This system has no "reality" but the one we create together with our "collective intentionality." Barrett discusses the way in which our mutually constructed social reality involves mental concepts. "We can look at a hammer, a chainsaw, and an ice pick and categorize them as 'Tools,' then change our minds and categorize them all as 'Murder Weapons.'"[8] This duality is where the Dark Triad cast doubt and confusion. Imagine that a target reports being harmed by a hammer, chainsaw, and an ice pick. The target details the damage suffered at the hands of these murderous weapons. The Dark Triad are consulted, and they act shocked that these concepts have been invoked when, in fact, they have only been using the hammer, chainsaw, and ice pick as tools. Tools to build with. If someone got hurt, they had no idea that these "tools" could be harmful. Dr. Jekyll's "tools" are Mr. Hyde's "murder weapons."

Montgomery's teacher yelling in his face and detaining him for more when he tried to get away—in repeat scenes of public humiliation—is categorized in law as "assault" (murder weapons). But the teacher was *not* charged because the lawyers said when a teacher does this to a student, it is "motivation" (tools). After two teachers held a student while one beat his legs black and blue, a precedent-setting ruling in the United States in 1977 declared the conduct was legal "discipline" (tools); whereas if it had happened in jail with an inmate and guards, it would be "aggravated assault" (murder weapons).[9] Once again, the position changes everything. If the victims are adults, not children, it also appears to change the "reality" of right and wrong. If the victims are women, not men, it also changes the "reality" of right and wrong in courtrooms.

At this juncture, amid this confusion, all kinds of other social realities are brought into play. Let's review Macfarlane's court case again and expand it to include how we construct "reality" from social training. The church's lawyers tried to assert that if the target really felt exposed to "murder weapons," she would have struggled and fought for her life. She would have run away. But the lawyers asserted that she found these "so-called weapons" simply to be "tools," so they were not "unwelcome" to her. It was her character (slut) and conduct (leading men on) that exposed her to these "tools" in the first place. And, as has been outlined in the book her domestic abuser referenced, she wanted these "tools" to hurt her. This reading of the situation is constructed on socially agreed upon beliefs that have no reality. And yet, if you're human and live in a "social world," then how your society constructs reality potentially has a life-and-death impact on you.

Social Constructs of Misogyny and Racism

Remember, our beliefs are what create "reality," and the reality for assault victims in the Porgeses' scenario are as horrendous as when we use "Eve-teasing" to assess a rape. As noted, it is institutional gaslighting. They explain: "The personal trauma that comes from surviving danger or tragedy is multiplied when victims feel like nobody is offering relief or compassion—or when victims cannot offer it to themselves because they are left doubting their own experiences."[10] When you are made to doubt your experiences, it's helpful to notice that you are being gaslit. The institution's response to reports of bullying can protect and repair or break and shatter. The institution can use gaslighting to erode your self-trust and belief in your perceptions of reality.

We have focused on misogyny as a belief system that creates a grim reality for women and all those who care about them. Let's look at what Barrett shows about racism as another example of how society wires our brains with a belief system about reality and its brutal impacts. Notice that our belief about reality—which is socially constructed—has unfair real-life consequences:

If a culture dictates that people with certain skin colors are less worth-while, this social reality has a physical effect on the group: they have lower salaries and their children have poorer nutrition and living conditions. These factors change the structure of their children's brains for the worse, making school harder and increasing the odds that the children will earn lower salaries in the future.[11]

Misogyny and racism are bullying constructs wired into brains that then *believe* that the emotion concepts they produce and the picture they construct of society and the world are "real." Gaslighting reinforces the illusion that the victims are the offenders, which is achieved through reversal. The bullying uses the two essential lies to sculpt our brains: women or people of color are not worthy and do not belong. The bullying is reinforced by gaslighting that normalizes injustice, such as women and those of color are in the out-group, which does not have the same rights as the in-group. We saw with the Met police force—that so badly maltreated Wilson—that these bullying and gaslighting lies even infect police, protectors of safety, so that marginalized Londoners do *not* feel safe. And yet, as Stephen Porges's research shows, the more people feel unsafe, the more they act in reactive and aggressive ways because their survival is under threat. The vicious cycle feeds itself.

We saw that it wasn't really that difficult to show that the concept "Eve-teasing" is simply unfair. We deconstructed the unjust concept—being mistaken for "reality"—by coming up with the opposite "Tereus-teasing." Our brains might not see the injustice if we supply it with facts, because the way they *see* is through their ingrained belief system (if food is in a jar, it's food; if food is in a diaper, it's poo). What your senses tell you is irrelevant once you've been wired to believe. That's why we used an opposite myth—not fact-checking—to show the construct's injustice.

Society has made "Eve-teasing" normal or "real" to the point where it's used as part of a whole misogynistic model in the courts of India, as well as influences other countries. The whole concept of justice is lopsided if only Eve-teasing is used and Tereus-teasing is not. How tragic that a woman is raped and then is offered to her rapist as a "wife." Her maltreatment results in further maltreatment at the hands of the institution. How tragic that a child's skin color can determine whether she gets nutritious food, has proper living conditions, does well in school, and earns a salary commensurate with her potential if given the same opportunities for health, shelter, and education as her Caucasian counterparts. "Racelighting"— constructed on lies—determines her future. It is the twenty-first century. We've run out of excuses for believing in our socially constructed "realities" that bully and gaslight targets with institutions being complicit.

It is hopeful and inspiring that we can change our brains, which means we can break the cycle. The cycle is created by society, and we can see that some social trainings that create belief systems mistaken for "reality" are not healthy, fair, or safe. As a society, we appear to believe in the lies of bullying and gaslighting on the smallest and grandest scale. It's trained into us by society; it's how we see "reality." *The Gaslit Brain* has shown that bullying is constructed on lies reinforced by the lies of gaslighting and institutional complicity. How much longer will we as a society continue to accept false constructs in place of a non-bullying, non-gaslighting reality? The good news is that we created this false construct, and we can deconstruct it. We can debunk these social trainings as outdated myths and create healthier, fairer, and safer ones.

Unsafe Workplaces, Unhealthy Employees

Expert in our nervous system's perpetual search for safety, Stephen Porges says that we must stop the fear fueling the aggression or the shutdown of our nervous systems. Instead, start asking questions. As soon as someone informs you about an "enemy" by means of disinformation, cyberbullying, gossip, smear campaign, from a bully pulpit in a church or political campaign, consciously override your threat response with critical thinking. Recognize that they are striving to instill a feeling of unsafety in you. Why? Because it gives them power over you. It shatters your ability to think critically and makes you easy to manipulate. Fight back against the feeling of fear; instead, start asking questions.

Who is telling you to be angry? Which politician is tossing you the red meat that tells you that it's okay to hate or even harm others whom they are casting as rivals? In effect: Who is exploiting your nervous system to make you physically and mentally unhealthy for their own cynical ends? Whether it's to hold on to power or simply to keep you focused and engaged through the commercial break.[12]

The critical question—when someone is riling you up, stoking fear and anxiety, threatening your overall sense of safety—is: Who is exploiting my nervous system? It's an important medical question because this exploitation can make you "physically and mentally unhealthy." The next key questions are: Why are they exploiting my nervous system? What do they want? Power, money, an advantage of some kind, cover-up of their negligence or of another wrongdoing? The workplace is a microcosm where, as we have seen, bullying and gaslighting lies can take hold. Using a whole host of destabilizing strategies from humiliation to pointing fingers at a trumped-up enemy, the goal is to stop you from asking questions and facing the crisis with critical thinking. The goal is to stop you from thinking at all. The best way to block your critical thinking is to trip up your brain by pushing it into survival mode.

Leaders, managers, and HR can create safer, healthier, higher-performing workplaces by protecting and supporting those who ask questions. As we saw in Mary Inman's work, far too often those who ask questions and speak up about safety, whether mechanical construction or bullying and gaslighting behaviors, are penalized and let go. Speaking up can quickly and abruptly put you into the position of "rival"; for those who are threatened, that means "enemy." The facts and truth in these instances becomes the "enemy," and gaslighting becomes what Rebecca Solnit terms "violence against the facts and truth."

Exploitation is believed to consolidate power and increase engagement. It might in the short term. Leading by fear is the foundation of the command-and-control model, but according to research, leading by making employees safe, even those who dare to speak up, in the long run creates healthier, more productive, more profitable workplaces. Stephen Porges's scientific research fully supports abandoning the outdated command-and-control leadership model because, as he points out, lack of safety, activating our nervous system's threat response, leads to poor health and mental health outcomes. Sick people can't perform at peak or fulfill their potential. Threats and stoking fears are infectious; more and more people fall ill.

THE CONTAGION OF FEAR

Carle, Wilson, and Macfarlane all excelled at work when they were connected to colleagues, leading teams, striving for best practices, collaborating with leaders in other institutions. They were top performers in workplaces that gave them the "ability to use social behavior as a calming neuromodulator." They were doing very challenging work, were healthy, were energized in workplaces that were built on "access to safe social behavior."[13] Stephen Porges sees their workplaces prior to bullying and gaslighting as ideal for the nervous system. He notes that when individuals do not get this kind of healthy social interaction, they may resort to addictive substances to self-medicate nervous systems that are stressed.[14]

Addiction isn't the only negative outcome of bullying and gaslighting workplaces that lack safety. Without healthy social interaction, our bodies can automatically feel threatened, panicky, aggressive, or immobilized.[15] The sympathetic stress response creates unsafe workplaces where employees struggle in states of fight, flight, freeze, fawn, and fabricate. These stress states are unconscious or autonomic reactions that fly beneath the radar and fuel the bullying social construct.

When people don't feel safe, we can literally see it in their faces and hear it in their voices. These physical expressions of safety and danger are contagious. Simply put: We tend to mirror the autonomic state of others. When other people look and sound threatened or threatening, it signals to our bodies (via our neuroception) that maybe we should be on edge too.[16]

In the bullying construct, the Dark Triad want us to *mirror* their power, credibility, and social standing. Behind closed doors or with the support of the institution to do it publicly, they unleash Mr. Hyde. He intensifies command and control into coercion and control: ignoring, smear campaigns, refusing feedback, ostracizing, put-downs, humiliation, public shaming, destabilizing lies, NDAs to silence reports of abuses, harassment, constructive dismissal, threats, berating, assault, violence, and gaslighting. The targets' fear that manifests in escapist behaviors, cowering poses, paralysis, silence, seeming unhinged, feeling unhealthy is all meant to accept the position of "loser" to mirror the Dark Triad as "winners." Dr. Jekyll maintains his position of power, credibility, and social standing when Mr. Hyde demotes and destroys rivals—"enemies."

Notice the gaslighting lie that hinges on taking social reality and shifting the terms to sow confusion and support their self-serving lies. As we've seen again and again, the brain struggles with these alternative facts and half-truths. These "enemies" *aren't* the corporate competitors Carle was meant to dominate; they *aren't* the terrorist threat that Wilson was meant to anticipate and halt; they *aren't* the law departments luring top prospects away from Macfarlane's university. These abruptly targeted "enemies" are within the institution because with their integrity, talent, and stellar track records, they threaten the Dark Triad. Are these "enemies" inside the institution tools or murder weapons? Are they baby food or baby poo? This is where our brains break down. These "enemies from within" are the truth tellers, the whistle-blowers, the ones who rival the false "reality" being paraded from on high. These individuals are coded as "enemies" because they identify lies and call them out. They ask questions. They demand transparency. They speak truth to power. They speak up. They report bullying, gaslighting, safety issues, and fraud. You can't buy their silence. They commit the truth. They are tools, but the strongman wants you to see them and label them as murder weapons. The strongman wants you to believe that he will protect you by locking up these dangerous "weapons," these threatening "enemies."

Which institution, which workplace turns out to be better? The one where whistle-blowers, or even just rivals, are coded as the "enemy from within" (murder weapons), or the one where it's safe to speak up and report dangers in any form? It's simple to imagine which workplace is more productive and profitable: the safe one, where whistle-blowers are allies with courage and integrity and are protected (tools). Research has confirmed this commonsense fact.[17]

Panning back out from the microcosm of the workplace to the macrocosm of politics, the Porgeses comment:

When we feel safe, we naturally express concern and altruism for others. But when we are in this Yellow state of fear (which is exacerbated by social isolation), feelings of personal survival trump all else. We act selfish, angry, and reactive—a truth that is hard to ignore as we look at the widening political and cultural schisms that have become a hallmark of recent years.[18]

The Red state of fear in Stephen Porges's theory is when we freeze or are paralyzed with fear and trauma. The goal is to create workplaces where employees are in the Green, which is homeostasis and depends on feelings of safety. When the neuroception system isn't on high alert, scanning for and responding to what it interprets as threat, then brains can fulfill their problem-solving, creative, innovative, analytical, productive potential. They flourish when they can engage socially with coworkers in healthy, safe ways.

FEAR CYCLE FUELS PROFITS FOR SOME

If we are born wired for empathy, what happens to our brains so that we live in a society suffering from a bullying epidemic? Fear begets fear, but it also is profitable. The Porgeses articulate the unhealthy cycle: "When we feel chronically threatened, our worst and most tribalistic tendencies surface. Like a scared dog, we see others as threats and perhaps act threatening ourselves."[19] Those in the Dark Triad often are scripted by abuse and neglect. They bully others with two essential lies: they are unworthy, and they don't belong. The Porgeses express this phenomenon on a macro level. "For an authoritarian or would-be strongman, convincing a large number of people that they are under threat is basically required to maintain power." The strategy is to cast their opponents as "outsiders and subhuman bogeymen."[20] The Porgeses make the gaslighting obvious. The offender issues threats about so-called offenders who are, in fact, victims. It's textbook reversal, but people fall for it and attack the victims while the offender walks away safely and nonchalantly, with impunity for harm done and a boost to his power.

Politicians may work hand in hand with state-controlled—or biased—media, which we have deplored in history for spreading propaganda. We now deplore it as "disinformation." When gaslighting earns profits, and regulators do not stop those who lie or have platforms where lies flourish and manipulation is well-documented, we find ourselves amid a war on truth. Social media have made this kind of false messaging grow exponentially with unheard-of profits. The Porgeses note that our nervous system, designed for survival, becomes manipulated by media and social media: "When we're scared, we are activated, engaged, and will continue to stare at our screens."[21] Fear, anxiety, threat are all addictive. The feeling is that if we do not watch our screens, we won't be prepared for imminent danger, and we're being fed the message that danger is everywhere. As we've noted throughout, and it's stressed by Stephen Porges, "trauma is contagious."

> *Just as a sense of social safety can spread to others, so too can a sense of danger and trauma. We mirror the autonomic state of others. So when we are aggressive and defensive, it signals to others that they should be as well. Today we are seeing this occur on a societal level, with many politicians and media figures using every opportunity they can to spread anger and outrage. They are, in effect, traumatizing an entire society by moving our baseline level of fear—or making such fear an omnipresent feature of our lives.*[22]

A politician gains power by identifying "enemies" who have the double role of threatening the populace and showcasing the power of the politician as strongman. The enemies are to be feared, which also increases the politician's bid for power and the capacity to save us all from this fearful "enemy." The politician promises to punish or rid society of the "enemies," thus positioning himself as a powerful savior. In this moment, the politician has taken the textbook position of the bully dictating who is unworthy and who doesn't belong. If the bully takes out the targets, then those who fawn and fabricate get to be beneficiaries. They get to steal the target's rights and hard-earned position. Let's take Stephen Porges's research from the macro level to the micro level in the workplace.

In the workplace, it simply happens on a smaller scale. The leader or manager, even a colleague, takes the strongman position. The target is transformed into an "enemy." For some, fear leads them to escape, ignore, look the other way (flight). For others, fear leads them to paralysis; they go silent; talk about anything else; feel powerless (freeze). We have those whose fear leads them to identify with the aggressor (fawn) and fight for the work bully against the target, become aggressive, violent, use manipulation and lies (fabricate), drive the "enemy" out of the workplace. And finally, we have the media and social media that disseminate the work bully's lies and profit handsomely (fawn and fabricate). On the political stage or in the workplace, even on the playground, the behaviors—the result of social constructs that we think are reality—rarely change.

THE BULLY SAVIOR

You should be on high alert the minute another says he will "save" you or knows a way for you to attain "salvation." It just requires you to *see* "the enemy" and follow the savior's lead in how to deal with this dehumanized figure or populace. The promise to protect and save you is a red flag: you're being encouraged to enter a bullying dynamic. You are being drawn into the illusion of gaslighting where offenders are always victims and victims are revictimized and doubt themselves. The Porgeses explain this dynamic in terms of domestic abuse, but it applies equally to a bullying strongman or a bullying colleague.

> *In many cases, the source of our perceived threat also acts as the salve for it. It is common for abusive partners to alternate between hot and cold. To act angry and aggressive one minute, and loving and calm the next. Through this cycle of threat and relief from threat, we might be sucked into abusive and harmful relationships that play on our nervous system's need for immediate relief from danger.*[23]

The strongman position—whether it's a politician, someone at work, a coach or educator, or romantic partner—reveals the dangerous Dr. Jekyll and Mr. Hyde dual persona when he cares and then abuses. Mr. Hyde ramps up the nervous systems of his listeners by telling them that they are at risk from "the enemy," especially the "enemy from within." Throughout history, this "enemy" siphons off money for his own benefit, takes away jobs from those who deserve them, brings disease, worships the wrong god, taints us with dirt or disease, even eats our beloved pets. Apparently, no outrage is too shocking for this threatening "enemy." Of course, this enemy is the offender's target and is being exposed to serious harm of all kinds, but the populace—in a textbook but mind-bending reversal—is led to believe that the victims are the enemy.

Just when we are positively ill with fear of this "enemy," in steps Dr. Jekyll, who knows exactly what to do. He is powerful. He can offer the remedy, the cure to the plague. He can command militia and military; he can have people locked up; he will protect us all from this terrible illness and cure our fear and suffering. The split personality indicates the Dark Triad at work. All these behaviors inform the playbook that is used over and over and amazingly enough, our brains fall for it over and over. It might have to do with the fact that the Dark Triad's manipulation and destabilization make brains very afraid, and as the Porgeses put it, when we feel unsafe, a "numbing fog" becomes the norm.[24]

As we have seen throughout *The Gaslit Brain*, our brains are confused by dual presentation. Our brains can understand Dr. Jekyll, choose winning emotion concepts, and act accordingly. Our brains are adept at understanding Mr. Hyde and likewise can select winning emotion concepts from a host of predictions and act accordingly. Now, where the brain breaks down is in Dr. Jekyll and Mr. Hyde appearing as a single contradictory figure. It does not make any sense to the brain that society—a society that tells us in no uncertain terms over and over that it has zero tolerance for bullying—that Mr. Hyde, an obvious bully, would be put into a position of power, credibility, and social standing. Gaslighting makes no sense to the brain, which doubts itself rather than try to figure out how victim and offender are the same person. The brain cannot answer the question: How did this happen? And as we learned from Michael Merzenich when the brain can't answer the question, in response, the brain degrades all systems. It stops working! This is why the dual presentation created brain fog in the past and still creates brain fog today. But now, with brain science, we can stop this cycle.

Why the Brain Falls Apart

Let's listen to Stephen Porges's research that offers an explanation about what is happening in the brain and body to be sure that we fully understand why the brain falls apart when confronted with the dual presentation of Dr. Jekyll and Mr. Hyde:

> *Our brains search for patterns that allow us to assess threats and safety, so that we know when to rev up as needed for survival, and when to wind down again to heal. If you want to cause a rat in an experiment to go crazy (or possibly drop dead), all you need to do is make everything random in terms of when and why things happen. When events—especially punishing or attention-sapping ones—occur at random intervals, our brains quickly learn that we always need to stay on high alert, and our bodies can never truly shut down or relax.*[25]

Knowing that the brain searches for patterns pertaining to threat and safety explains why abusive individuals employ grooming, love bombing, and behave both hot and cold. The pattern of safety is established and suddenly, the pattern is upended. Romance morphs into insults and anger. Caring gestures turn violent. Apologies are issued. Flowers are bought. The honeymoon phase starts again, only to be randomly overturned by yelling, humiliating, and threatening behaviors. The brain can't find a pattern but searches frantically for it. The brain and body cannot rest. They can't shut down. They can't relax.

Montgomery was given one-on-one time with the teacher, opportunities to play up with the seniors at the provincial championships, sent many texts about his game, and given many talks about how he played. The pattern communicates safety. The pattern is the same whether the individual is a pedophile or a domestic abuser: draw in the victim as Dr. Jekyll (safe) and then unleash—without warning—Mr. Hyde (threat). One minute the teacher is fun and laughing, the next minute he's screaming at Montgomery and another boy, "stop fucking touching each other." Wait—what? Basketball players joking around with the team occasions that kind of reaction? The brain cannot understand it. All systems degrade. And the pattern continues in its random way—shuttling between safety and threat without a pattern—which can make a lab rat lose its mind or simply drop dead. It can block a human from rest and relaxation critical to health and survival.

The brain quickly learns in an unpredictable workplace where bullying is enabled that it must stay on high alert, which is incredibly damaging to our health. If you speak up about bullying, you enter gaslighting's hall of mirrors where you are told *you* are the problem. *You* must be gotten rid of and take the plague of the truth with you.

We are caught in an outdated social concept still reflected in our laws, but hopefully that is changing. We think that the more physical the violation, the more harmful. But the body heals more quickly than the brain. The body often shows its wounds to the naked eye, whereas the brain requires noninvasive technology to show its neurological scars, and we rarely employ this measure or assessment. If we listen to scientists, we learn that we don't need our leg broken, all we need is "biological rudeness" to have a "bodily reaction" that negatively impacts our health. Stephen Porges's research documents why mere rudeness harms our health:

> *As humans, we evolved to anticipate reciprocal social interactions from others. When our nervous system believes we are about to be social, it prepares our body by downregulating our defenses and activating the features of the Social Engagement System. When the neural expectancy of friendly socialization is violated, there might be an immediate and massive shift in our nervous system toward a state of defense.*[26]

The Porgeses' description of what occurs in our brain and body when we are exposed to biological rudeness helps us understand why social-emotional bullying and emotional neglect can be so devastating to our health. Lawmakers are exploring new workplace regulations that factor in not just physical safety but also psychological safety. If we read the research of a scientist such as Stephen Porges, we realize that psychological safety is more fully understood as neurological safety (brain) and physiological safety (body). To be healthy and high performing, we need to factor in the way our nervous system assesses safety and threat through neuroception.

Normalized Bullying

The hard part about change for our brains is that they believe lies, socially constructed and wired in, much more easily than they believe science. Our brains fall for gaslighting; even the brains of psychiatric experts are vulnerable to the lies of the Dark Triad.

Is it possible that bullying has become so normalized that we no longer recognize it as harmful? Has our society taught us, wired into our brains, a belief system that bullying is "real" and not constructed on lies? Are we unable to *see* bullying because our society's training has led us to ignore its damaging effects (murder weapons) and morph them into something benign (tools)? Is it possible that we are so steeped in the possibility that we can be thrown into the out-group as an "enemy" for something as simple as being female (50 percent of the population) or not being Caucasian (90 percent of the population) that we go to work in a compromised state of fear?

Many of us were wired to *believe* that instilling fear was a way to motivate employees. Pitting employees against one another—pushing them to compare themselves to each other and compete against each other—was also seen as a way to achieve top results. We even do this with children in school and sports. We keep an eye on employees by tracking their productivity, emails, sick days; do frequent performance reviews; keep them on their toes with so much work that they don't have a moment to interact or have fun. That has been wired into us as a way to excel. The Porgeses explain the impact of all this watching and judging: "On a primal level, it triggers our survival instincts. When we know we are being watched, we are instinctively activated into a state of alertness."[27] The alertness is an activated stress response system, with cortisol being released repeatedly into brain and body, which is extremely unhealthy and limiting, as is discussed in detail in *The Bullied Brain*.

We appear to be at a breaking point, which has led to "The Great Resignation." In child populations, our social construct has led to an urgent public health crisis. It's not just violence; it's not just depression and anxiety; note the statistic on youth suicide. From 2000 to 2018—a time of the internet, disinformation, the war on truth, the bullying epidemic, gaslighting as the most-looked-up word of 2022, suicide among those ages ten to twenty-four increased 57 percent.[28] A 57 percent increase in children killing themselves. If nothing else tells us that our social constructs need an overhaul, this statistic should do it.

Of course, many complex factors affect disengagement at work and youth mental health declines, but we have never seen such high levels of unmotivated, burned-out, mentally ill individuals—including children—in our society. Could the crisis be informed by a fundamental lack of safety, not from physical harm but from social harm? Have normalized bullying and gaslighting led to more individuals suffering abuse and neglect and becoming those categorized as the Dark Triad? Has the contagion infected more people, which is why we see it as an epidemic? Do we fail to stem the tide, quarantine those who are infected, get them better because we have been wired to think that bullying and gaslighting are "reality" even though they are socially constructed lies?

We complain about pathological liars, but if they are mainstream and in positions of power, credibility, and social standing, then we must admit at some point that we believe the lies. We complain about pathological liars, but institutional complicity tells us that they are victims while those who tell the truth are offenders. When you examine the fate of whistle-blowers, this gaslighting reversal is not surprising. It's just a fact.

Psychologically Safe Workplaces

We have a great deal of knowledge about how to create flourishing workplaces. It's not cutting edge or state of the art, challenging or cost prohibitive; it's pretty basic. For our brains and bodies to flourish, we need kindness. As the Porgeses express it, "Being around safe-seeming others is how our bodies heal and build resilience. It unlocks the Green state, which is crucial for our body's ability to funnel resources toward the systems that facilitate health, growth, and restoration."[29] Yellow and red in Stephen Porges's research into the nervous system, as we've noted before, are fight and flight (yellow) and freeze (red). Green is when our sympathetic nervous systems are not activated by threat and stress, and we are in homeostasis (green). Homeostasis is when we are balanced, and our bodily systems are functioning in harmony. When we're in the green, we can fulfill our potential as employees and dedicate our energy and brainpower to work. Unfortunately, many workplaces do not know how to create the conditions for homeostasis, and as the Porgeses say, "The modern workplace seems almost scientifically engineered to make us feel unsafe."[30]

Why should leaders, managers, and HR want to invest in creating psychologically safe workplaces engineered to make us feel safe? Because their employees will be "more creative, productive, and stick around longer. The modern workplace's tendency to be dismissive of this fact is shortsighted and self-defeating. It is a lose-lose for both employers and employees."[31] We can drive human beings at work and children at school or sports to do more and more, avoiding fun, play, social interaction, and engagement, but this avoidance blocks their systems from attaining homeostasis. They burn out, lose their motivation, see health repercussions.[32]

What does a scientist such as Stephen Porges mean by social interaction? Essentially, he means the opposite of bullying, gaslighting, and institutional complicity. For Stephen Porges, social interaction is "all about facilitating co-regulation." He defines coregulation as our body's innate ability to send out and receive "signs of safety with others," ones you already know. We look into one another's eyes to see with empathy. Signs of safety are conveyed in physical posture that is open and welcoming, as opposed to closed and threatening (of course, we need to factor in cultural differences). Signs of safety come through our tone of voice, using a singsong, animated voice just as we speak lovingly to infants or pets. This coregulation in our interactions gets lost online and it is having dire impacts on our health and mental health. We need these physical interactions to "regulate our nervous system so as to experience the states conducive to health, growth, and restoration." Stephen Porges stresses that coregulation—our social interaction—is a "biological imperative" that we need as much as food and sleep for optimum health and wellness.[33]

When we engage face-to-face, speak to one another, and hear one another, our system experiences "a rewarding rush of neurotransmitters and a feeling of satisfaction—not to mention better physical and mental health."[34] As I wrote about extensively in *The Bullied Brain*, all forms of bullying and abuse—including all forms that do not touch the body—can lead to physical damage to brain architecture and function. The chemical faulted for a great deal of this harm is the stress hormone cortisol. It is a healthy, necessary part of our system, but our twenty-first-century social constructs—specifically our belief that the lies of bullying and gaslighting are real—lead to way too much cortisol being released. As discussed, a system out of balance goes into fight and flight (yellow) and freeze (red); it cannot return to the homeostasis (green) that it desperately needs for rest and recuperation. The antidote to the stress hormone cortisol is the hormone oxytocin. The way it works is extremely complex. It depends on other chemicals that it interacts with such as vasopressin, but for our purposes, we simply need to understand that cortisol can have negative impacts on us when released too often, whereas oxytocin can do positive, reparative work on our struggling systems.

OXYTOCIN

Our coauthors, father Stephen Porges—a brilliant scientist but difficult to understand—and son, Seth Porges—a fabulous communicator, so we nonscientists can learn along—draw from the research of a scientist who leads the field in oxytocin research, none other than Stephen's wife and Seth's mom, Dr. Susan Carter. When I presented at the Masters Events at the University of Oxford on *The Bullied Brain* in the fall of 2024, one of the main draws for me was to hear Carter speak about her research on oxytocin. At her lecture, she coined the term "socioception," further building on her husband's coining of the term "neuroception." It reinforces the importance of our socially constructed, socially agreed upon world that becomes our "reality."

Scientists have learned recently that oxytocin isn't only a "love hormone" released during sexual encounters and when mothers nurse babies. It can also be released in social interaction. Oxytocin is fundamental to the healthy workplace that creates time and space for "face-to-face interactions" because it is now known to be critical for our health. Scientists such as Carter are doing research that charts oxytocin's positive effects on illnesses ranging from heart disease to schizophrenia to diabetes and some kinds of cancer.[35] Oxytocin—released through caring, engaging, social interaction—not only can heal, but it is a preventative keeping the autonomic nervous system resilient. Oxytocin "helps protect us against the stresses and illnesses the world throws at us."[36] As her husband and son concur, "Carter goes so far as to argue that both oxytocin and 'love' are biological metaphors for safety and trust, and exist as both conduits for and expressions of this deeply ingrained biological need."[37] When someone tries to make you feel unsafe, creates anxiety, plays upon your fears, and then designates an identifiable enemy to be a recipient site for your panicky emotions, you are not in the realm of safety and trust. See the red flag of being unsafe and exposed to untrustworthy lies. Start asking questions and maintain your critical thinking at all costs. Refuse to be manipulated.

The lies of bullying, gaslighting, and institutional complicity are toxic to body and brain health, but if we take it another step further in terms of creating healthy, highly productive workplaces, we need to stress just how critically important positive, kind, caring social interaction is. Considering what we have learned about the harmful effects of cortisol and the healing effects of oxytocin, it's worthwhile seeing just how much kind, respectful, caring social interaction impacts the workplace.

> *The human nervous system craves social interaction, to the point that it can be viewed as a biological imperative. When we are given the opportunity to be truly social, the wrappers of defense disintegrate in favor of the warm and welcoming Green state. Our brains operate with more clarity and creativity. Time flies by and things feel fun. We become more creative, better able to solve problems and likely more productive.*[38]

Leaders, managers, and HR might have been wired like so many of us to view social interaction as wasting time on the company payroll, but it's a key component to a flourishing workplace.[39] In the 1980s, remember, we learned that aerobic fitness—which took up precious work time—was a fabulous investment in employee health and productivity. We're now at the tipping point to building in brain fitness as a vital part of company culture.

Brain fitness means working out in Merzenich's *BrainHQ* gym. It means deconstructing Barrett's emotion concepts that are not healthy and replacing them with new vocabulary to express concepts backed by science and not myth. Brain fitness for the Porgeses means creating workplaces where we can feel socially and emotionally safe with one another and engage in collaborative, trustworthy, supportive ways.

We might have brains wired by society, but we also have neuroplasticity. We can change our brains. We can unwire what society has taught us is "real" and rewire it into something real for all of us, not just those with an agenda, who resort to self-serving lies, who bully others into an outgroup, who gaslight, who are complicit in the whole illusion. It's a choice.

Barrett encourages us: "If your brain operates by prediction and construction and rewires itself through experience, then it's no overstatement to say that if you change your current experiences today, you can change who you become tomorrow."[40] What would our workplaces be like if we predicted that everyone was worthy and belonged? What would our workplaces be like if we designed them to be safe from fire *and* to be psychologically safe? How would our workplaces improve if instead of the stress hormone cortisol coursing through brains and bodies doing damage, we had the healing hormone oxytocin? What would happen if we constructed a "reality" where we *all* felt safe at work? What would happen if we could channel our considerable brainpower into solving problems, being innovative, tapping creativity rather than just being on high alert, scanning for the next threat?

NOTES

1. Stephen Porges and Seth Porges, *Our Polyvagal World: How Safety and Trauma Change Us* (New York: Norton, 2023), xix.

2. "Our nervous systems are very good at responding to the people and cues around us. So, if we are threatened by somebody, we're likely to reflexively respond to their aggressive state by either mirroring this aggression or reacting with hurt and vulnerability. But while the Polyvagal Theory helps explain the real harm that bullying can cause, it also recognizes that this behavior often comes from a place of real pain or trauma." Porges and Porges, *Our Polyvagal World*, 158.

3. Porges and Porges, *Our Polyvagal World*, xx.

4. Porges and Porges, *Our Polyvagal World*, 16.

5. Porges and Porges, *Our Polyvagal World*, 17.

6. Daniel Kahneman, *Thinking, Fast and Slow* (Toronto: Anchor Canada), 370.

7. As Daniel Kahneman explains, "money is a proxy for points on a scale of self-regard and achievement. These rewards and punishments, promises and threats, are all in our heads. We carefully keep score of them. They shape our preferences and motivate our actions, like the incentives provided in the social environment." *Thinking, Fast and Slow*, 342.

8. Porges and Porges, *Our Polyvagal World*, 135.

9. Jennifer Fraser, *The Bullied Brain: Heal Your Scars and Restore Your Health* (Lanham, MD: Prometheus, 2022), xi–xxii.

10. Porges and Porges, *Our Polyvagal World*, 17.

11. Porges and Porges, *Our Polyvagal World*, 153.

12. Porges and Porges, *Our Polyvagal World*, 30.

13. Porges and Porges, *Our Polyvagal World*, 108.

14. Porges and Porges, *Our Polyvagal World*, 108.

15. Porges and Porges, *Our Polyvagal World*, 126.

16. Porges and Porges, *Our Polyvagal World*, 62.

17. Kyle Welch and Stephen Stubben, "Throw Out Your Assumptions about Whistleblowing," *Harvard Business Review*, January 14, 2020, https://hbr.org/2020/01/throw-out-your-assumptions-about-whistleblowing.

18. Porges and Porges, *Our Polyvagal World*, 126.

19. Porges and Porges, *Our Polyvagal World*, 28.

20. Porges and Porges, *Our Polyvagal World*, 28.

21. Porges and Porges, *Our Polyvagal World*, 29.

22. Porges and Porges, *Our Polyvagal World*, 103.

23. Porges and Porges, *Our Polyvagal World*, 104.

24. Porges and Porges, *Our Polyvagal World*, xix.

25. Porges and Porges, *Our Polyvagal World*, 137.

26. Porges and Porges, *Our Polyvagal World*, 83.

27. Porges and Porges, *Our Polyvagal World*, 140.

28. Sally Curtin, "State Suicide Rates among Adolescents and Young Adults Aged 10–24: United States, 2000 to 2018," *Centers for Disease Control* 69, no. 11 (September 11, 2020), https://www.cdc.gov/nchs/data/nvsr/nvsr69/nvsr-69-11-508.pdf.

29. Porges and Porges, *Our Polyvagal World*, 126.

30. Porges and Porges, *Our Polyvagal World*, 138.

31. Porges and Porges, *Our Polyvagal World*, 139.

32. Porges and Porges, *Our Polyvagal World*, 141.

33. Porges and Porges, *Our Polyvagal World*, 78.

34. Porges and Porges, *Our Polyvagal World*, 81.

35. Porges and Porges, *Our Polyvagal World*, 89.

36. Porges and Porges, *Our Polyvagal World*, 89.

37. Porges and Porges, *Our Polyvagal World*, 90.

38. Porges and Porges, *Our Polyvagal World*, 144.

39. Porges and Porges, *Our Polyvagal World*, 145.

40. Porges and Porges, *Our Polyvagal World*, 174.

Chapter Twelve

Become a Dishabituation Entrepreneur
Proven Way #4: Choose Perception

The fourth proven way to strengthen our brains and make them ready to battle the lies of bullying, gaslighting, and institutional complicity focuses on perception, the process by which our brain pays conscious attention to what it is seeing. We use perception in this chapter to contrast it against habituation, which is when your brain is on autopilot.

Once you've driven a car for a few years, you don't really pay conscious attention to going from A to B unless something unexpected snaps you to attention. This is autopilot, and we navigate automatically, unconsciously through many other aspects of our lives, including when we're at work. If every time we drove our car required our brain to really engage and perceive what we were doing, we would become exhausted and deplete our neurological resources. One of the ways we manage our brain and body budget is by putting tasks that are repetitive, environments that are frequent, interactions that are expected on autopilot to reduce demands on our energy.

Our brains are very good at habituating. They treat what they deal with regularly as normal or real, but they become surprised and more alert when they encounter something out of the ordinary. Because our brains tend to approach our lives from a resource-saving autopilot, we are susceptible to those who want to normalize abusive or fraudulent practices. Cognitive neuroscientist Tali Sharot and legal scholar Cass Sunstein lead us through research that shows how our brains are vulnerable to falsehoods while providing strategies to make them less habituated and more perceptive. In a workplace at risk from the lies of bullying and gaslighting, this information is very useful for leaders, managers, and HR.

Sharot and Sunstein stress that becoming knowledgeable about how our brains construct reality by discerning between truth and falsehood is empowering.

> *The combination of the truth bias and the easier, truthier heuristic can make us vulnerable to misinformation, fake news, and scams. But knowledge of these biases and heuristics also gives us power. We cannot override them, as they are well ingrained in the architecture of our brains, but once we are aware of them, we can put policies in place to protect ourselves.*[1]

Throughout *The Gaslit Brain*, we have learned that our brains are vulnerable specifically to lies and manipulations. The overarching goal of the book is to become well-informed about how easily our brains are deceived and traumatized by falsehoods and betrayals to prevent their likely harm. The very architecture of our brains puts us at risk to fall for the lies of the con man, gaslighter, and traitor, but research shows that awareness is a game changer. We can turn the tables on those who lie and manipulate by refusing to be pawns in their game.

As we know from history, our brains can habituate to the most horrifying and obscene behaviors that we believe in the moment are normal or necessary for survival. However, we can also train our brains to be perceptive. We can bypass the manipulative encouragement to turn a blind eye, defer to business as usual, normalize a workplace on autopilot, and instead, include and encourage what Sharot and Sunstein call those who are perceptive, namely, "dishabituation entrepreneurs." These are the rare individuals who question the status quo, wonder why things or statements are treated as "real" or the only way, imagine and invent different approaches, and find ways to communicate it to those who are more complacent.

If our brains are in the habit of habituating us to our environment, we need to become aware of how that works and how to become far more alert and intentional. Our goal in this chapter is to look at habituation, then ways to replace it when needed with perception. Perception is a way to regard, understand, or interpret something with an awareness of one's focused activity. To recognize, understand, and interpret the confusing duality of Dr. Jekyll and Mr. Hyde, perception needs to function like progressive lenses so that we don't only see up close, but also from a distance. To avoid being blind to betrayal, perception needs to expand to encompass *both* the respectable doctor and the psychopathic liar.

What Leads the Brain to Habituate

Remember the research we discussed in the introduction on people who tell self-serving lies? Sharot was one of the researchers, and she and Sunstein discuss the study in their book *Look Again*. It's a prime example of how the brain can habituate to almost anything, including falsehoods. If you recall, the study showed that individuals who tell self-serving lies stop getting alarm signals from the threat detection region of the brain, the amygdala. You can see how this applies to other instances of wrongdoing. It's critical research for us with our focus on the self-serving lies of bullying, gaslighting, and institutional complicity.

Sharot and her neuroscience colleagues found in their study on self-serving lies—focusing on one participant, "Leonora," who represented the others—the "greater the drop in her brain's sensitivity to her dishonesty, the more she lied the next time she had the chance." With the lack of reaction in her amygdala, they saw that "there was nothing to curb her dishonesty" and that this response was "typical."[2] Leonora told the researchers she "was completely unaware that her lies were snowballing." Sharot concludes that she "had habituated to her lies to such an extent that she did not even notice what had happened."[3] I am not sure I believe Leonora completely. I mean, maybe the stakes were low—it was just a research project, just a game, not really going to hurt anyone, and she played it like a game and tried to win.

In the real world, with the Dark Triad, they are quick to claim they didn't notice how harmful their lies or other bullying acts were. Don't believe them. It's important to *perceive* how adept they are at changing their behavior depending on who is watching. This indicates a clear understanding that they know they are telling self-serving lies, and they know they are harming others. They do not abuse higher-ups in the same way they abuse those over whom they have power. They do not tell higher-ups or beneficiaries that they are unworthy and do not belong. These self-serving lies are only for targets. They learn to control their self-serving lies and other destructive behaviors depending on who is receiving them. Sharot notes, "Without a negative emotional reaction to your lies, you are more likely to lie," and this certainly makes sense with the Dark Triad, who, as noted, do not feel emotions, including negative ones.[4] They do not suffer from guilt, regret, or anguish over their lies the way people whose brains are healthy and intact do. Groomed higher-ups often don't hold the Dark Triad accountable. They believe their denials, dismissals, and then promises to be better. Targets are often in less powerful positions. Due to their own integrity, they are quickly confused by the Dark Triad's amorality. It's very important to consider environment in the way employees behave. Habituation is a key component.

If your workplace allows homophobia and misogyny, over time you are unlikely to react strongly to it. Your brain habituates. It becomes your normal, and as we saw with Lisa Feldman Barrett's research, you come to believe it's "reality." The reality you exist in and believe in is that individuals in the LGBTQ+ community, along with women, can be objectified, blocked from opportunities, earn less, have fewer rights, have no rights, are OK to mock or humiliate or assault. In contrast, if your workplace does *not* allow microaggressions, let alone full-on discrimination, you would have a strong, shocked, and distressed reaction to homophobia and misogyny. All too often, however, we discover advanced workplaces where the lies of bullying, gaslighting, and institutional complicity rule the day. Reactions are muted, or nonexistent, which is why whistle-blowers are such unusual outliers. They are *not* the norm. They are dishabituation entrepreneurs.

Sharot and Sunstein do not have research on what makes someone speak up, but in their experience, individuals such as Montgomery, Carle, Wilson, and Macfarlane work from "a combination of nature and nurture" that "generates individuals who are less conformist, more skeptical, more courageous, and more perceptive."[5] All these skills and traits can be trained. Workplaces that privilege and reward these qualities will create more dishabituation entrepreneurs.

Sharot and Sunstein pose this concerning question: "Why, despite being sophisticated creatures, are we relatively quick to accept dreadful things that become the norm, such as cruelty, corruption, and discrimination?"[6] This has been the pressing question behind my work, which began twelve years ago when Montgomery and the other students were being cruelly treated by teachers while the leader, board, and chaplain chose to cover up rather than fulfill their duty to protect victims. The ultimate corruption is to revictimize, especially children who have asked for protection. The leader, board, and chaplain were sophisticated creatures, but all of them accepted and tried to normalize dreadful things, specifically daily cruelty meted out to students.

The transfer of knowledge from teacher to student underpins a functioning society and its values. Imagine what happens when teachers who have power, credibility, and social standing teach bullying, cruelty, cover-up. As Sharot and Sunstein reveal, "people get used to gender and racial discrimination and even to the gradual rise of fascism, until 'dishabituation entrepreneurs'—rebels who combat the norms—make them salient."[7] Montgomery and the other students rebelled against abusive teachers who wanted to habituate them to an onslaught of gender and racial discrimination. One Indigenous player on the team they called "lazy"; they even sent an email to the team saying they were going "scalp hunting." This player, like Montgomery, was targeted for intense berating. He was by far the best three-point shooter, on full scholarship, and in boarding. Far from his family, he was brutally maltreated. One wonders what kind of teaching youth—who embrace contemporary misogynistic or fascist ideals today—have encountered. Montgomery and the other students perceived a serious problem, and they acted. They are in the camp Sharot and Sunstein refer to as "dishabituation entrepreneurs."

When the team huddled around the coaches during games, Montgomery would stand at a distance. They would be crouched, and he would stand fully upright. He appeared to be distracted, hands on his hips. After taking testimonies from other players and understanding the abusive regime they were subjected to, I asked Montgomery why he took this stance. He told me the coach would say things like "we're going to take them to the crematorium," and he didn't want anything to do with it. This is what Sharot and Sunstein identify as choice. Montgomery *chose* to dishabituate, consciously rejecting the abusers' habituation techniques.

Abuse Addiction

Just as addicts may start with a gateway drug and then need more, then stronger drugs to get the relief or the high they seek, those who abuse—because of our brain's innate habituation—need to intensify their targeted attacks. As Sharot and Sunstein point out, "Because people have a weaker emotional response to a repeated stimulus, they need larger and larger quantities of that stimulus to achieve an equivalent high."[8] When the Dark Triad hold up a mirror to their targets, they need the targets to reflect back their power but more elaborate, more grandiose, more exaggerated or it doesn't provide the hit that the normalizing brain needs.

The brain's habituation is exactly why grooming, luring, love bombing that slides into gaslighting, subtle harassing that increases, the honeymoon phase that collapses into emotional and physical violence, the jealousy that morphs into stalking, are all in the abusers' playbook. One minute you think you're accidentally overlooked at a board meeting or dealing with difficult people; the next, you're at a breaking point and leaving your cherished, hard-earned position with a workplace community you thought cared about you. If it can happen to Carle, Wilson, and Macfarlane, it can happen to any of us. This slippery slope is why we need to turn the brain's habituation into perception—a specialized dual perception that factors in the risk of Dr. Jekyll *and* Mr. Hyde.

Repetition is all it takes for the brain to normalize something. Sharot and Sunstein define the term this way: "We *habituate*, which means that we respond less and less to stimuli that repeat."[9] When we repeatedly drive a car, we stop being aware of all the complex brain tasks we do to drive. Remember, our brains conserve energy by going on autopilot. In the workplace that has habituated toxic behaviors, the repeated lulling effect puts us at risk. It can lead to ethical and empathic inertia.

When we habituate to the bad things, we are less motivated to strive for change. That Tuesday's nightmare is Sunday's snore becomes a serious challenge for fighting foolishness, cruelty, suffering, waste, corruption, discrimination, misinformation, and tyranny.[10]

Think of the diverse workplaces we've looked at, all behaving in the same textbook way in normalizing bullying and using gaslighting to cover up. There is not a lot of fighting to stop the rampant lies that prop up bullying, not a lot of challenge to gaslighting victims, certainly a failure in institutional integrity when the target is ousted, and the perpetrators are protected. These workplaces are on autopilot, which leads them directly into institutional complicity. They snore right through losing yet another talented employee, with an exceptional track record, who is devoted to the institution. They snore while those who tell self-serving lies hunt for their next targets. They snore through the perpetrators ramping up the enabled abuse because they need a bigger hit. They find new targets, hit repeat, but with a more unbridled attack. Repetition is all it takes for heinous acts to become normalized reality. Michael Merzenich cautions us about "sleepwalking" through our lives, and these are particularly ominous examples of it.

What happens to these institutions? In my case, they end up on the front page of the most widely read newspaper in the country and are featured on a national TV show where investigative journalists expose corruption. In Carle's case, female employees issue a survey that exposes rampant bullying, and the executives doing the harm are fired. In Wilson's case, the cover-up of rampant bullying by the Met police is exposed in Baroness Casey's excoriating public report. In Macfarlane's case, her university law department is now known as signing an NDA with a professor preying on female students whom they passed on to other unsuspecting victims at another university. They are one of the catalysts for the legal movement launched by Zelda Perkins and Julie Macfarlane, Can't Buy My Silence.

LET'S LOOK THROUGH THE LENS OF BRAIN SCIENCE

If we sidestep the moral framework for a moment and study these institutional crises through the lens of brain science, we can understand how this harmful cycle happens and set in motion ways to avoid it.

Have you ever heard someone at work say, "Oh, that's just so-and-so"? Maybe this colleague tends to tell jokes that embarrass people. Maybe she makes sexual comments about others. Perhaps he gossips behind the backs of coworkers he pretends to befriend. Maybe she has a history of not meeting your eyes, ignoring you when you speak, forgetting or mispronouncing your name, commenting cruelly on your clothes or work performance. It's all so subtle and easily dismissible—until it isn't. Once you encounter any of these behaviors, you notice it each time thereafter. "But after a while your brain creates a 'model' (that is an internal representation) of the situation."[11] You anticipate this model. In other words, your brain *predicts* this model. "If the experience matches the model, your response (neural, emotional, behavioral) is inhibited."[12]

Let's rewrite this for our purposes: If the bullying experience matches the model (of the bullying lies you're regularly subjected to), your response is dumbed down. You've grown accustomed to maltreatment; your brain has habituated; other people aren't speaking up or defending targets; as a result, your own neural, emotional, and behavioral response is neutralized. You don't react, don't feel it, and certainly don't act to stop it. It's the beginning of freeze or paralysis where you develop what's called in psychology "a perception of inescapability" or "learned helplessness." Sharot and Sunstein describe in brief why we allow horrendous harm to occur: "Habituation, confusion, distraction, self-interest, fear, rationalization, and a sense of personal powerlessness make terrible things possible."[13]

It used to be that callous, rude, hurtful behaviors made you uneasy. Not anymore. "You have become habituated."[14] You hear so-and-so telling a cruel joke that mortifies a secretary. Your brain has seen this before and matches this experience to the model. What happens? Inhibited or neutralized response. No need to react. Business as usual. You meet with the boss who makes a sexualized comment about a colleague. Your brain has heard this before, too, and matches this experience to the model, the internal representation. What happens? Inhibited, neutral response. No need to say anything or react in any way. Business as usual. And so on. Press repeat. The brain is habituated to this workplace. It doesn't see any reason to fight for change. Besides, when these behaviors come from those in positions of power, credibility, and social standing, you feel confusion. They unleash distraction when you question what's happening. They spark your anxious self-interest. They play on your very real fears. You find yourself rationalizing harm to others. You collapse into a sense of personal powerlessness as terrible acts unfold before you. It's shocking to targets, but research shows that these responses of colleagues to bullying and gaslighting are textbook.

Who Disrupts Habituation?

Predicting correctly is easy and comforting, and it requires little energy or resources. It's like driving while thinking of other things. This routine feeling, this habituation happens, when you drive the same route to work every day. You listen to podcasts, or the news on the radio, and your brain tunes out the driving while paying attention to "what recently changed, not about what remained the same." It's an automatic brain process: "To make the new and unexpected stand out, your brain filters out the old and expected." The podcast and radio information are new and unexpected. Your brain cares about this surprising newness, and with its limited resources filters out the same old route to work.[15] Merzenich stresses that surprising or new experiences are the key to neuroplasticity.[16] If we want change on a brain level, we need to get out of our rut and allow for innovation, surprise, and different ways of operating:

> *Sharot and Sunstein describe how this habituation looks in the workplace. . . . Bureaucrats often find themselves in a rut. Public servants who have worked in the same job, day after day and year after year, tend to be terrific at what they do, and highly professional, but they sometimes find it difficult to imagine doing things differently. Because they are habituated to certain ways of operating, they take long-standing patterns and practices for granted. This is due not only*

to risk aversion, but also to a failure even to consider what risks one might take.[17]

Consider that we are moving into an era of legal change in the workplace. With legislation around psychological safety on the horizon, it would be wise for leaders, managers, and HR to get ahead of the curve and educate on why and how our brains struggle to address, in a healthy and effective manner, the lies of bullying and gaslighting. Having seasoned employees knowledgeable about long-standing practices and the importance of risk aversion could be balanced with employees who are "dishabituation entrepreneurs" who pose questions, who imagine something other than "this is the way we've always done things," who innovate and offer alternatives.

Sharot and Sunstein explain how it works:

> *Dishabituation is often triggered by newcomers, who inject new ideas into organizations not because they are smarter or more creative by nature, but because they have not yet settled into the usual patterns. Instead of doing what has always been done, they look at things sideways or from a distance, or from very different starting points.*[18]

At the start of the chapter, we asserted how important it is to look at a situation from different angles. We used the analogy of progressive lenses that allow us to read what's happening up close, but *also* from a distance. The hope is that this multifaceted assessment of what's happening would put us in a better position to recognize not only Dr. Jekyll, but also Mr. Hyde. In the context of the Dark Triad, we would benefit from X-ray vision that allowed us to see behind closed doors. The way we can get this perspective is by listening to and recording what targets and witnesses tell us rather than resorting to counter facts that our brain supplies to normalize an abnormal crisis.

Sharot and Sunstein's research into the way highly "successful companies get into a rut," staying on the well-traveled path full of habituated brains doing the routine demands without question, helps us understand why a teenage Montgomery could far more quickly see through gaslighting than adults such as me, Carle, Wilson, and Macfarlane. His advantage was being young, not yet lulled by the brain's habituation.

But Montgomery has another quality that lets him see what others miss. One of his family nicknames is "Eagle Eye" because he has always been an incredibly sharp observer. He not only perceives detail that escapes many of us, but he also can imagine multiple perspectives and angles on what many of us see with a singular vision. Neuroeconomist Daniel Kahneman sees this skill as invaluable to institutions: "It is much easier to identify a minefield when you observe others wandering into it than when you are about to do so. Observers are less cognitively busy and more open to information than actors."[19] The combination of youth—so that he was still able to dishabituate—coupled with his sharp observation put Montgomery in an enviable position to perceive the minefield masquerading as a private school.

The Post-Truth Era

We have noted the challenges we face in an era of disinformation, conspiracy theories, and outright lies coming at us from all directions. Sharot and Sunstein note that from 2004 to 2018, "the number of Americans who said it was fine to exaggerate facts to make a story more interesting grew from 44 percent in 2004 to a staggering 66 percent."[20] Put this statistic, which they find "staggering," side by side with the impact of manipulation and destabilization of the truth on youth populations. They are a powerful indicator of a vulnerable population, but also a population that is scripted in their formative years by the post-truth era. In short, they don't know any different. What has it done to their brains?

Depression increased 83 percent after Facebook was accessible to all American college populations, and as we noted previously, youth suicide increased 57 percent from 2000 to 2018.[21] These are not meant to be in-depth analyses of what's happening to today's youth, but we can use them as red flags: our increasingly online world of social media, its exponential capacity to spread disinformation as well as separate us from much needed in-person connection, our disregard for the truth, the "violence against facts and truth" that Rebecca Solnit warns against, have serious repercussions. It leaves us with a lingering question: What happens when lying is the new norm? What happens when our brain can no longer distinguish between truth and falsehoods? Isn't the ability to know what's real and what's fake a critical component of mental health and stability?

Have we burned through the gateway drug of lying and need it to dominate more and more, become more outlandish, more divorced from common honesty or decency? Do we need stronger, more exaggerated hits to get high? Sharot and Sunstein remind us, "When ethical erosion is gradual, people are less likely to take notice and more likely to engage in wrongdoing."[22] It seems that there is a parallel between empathy erosion and ethical erosion; not surprisingly, both indicate psychopathology on a brain level and a behavior level.

That's the double whammy that we find with Dr. Jekyll and Mr. Hyde. On the one hand, the doctor with power, credibility, and social standing is very adept at grooming us, luring, us, numbing us into believing he cares about us. He is our medical savior. He can cure what ails us. But behind closed doors his manipulation fuels Mr. Hyde, who is more and more likely to engage in wrongdoing as he isn't noticed and isn't stopped. Hyde is the toxicity, the poison, the cover-up, the pathological lies that make people ill. Dr. Jekyll is critical to Mr. Hyde's contagion.

TRAILBLAZE A NEW PATH

Must our workplaces succumb to the post-truth era or can they trailblaze their own path in this precarious time? Sharot and Sunstein are clear—and considering their combined expertise in neuroscience, law, and economics, it's probably worth hearing them out—"In the workplace, you might well be better off and avoid much bigger problems by creating an atmosphere where minuscule lies (such as cheating by a few dollars on expenses) are not acceptable."[23] This advice stems from Sharot's research into self-serving lies. Rather than letting them proliferate, how about stopping them. How about making them unacceptable on multiple levels? Sharot and Sunstein concur:

> *Norms are often rigid: do not lie (ever), do not steal (ever), do not be disrespectful toward your parents (ever), do not reveal confidential information (ever), do not break your promises (ever). The rigidity of the norms may seem a bit extreme, but that is the point. They ensure*

an intense emotional reaction that makes it more difficult for people to get comfortable with their moral transgressions.[24]

This code of ethics works powerfully for workplaces but breaks down when you deal with Dr. Jekyll and Mr. Hyde. It's important to note here just how adept the Dark Triad are at using these norms to their advantage. Their modus operandi is to lie and steal (not just money, but people's work, opportunities, livelihood, career) through advanced manipulation and a confusing split personality. They champion the rigid norms to cover up what happens behind closed doors. They act as if they are a gift to the institution when instead they are a Trojan horse. This is why we need double norms or double emotion concepts if we encounter the Dark Triad, as we learned in studying Barrett's research.

Remember how we examined the Trojan horse to show that norms can be misleading. Do not be ungrateful (ever). Do not reject a gift (ever). Well, what about when the gift is designed to make you trusting and vulnerable, then destroy you? Do not be disrespectful toward your parents or teachers or managers or leaders (ever), but what about when they are abusive? We've used this model in the employer (parent) and employee (child) context and learned that the training, the habituation to obey and *not* ask questions, can be detrimental. If we believe that hierarchies of power are "real," not socially constructed by our collective agreement, then our brains struggle to speak up because it goes against the norms, the "reality," which is that we must respect those with more power. How about the normalized warning not to reveal confidential information (ever)?

From Julie Macfarlane and Zelda Perkins's mission to halt the misuse of NDAs to cover up perpetrators' wrongdoing we realize that sometimes keeping silent is wrong and dangerous. Although the intent of Sharot and Sunstein's norms is clear, it is a great exercise for workplaces to learn why strict norms are valuable, as the brain has a strong emotional reaction when they are broken. We also need to be dishabituation entrepreneurs and ask challenging questions to ensure that the Dark Triad don't use our own norms to manipulate us.

I'll leave you with one clarifying and sobering example of how an abusive individual can harm us with our own ethical norms. Research has documented extensively, and I discuss it in depth in *The Bullied Brain*, that we are trained from an early age to obey authority, beginning with parents, teachers, and coaches. It extends to authorities such as doctors and workplace leaders. As you're now well aware, our brains are scripted and sculpted by society. They become wired to believe and behave in wired ways that can be very difficult to change. Dr. Larry Nassar used this training to abuse his victims right in front of their mothers. The mothers believed in his authority as a doctor so conclusively that they could not fathom that he was sexually abusing their daughters, not healing them. The mothers could only *see* Dr. Jekyll, not Mr. Hyde. You can also envision how Nassar made his child victims—and don't forget, there were hundreds—believe that his conduct was normal, so if they felt hurt, violated, or traumatized, the issue must be with them. While he was abusing, he was gaslighting. The children learned *not* to trust their own perceptions and emotions. What the doctor was doing had to be *normal* because their own mothers were not stopping it. This awful story is a good one to remember when we become complacent about the way the Dark Triad are adept at manipulating even our own ethical norms.

HABITUATING TO OUR OWN MALTREATMENT

Sharot and Sunstein use discrimination against women as one way to teach us how we habituate to injustice. It's another way of thinking about being blind to betrayal. They look at the history of women's lack of rights whereby, up until the 1960s, it was normal and "real" for women—based on their gender—to be denied a job, not allowed to own property, not allowed on a jury, and so on. "They were chained. While some women fought these chains and made important progress, the overwhelming majority accepted life as it was. Habituation did its thing . . . most women did not rebel."[25] When you do not believe you have equal rights—when you believe the bullying lies that you are unworthy and do not belong—then you accept them as true or real. Sharot and Sunstein examine research that documents how "people adapt to deprivation." Our habituation or adaption to maltreatment, in the researcher's words, "have both a numbing effect and a paralyzing effect: they alleviate the pain while also blunting any urge to act."[26] This survival mechanism sounds similar to Jennifer Freyd and Patricia Birrell's concept of being blind to betrayal.

Sharot and Sunstein explain that women were not unhappy with this oppression because they thought it was just how things were. They were not unhappy with "reality." It's a great example of the way our brains habituate to almost anything. But then dishabituation entrepreneurs fought tooth and nail for women's equality, and they succeeded in bringing about significant change.

Sharot and Sunstein note that women are now less happy. The reason for women's frustration lies in what neuroscientists call "prediction errors"—the gap between what is promised (namely, equality) and what is happening (ongoing inequality).[27] We have learned how our brains always predict next steps. Women today predict fairness but bump up against being paid less or having to do more unpaid domestic labor than men, and so on. It's frustrating, but as Sharot and Sunstein explain, "while prediction errors induce unhappiness in the short term, they are critical for progress."[28] This insight can be applied in the workplace to transform outdated bullying and gaslighting cultures into cultures that prioritize connection, equality, and brain health. It might be challenging, creating distress or unhappiness in habituated brains, but in the long run it results in progress.

Sharot and Sunstein note, "These mistakes (or prediction errors) are important—they are 'teaching signals' from which you can learn about the world around you and correct your expectations."[29] But these mistakes can also lead to debates and discussions around why we have high expectation and low reality. We noted previously that workers lose trust in their leaders, managers, and HR when there is a gap between stated policy and procedure and what actually takes place. Being told that the anti-bullying policy is strong but perpetrators revictimize targets causes immense unhappiness and lack of trust. Workplaces can use this gap between expectation and actuality to become aware and articulate about how our brains can habituate to maltreatment. We can teach that prediction errors are helpful alerts to gaps, and we need to address them, not sweep them under the rug. As Sharot and Sunstein advise, "So while unmet expectations cause unhappiness, unhappiness might be necessary for change."[30]

Why Do Our Brains Believe Lies?

At the outset, we learned that repetition is all it takes for our brains to habituate. Amazingly enough, they even habituate to lies. In other words, they *reverse* a lie into a truth if it is repeated. Sharot and Sunstein state, "Whenever a falsehood is repeated, people tend to think it is true."[31] This brain tendency offers exceptional opportunities for the Dark Triad to manipulate us. All they need to do is say their lies over and over, lo and behold, the brains of listeners in the workplace come to believe that the lies are true. As noted, the leader at Montgomery's school would repeat the mission statement at every opportunity including the line "we are a community shaped by the pursuit of truth and goodness." You might assume he repeated the mission statement because he believed it, but it's now clear to me that it's far more likely he repeated the mission statement to make us *believe* he was a truth teller when he was a liar and a manipulator.

Sharot and Sunstein quote Adolf Hitler at the start of the chapter titled "(Mis)Information: How to Make People Believe (Almost) Anything," which could be a slogan for *The Gaslit Brain*. Hitler ascribed to the principle, "Slogans should be persistently repeated until the very last individual has come to grasp the idea."[32] Notice he uses the term "idea," which sounds like a new concept, something challenging for the populace, but he didn't have an idea per se that could stand up to scrutiny. His plan wasn't to supply research and evidence to back up his idea. He was simply going to repeat a lie from a position of power, credibility, and social standing. That's all it took for the populace to *believe*.

What effect does repetition have on the brain? Sharot and Sunstein explain that "when a statement is repeated again and again, your brain processes it less and less as it is no longer surprising or new. The result is that you are more likely to accept it as a given."[33] They note that psychologists call this "the illusory truth effect."[34] It's an excellent contradiction (illusion is the opposite of truth) to remember, as it can remind us that our approach to the Dark Triad is safer if double. Dr. Jekyll is an illusion when he shares a self with the terrifying truth that is Mr. Hyde. As an individual, they are an illusory truth. The fact that we fall for them so often is an example of the illusory truth effect. The effect they have on us is to make us believe that an illusion is "real," not a self-serving manipulation. We tend to think that those who are tricked and gaslit are not educated or are gullible. Sharot and Sunstein comment that the "illusory truth effect appears to be a feature of all minds."[35] No matter how experienced, how educated, how advanced, we are all susceptible to manipulation.

Remember how the Dark Triad's brain regions—that activate when shown images that make healthy brains feel empathy and emotion—are language and cognition? Imagine now how they use language and repetition to make you think that what's false is true. Sharot and Sunstein point out, when "you have heard a statement many times before, you take it for granted and respond to it less—you are habituated to it. It does not produce surprise. But when you hear an unfamiliar statement, you feel jarred and so you question it."[36] When the falsehoods being repeated are the lies of bullying, the tendency is to question *yourself*. When these lies are followed by gaslighting's reversals, once again, you don't question the unfamiliar statement; instead, you question your perception. These highly specific forms of manipulation lead you to take the surprising information and turn it on yourself. When information is disseminated from a position of power, credibility, and social standing, you aren't jarred by what's spoken, but you feel unsure of your worth or whether you belong, whether your reading of the situation is off or incorrect.

Sharot and Sunstein aren't talking about the lies of bullying and gaslighting, but they explain why our brains mistake the repetition of lies for truth, which applies powerfully to what happens during manipulation. The term psychologists use is "metacognitive myopia." it describes the way our brains are "highly attuned to primary information" but "less attuned to 'meta-information.'" In other words, they absorb the lies but don't wonder whether "the primary information is accurate."[37] Primary information could be slogans or insults frequently repeated or put in all capitals, bolded, or in a bright font. The emotionality, the eye-catching form, and the repetition work to make this primary information seem true. Meta-information requires looking at the source and reflecting on whether they have an agenda, are biased, benefit from issuing the slogan or insult, or have a track record of telling the truth or disseminating lies.

Myopia or nearsightedness works perfectly for Dr. Jekyll and Mr. Hyde. It means you see Dr. Jekyll with his power, credibility, and social standing sharp and clear, but Mr. Hyde with his destructive impulses appears at a distance, out of focus. Considering that we have habituated children to screens and the small screens of phones, it's hardly surprising that they are developing myopia or short-sightedness at exponential rates. Our brains tend to fall prey to the illusory truth effect, especially when the lies are told by someone in a position of power, credibility, and social standing like Dr. Jekyll. It's not difficult—when you think of how our brains function—for the Dark Triad to manipulate us with false-hoods. This faultiness in our vision is why we must consciously choose perception: see what's near but also train our eyes to see what is in the distance or even behind closed doors. We must learn to see beyond the facade of the position to the person and how he speaks and behaves. A discrepancy between the two raises the red flag.

Our brains accept primary information with ease. It's like being on autopilot; it's our brain's tendency to habituate. Unfortunately, this energy-saving function of the brain puts us in danger when it comes to believing lies. "When it is effortless for you to process information because of repetition (i.e., less neural response), you are more likely to accept it as true. Effortless means there is no 'surprise signal.' You don't stop to ponder; you just accept."[38]

Imagine you're in a workplace with a pathological liar who no longer hesitates to lie because her amygdala doesn't give her alerts or surprise signals. You believe her lies—along with most everyone else—because their repetition creates a sense of familiarity, and you translate this into belief. When bullying occurs in the workplace, it can escalate into mobbing when coworkers participate in the maltreatment. Seeing this behavior from a brain perspective, it's not surprising. Coworkers *believe* the bully's lies because all it takes is repetition, causing a sense of familiarity. Falsehoods about the target are taken as truths, and the believers repeat and amplify the message. The harm done to the target can be hellish—the more people turn against you, the more you may think the fault lies with you.

Sharot and Sunstein use the phrase "easier, truthier!" to describe this weakness of the brain that leads it to "associate the ease with which information is processed with its truthfulness."[39] Think about it: the brain decides that the more in-depth, more complex, more layered communication is untrustworthy while something shallow, simple, limited to one viewpoint is believable. You can see now why fact-checking may well be ignored because it's seen as irrelevant. The truth is the truth. It makes you worry about the brain when you learn from research that all it takes is a bigger font and a brighter color for the brain to give written material the stamp of truth. It's *not* content that convinces. In fact, content that challenges the brain might be rejected as truth because it's too difficult. It's *form* that carries the truth (position, repetition, font, ink color). We are in the realm of philosopher Marshall McLuhan, who taught us in the 1960s that "the medium *is* the message." If you want a lie to sound like the truth, make it easy to digest and simple to understand. Use all capitals and colorful ink. Then, repeat it over and over.

THE EASIER, THE MORE BELIEVABLE

The brain's habituation, its autopilot, its tendency to automatically "believe information more if it can be easily processed" helps us understand why the brain is completely floored and flummoxed by the immensely complicated presentation of Dr. Jekyll who somehow is also Mr. Hyde. According to Sharot and Sunstein, the brain's decision-making apparatus around truth and lies can be used to advantage by those who repeat "false or unsubstantiated claims."[40]

Our brains have built into them the "truth bias," which ironically facilitates manipulation. Our brain usually is told the truth; it habituates to the pattern that if someone tells me something at work, it is true. And then the brain encounters the Dark Triad; it also believes they are telling the truth. Sharot and Sunstein acknowledge that the truth bias makes working together possible. It's a key component for a "functioning society," but with serious risks.

> But the truth bias can get us in real trouble, as evidenced by the billions of dollars lost every year to phishing scams and other incidents of fraud. Again, it's not only the tech illiterate, the elderly, or teenagers who fall for the truth bias and therefore for scams. Many savvy

businesspeople, and sophisticated people of all other kinds, have been victims.[41]

Falling for online manipulation is easy enough; imagine how easy it is for the brain to be manipulated by Dr. Jekyll and Mr. Hyde. We've looked at how they turn the truth into lies from many different angles; now add this research-based insight to see why any of us could be a victim, especially when we are not trained to understand how the Dark Triad work. "The default assumption of truth is so robust that it can override strong clues of lying"; even more distressing, "Studies show that even when information is discredited . . . or explicitly said to be false, we may still rely on it to guide our choices."[42] Our brain's preference for easy information, mistaking position for the person, its tendency to normalize what happens frequently, including lies and lying, sets us up to choose falsehood over truth. Our brain makes fact-checking only effective for those who recognize that we must dedicate precious resources to "meta-information." We easily gobble up primary information (true or false) but must work harder to assess accuracy, the meta-information. Too many brains appear to lack the energy required to work harder for the truth conveyed through meta-information.

THE BRAIN SCIENCE OF CHANGE

It may feel overwhelming to get a workforce on autopilot to change. But when what's become normal is also harmful, it must be done. You might have tried the carrot-and-stick approach but feel like you're running out of options. Those who do harm get accustomed to the lecture, claim they had no idea they were being destructive, promise not to do it again, and take a workshop on boundaries or anger management until the next time. They have a host of excuses, lean on a series of reversals. Maybe they're the victim? It seems like you're going in circles.

But here's good news: the brain does not get habituated to "the joy of learning because learning by definition is change. One cannot habituate to change."[43] That brain fact is fabulous news for leaders, managers, and HR. Instead of reward and punishment, have your employees step out of the moral framework for behavior and step into a brain-informed paradigm.

They can learn why the brain harms others. They can learn that normalized bullying behavior can do physical damage to brain architecture and function as is detailed in *The Bullied Brain*. This kind of learning is eye-opening, turns off the autopilot, and turns on the fighter pilot. It galvanizes brains to change because they have new knowledge that is surprising, even startling, and cries out for action. Employees can be taught that we can all strengthen our brains if we do it in a collaborative, supportive way. We will put our brains into the homeostatic state that helps it learn (as we discovered in the previous chapter). Sharot and Sunstein explain, "When we cannot learn, we get bored and unhappy." Even more concerning: "When change halts—when you stop learning and progressing—depression kicks in."[44] Depression can be an underlying cause of the burnout employees feel and express. We could turn around this downward spiral by introducing brain health and brain fitness into our workplaces. Channeling resources into educating employees on how to keep their brains healthy, happy, and high performing is likely to bring positive rewards. According to Sharot and Sunstein, "While satisfaction with material goods falls sharply over time, satisfaction with experiences does not decline. Research shows that it often increases!"[45] An excellent way to shift negative, bullying cultures into positive, brain-informed cultures is to offer employees experiential learning where they connect and collaborate on how to have psychologically safe workplaces, ones where transparency and empathy are the norm and bullying and gaslighting are seen as harmful, counterproductive, and outdated.

I don't want to make this culture change sound easy. I do want us to see it as doable. The tricky part is that you don't feel motivated to create change when you cannot perceive that anything is wrong. Social media is an ideal contemporary example. Facebook was released initially at Harvard and had an air of exclusivity about it. It was available to all colleges in 2008. As noted, for "the next ten years, depressive episodes in the college-age population increased by a staggering 83%!"[46] For colleges, students, and families, youth depression became "normal," and it was not linked to Facebook as a worrisome cause. Remember the other stat we looked at in the last chapter: the 57 percent increase in youth suicide from 2000 to 2018. Again, it's like young people killing themselves is a new normal; only now do we see widespread reactions such as banning phones in schools. These stats are sharp reminders of how our brains normalize social media, and it takes learning a new shocking piece of information about how harmful it is to pull us out of our lull, more accurately, our brain's habituation.

Sharot and Sunstein hammer home the important point that when we habituate, we no longer perceive. We become untroubled by what we witness. How could we possibly be unperturbed by an 83 percent increase in a serious mental illness in our youth? Because of habituation—collectively across our brains—it is difficult to assess how "online noise" really affects your life. Noticing the impact of things that are constant is hard. "We may not notice the interference caused by a TV that is on in the background until someone suddenly turns it off."[47] We are likely to see more and more people unplug from social media, keep children away from screens, write on paper, attend meetings in person, and question the normalization of an online world. Remember, Merzenich has warned us about the impact of "noise" and "chatter" on the brain. It distracts and confuses, and we might not even notice what's happening to us.

BRAINS THAT *DON'T* HABITUATE

Remember Sam Bankman-Fried's apparent belief in the utilitarian model that if the majority are happy, then a minority of suffering individuals can be ignored? And as you recall, the leader at Montgomery's school tried the same ruse. If most students were not maltreated, their position drowns out the concerns of the students who were abused. He literally used "happy" versus "unhappy," so perhaps he, too, had been reading up on utilitarian theory. In totalitarian dictatorships, the model flips to favor a happy minority while an unhappy majority suffers. Regardless of whether happiness is treated as a right for the minority or the majority, notice how these models apply the bullying playbook that uses fear, favoritism, and humiliation to command and control. In institutions where corruption flourishes, these approaches are textbook, just like silencing truth tellers and whistle-blowers. But even with the challenges our brains present us with, couldn't we strive for a better model?

When it comes to culture change, listening to the outlier voices can provide an excellent strategy. Only a minority have the capacity to *dishabituate* and perceive the problem. They turn off the TV for the rest of us and remind us what it was like without a constant buzz of online noise. The ones who speak up don't have to be a target or victim to do it either. "For social movements to arise, there must be someone who does not entirely habituate—who is uncomfortable with some practice, or some situation, and who is willing to say or do something about it."[48] They can report safety concerns, the abuse of others, fraudulent practices, and so on. But they will never be a majority. These are what Sharot and Sunstein call the "dishabituation entrepreneurs," and they believe this mind-set can be taught.[49] "The hope though, is that awareness of all the ways our brains blind us to the constant and expected will help you distinguish the 'chains' you accept from those you should try to break."[50] This suggests a great learning opportunity at work. Which chains do we accept, and which do we need to break?

At the beginning of this chapter, we distinguished between habituation and perception. Let us hear one more time from Sharot and Sunstein why perception, though it takes more brainpower and is harder work, is necessary.

> In a world where bias and discrimination are the norm, most people become habituated to them. We do not perceive the discrimination around us because we expect it. One more time: we notice what is surprising and different, but gloss over what is the same and anticipated. And here the problem lies: we cannot work to change what we do not perceive. Until someone comes along and makes what is in front of us clear and salient.[51]

If we reduce discrimination to its essential form, it issues bullying lies: you are not worthy; you do not belong. From that position, all kinds of destructive behaviors are condoned, and all kinds of elaborate falsehoods can be used to justify degrading, demeaning, and dehumanizing. It requires a conjured "social reality" that people agree on and mistake for actual reality. We now know that this is easy work for our brains that feel comfortable with repetition and familiarity. Our brains are much less concerned about whether what we believe is true or false, real or fabricated. Our brains habituate to the world of "illusory truth," where illusions can have as much influence as facts. Remember that in 2009 author Chris Hedges titled his book on American society's concerning demise *The Empire of Illusion*. Like Sharot and Sunstein, Hedges thinks the truth is worth fighting for, and illusion is toxic. Hedges's subtitle, *The End of Literacy and the Triumph of Spectacle*, offers a prime example of primary information (spectacle) versus meta-information (literacy). The ease of spectacle makes our brains believe it is true. Reading an article or a book takes more work and energy for our brains. When we replace the truth with illusion and spectacle, we enter into the manipulations of illusory truth.

In our focus on the manipulation of split personalities that dominate the Dark Triad, we can add here that we do not *perceive* bullying done behind closed doors. We don't believe reports when it happens because we confuse the position for the person. We see Dr. Jekyll up close but fail to see Mr. Hyde in the distance. We cannot perceive in these dual ways until we recognize our cognitive myopia and put on progressive lenses, which only happens when someone exposes the lies of bullying and gaslighting, rather than repeats and amplifies them.

THE RISK OF HABITUATING TO RISK

Leaders, managers, and HR can create workplace cultures that encourage dishabituation entrepreneurs. They can train individuals at all levels to trust their emotional reactions, not let them become numbed by familiarity. Knowing that manipulators, especially gaslighters, strive to make us doubt our perceptions, educating employees to trust their instincts and trust in safe, secure ways to report concerns is an excellent way to dishabituate quietly growing risk factors.

Anonymous surveys with surprising questions, not always the same ones, is another way to deactivate the lulling force of habituation. Make people think. Make them wonder what they believe. Ask them about illusory truth effect, how often they check the source and evidence for what they believe. Make them question why they believe something. Is it the font, the colored ink, the repetition, or the position from which it was spoken?

Pose questions around halo effect. Is the person's appearance, just like their position, the reason doubt or belief occurred? These surveys can provide interesting information to discuss and allow individuals to be provoked and honest in their replies because they're anonymous.

Rather than a casual day, have a day where individuals leave their comfort zone and dishabituate to their position. What is it like to spend an hour in a leader's shoes, or at a colleague's desk? What is it like to put in time in HR and deal with their responsibilities? Dishabituation exercises can create that entrepreneurial mind-set. As Sharot and Sunstein put it, "The answer to dishabituation was *change*. Change the environment, change the rules, *surprise* people, and habituation will break."[52] Make people shift their attention and challenge them to see with progressive lenses, not just what's right in front of them, but also what's in the distance. Replace habituation with intentional perception. Replace spectacle with literacy. Have employees share how their beliefs changed when they went beyond primary information and drew on meta-information.

Research shows that most accidents on construction sites occur when the project is almost finished. It's like when you're driving home, and you stop paying reasonable attention for the final few miles as you think about your impending arrival. This is when risks are heightened, not minimized. Sharot and Sunstein show that as "the days pass, workers habituate. They feel less and less fear, so they take fewer precautions."[53] All workplaces are susceptible to habituation. It's not a bad idea to bring in outside evaluators to assess risk—not just the fire exits but also the interactions, the language, the normalized treatment of all employees.

Notes

1. Tali Sharot and Cass Sunstein, *Look Again: The Power of Noticing What Was Always There* (London: Bridgeport Press, 2024), 137.

2. Sharot and Sunstein, *Look Again*, 105.

3. Sharot and Sunstein, *Look Again*, 106.

4. Sharot and Sunstein, *Look Again*, 107.

5. Sharot and Sunstein, *Look Again*, 201.

6. Sharot and Sunstein, *Look Again*, 4.

7. Sharot and Sunstein, *Look Again*, 9.

8. Sharot and Sunstein, *Look Again*, 64.
9. Sharot and Sunstein, *Look Again*, 2.
10. Sharot and Sunstein, *Look Again*, 3.
11. Sharot and Sunstein, *Look Again*, 6.
12. Sharot and Sunstein, *Look Again*, 6.
13. Sharot and Sunstein, *Look Again*, 218.
14. Sharot and Sunstein, *Look Again*, 7.
15. Sharot and Sunstein, *Look Again*, 8.
16. "The surprise results in a complex pulse of the alerting stimulating chemical noradrenaline. Clarion calls tell his brain that 'something surprising has happened. We'd better figure out if it's important, or not.' A second neuromodulatory area has contributed acetylcholine to that pulse. By its release, it's telling almost the entire forebrain that 'something important may happen soon. Be open for brain change.'" Michael Merzenich, *Soft-Wired: How the New Science of Brain Plasticity Can Change Your Life* (San Francisco: Parnassus Press, 2013), 99.
17. Sharot and Sunstein, *Look Again*, 98.
18. Sharot and Sunstein, *Look Again*, 98.
19. Daniel Kahneman, *Thinking, Fast and Slow* (Toronto: Anchor Canada, 2013), 417.
20. Sharot and Sunstein, *Look Again*, 109.
21. Sally Curtin, "State Suicide Rates among Adolescents and Young Adults Aged 10–24: United States, 2000 to 2018," *National Vital Statistics Reports* 69, no. 11 (September 11, 2020), https://www.cdc.gov/nchs/data/nvsr/nvsr69/nvsr-69-11-508.pdf.
22. Sharot and Sunstein, *Look Again*, 110.
23. Sharot and Sunstein, *Look Again*, 115.
24. Sharot and Sunstein, *Look Again*, 115.
25. Sharot and Sunstein, *Look Again*, 181.
26. Sharot and Sunstein, *Look Again*, 186.
27. Sharot and Sunstein, *Look Again*, 183.
28. Sharot and Sunstein, *Look Again*, 183.
29. Sharot and Sunstein, *Look Again*, 184.
30. Sharot and Sunstein, *Look Again*, 187.
31. Sharot and Sunstein, *Look Again*, 121.
32. Sharot and Sunstein, *Look Again*, 121.
33. Sharot and Sunstein, *Look Again*, 121.
34. Sharot and Sunstein, *Look Again*, 122.
35. Sharot and Sunstein, *Look Again*, 124.
36. Sharot and Sunstein, *Look Again*, 125.
37. Sharot and Sunstein, *Look Again*, 127.
38. Sharot and Sunstein, *Look Again*, 129.
39. Sharot and Sunstein, *Look Again*, 130.
40. Sharot and Sunstein, *Look Again*, 131.
41. Sharot and Sunstein, *Look Again*, 134.
42. Sharot and Sunstein, *Look Again*, 136.
43. Sharot and Sunstein, *Look Again*, 23.

44. Sharot and Sunstein, *Look Again*, 24.
45. Sharot and Sunstein, *Look Again*, 28.
46. Sharot and Sunstein, *Look Again*, 57.
47. Sharot and Sunstein, *Look Again*, 67.
48. Sharot and Sunstein, *Look Again*, 188.
49. Sharot and Sunstein, *Look Again*, 189.
50. Sharot and Sunstein, *Look Again*, 190.
51. Sharot and Sunstein, *Look Again*, 193.
52. Sharot and Sunstein, *Look Again*, 154.
53. Sharot and Sunstein, *Look Again*, 150.

CHAPTER THIRTEEN

Learn to Avoid Shortcuts and Think Slow

Proven Way #5: Seek Proprioception

THE FIFTH PROVEN WAY TO STRENGTHEN OUR BRAINS AND MAKE THEM ready to do battle against the lies of bullying, gaslighting, and institutional complicity focuses on proprioception, which usually is applied to body awareness, but we will extrapolate it to focus on brain awareness. Proprioception gives us the ability to perceive the location and movements of our body; here, we apply it to the way our brains perceive our position in the narrative that we tell about our decisions and ourselves.

Drawing on the work of psychology professor Daniel Kahneman, an expert in neuroeconomics, we examine bullying, gaslighting, and institutional complicity in the context of his knowledge and insight into the way our brains make decisions. In chapter 12, we learned from Stephen Porges's research how important homeostasis—a state of balance among all our body systems—is to our ability to establish health, recover from being unwell, repair past stresses and traumas. Likewise, proprioception is imagined in this chapter as another component in our quest to attain balance in the ways we handle immensely challenging issues at work that have lying and manipulation at their core.

In essence, Kahneman's work reveals the risks we run when our brains move fast, and he makes a compelling argument for slowing down our thinking to make more accurate decisions. Kahneman's overarching goal is to "improve the ability to identify and understand errors of judgement and choice."[1]

SIX PROVEN WAYS TO SEE THE TRUTH

Our goal to learn why we fall for the essential lies of bullying—
namely, that targets are not worthy and do not belong—benefits from
being positioned as an error of judgment and choice. Likewise, our goal
to understand the tendency to fall for the lies of gaslighting benefits from
knowing why our brains falter when they move too quickly and how they
can become more resilient and resistant if we intentionally *think* slower.
Kahneman's shift from the moral universe to the medical one reinforces
our approach. He likens his work to that of a doctor who requires "richer
and more precise language" to offer "an accurate diagnosis." The diagnosis
can suggest "an intervention to limit the damage that bad judgements
and choices often cause."[2] Kahneman offers an extensive array of the
ways in which our brains make poor judgments, but we only examine the
ones relevant to bullying, gaslighting, and institutional complicity.

Scientists used to think that we were rational creatures who could
be tripped up by emotional upheaval (the crime-of-passion argument).
Kahneman has been a leader in the field of showing that we make errors
and poor choices, not because of "the corruption of thought by emotion"
but due to the "design of the machinery of cognition."[3] The more we
know about how the brain's machinery works, the less likely we are to fall
for its weaknesses instead of harnessing its strengths.

Reinforcing the approach that we focused on in the previous chapter,
our brains have an unfortunate tendency to choose the easy rather than
the difficult path. This tendency makes us vulnerable to manipulation
because all a liar must do is repeat simple falsehoods; our brains easily
come to believe they are true. We absorb this "primary information"
quickly but do not put in the slower work to attain the "meta-information"
that checks the source, poses questions about agenda and bias, and strives
to figure out if the source of the information benefits from issuing it.
Kahneman explains that "when faced with a difficult question, we often
answer an easier one instead, usually without noticing the substitution."[4]
As noted, we substitute illusion for truth and spectacles for literacy.
Kahneman calls the brain's defaulting to easier answers an "heuristic," a
shortcut we take to reach a decision.

300

SUBSTITUTION WORKS LIKE REVERSAL

Substitution is one of the key manipulations Dr. Jekyll and Mr. Hyde use, as Lisa Feldman Barrett explains. You confront the Dark Triad with "murder weapons" (hammer, ice pick, chainsaw); they label them "tools"—everyone agrees—so, it must be a problem with you and how you see the world (gaslighting). You're "too sensitive." The substitution deflects attention from the harm done and reverses offender and victim. This is another kind of substitution that confuses the brain. What's concerning is Kahneman's emphasis on how we don't even notice our brains doing this quick substitution. These shortcuts or heuristics belong to what he calls "the secret author of many of the choices and judgments you make."[5] To understand bullying, gaslighting, and institutional complicity, the goal is to replace secrecy with transparency.

Kahneman describes intuition as operating "automatically and quickly, with little or no effort and no sense of voluntary control."[6] In contrast, metacognition pays "attention to the effortful mental activities that demand it" and that we associate "with the subjective experience of agency, choice, and concentration."[7] In other words, it's the shift from habituation to perception. Echoing Barrett, Kahneman notes that it takes energy for our brains to work slower and dedicate resources to metacognition rather than taking the intuitive shortcut.[8] He references the famous experiment of the "invisible gorilla," which revealed how we can be blind to what's right in front of us when our attention is directed elsewhere.

In brief, the experiment designed by two psychologists had viewers of a video count the number of times players in white shirts passed a basketball to other players. There were also players in black shirts passing a basketball, and viewers were told to ignore them. Amid the players, a person wearing a gorilla suit walked to the center of the ball passing, thumped his chest, and left. The researchers asked for the tallies, waiting to see who identified or mentioned the gorilla. Approximately half of the viewers were concentrating so hard on counting the passes that they did not see the gorilla. Kahneman's take: "The gorilla study illustrates two important facts about our minds: we can be blind to the obvious, and we are also blind to our blindness."[9] I would add a third important point that the study illustrates: we see what we are told to see. This is another way of saying what Barrett explains: we see what we believe because oftentimes what we believe has been wired into our brains by others, by our culture.

We See What We're Told to See

The gorilla study illustrates how susceptible we are to doing as we're told, obeying orders, fulfilling mandates when directed to do so from an authority. I examined this phenomenon in detail in *The Bullied Brain* with the equally famous Milgram experiment on obedience to authority.[10] Like Milgram's study, the gorilla study did not have high stakes. It was just a research study with participants. The authority had no real power over the participants. Nothing was stopping them from refusing to do as they were told. Nonetheless, they did as they were told and kept their focus where the researchers directed.

Now imagine a high-stakes environment: the workplace where the authority is your employer, a leader or manager who can terminate your contract. You are in a highly dependent position, like a child to a care-taker. When your employer tells where to focus—like the viewers in the gorilla experiment—you do it. When the authority can threaten you or your family by firing you, taking away your livelihood, derailing your career path, harming your reputation, you are even more likely to *see* what you are told to and ignore the rest. The "blindness" that occurs in the gorilla study is another example of why we may don blinders and be blind to betrayal. Perhaps our intuition tells us to only see Dr. Jekyll and ignore Mr. Hyde. Our survival instincts tell us that it's best not to think too much or too slowly, just keep substituting the one who has power, credibility, and social standing in order not to see the one who is doing harm.

Psychopathic Charm

Kahneman tells the story of being a young psychologist and learning from his teacher to resist falling for "psychopathic charm." A patient was described as coming to a therapist and regaling him with detailed stories about the failure of other therapists to help him in the past. The key message was that they didn't understand him, but the therapist hearing the tale of others' mistakes would be able to help. The teacher took it for granted that the psychologists would have "sympathy" for this patient, not recognize that he was likely a "psychopath," and the psychologists "will not be able to help him." The key to recognizing the "cognitive illusion" here was the feeling of "strong attraction" to the patient—a red flag something was wrong.[11] We recognize the love bombing, grooming, and luring to which we are susceptible. We can also see the messaging that others—in this case, the psychologists who didn't understand the patient—are wrong, untrustworthy; in a sense, losers. They are rivals to the psychologist, sliding into the territory of being enemies.

The patient creates a loyalty bind with the new potential therapist with the promise that he will be the powerful one who brings about a cure. He'll be the savior. It's interesting to see Kahneman's teacher expose this dynamic as a Trojan horse: it looks like a gift, you're scripted with the emotion-concept gratitude for that, but it will go off like a bomb, and you'll lose. Remember how Sinon bonded with the Trojans by presenting himself as a victim? The psychology teacher's advice: "Do not even *think* of taking on this patient!"[12]

If we apply Kahneman's diagnostic vocabulary, we now can understand that our intuition, our quick-thinking brain, the one that reverts to autopilot and thereby preserves resources, does not *see* the dangers of "psychopathic charm." Most of us have been introduced to the "halo effect," which could be at play in this scenario. Namely, if the patient were attractive, our sympathy for his plight would increase. We would be more likely to believe his words. Less well known but just as useful, our quick-thinking intuitive brain that likes shortcuts does *not* recognize the "cognitive illusion" the patient offers.

We can add this vocabulary to Tali Sharot and Cass Sunstein's "illusory truth effect," which reminds us how easy it is for us to substitute an illusion for the truth. Kahneman also reminds us that all it takes is repetition for us to substitute a falsehood for the truth: "A reliable way to make people believe in falsehoods is frequent repetition, because familiarity is not easily distinguished from truth."[13] Familiarity takes little thought; it can be consumed on autopilot. Movement takes energy, and changing position draws on resources; staying put is just so much easier. Sharot and Sunstein showed that we were quicker to believe the truth of a statement if it was in a larger font or brighter color. Kahneman adds to this with research on how all it takes for us to attribute more truth to a message is using bold.[14] It's just that much easier to notice, remember, and believe.

Getting to the truth isn't easy. It requires work and metacognition. The second you find yourself leaping to conclusions, passing judgments, making choices—without evidence, research, or thought to back it up—pause. This is the moment to replace your intuitive shortcut with the resource-depleting, meta-cognitive powers of your brain. Demand accuracy: you want to put this target or group of targets into the dehumanized out-group? Based on what evidence? I don't just want to hear about it. I need to see it. For the one making the intuitive judgment followed by a choice, ask: can I share this judgment and choice publicly, or do I need to cover up the "secret author" who acted here? If what I am doing is fair and safe, and has been thought through fully and complexly, why can't I share it far and wide, with regulators and the media?

Although it's hard work, and even though it depletes our precious brain resources, the goal is to recognize "cognitive strain." This can save an individual and a populace; it can save an employee, employer, and an institution. When the stakes are high, we are better off *not* taking the easy path our brains encourage us to take. Cognitive strain "mobilizes" our metacognition and pushes us to ask difficult questions about why we believe certain messages and ignore others. Why do we see only one component and are blind to the others? When we take the more challenging path we shift "people's approach to problems from a casual intuitive mode to a more engaged and analytic mode."[15] When confronted with the lies of bullying, we may panic and take what looks like the easiest steps to resolve the issue as painlessly, as easily as possible. But if we choose a more engaged and analytic mode, we may find that protecting perpetrators who deal in falsehoods while ousting targets who are truth tellers isn't the fairest, healthiest, best long-term decision for the institution.

Affect Heuristic

Another relevant diagnostic label we can apply from Kahneman's research is the "affect heuristic." Remember, heuristic is the brain taking an intuitive shortcut. Affect heuristic is similar to the halo effect. He describes it as "where judgements and decisions are guided directly by feelings of liking and disliking, with little deliberation or reasoning."[16] As you can see, this is the brain replacing a difficult question with an easier one, and as we learned, this is a substitution we don't usually notice. The difficult question would be, "Why do you *dislike* this rival, and why are you positioning her as an enemy? What are the reasons, where is the evidence, can your evidence withstand fact-checking from a non-biased source?" Put another way, "Why do you like this leader and judge him to be safe, healthy, and fair? What are the reasons, where is the evidence, can your evidence withstand fact-checking from a non-biased source?" Another difficult question is: "What is the person's track record that supports your liking or disliking?" Taking the time to deliberate and reason about our impulsive, emotional reactions might save us when face-to-face with the Dark Triad who have put on the "fictional mask."

Here's a quick way to deliberate: Does this individual reflect back what I *want* to see, and does this reflection shift and change for different viewers or audiences? In other words, if I am a higher-up, is the mask one of respect, thoughtfulness, intentional practice? But if I'm an employee, does the mask morph into a degrading, thoughtless, irrational practice? If I am a female executive, do I find a sexually harassing mask that turns into a brotherly mask if I am a male executive? If I am a member of the Anglican Church, does the minister show me a mask of spiritual integrity that collapses into the mask of a pedophile when he is alone with a child? If I am a Christian, do I find myself face-to-face with the mask that purports to be a religious savior? If I am a bigot, do I look into the mask that puts others into the out-group? If I am a woman, does the mask promise to protect me? If I am the founder of a tech company, does the mask insist that it will loosen regulations? Does that mask switch if I'm an oil and gas tycoon who wants environmental regulations eased or removed?

The deliberating and reasoning response is to feel concern that no solid identity or set of values is behind the ever-changing fictional mask, one of the red flags of the Dark Triad. You can see the importance of always asking: What is the track record behind the mask that is reflecting my hopes and desires?

As you'll recall, this question would have stopped the bullying of Carle, Wilson, and Macfarlane. It would have made the insinuation that Montgomery and the other students were liars highly problematic. These individuals had stellar track records that cut through the lies of bullying, gaslighting, and institutional complicity. Colleagues who depend on the leader likely will choose survival over sacrifice; and if that means joining the leader in *not* looking at the target's track record, ignoring it, being satisfied with the leader's fictional mask, so be it. They do as they're told and choose illusion over truth.

Oftentimes, when the Dark Triad want you to replace a difficult question with an easier one, generated by the brain's "secret author," they draw your attention away from the target's track record and focus it on the future *they* promise you. They do not want you to notice the gorilla. They don't want you to use your metacognition. They want you to think fast because that's how their substitutions go unnoticed. Kahneman stresses that jumping "to conclusions is risky when the situation is unfamiliar, the stakes are high, and there is no time to collect more information."[17] This can be an effective checklist when bullying and abuse are reported. Is this an unfamiliar situation? Are the stakes high? Is there no time to collect more information? If a leader, manager, or HR is going to derail a previously trusted employee's career or future, remove their livelihood, negatively impact their health and mental health, the stakes are high. And unless a natural disaster is looming or a massive workplace crisis is on the horizon, there's always time to collect information properly.

In the case studies we looked at, jumping to conclusions—where they never dealt properly with institutional abuses (of power, emotion, finance, safety)—lead to serious harm for targets in the ongoing abusive environment. The failure to halt the abusive practices puts the institution into the position of thinking fast, not just as an unconscious intuitive shortcut, but as a strategy to encourage others to think fast. The institution presents the crisis as "unfamiliar" when it's far more likely that their failures to address it have been piling up. There's never just one report, one victim, one unfamiliar situation. But the institution gaslights targets and the community to believe it's an isolated incident and not what they think, have heard about, or even seen. "Look where we tell you" is the directive, and we are trained to obey. The institution reinforces that training by making it clear that disobeying may result in reprisals. It's better to doubt the targets and your own perceptions than doubt those with power, credibility, and social standing based on their position.

When employees think fast, they're not asking questions, requiring evidence, insisting on more information. How does that play out? In the case studies we looked at, the easy institutional path—a strategy to cover up—was to reverse or substitute the victim for the perpetrator. The institutions all chose to scapegoat the victim and protect and enable the abusers. The institutions chose to gaslight and privilege falsehoods over truth.

In all cases, when more information was collected, injustice was exposed. At Nike, the women did their own survey on abuse and found it was widespread. At Montgomery's school, national investigative journalists revealed how the private school was supported by a complicit government regulator in covering up abuse. At the Met police, Baroness Casey's investigation identified rampant abuse. At the University of Windsor, their NDA—used to cover up a perpetrator, given carte blanche to harm other victims—was disclosed through Macfarlane's integrity and powerful sense of duty. These institutions banked on the illusory truth effect whereby institutional positions of power, credibility, and social standing allowed them to do violence to facts and truth and immeasurable harm to victims. Institutions that take a path to prioritize talent retention, employee engagement and trust, productivity and profitability, community respect, protection from the Dark Triad with an eye to succession planning and legacy can follow Kahneman's advice instead.

INSTITUTIONAL COMPLICITY DEPENDS ON INTUITIVE SHORTCUTS

Kahneman contrasts the way our fast-thinking brain is gullible, and our slow-thinking brain is not. The power of our metacognition is that *if* it is allowed to do its work, it does not believe falsehoods. It does not fall for repetition or simplicity, or someone's good looks, or other illusions put before it. Our slow-thinking brain is "in charge of doubting and unbelieving." The problem lies in the way it can be thrown off the scent when otherwise occupied. Those who bully and gaslight use distraction, red herrings, deflection, reversals, foot dragging, filibustering, and any other means to confuse our slow-thinking metacognition.

Our fast-thinking, shortcut-taking brain suffers from "confirmation bias": it looks for information to confirm what it already believes. It is similar to the way we can be seduced by the Dark Triad's fictional mask, which reflects our own hopes and desires. Confirmation bias "favors uncritical acceptance of suggestions and exaggeration of the likelihood of extreme and improbable events."[18] When it comes to the lies of bullying, you can see how dangerous this aspect of the brain can become. If we take the easy route—believe what we're told; do what we're told; tend to think that exaggerated, extreme, and improbable events could occur—those we target as rivals, losers, and enemies are put at serious risk. In these high-stakes situations—where we are being encouraged to lash out or look the other way while someone is victimized—we want to galvanize our critical thinking. Instead, we may default to "uncritical acceptance." You can see how the shortcut of confirmation bias fuels conspiracy theories—exaggerated, extreme, and improbable—that do not stand up to deliberation, reasoning, seeking evidence, gathering information, or other plodding work of metacognition done by the slow-thinking brain. We need to fight against this tendency. A quick way to push back against this tendency is *not* to seek confirmation of what you already believe; seek information that questions, puts into doubt, or flatly rejects your belief.[19]

When it comes to Dr. Jekyll and Mr. Hyde, the fast-thinking brain puts us at risk because our confirmation bias is quick to supply many examples of good Dr. Jekyll. Further, he makes a good first impression, and the halo effect that emerges from his power, credibility, and social standing *confirms* our belief in his goodness even more. The halo effect comes first in the sequence, and it can drown out other information that follows. We dismiss and ignore what follows in the troubling reports we get about Mr. Hyde. Research documents that this is how our intuitive shortcuts work.[20] This is why they lead us to believe the lies of bullying and gaslighting. We *like* Dr. Jekyll, which is where the affect heuristic comes in: to keep us from facing the truth of Mr. Hyde. To remind you, affect heuristic is similar to the halo effect. It's when our judgments and decisions are guided directly by feelings of liking and disliking, with little deliberation or reasoning. We like nice Dr. Jekyll, and our feelings of liking him blind us to Mr. Hyde. Further, as we saw with the gorilla study, when the institution tells us to look elsewhere, not see to Mr. Hyde, then we become blind to his harm and do not experience feelings of dislike. We are told *not* to see him, so we don't.

RESIST INFLUENCERS

Our brains are easily influenced by random people on social media. Likewise, as we've seen throughout *The Gaslit Brain*, our brains are easily influenced by people in positions of power, credibility, and social standing. Our brains are easily influenced by individuals who could fire us, take away our livelihood, and ruin our careers. But when the stakes are high, and our livelihoods, health, and lives are on the line, we need to know how to resist those who seek to influence us, making us substitute falsehoods for truths.

Kahneman provides a simple solution that we can apply to avoid leaping to conclusions and believing illusions rather than seeing reality. We noted the power of an anonymous survey to find out what is happening without fear of retribution. Another way is to have individuals involved write down—based on information, not hearsay—what they believe is the most effective strategy to stop the bullying, hold perpetrators to account, decide whether to rehabilitate or terminate, create cultural change that makes it more difficult for these destructive behaviors to occur in the future. A discussion that follows offers the opportunity for transparency to replace the "secret author" who pushes us to take the easy path. It provides an opportunity to gather more information, think slowly, set in motion our meta-cognitive powers, reach a far better decision, and develop a far better plan of action. The goal is to encourage "independent judgments" to have "diversity of knowledge."[21]

ONE-SIDED EVIDENCE DOES NOT FACTOR IN MR. HYDE

If our brains are to deal with Dr. Jekyll and Mr. Hyde, they need double-emotion concepts. The Trojan horse makes me feel gratitude, *but* it should make me feel fear. We need to wear progressive lenses to see the doctor up close *and* see the abuser in the distance or behind closed doors.

Likewise, we must use our second brain system—our meta-cognitive slow brain that does *not* believe. Instead, it doubts, asks questions, seeks more information, wants accuracy—necessary if we want to include Mr. Hyde in our reality. Otherwise, the "secret author" hides Mr. Hyde and manipulates us to do violence to truth and facts (not to mention people). One of the many challenges posed by our fast brain, which wants us to take intuitive shortcuts, is that it is a storyteller (of course, the "secret author" is a storyteller). As we've seen, our fast brain "operates as a machine for jumping to conclusions," and it "excels at constructing the best possible story that incorporates ideas currently activated."[22] Kahneman provides an example that supports exactly why Dr. Jekyll is foregrounded and Mr. Hyde is overlooked.

> *Consider the following: "Will Mindik be a good leader? She is intelligent and strong . . ." An answer quickly came to your mind, and it was yes. You picked the best answer based on the very limited information available, but you jumped the gun. What if the next two adjectives were corrupt and cruel?*[23]

Not only do we see our fast brain jumping to conclusions, but we can also see that our fast brain will reject more information such as "corrupt and cruel" outright. It cannot think fast *and* include confusing, contradictory material. When we looked at Paul Babiak and Robert Hare's research into psychopaths, they found exactly these kinds of contradictory presentations. The psychopath presented almost as if he were two different people. He was "intelligent and strong" like Dr. Jekyll but "corrupt and cruel" like Mr. Hyde. The higher-ups and beneficiaries only saw the intelligent, strong behavior; the corrupt and cruel behavior was directed at targets behind closed doors. One-sided evidence (intelligent and strong) creates what the fast brain likes, a coherent story that makes for "cognitive ease."[24]

Our fast brain is easily used in service of bullying and gaslighting. It is one reason why institutions choose to be complicit in wrongdoing rather than stop and remedy it (oftentimes until it is too late, and disaster strikes). The fast brain "suppresses ambiguity and spontaneously constructs stories that are as coherent as possible" producing the work of the secret author. And as we have seen repeatedly, unless "the message is immediately negated, the associations that it evokes will spread as if the message were true."[25] The fast brain is why the lies of bullying and gas-lighting are so easily used to destroy innocent truth tellers' lives. It makes sense that the impulse is to shoot the messenger. The whistle-blower, the truth teller, the messenger interjects ambiguity, threatens the coherent story. Rather than grapple with the reality of a Dr. Jekyll compromised by reports of Mr. Hyde, it's easier for the institution and the brain to simply silence the messenger and suppress the truth.

By speaking up about abuse or fraud, the truth teller requires the full force of the meta-cognitive slow brain. The truth teller questions one-sided evidence and activates ambiguity by telling the other side of the story, thereby making the institution's story incoherent. The master narrative that drives the institution and its reputation is put at risk when the truth teller becomes a whistle-blower. You can see why the secret author or fast brain wants to suppress all the doubts raised and simply return to the easy, comfortable story. If the institution fails to activate the meta-cognitive slow brain the first time it hears reports of abuse, fraud, or safety issues, it must become an active agent of cover-up the next time it hears, and the next.

It's hard to choose the slow brain path. As Kahneman puts it, "sustaining doubt is harder work than sliding into certainty." But that's the beauty of metacognition and slow brain movement. Its power in the long run for the institution is that it "is capable of doubt, because it can maintain incompatible possibilities at the same time."[26] This is an apt definition of empathy: it requires holding simultaneously the thoughts, feelings, and intentions of others, not just oneself. Empathy is cognitively and emotionally demanding and a critical component of the slow brain. It's hard work. It requires cognitive strain. It takes our precious brain resources, but it's worth it. If an institution does not want to be at the beck and call of the unempathic Dark Triad, it needs to consciously resist the "coherent story" dependent on one-sided evidence supplied by the secret author. Kahneman concurs: "Maintaining one's vigilance against biases is a chore—but the chance to avoid a costly mistake is sometimes worth the effort."[27] Institutions seem to act as if the whistle-blower's truth is expensive to deal with when, in fact, it is the lies told in bullying, gaslighting, and institutional complicity that are far more likely to be costly.

We discussed the "affect heuristic," when our fast brain takes an intuitive shortcut and passes judgment on people based on whether they're likable. If we *like* them, and we all *like* powerful, credible, and high in social standing Dr. Jekyll, we do not believe he could commit harm. Just think for a quick minute how effectively this affect heuristic worked to cover up the abuses done by coach Jerry Sandusky, actor Bill Cosby, doctor Larry Nassar, producer Harvey Weinstein, entrepreneurs Sam Bankman-Fried and Elizabeth Holmes, and nurse Heather Pressdee. If these individuals had been *disliked* more regularly, we might have stopped their abuse far more efficiently. Kahneman applies this same intuitive distortion to the way we think about and plan for risks. Bullying is a common risk that needs to be addressed by institutions, and when we look at the statistics, it's apparent that we struggle to do effective risk management.

IMPROVING RISK MANAGEMENT

Research shows we frequently make decisions *not* based on rational thought but instead, based on emotion as basic as "Do I like it? Do I hate it?"[28] Kahneman explains that the affect heuristic "is an instance of substitution, in which the answer to an easy question (How do I feel about it?) serves as an answer to a much harder question (What do I think about it?)."[29] A major substitution occurs in bullying that parallels the substitution from hard to easy. We treat bullying as a behavior that occurs in childhood. It's *easy* to condemn behavior in child populations. We do not treat bullying as a behavior that occurs in adulthood or is transferred from adults to children. We often fail to educate, train effectively, or discipline bullying and abuse properly in the moment. Instead of stopping it, too often we gaslight, revictimize, cover up the abuses, and thereby enable the lies and manipulations of bullying to continue. This approach is not effective risk management.

It's much harder to tackle a problem in adult populations. Moreover, we are influenced by cultural scripting and past wiring that led us to feel in ambiguous and conflicted ways about bullying. On the one hand, we deplore it and know it's very harmful (so we are appalled by child bullying). On the other hand, we grudgingly admire it and believe it's a necessary evil for greatness as detailed in *The Bullied Brain*.[30] How many workplaces discuss this contradictory, two-sided aspect to bullying in our culture? When an institution is striving to do risk management around bullying, if it resorts to the intuitive shortcut, it treats bullying as a childhood issue that doesn't require frequent training, strict policies, and effective, well-established procedures. How many leaders, managers, and HR have well-informed, clear-cut ways to handle bullying? The policy and procedure manual in most workplaces isn't worth the paper it's written on if we recall what Baroness Casey discovered at the Met police.

When I was working on a task force to write new terms of reference to stop rampant abuse in gymnastics in Canada, we consulted with other countries that had done similar work. It turns out that abusing athletes is an entrenched international phenomenon. We heard again and again that a new policy and procedures manual had been written but now was gathering dust in the offices of those who had power to protect. If we look at our recent case studies, we see the same pattern. Each workplace, of course, had rules and regulations, bullying was not tolerated, and so on, but on the ground, employees weren't invited to discuss, get educated, undergo frequent training to ensure a bully-free culture. Carle did not even recognize her repeat maltreatment as "bullying." Wilson did not know the term "gaslighting." Macfarlane assumed that her colleagues would never send a predatorial professor on to unsuspecting students at another university. The lack of education and training in workplaces is not an effective way to manage risk. Education and training require conscious thought, not unconscious feeling, and the metacognition of the slow brain, not the quick fix of shortcuts. It's well established in brain science that we cannot make good decisions without emotional knowledge. Our rational and emotional decisions are inextricably entwined. It is when feeling—mostly focused on stressed and panicky feelings about oneself—informs leadership's failure to halt the lies of bullying and gaslighting that it will find itself participating in institutional complicity.

DEFINING RISK

Kahneman stresses how researchers understand that "defining risk is an exercise in power."[31] Risk is part of our social reality that we agree on or that someone tells us to believe. The media influence our thoughts on risk, and our workplace culture influences how we understand the concept of risk. We can agree that tools (hammer, ice pick, and chainsaw) are risky and require skills and safety measures to use them. We can fully change that risk assessment and agree that murder weapons (hammer, ice pick, and chainsaw) are extremely risky and need to be locked up. The "real" objects do not change, but our social agreement about their risk and their impact on our reality does. This more complex understanding of risk is critically important for institutions.

Those in power can define risk in workplace culture. They can tell you, "We don't have any bullying" in our institution. There is no risk. In these institutions, you may worry that the only "reality" is Dr. Jekyll; and when Mr. Hyde does his harm, it will result in gaslighting and institutional complicity. Or those in power asked to define risk tell you, "we have informed, regularly practiced, and discussed policies and procedures to deal with *all* forms of bullying in our institution. Just like we ensure that the fire department finds our buildings and emergency plans up to code, we ensure that the psychology department finds our policies and procedures on bullying, abuse, and harassment up to code. We risk manage and care about psychological safety just as much as we do about physical safety in our workplace." Now that is an informed and intentional workplace that understands how tools can be used by some as murder weapons. It's a workplace prepared for likable Dr. Jekyll to be unleashing Mr. Hyde on targets behind closed doors and has a plan to deal with such a shocking and challenging crisis.

When you press leaders, managers, and HR for more information in this workplace, they talk about how they do extensive education on the lies of bullying and the harm they can do to the brain and body; they explain that they conduct biannual anonymous surveys to gather as much information as possible from all voices in the workplace; they use these surveys to avoid fear of retribution for speaking up; they discuss how they have a trauma-informed way to take reports; they share their knowledge of the brain's challenges to assess what's true and what's false; they provide insights into how there's a tendency to revictimize those who speak up, but they follow the research that shows whistle-blower respect, and protection is better for productivity and profitability. Finally, they privilege the work of the slow brain even when it destabilizes the coherent narrative that the institution wants to believe. They privilege diverse approaches, the use of empathy, the asking of questions, deliberating, and reasoning. They are aware of the brain's tendency to habituation and shortcuts. They encourage dishabituation entrepreneurs, and they replace the brain's shortcuts with slow thinking.

DISCARD THE OUTDATED PARADIGM AND ENTER THE NEW NEUROPARADIGM

To discard the old framework of how we've always done things and begin a new way of handling problems that are *not* going away in the old system is very difficult. We must admit to ourselves that the way we approach the lies of bullying and gaslighting in the workplace is far too often a failure. It doesn't work, but this shift into a brain-informed model is difficult (ironically) for our brains. As Kahneman says, "we humans constantly fool ourselves by constructing flimsy accounts of the past and believing they are true."[32] Kahneman's research documents the way in which we have two selves operating within us: our remembering self and our experiencing self. Our dual self—remembering and experiencing—is manipulated effectively by the Dark Triad. They know that when reports come in, it baffles the brains of leaders, managers, and HR. They know that all kinds of mental and neurological confusion—as Kahneman's research showed—will lead those in the workplace to "repeat the episode of which they had the less aversive memory."[33] They remember Dr. Jekyll very well. He's likable, powerful, credible, and has social standing. Strangely, he also has reports from multiple sources about his abusive behavior. He's never or rarely displayed this abusive behavior in front of leaders, managers, and HR. It's very difficult to include the reports of this alter-ego Mr. Hyde, especially when our remembering self prefers the "less aversive memory" of Dr. Jekyll. Doesn't this help explain the decades when abusers are protected in institutions while reports of their abuse pile up and are silenced?

Babiak and Hare see the way our brains process others at work as a weakness psychopaths exploit. The remembering self is highly influenced by a person's first impression to the point that it seeks to reinforce it, rather than factor in confusing, conflicting information. The secret author clings to its coherent narrative. The Dark Triad specialize in impression management, and they are sure to make an exceptional first impression that is not easily shaken by reports of abuses.

> *The problem is that all of us form first impressions of others very quickly, perhaps during the first seconds of meeting someone for the first time. Once formed, people solidify their first impressions by filtering out new information that contradicts their early impressions, and preferentially let in information that is supportive.*[34]

What's disturbing is that once again we find ourselves believing in and even defending a "reality" that is false. We are staunchly committed to our memory of Dr. Jekyll, and when we hear reports—aversive, troubling, serious reports—about Mr. Hyde, we revert with the help of our remembering self to the comforting recollection of the good, respectable doctor. Babiak and Hare remind us that the good doctor is a fiction. How does abuse that psychopaths do flourish for years in institutions?

> *The answer lies in their ability to create a fictional story about themselves that fulfills the global requirement and expectations of the company and its members. Once the fiction is firmly established in the collective mind of the group, it is easy to hide negative, counterproductive traits.*[35]

The fictional story of Dr. Jekyll makes it easy to hide Mr. Hyde. Mary Inman describes this kind of groupthink in the wishful "reality" we construct around corrupt entrepreneurs such as Elizabeth Holmes or Sam Bankman-Fried. It's comparable to how we fall for the fictional mask of the Dark Triad even though it perpetually changes to lure in a variety of victims.

Kahneman's research takes our understanding to the next level.

Confusing experience with the memory of it is a compelling cognitive illusion—and it is the substitution that makes us believe a past experience can be ruined. The experiencing self does not have a voice. The remembering self is sometimes wrong, but it is the one that keeps score and governs what we learn from living, and it is the one that makes decisions. What we learn from the past is to maximize the qualities of our future memories, not necessarily of our future experience. This is the tyranny of the remembering self.[36]

Once again, we find substitution or reversal at work. It's understandable and relatable that leaders, managers, and HR do not want "a past experience"—namely, their work history with Dr. Jekyll—to be ruined by acknowledging Mr. Hyde's contradictory and abusive work history. They can erase the experience of witnessing or receiving reports of abuses, with a compelling cognitive illusion that allows them to substitute the story being told by the remembering self. This substitution is not difficult when we realize that the experiencing self does not have a voice. Within all of us lies the secret author fueled by the tyrannical remembering self whose goal is to maximize the qualities of our future memories. What do we want to remember, Dr. Jekyll or Mr. Hyde? Do we want to remember our leadership as stellar or as a failure? Do we want to remember our institution's story and preserve its legacy as ethical and caring? The remembering self is keeping score and is the one who makes decisions. Imagine how incredibly difficult it is to give the experiencing self—who has learned about Mr. Hyde—a role in this cognitive process that's unfolding in our brains.

How does the cognitive illusion work, and why is it so attractive? The remembering self, who makes the decisions, decides against mounting evidence that Mr. Hyde is the real illusion. He simply didn't exist in the way he's being reported on. In fact, the victims who reported, the whistleblower who spoke up, *they* were the problem. The remembering self has removed the truth tellers, in many cases with compensation, because the remembering self is ethical and caring. The cognitive illusion generated by the remembering self thereby preserves a future memory of self and the institution as stellar and not tarnished. Unfortunately, this carefully constructed narrative is at risk; and thus, we see decisions like firing, or the convenient "retiring early" of Mr. Hyde, along with strategies to keep it quiet by using NDAs of one kind or another. If needed, a smear campaign is conducted to ensure that the community, the collective mind of the group, believes that the one reporting abuse is the untrustworthy one.

THE REMEMBERING SELF IS ADEPT AT GASLIGHTING

For the leader to tell a good story with her remembering self, all that's required is to substitute an easy question for a hard one. The secret author, the fast brain's substitution is comparable to gaslighting's reversal and shows the way gaslighting is a key component of institutional complicity. Kahneman explains that "we all care intensely for the narrative of our life and very much want it to be a good story, with a decent hero."[37] Let's try to imagine what is happening in the mind of the leader's remembering self. How will he construct and frame his future memories? Notice how the remembering self uses substitution of victim for perpetrator. This parallels Jennifer Freyd's DARVO that exposes the way we reverse victim and offender. These mind-bending substitutions and reversals maintain the remembering self's story that positions the leader as a decent hero and creates future memories of decency, not cover-up and collusion.

- Did I fulfill my duty or was I negligent? If the past and present victims are reversed into perpetrators (liars), then abuse never took place. Check: I dismissed the perpetrators. I fulfilled my duty. Phew, I'm a decent hero.

- Was I a protector or punisher? If the victims are reversed into perpetrators (liars), then abuse never took place. Check: I dismissed the perpetrators. I protected accused employees. Decent hero.

- Was I loyal or a betrayer? If the victims are reversed into perpetrators (liars), then abuse never took place. Check: I dismissed the perpetrators. I am loyal to my employees. Decent hero.

- Do I run a tight ship or is it running amok? If the victims are reversed into perpetrators (liars), then abuse never took place. Check: I dismissed the perpetrators. I run a tight ship. I am, once again, a decent hero in my own story, which I constructed with the remembering self. The experiencing self did not disagree because it has no voice.

In the present, the experiencing self actively covers up abuses; revictimizes targets; shoots the messenger; causes betrayal trauma; refuses to take accountability for negligence; loses dedicated and talented employees; strips innocent victims of livelihoods, health, and careers; and puts the institution at risk for exposure. The remembering self uses gaslighting to cling to a Dr. Jekyll version of perpetrators and a Dr. Jekyll version of himself. He can use cognitive illusion to tell a coherent story that ensures that victims, whistle-blowers, and Mr. Hyde are all silenced and that the experiencing self "does not have a voice." The remembering self controls the secret author's narrative and gaslights all others who see Dr. Hyde into no longer seeing him.

Kahneman provides a key takeaway for this kind of autobiography that the "remembering self" constructs: "He is desperately trying to protect the narrative of a life of integrity which is endangered by the last episode."[38] When the last episode exposes that abuses are occurring, the leader feels endangered. Montgomery, Carle, Wilson, Macfarlane *endangered* the leadership's life story, which is supposed to be a "life of integrity" that positions him as a "decent hero." Those who report abuse must be silenced and dismissed because they threaten what the leadership is "desperately trying to protect"—not victims, not safety, not transparency, not honesty, not the institution—but his own life story.

Psychological research teaches us how reversal and substitution occur. The secret author, the fast brain's remembering self, just needs to generate a cognitive illusion to swap positions: murder weapons to tools, Mr. Hyde to Dr. Jekyll, the present (reports of abuses) to the past (when reports of abuses had been unknown or effectively silenced), truth to illusion, fact to fiction. It requires a kind of violence, but it is easily dismissed and forgotten by the remembering self whose focus is on good future memories about herself.

The illusion that one has understood the past feeds the further illusion that one can predict and control the future. These illusions are comforting. They reduce the anxiety we would experience if we allowed ourselves to fully acknowledge the uncertainties of existence. We all have a need for the reassuring message that actions have appropriate consequences and that success will reward wisdom and courage.[39]

Covering up abuses may lead to exposure and a hit to the institution, but the illusion still holds and leads decision-makers to make poor decisions. Kahneman explains this succumbing to belief in oneself—one's courage and wisdom—by noting that research shows those who have power—*or* are simply reminded of a time when they had power—trust their intuition more.[40] Power increases your tendency to take an intuitive shortcut, and as noted, it lowers your empathy. For those reporting abuses, this combination is worrisome.

THE LEADER'S NEED TO CONTROL THE NARRATIVE

Let's start with how the halo effect contributes to the construction of comforting narratives. Kahneman says that the "halo effect helps keep explanatory narratives simple and coherent by exaggerating the consistency of evaluations: good people do only good things and bad people are all bad."[41] The Dark Triad use this intuitive shortcut to their advantage. They always surround themselves with beneficiaries of their abusive ways who defend them when targets report. These beneficiaries receive opportunities in the moment or promises of future "gifts" if they do the Dark Triad's bidding. When reports come in, the Dark Triad exclaim that they can't possibly be true because—cue the halo effect—they have done so many good things. The brain is already confused by the reports that Dr. Jekyll is also Mr. Hyde. Now another illusion is being shattered by this idea that someone like Harvey Weinstein—who championed opportunities for women directors and marched for women's rights—is simultaneously being accused by multiple victims of emotional and sexual abuse. Weinstein is quick to say: they lie because here, look, I do good things for women, so I cannot be bad. Although this illusion works for the perpetrator, it is denied to the victim. The leader wants so badly to cling to the illusion of "good people only do good things" that when it comes to the victim, his history of doing good things has to be erased as it causes more confusion. It's hard to do because many targets have fabulous track records, but when a leader is falling prey to cognitive illusions and the need to construct a narrative of integrity with himself as the decent hero, this track record that upends the coherent narrative must be erased. As Kahneman puts it, "Changing one's mind about human nature is hard work, and changing one's mind for the worse about oneself is even harder."[42]

Changing from the outdated bullying paradigm into a new brain-informed neuroparadigm is hard, but not nearly as hard as leaders taking accountability for failing victims and whistle-blowers. Negligence can blow up the leader's narrative of integrity, and it must be covered up at all costs.

PUTTING THE INSTITUTION AT RISK TO SAVE ONE'S FUTURE MEMORIES

Kahneman's research examines leaders' decisions when it comes to financial errors. We see this same pattern of putting the institution at risk to save one's own "future memories." It's another gaslighting reversal at work because the leader acts as if she must cover up abuses and get rid of victims and whistle-blowers because she's doing everything in her power to save the institution's reputation. You can imagine how this utilitarian model, which Sam Bankman-Fried championed, makes this commitment to the institution believable: the happiness of the majority at the institution will be saved if we oust these vocal, problem employees.

In an institution that strives for maximizing profit for those at the top while paying the majority as little as possible, you see the model flip: the happiness of the minority justifies the unhappiness of the majority. Once again, the minority's commitment to the institution is the illusion that covers up the truth of inequity and injustice. The same spectacle is used in a totalitarian dictatorship. Citizens are told that the minority's happiness is a necessary evil (since it depends on the majority's unhappiness) because it demonstrates commitment to the great nation. Those who question the illusion are labeled as losers, enemies, and traitors who must be silenced and even locked up. They are also labeled via gaslighting as deranged or crazy in order to cast doubt on their assessment of reality. Truth tellers and whistle-blowers have no place in the totalitarian dictatorship's spectacle.

Now, contrast this cognitive illusion being offered to employees by the leader, when in fact the leader is putting his energy into saving himself and his narrative of integrity, which is key to preserving his future memories. "All too often a company afflicted by sunk costs drives into the blizzard, throwing good money after bad rather than accepting the humiliation of closing the account of a costly failure." Just as we saw with abuses being exposed, the goal is to avoid humiliation at all costs. And it's all about the leader's life story:

> Canceling the project will leave a permanent stain on the executive's record, and his personal interests are perhaps best served by gambling further with the organization's resources in the hope of recouping the original investment—or at least in an attempt to postpone the day of reckoning.[43]

Institutional protectionism may actually be the leader protecting himself. National protectionism may actually be the leader protecting himself. The leader's attempt to protect his track record can be disastrous for the institution and for the nation. Let's use the president of Rutgers University as an example. Leadership was informed of coach Mike Rice's abuse of players, mostly in the form of hurling homophobic slurs. They saw a short video an assistant coach made that revealed Rice berating athletes with homophobia and throwing basketballs at them in an apparent fury. Instead of firing him, leaders did a series of strategies to mitigate the risk he posed to them and the institution but still allowed them to cling to the coherent narrative of their own integrity and status as decent heroes. They suspended the perpetrator, fined him, and covered up. As is textbook when the institution colludes with an abusive individual, the assistant coach—who put together the incriminating video to see athletes protected—took the hard path of the whistle-blower, gave the video to ESPN, and did not have his contract renewed.[44]

Gaslighting swirls through this abuse crisis, as it does in so many others. The idea that the Dark Triad, who abuse those over whom they have power, will respond to a punishment such as taking an anger management course, a workshop on boundaries, or even accepting a three-game suspension and a fine is completely ignorant of psychological research. If an institution discovers that an employee is an arsonist, would it send the arsonist to a course on how fire is dangerous? The gaslighting revolves around exposing abuse victims—in this case basketball players completely dependent on the coach who has power, credibility, and social standing—once again to the abuser's mental illness, which is contagious. If Mike Rice had a life-threatening virus and covered it up, exposing student athletes, would he be sent to a course on why quarantine is a safer option? All the decisions around Mike Rice's abuse display leaders pretending that they are making decisions about tools when, in fact, they are dealing with murder weapons. They believe and want to ensure that everyone believes—including the victims who are exposed to the significant danger of the manipulative Dark Triad in the form of Mike Rice.

When ESPN released the video, the gaslighting fell to pieces. Leaders could no longer cover up what Mike Rice had done and had been enabled—by them—to continue doing. Rice was fired immediately. Another assistant coach, who had mimicked Rice's abuse, resigned ahead of also being fired. Rutgers's athletic director resigned; he had seen the video and failed to protect athletes. The legal advisers at Rutgers resigned; they had advised on the suspension and fine rather than advising Rice be fired. Loud calls demanded that the president of the university, who had seen the video, step down, but he hung on to his position. The university was subjected to brutal media coverage, significant reputational losses, and the cost of terminated contracts for multiple employees. If we believe that the president and others were doing their best to protect the institution, it's hard to understand how it reached this outcome. Was the president gambling his institution's reputation to protect a narrative about his own integrity that positioned him as the decent hero?

LET'S CHANGE THE NARRATIVE TOGETHER

If leaders, managers, and HR were educated in the Dark Triad, perhaps they would identify them more easily, be less manipulated by their illusions, and not treat their failure to act earlier as a humiliation. If the leader could still be the hero in his own story by stopping the Dark Triad and admitting past failure, he would be far more likely to protect victims, stop fraud, accept accountability for being gaslit, and do damage control. When we know that the Dark Triad are adept at manipulating psychiatric experts, we can acknowledge that we, too, can be tricked. We can admit that we made errors but now are intervening to address the crisis fully and effectively going forward.

Kahneman concurs with Barrett that developing a more accurate vocabulary will be a key component of changing for the better. He writes, "By providing a distinctive vocabulary, organizations can also encourage a culture in which people watch out for one another as they approach minefields."[45] Likewise, Barrett would encourage us to develop a series of emotion concepts—with an eye to a nuanced and distinctive vocabulary—that allows us to see through the illusions of the Dark Triad. In the last chapter, we quoted Kahneman on the way in which we should trust observers who are less cognitively busy and better able to see through the illusion (Dr. Jekyll) to the minefield (Mr. Hyde). Montgomery is an observer.

Merzenich would encourage us to use the language of neuroplasticity to get in the practice of doing daily brain fitness and going to the brain gym to keep our mental faculties sharp, far less easily distracted and misled by the noise and chatter deployed by the Dark Triad. Stephen and Seth Porges would have us become conversant in the vocabulary of neuroception so that we are aware of our need for homeostasis to recover from bouts of activation leading us into fight and flight or freeze. Sue Carter would remind us that coregulation—our deep-seated need for connection and community—should make her concept of "socioception" vitally important in the workplace. A vocabulary that has terms like the stress hormone cortisol and the bonding hormone oxytocin would be useful in establishing psychological safety and thereby being more adept at risk management. Tali Sharot and Cass Sunstein would want us to develop the kind of vocabulary used by dishabituation entrepreneurs to jolt us out of the brain's tendency to operate on autopilot. Kahneman would have us switch from a morally informed terminology to a medically informed one that helps us see through our "descriptions of reality" to facts and truth. The more we diagnose our impulses to believe in our own hero story and our secret author's wish for a predictable, coherent narrative, quickly and easily constructed by our fast brain, the less susceptible we are to the intuitive shortcuts that cover up the chaos and mayhem we live in.

Kahneman makes a compelling argument for how we can be better balanced if we can just find the courage to listen to those who speak truth to power, those who offer constructive criticism, and take a deep breath that allows for slow thinking and accurate vocabulary.

Ultimately, a richer language is essential to the skill of constructive criticism. Much like medicine, the identification of judgement errors is a diagnostic task, which requires a precise vocabulary. The name of a disease is a hook to which all that is known about the disease is attached, including vulnerabilities, environmental factors, symptoms, prognosis, and care.[46]

Mary Inman's work with whistle-blowers confirms Kahneman's insights; and the fifteen years of data analyzed by Kyle Welch and Stephen Stubben, discussed in *Harvard Business Review*, tell us that listening to truth tellers, respecting and protecting whistle-blowers increases productivity and profitability.[47] Letting leaders see themselves as part of a medical rather than moral narrative allows them to act more like physicians and less like decent heroes. Richer language about how our brains and bodies function—with a specific focus on the lies of bullying, gaslighting, and institutional complicity—can help us articulate the many minefields we need to cross when dealing with the Dark Triad.

Dark Triad itself is a shorthand for mental diseases that an individual usually catches in a childhood rife with abuse and neglect. A medical vocabulary for what they are suffering allows us to see them as unwell and needing medical attention. It makes us understand why it is irresponsible and dangerous to allow them to infect others in the institution. At the same time, it allows leaders, managers, and HR to know that a defining feature of this disease is the difficulty in diagnosing it. That shifts their focus from their own failure story to channeling their attention and energy into figuring out vulnerabilities, environmental factors, symptoms, prognosis, and care.

The question no longer is about how I can use intuitive shortcuts with my remembering self to construct a narrative with me as the decent hero of the story. The questions become: What institutional vulnerabilities led to the Dark Triad committing abuses? What environmental factors created an opportunity for the Dark Triad to flourish? What were the Dark Triad symptoms that we missed so that our diagnosis came later than we would have liked? Does the prognosis require the intervention of a mental health professional? Should the institution learn whether others have been infected? How will the institution care for the Dark Triad and others who may have caught the disease? How will they ensure that the targets recover their health?

These kinds of questions and this kind of medical language respects the Dark Triad but also the targets. It foregrounds the health of the institution going forward. Kahneman's research shows that leaders or decision-makers "will make better choices when they trust their critics to be sophisticated and fair, and when they expect their decision to be judged by how it was made, not only by how it turned out."[48] Notice that listening to abuse reports, to critics, to truth tellers, to whistle-blowers shifts the focus from the remembering self to the experiencing self. The attention is on how we ask precise questions, how we reach decisions, who we listen to. Are we silencing anyone? Are we constructing descriptions of reality or bravely trying to address reality in all its chaos? Are we taking intuitive shortcuts with our fast brain or being disciplined in dealing with difficulties and challenges with our slow-thinking brain? You can still be the decent hero in this new story, but it requires deliberation and reasoning with your slow-thinking brain.

NOTES

1. Daniel Kahneman, *Thinking, Fast and Slow* (Toronto: Anchor Canada, 2013), 4.
2. Kahneman, *Thinking, Fast and Slow*, 4.
3. Kahneman, *Thinking, Fast and Slow*, 8.

4. Kahneman, *Thinking, Fast and Slow*, 12.
5. Kahneman, *Thinking, Fast and Slow*, 13.
6. Kahneman, *Thinking, Fast and Slow*, 20.
7. Kahneman, *Thinking, Fast and Slow*, 21.
8. Kahneman, *Thinking, Fast and Slow*, 23.
9. Kahneman, *Thinking, Fast and Slow*, 24.
10. Jennifer Fraser, *The Bullied Brain: Heal Your Scars and Restore Your Health* (Essex, CT: Prometheus, 2022).
11. Kahneman, *Thinking, Fast and Slow*, 28.
12. Kahneman, *Thinking, Fast and Slow*, 28.
13. Kahneman, *Thinking, Fast and Slow*, 62.
14. Kahneman, *Thinking, Fast and Slow*, 63.
15. Kahneman, *Thinking, Fast and Slow*, 65.
16. Kahneman, *Thinking, Fast and Slow*, 12.
17. Kahneman, *Thinking, Fast and Slow*, 79.
18. Kahneman, *Thinking, Fast and Slow*, 81.
19. Kahneman, *Thinking, Fast and Slow*, 81.
20. Kahneman, *Thinking, Fast and Slow*, 83.
21. Kahneman, *Thinking, Fast and Slow*, 85.
22. Kahneman, *Thinking, Fast and Slow*, 85.
23. Kahneman, *Thinking, Fast and Slow*, 85.
24. Kahneman, *Thinking, Fast and Slow*, 87.
25. Kahneman, *Thinking, Fast and Slow*, 114.
26. Kahneman, *Thinking, Fast and Slow*, 114.
27. Kahneman, *Thinking, Fast and Slow*, 131.
28. Kahneman, *Thinking, Fast and Slow*, 139.
29. Kahneman, *Thinking, Fast and Slow*, 139.
30. Fraser, *The Bullied Brain*.
31. Kahneman, *Thinking, Fast and Slow*, 141.
32. Kahneman, *Thinking, Fast and Slow*, 199.
33. Kahneman, *Thinking, Fast and Slow*, 383.
34. Paul Babiak and Robert Hare, *Snakes in Suits: When Psychopaths Go to Work* (New York: Harper, 2006), 71.
35. Babiak and Hare, *Snakes in Suits*, 120.
36. Kahneman, *Thinking, Fast and Slow*, 381.
37. Kahneman, *Thinking, Fast and Slow*, 387.
38. Kahneman, *Thinking, Fast and Slow*, 390.
39. Kahneman, *Thinking, Fast and Slow*, 204–5.
40. Kahneman, *Thinking, Fast and Slow*, 135.
41. Kahneman, *Thinking, Fast and Slow*, 199–200.
42. Kahneman, *Thinking, Fast and Slow*, 172.
43. Kahneman, *Thinking, Fast and Slow*, 346.
44. Don Van Natta Jr., "Video Shows Mike Rice's Ire," *ESPN*, April 2, 2013, https://www.espn.com/espn/otl/story/_/id/9125796/practice-video-shows-rutgers-basketball-coach-mike-rice-berated-pushed-used-slurs-players.

45. Kahneman, *Thinking, Fast and Slow*, 418.

46. Kahneman, *Thinking, Fast and Slow*, 418.

47. Kyle Welch and Stephen Stubben, "Throw Out Your Assumptions about Whistle-blowing," *Harvard Business Review*, January 14, 2020, https://hbr.org/2020/01/throw-out-your-assumptions-about-whistleblowing.

48. Kahneman, *Thinking, Fast and Slow*, 418.

CHAPTER FOURTEEN

Keep the Opportunist in Check

Proven Way #6: Balance Lateralization

THE SIXTH PROVEN WAY TO STRENGTHEN OUR BRAINS AND MAKE THEM ready to do battle against the lies of bullying, gaslighting, and institutional complicity is lateralization, the way the brain functions as two distinct hemispheres. Drawing on the work of psychiatrist Dr. Iain McGilchrist, we are provided with startling insight into the way in which our brains construct reality "from two incompatible world views."[1]

One of these worldviews—generated by the brain's left hemisphere—is correlated with a narrow self-focus that can jeopardize an institution's health and high performance. In contrast, the brain's right hemisphere is correlated with a worldview that can act as a preventative and an antidote when the two hemispheres work together. Knowledge of how our brains work in this regard allows us to make far better choices and decisions about ourselves, our colleagues, and our world.

McGilchrist expresses profound concern that our left hemispheres are taking over and constructing an unhealthy, unsustainable world of competition and exploitation. His concerning view—which Chris Hedges shares in his *Empire of Illusion*—provides insight into why so many suffer in the workplace from environments that normalize bullying, gaslighting, and institutional complicity. Knowledge of how our brains work grants us the ability to make balanced decisions going forward. If we keep in mind Michael Merzenich's research into all the ways we can overcome neurological deficits and strengthen our brains, learning about the left hemisphere's dominance of the right does not have to signal our decline. Instead, we can galvanize our neuroplasticity, our brain's innate ability to change based on what we practice. We can create a better future in which bullying is replaced with empathy, gaslighting transforms into transparency, and institutional complicity becomes collaboration built on the foundational understanding that we are stronger together. That's the right hemisphere talking.

Distance Is Our Greatest Strength and Weakness

According to McGilchrist, the evolution of neuropsychology reveals the inextricability of our divided brains. Although the two hemispheres work in distinct ways as they interact with the world, they are designed to work in tandem. McGilchrist describes "our ability to stand back from the world, from ourselves and from the immediacy of experience." This detachment or distance "enables us to plan, to think flexibly and inventively." It also enables us "to take control of the world around us."[2] A planner who is flexible and inventive brings wonderful qualities in any workplace, but taking control of the world around us may lead to issues, especially when this impulse to control and dominate is out of balance with our brain's foregrounding of social and environmental connections.

McGilchrist emphasizes that our two brain hemispheres, specifically the frontal lobes—with their distance from the world and one another—can lead us to use and exploit others and at the same time, become more empathic. Although he does not highlight the two empathy neural circuits, which we examined in detail through the work of Simon Baron-Cohen, it's worth applying that knowledge here to his description. When it comes to our cognitive empathy, distance "can yield detachment, as when we coldly calculate how to outwit our opponent, by imagining what he believes will be our next move." The distance emerges as if we are competitors in a game where the goal is to read our opponent like a book and outwit him. If we succeed, then we are winners. As we've seen with the Dark Triad, winning is a driving force; not surprisingly, it is a left-hemisphere priority. Note how this drive to win, as Paul Babiak and Robert Hare report, manifests in a workplace that enables psychopaths to take hold.

Winning almost always involves financial and power rewards, such as a steady paycheck for work rarely completed, and promotions into increasing levels of authority. It can also include derailing the careers of coworkers up to and including their unjust termination.[3]

I wonder whether the left-hemisphere approach to my workplace and that of Carle, Wilson, and Macfarlane would be healthier and more balanced if it questioned this lopsided protection of those who abuse and lie while abandoning those who care and tell the truth. I wonder whether it's a left-hemisphere approach degrading our culture into an illusion that Chris Hedges sees as revolving around the "cult of the self" with its privileging of the "ability to lie and manipulate."[4]

As McGilchrist says, the left hemisphere "is always a winner: winning is associated with activation of the left amygdala, losing with right amygdala activation. There are links here with the right hemisphere's tendency to melancholy."[5] We experience a different reality when it comes to our affective empathy that can lead to feelings of sadness or melancholy due to concern and care for others. McGilchrist writes, "By standing back from the animal immediacy of our experience we are able to be more empathic with others, who we come to see, for the first time, as beings like ourselves."[6] Distance from the world and one another can "teach us to betray" as well as "to trust."

Listen to McGilchrist's description as it applies to the workplace. He is wearing progressive lenses in the sense that he does not only see Dr. Jekyll but also Mr. Hyde. He understands and speaks about the brain and thus humanity as a dual figure that can tip in different directions using the same defining neurological mechanisms.

The evolution of the frontal lobes prepares us at the same time to be exploiters of the world and of one another, and to be citizens one with another and guardians of the world. If it has made us the most powerful and destructive of animals, it has also turned us, famously, into the "social animal," and into an animal with a spiritual dimension.[7]

To allow both brain functions to coexist, yet perform their distinct roles, our brains allocated the grasping, getting, and feeding needs of the brain—that make us exploiters of the world and of one another—into the left hemisphere, while expanding this intense survival focus as widely as possible in the right hemisphere, where we are citizens one with another and guardians of the world. In short, our brains appear like an indivisible Dr. Jekyll (altruist who cares) and Mr. Hyde (opportunist who exploits). If the brain hemispheres are in balance, and each fulfills its role without dominating the other, the self achieves homeostasis. But if the left hemisphere takes control and begins using Dr. Jekyll to camouflage the exploiting of others and the world, then we are in serious jeopardy. As we will examine, McGilchrist ultimately shows how our world is tilting toward a domineering left-hemisphere approach that puts us and our world in danger.

The Left and Right Hemispheres of the Brain

The left and right hemispheres of the brain function in diverse ways and envision the world differently, but as McGilchrist explains "both hemispheres take part in virtually all 'functions' to some extent, and in reality both are always engaged."[8] The goal is not to try to limit functions to one side or the other. The goal is to avoid what McGilchrist calls "interhemispheric imbalance."[9]

Throughout *The Gaslit Brain*, we have seen the destabilizing force of lies as they unbalance our brains, our careers, and our lives. Keeping in mind the brain's inextricable way of constructing reality, distinguishing the left and right hemispheres reveals the vital importance of balance and the proven ways we can achieve it. For the sake of ease and clarity, we refer to the left hemisphere as the "opportunist" and the right hemisphere as the "altruist." *Both* are critical to our survival. The opportunist sees reality in such a way that we do not miss opportunities, whereas the altruist belongs to a reality where we engage empathically and emotionally with otherness. For a safe and sane workplace, we clearly need to strike a balance between these two opposing forces within our brains.

McGilchrist characterizes the opportunist side of the brain as paying "attention to the virtual world it has created, which is self-consistent, but self-contained, ultimately disconnected from the Other, making it powerful, but ultimately only able operate on, and to know, itself."[10] This hemisphere parallels what Daniel Kahneman terms "the remembering self" that invests its energy into being "the decent hero" of a story constructed on integrity. This side of the brain is focused, organized, disciplined, able to act efficiently and pragmatically. It has the kind of power that we associate with leaders who can manage complex institutions and even nations. However, you can quickly see how this side of the brain—if it dominates or becomes unbalanced—may lead us down the path of the Dark Triad. Disconnection from the Other can lead to objectifying others, seeing them merely as pawns in one's own virtual world. As Kahneman explains, this remembering self dominates and erases the "experiencing self" when it puts in doubt the coherent narrative of integrity that the opportunist side of the brain relies on. The experiencing self does not have a voice, and it can easily be put into an out-group if it gets in the way of opportunities for the remembering self to script a legacy of heroic decency and integrity. This side of the brain channels energy into a virtual world it creates that increases control and power because it is self-consistent and self-contained. It almost sounds as if the opportunist side of the brain participates in the world with a gamelike fascination, as Babiak and Hare saw as a key quality in psychopaths.

The opportunist side of the brain functions like a narcissist, limited by only being able to operate within his own virtual world where he only knows himself. Babiak and Hare describe psychopath brains in a similar way.

Psychopaths lack empathy and possibly even the most basic understanding of human feelings. Characteristically, the economic and emotional impact of their selfish behavior on others is irrelevant to them, in part because they believe everyone in this dog-eat-dog world is as greedy and unfeeling as they are.[11]

It's as if psychopaths are trapped in the left hemisphere and have lost the ability to switch focus and return to the right hemisphere, which has a larger, more compassionate and encompassing vision of self as part of humanity and the world. What Baron-Cohen identifies as their "empathy erosion" reduces their perspective to a handheld mirror that they gaze into, believing it to be "reality." When they see others, it's only in a larger mirror magnifying their image and power. From a brain perspective, it makes sense that the opportunist—when reported on for bullying or gaslighting—acts as if she is outraged at such an unjust accusation. Opportunists *deny* having done harm as part of their textbook response—the "D" for Denial in Jennifer Freyd's DARVO acronym. Perhaps on one level, so much in the world is their own narcissistic construction, they truly believe in their innocence. If they have deficits in the right hemisphere, which narrow their vision to only see their psychopathic needs, that makes sense. As McGilchrist notes, "Denial is a left hemisphere speciality."[12]

As we saw in the work of Babiak, Hare, and Baron-Cohen, the Dark Triad lack empathic and emotional activation. Instead, they experience cognitive and language activation, ideal for charismatic liars who can shapeshift easily from Dr. Jekyll to Mr. Hyde and back. Their intelligence and skill with words are ideal for the lies of bullying and gaslighting. In contrast, McGilchrist notes that the right hemisphere harnesses the power of language for connection and community. He says that the altruist right hemisphere "uses language not in order to manipulate ideas or things, but to understand what others mean."[13]

As we saw in the work of Lisa Feldman Barrett, a rich vocabulary for emotions is key for understanding self and others. The Dark Triad appear to lack this understanding as their drive is to manipulate with words, not learn or create emotion concepts. Hence their satisfaction, maybe even fascination, with repetition to secure opportunities for themselves. They abuse over and over in identical ways, the only difference being a revolving door of victims. They use repetition to make others believe that their falsehoods are true. This doesn't bore them. Merzenich describes them as becoming caricatures of humans, perhaps the result of having left-hemisphere dominance that deprives them of the capacity to recognize that they are a part of a whole, an individual among humanity, an organism in a natural environment.

One of the most striking and dangerous features of the Dark Triad is their lack of empathy and emotions. The Dark Triad are quick to humiliate those with emotions as "too sensitive," "pathetic," "soft," "pussy," linking weakness with the feminine and thus demeaning emotions with misogynistic and homophobic slurs. Likewise, empathy is seen as a weakness, but in textbook psychopathic reversal, empathy, despite the weakness it shares with emotions, is also seen as opening up society to exploitation and is thus categorized as a weapon. As shown by Babiak and Hare on brain scans, the Dark Triad replace empathy and emotion activation with language and cognition activation. It is as if the Dark Triad's focus on language to manipulate has denied them the capacity to experience emotions and name them with concepts many of us take for granted. Their brains default to lying and scheming in place of affective empathy. McGilchrist shares insight into the psychopathic brain contrasted with the way in which healthy brains experience emotion.

There is also a direct correlation between sadness and empathy, on the one hand, and feelings of guilt, shame and responsibility, on the other. Psychopaths who have no sense of guilt, shame or responsibility, have deficits in the right frontal lobe, particularly the right ventromedial and orbitofrontal cortex.[14]

Imagine how different our workplaces would be if we recognized that perpetrators of bullying and gaslighting had brain deficits. Not only does their behavior manifest empathy erosion in the brain, but it also shows symptoms of right-hemisphere deficits. How many workplaces respond to bullying and gaslighting reports by having the perpetrator assessed by a psychologist, psychiatrist, and neuroscientist? How many workplaces require a clean bill of health—namely, a brain scan and professional assessment—before this individual is allowed back to work? If they are wrongly accused, the brain scan should quickly indicate a healthy brain, but if they have deficits and erosion in key areas correlated with psychopathology and abuse, then they need to be quarantined. They should certainly *not* be allowed to infect others in the institution. And why should they be enabled and empowered to take a colleague's livelihood, health, and career simply because they are unwell? These questions are not being asked, let alone answered, yet they are key questions for the workplaces now and in the future. Considering the extensive science, we must make informed and healthy changes.

The Altruist Is Empathic

In contrast to the emotional deficits of the opportunist left hemisphere, McGilchrist characterizes the altruist right side of the brain as paying "attention to the Other, whatever it is that exists apart from ourselves, with which it sees itself in profound relation. It is deeply attracted to, and given life by, the relationship, the betweenness, that exists with this Other."[15] You can see that the right side of the brain is how we experience intense bonds with nature, a feeling of awe about the universe, humble adoration for the divine, love for animals, and a deep-seated care for humanity. You can imagine the altruist right side of the brain being a professor, an environmentalist, a poet, or a philosopher, with its head in the clouds and an inability to get through its to-do list. This side of the brain might struggle to put food on the table and pay the bills on time. As you can see, both brain hemispheres are essential, but when it comes to the lies of bullying, gaslighting, and institutional complicity, workplaces might become dominated by the opportunist left side of the brain and thereby put our balance, safety, and sanity at risk.

The teachers who Montgomery and the other students reported as abusive had an odd feature reported by numerous victims. The abusive teachers couldn't look them in the eye. McGilchrist discusses avoiding the eyes when looking at a face as indicative of the opportunist left-hemisphere approach:

> It seems that the left hemisphere reads emotions by interpreting the lower part of the face. Though the left hemisphere can understand emotional display, it looks not at the eyes, even when directed to do so, but at the mouth. The right hemisphere alone seems to be capable of understanding the more subtle information that comes from the eyes. Empathy is not something one reads in the lower face, where relatively blunt messages—friend or foe—tend to be conveyed.[16]

This description reminds us that frequently those in the Dark Triad who abuse are those who suffered abuse or neglect in their formative years. They may suffer from hypervigilance, perpetually trying to assess whether someone is safe or dangerous, friend or foe. In this context, it is reasonable that they are scanning the environment for threat. They can't look into the eyes and connect with others to see their individual uniqueness. Instead, they look to their mouths to see whether they are friend or foe, safe or harmful.

The opportunist left hemisphere's way of seeing is to ignore individual or unique characteristics and instead, put others into categories and then arrange them or re-present them for their own needs. One of the notable features in a lot of abuse cases is that perpetrators don't have authentic relationships with targets. They treat them simply as objects, so they dress the same way, go to the same place to abuse, say the same words, use the same gestures. It's as if they are in a one-sided play that they wrote for themselves, and they act out the abuse drama for years if enabled. It makes sense when you understand that their interaction with others is likely through the left hemisphere, which is "emotionally relatively neutral," whereas the right hemisphere "plays a vital role in emotional expression."[17]

The right-hemisphere altruist is better at "detecting deceit" because the left hemisphere "does not attend to the eyes." Those who report bullying appear to operate from a right-hemisphere approach that "picks up subtle clues and meanings." McGilchrist states that "because it can understand how others are feeling and thinking, we rely on it when we judge whether people are lying."[18] Those who report the lies of bullying and gaslighting often explain their motivation as being to protect others and the institution. Their encompassing, empathic, altruistic approach recognizes the dangerously narrow, self-serving focus of the opportunist. At the same time, the left-hemisphere opportunists are unaware of just how much they are missing in the emotional realm. The opportunist attacks what it does not experience or understand. Both sides of the brain have key roles to play, but when it becomes unbalanced or lopsided with the left hemisphere taking over the whole stage, not allowing the right hemisphere a role, then individuals, whole workplaces, and even whole populaces can become unstable.

Why Do Our Brains Have Two Hemispheres?

McGilchrist offers a succinct response to this complex question:

> *It might then be that the division of the human brain is also the result of the need to bring to bear two incompatible types of attention on the world at the same time, one narrow, focussed, and directed by our needs, and the other broad, open, and directed towards whatever else is going on in the world apart from ourselves.*[19]

Essentially, McGilchrist documents how the left hemisphere developed to capitalize on opportunities. As he articulates it, "I need to use, or to manipulate, the world for my ends, and for that I need narrow-focus attention."[20] To survive and flourish, I depend on the opportunist's "wilfully directed, narrowly focussed attention."[21] Like other creatures on the planet, in general, "the left hemisphere yields narrow, focussed attention, mainly for the purpose of getting and feeding."[22] Imagine the concentration one needs to hunt, the eye for detail one needs to forage, along with the drive and focus to secure water, shelter, safe places to sleep. These skills in the contemporary workplace compare to the concentration one needs to invest or land deals, the eye for detail one needs to build a bridge or repair mechanical malfunction, the laser focus to identify legal or financial errors, along with the drive and attention to locate a client base, secure property, create content, acquire insurance, and so on.

In contrast, the altruist right hemisphere developed to have awareness and bonds with a wider natural and social network.

> *The right hemisphere yields a broad, vigilant attention, the purpose of which appears to be awareness of signals from the surroundings, especially of other creatures, who are potential predators or potential mates, foes or friends; and it is involved in bonding in social animals.*[23]

The opportunist can afford to laser in on the task at hand, on getting and feeding, because it has the right brain on the lookout. While the left brain zooms in on the details and tasks, the right brain pans out to encompass the bigger picture, which includes the complexity of human bonds. To survive on the far-larger scale of the altruist right hemisphere, it is vital to bring awareness to one's social group. McGilchrist's longer description of the right hemisphere's world gives us a sense of how much bigger and more complex it is than the singular, narrow focus of the opportunist left hemisphere.

> *I need to see myself in the broader context of the world at large, and in relation to others, whether they be friend or foe: I have a need to take account of myself as a member of my social group, to see potential allies, and beyond that to see potential mates and potential enemies. Here I may feel myself to be part of something much bigger than myself, and even existing in and through that 'something' that is bigger than myself—the flight or flock with which I scavenge, breed and roam, the pack with which I hunt, the mate and offspring that I also feed, and ultimately everything that goes on in my purview.*[24]

In the workplace, many of us recognize this perpetual sense of self as a larger whole. While we do our tasks, concentrate, focus, and apply our eye for detail, we also have a running narrative about our social world: picking up the kids from day care or school, getting them to sports or arts, ensuring that the dog gets fed, being tuned into colleagues who might be struggling, neighbors who may need help, friends we love to laugh with, romantic interests, concerns about a certain colleague's unkindness, worries about politicians or economists' decisions, fears and anguish about wars, anxiety about the loneliness of aging parents, faith in our spiritual community. We are aware of a leader's potentially threatening ideas, a belief in a manager's integrity, while we depend on a colleague in HR who has a proven track record of empathy and fairness. Then in broader circles, we have feelings for nature and the divine with all the relationships involved. Our left hemisphere's laser focus can sometimes tune out the right hemisphere's sense of being part of a tribe and part of a natural environment but not for long.

THE BRAIN'S DUAL VISION

To survive and flourish, we need this dual vision of the left and right hemispheres. Remember in chapter 12, when we were thinking about the demands of today's workplace, especially when faced with the risks of bullying and gaslighting, that we needed vision like progressive lenses. We need to focus up close on position (Dr. Jekyll), but we also need to pull back and draw on a wider, more distanced view, that could incorporate the reality of threat (Mr. Hyde). With our two brain hemispheres constructing two visions of our "reality," once again we see the advantage of maintaining both ways of seeing, not just allowing one to take over. We might even think about how Dr. Jekyll parallels our right hemisphere as he cares for others, acts as a healer, is a trusted figure in the community. In contrast, Mr. Hyde parallels an intense version of our left hemisphere, which is about grasping, getting, and feeding regardless of the wider net and needs of others. It's as if the intensity of Mr. Hyde's focus to secure the opportunity to fulfill what he wants is too intense so that all else fades away, including his empathy.

Notably, opportunist left-hemisphere impulses sound comparable to the modus operandi of the Dark Triad at work as described by Babiak and Hare: "Because they do not see others as equals or as having any legitimate claim to resources, psychopaths (as well as some narcissists and Machiavellians) see no need to share resources. In fact, their parasitic, competitive nature drives them to actively siphon off resources from others."[25] You can see why McGilchrist has such a serious concern that the opportunist left hemisphere—with its intensive self-focus and unbridled getting and grasping—has begun to slowly but surely take over our engagement with one another and with our planet. The rise of billionaires who seem rarely satisfied with their insane wealth, disinterested in altruistic or planetary investment, and instead perpetually seek more for themselves perhaps signifies our tilt toward opportunist left-hemisphere dominance.

Empathy and emotional engagement are associated with the altruist right hemisphere's way of envisioning and being in the world. McGilchrist writes "that the capacities that help us, as humans, form bonds with others—empathy, emotional understanding, and so on—which involve a quite different kind of attention paid to the world, are largely right-hemisphere functions."[26]

McGilchrist shows that the left and right hemispheres don't simply *see* the world differently; they live in different worlds. He contrasts the altruist right hemisphere's "breadth and flexibility of attention" with the laser focus of the opportunist left hemisphere. The right "sees things whole, and in their context"; whereas the left "sees things abstracted from context, and broken into parts, from which it then reconstructs a 'whole': something very different."[27] The opportunist left hemisphere's breaking down and building up sounds like one of the textbook arguments for bullying.

In the bullying paradigm, individuals must be broken through violent humiliation with the overarching goal of turning them into a fighting machine, an unbeatable team, or a program that identifies talent. Instead of seeing the whole in context, the opportunist left hemisphere constructs a narrative with the remembering self as we saw in the previous chapter. He is the biggest focus of his own attention, the decent hero of the story, and he "reconstructs" a new whole—very different from what's happening in experience—that serves his future memories. Is it possible that the left hemisphere's approach to the world and way of being is what fuels the lies, or could we say "reconstructions," of bullying, gaslighting, and institutional complicity?

The Left Hemisphere Has Tunnel Vision

The opportunist left brain is unaware of the altruist right brain. In other words, it believes in its own limited view of the world, a view that places it at the center of the universe, the decent hero. When we see the left hemisphere in action, it appears to believe its reconstructions. No amount of fact-checking makes any difference because glaring "lies" about the way the right hemisphere sees the world are the reassembled parts of a whole, designed to make sense to the narrow focus of the left hemisphere. For this reason, McGilchrist is profoundly worried about the way in which the left hemisphere now dominates how we see and live. He depicts the left hemisphere as "more conscious, more willed, more deliberate" in keeping with its "need to influence and manipulate, as well as its role in re-presenting experience."[28] The opportunist left hemisphere uses reversal, substitution, and shortcuts to re-present a simple, coherent spectacle to replace the far more complex and authentic experience seen by the altruist right hemisphere. The opportunist substitutes illusion for reality.

Our case studies show that oftentimes the workplace protects the vision and resulting conduct of the opportunist left hemisphere. We saw again and again that conscious, deliberate, willful attacks were covered up and enabled by the institution. Those who sought to influence and manipulate were empowered through institutional complicity. The use of lies to re-present experience in such a way that it served the perpetrator resulted in bullying and gaslighting objectified targets, where they suddenly found themselves given fabricated roles in the perpetrator's drama. With the institutional audience accepting this new "reality," broken down and built back up—in the image of the perpetrator as the decent hero and the targets as the deranged enemies—the opportunist left hemisphere obviously has taken a dominant role.

McGilchrist notes that "individual self-belief" is "preferentially treated by the left hemisphere," whereas bonding and empathy are "preferentially treated by the right hemisphere."[29] The traumatic shock bullying targets experience makes more sense when we realize that they are operating in the right-hemisphere world of bonding and empathy and are thus ill-prepared for the opportunist's individual self-belief. The altruists operate in a world where individuals are *not* objectified into parts to be moved around with a "gamelike fascination" to serve the grasping, getting, and feeding needs of the opportunist left hemisphere.

The left hemisphere is just as vital as the right. It plays a needed role. The left hemisphere is not "bad" or negative, just like the stress hormone cortisol is not "bad" or negative. Both are critical functions of a healthy brain, but when our society tilts into unbalance, privileges one hemisphere over the other, allows cortisol into our brains and bodies far too frequently due to toxic stress, then it's helpful to understand what's happening and change course. To make this clearer, McGilchrist charts the way we live in the world via the right hemisphere and contrasts it with the left.

Our brains have two distinct ways of envisioning and operating within the world that "bring two different worlds into being." The right hemisphere brings into being a world that we know most fully from Indigenous peoples across the globe where "we experience—the live, complex, embodied, world of individual, always unique beings, forever in flux, a net of interdependencies, forming and reforming wholes, a world with which we are deeply connected."[30] The altruist right hemisphere positions humans as unique beings in a deeply connected community where nature is their shared home. This approach is obviously the opposite of the command-and-control model normalized in many workplaces. The way the altruist right brain envisions work relationships explains the traumatic shock of targets who had histories with the workplace community where they saw others as "unique beings" and assumed that they were known as unique beings. Instead, their individual track records were erased and silenced as they threatened the overarching story of the decent hero who only displays integrity. When we look at the opportunist way of being in the world, we can see how this unjust erasure and silencing can occur.

POSITIONS AND PARTS VERSUS A HOLISTIC PARTICIPATION

McGilchrist explains that via the opportunist left hemisphere "we 'experience' our experience in a special way: a 're-presented' version of it, containing now static, separable, bounded, but essentially fragmented entities, grouped into classes, on which predictions can be based."[31] Some workplaces constructed on hierarchies do not consider individuals, or the rights of unique beings, when bullying is reported; instead, they envision "fragmented entities" to which they assign a cost-benefit analysis. This privileging of classes or positions—the higher, the less likely to be held accountable—serves the command-and-control management strategy that seeks a predictable outcome rather than seeing situations or individuals as unique.

The reality of the experiencing self is overwritten by a "re-presented" version narrated by the remembering self whose focus is lasered in on herself and strives to keep herself as the decent hero of the story. This version does not *feel* guilt or anguish at the harm and injustice done to others or for that matter, the harm and degradation done to the environment. Instead of a deep connection to the community and a natural web of interdependencies experienced by the right hemisphere, the left hemisphere narrows its focus for the necessary acts of grasping, getting, and feeding.

This kind of attention isolates, fixes and makes each thing explicit by bringing it under the spotlight of attention. In doing so it renders

343

things inert, mechanical, lifeless. But it also enables us for the first time to know, and consequently to learn and to make things. This gives us power.[32]

Few of us would want to give up on knowledge, learning, and the act of creativity or the power that accompanies it. But we must be wary of the tendency of these impulses to overwhelm the living, breathing, changing connections we have with one another, with humanity as a whole, and with the planet itself. We can now more deeply understand why power is in an inverse relationship with empathy. When the world and everything in it—including others—become lifeless objects, it's easy to manipulate them and maneuver them, have power over them and control them. The attention on oneself, on one's opportunities and version of reality, does not leave space and time for empathy, emotions, or ethics.

The anguish the altruist right hemisphere feels for environmental degradation can easily be ignored or dismissed by the left-hemisphere opportunist. The suffering of others causes emotional pain for the right-hemisphere altruist whereas the opportunist does *not* feel this pain and instead channels its energy into preserving the heroic narrative at all costs. If this requires lies and manipulation, so be it. The right hemisphere's deep sense of connection is the left's strategic sense of detachment.

The Opportunist Strives to Control the Narrative

In the previous chapter, Kahneman contrasted the incompatible world-views of the remembering self and the experiencing self. As we have noted, these two selves parallel the storytelling approaches of the opportunist and the altruist. When institutional complicity occurs, we see the opportunist and the remembering self at work. The narrative that dominates is one where the leader sees the story of his leadership and legacy (future memories) endangered by those who report abuses and therefore eliminates, silences, erases the voice of the targets or whistle-blowers. Let's look at this impulse to control the narrative from the perspective of the opportunist.

McGilchrist explains that the opportunist left hemisphere's modus operandi is to "step outside the flow of experience." Kahneman would rephrase this as stepping outside the flow of the "experiencing self." It doesn't matter to the opportunist or remembering self that truth is being sacrificed for the consistency and clarity required to position himself as the decent hero. This worldview, this narrative's job, is to "re-present the world in a form that is less truthful, but apparently clearer, and therefore cast in a form which is more useful for manipulation of the world and one another."[33] If command and control are the motivators, then tampering with the truth is expected, especially when it's "more useful for manipulation." Perhaps funds have been misappropriated, safety requirements ignored, environmental harm covered up, negligence swept under the rug, bullying dismissed, the truth of these abuses does *not* matter to the opportunist; the successful manipulation does. When you're dealing with someone operating from the left hemisphere, he might be appalled that you called into question his coherent version of events. Speaking up about the gaps between his self-serving narration of what is being remembered and what was actually experienced may position you as a threat. Suddenly, there is a lot of emotion—outrage and a desire for vengeance. Your questions quickly are re-presented (the work of the left hemisphere) as a "witch hunt." The discrepancies you've exposed in his narrow vision of the "truth" are no longer the focus. The spotlight has turned full force on the one casting doubt who is quickly positioned as the enemy. Your experience, your track record, your emotions, your health, your rights even, do not matter in the left hemisphere's version of "reality."

The opportunist side of the brain, manifested in our remembering self, exists in a world McGilchrist details as "explicit, abstracted, compartmentalized, fragmented, static." In short, he calls it "essentially lifeless."[34] When this side of the brain dominates, unique individuals don't matter. They're easily abstracted into categories like their position, or by an identifying number. They become known by the amount of compensation they will receive once dismissed. The job is not done by living, breathing others. It's done by "faceless bureaucrats." What is the payoff for the loss in humanity, empathy, and connection? Power. As McGilchrist says, from "this world we feel detached, but in relation to it we are powerful." As we have seen, the payoff is power. The remembering self wants to position himself as the hero of the story, and heroes are powerful. The remembering self convinces everyone that he must make tough decisions to save the institution, but the institution is a substitute for himself. Think about it. The institution is the realm of the altruist right hemisphere whose view pans out to encompass the whole, who cares about the complex, dynamic, community of unique people who are part of an even larger always-changing global reality. There's no spotlight on the "hero," especially not one leading the whole institution into high-risk territory by enabling the lies of bullying, gaslighting, and institutional complicity. The opportunist left hemisphere is gambling away the institution to preserve the leader's future memories.

How would this workplace crisis be different if the altruist right hemisphere of the brain dealt with it? McGilchrist describes the brain's right side as being developed so that we could experience things as "*present* to us in all their embodied particularity, with all their changeability and impermanence, and their interconnectedness, as part of a whole which is forever in flux."[35] The experiencing self does not need to control the narrative. The altruist right hemisphere allows for the incoherent, complex, changing truth to simply unfold. There is no need to silence reports of abuses because they are part of an imperfect, unstable reality. There is no impulse to command and control. The altruist is not on a pedestal looking down at the world; he is a part of it. He gives up the power of the opportunist left hemisphere and in return, he belongs to the whole and is liberated through connection. McGilchrist writes, "In this world we, too, feel connected to what we experience, part of that whole, not confined in subjective isolation from a world that is viewed as objective."[36] The right hemisphere is the realm of Martin Buber's "I and Thou."

When we treat one another and our planet as objects, we gain in power, but we lose connection. Providing extensive research, Stephen Porges and Susan Carter show that connection is fundamental to brain and body health. Unhealthy relationships to others and to our natural world may increase a heroic, even godlike sense of selfhood, but the objectifying force of our thoughts and actions can also make us and the planet profoundly ill—physically and mentally ill. As we have seen, objectifying others is a mark of the Dark Triad. Objectifying others is the mark of psychopathology. When the lies of bullying and gaslighting lead to institutional complicity, the opportunist left hemisphere of the brain is dominating. Just as violence is easily done to others and to our global environment, so, too, is it done to facts and truth.

THE OPPORTUNIST CONFABULATES

Throughout the case studies and in the different neuroscientific approaches, we have seen how frequently the lies of bullying, gaslighting, and institutional complicity hinge on substitutions and reversals that hide what's going on. In the work of the secret author, lies are substituted for the facts, the offender is reversed with the victim(s), social agreements are manipulated so that one category (tools) is used to cover up another (murder weapons), a gift (wooden horse offering to the goddess) is used to cover up another (vehicle to transport murderous soldiers), and positions of power, credibility, and social standing cover up the harmful individual beneath (wolf in sheep's clothing, snake in a suit, false prophet). All these reversals hinge on substitution, and many of them relate to brain functions. The brain substitutes an easy route for a difficult one. It employs an intuitive shortcut rather than deliberating, gathering information, and reasoning fully. It mistakes the position for the person. It can't even *see* the person because it only focuses on the position. It mistakes repetition, all caps, bolding, or bright ink for facts. It puts a halo on attractive individuals as if their appearance makes them trustworthy. Once it has made a decision, it refuses further information that is contradictory. It normalizes or habituates everything and anything, even the craven cruelty of psychopaths. Those who want power dismiss the experiencing self and replace it with a remembering self who writes a coherent story about future memories, positioning themselves as the decent hero.

In this context, we are not surprised that the left hemisphere doesn't hesitate to fabricate details to fill the gaps in its own understanding. McGilchrist refers to this substitution as "confabulation," which occurs when "the brain, not being able to recall something, rather than admit to a gap in its understanding, makes up something plausible, that appears consistent, to fill it."[37] For instance, if due to injury the right hemisphere cannot provide "the contextual information that would help it make sense of experience," the left hemisphere begins to confabulate. It substitutes its own version of the experience. It "makes up a story, and lacking insight, appears completely convinced by it."[38] McGilchrist notes that even when there isn't a brain lesion, amnesia, or other neurological issue, "the left hemisphere exhibits a strong tendency to confabulate: it thinks it knows something, recognises something, which it doesn't, a tendency that may be linked to its lack of ability to discriminate unique cases from the generalised categories into which it places them."[39] We have seen the way that the left-hemisphere opportunist reverses the categories perpetrator and victim regardless of reports by unique victims to the contrary. We've noted the ways in which less powerful categories are sacrificed to more powerful ones in the workplace when abuses are reported, especially when the experience being shared endangers the master narrative of the most powerful individual whose remembering self prioritizes the category "hero" for herself. It's a shock to the individuals who believe that they are "unique cases," and they are experienced as individuals, but that is a right-hemisphere altruist vision that can be replaced quickly by the confabulating of the left hemisphere.

If leaders, managers, HR, and employees do not know that the brain may well substitute fiction for fact or create a false story from the opportunist left hemisphere that lacks context, doesn't privilege relationships, is narrowly focused by its own grasping, getting, and feeding, you can well imagine that targets and whistle-blowers will be at risk. We've seen how the brain can become careless or distracted by noise and chatter when it's not going to the brain gym regularly (chapter 9). We already noted the brain's inability to understand a concept or apply an accurate emotion if it lacks the right language (chapter 10). We learned that the brain is very susceptible to stress and can slide into fight, flight, and freeze, which blocks it from thinking clearly and opens itself up to being easily manipulated (chapter 11). We've seen how the brain habituates even heinous behavior and can trust a falsehood as the truth by something as simple as repetition (chapter 12). We've discovered that our brains try to save resources by using shortcuts that lead us to make serious mistakes that could be avoided by applying the metacognition of our slow-thinking brain (chapter 13). In this chapter on lateralization, we are being shown that we run the risk of a deadly imbalance when our opportunist left hemisphere takes over and drowns out the bigger vision of connection that we have with the altruist right hemisphere.

Factor in all these brain vulnerabilities, then imagine how the Dark Triad capitalize on them. The lies of bullying and gaslighting destabilize the target, and a brain that's unbalanced truly struggles with what's real and what's fake, the facts and falsehoods, who to trust and who to fear. Into that chaos stride the Dark Triad who promise to save everyone by putting on a fictional mask that positions them as the saviors of all except the rivals, losers, and enemies.

WHEN POSITION COVERS UP PERSON

We have examined the way our brains make serious errors when we substitute the position or category for the person or thing itself. We used the example of the Anglican priest: as a position and category, our left hemisphere can bank on this partial knowledge and make decisions accordingly. It can decide whether it's safe for children and vulnerable adults to be with this position or category. Because the opportunist can only envision category, the answer is yes, he is safe. The institution, the Anglican Church, can protect the priest and defend him on these grounds. Parents can choose to hand their children over to his caretaking also using the left hemisphere of the brain. As history and continuing stories attest, all those decisions were far too often serious mistakes without the larger picture supplied by the altruist right hemisphere. McGilchrist makes clear the way in which the left only sees categories whereas the right sees distinct individuals.

> *The right hemisphere presents individual, unique instances of things and individual, familiar, objects, where the left hemisphere represents categories of things, and generic, non-specific objects. . . . In fact it is precisely its capacity for holistic processing that enables the right hemisphere to recognise individuals. Individuals are, after all, Gestalt wholes: that face, that voice, that gait, that sheer "quiddity" of the person or thing, defying analysis into parts.*[40]

Individuals who were subjected to the lies of bullying and gaslighting could not believe their institution positioned them as a category that could be dismissed. They went from being human beings to being dehumanized. They were individuals with track records before they spoke up; afterward, they were categorized as threats, reduced to employee numbers for HR to sort out. Their quiddity, their inherent nature, their essence as holistic beings was simply erased. Leaders, managers, and HR have an immense advantage in not succumbing to the limited worldview of the opportunist left hemisphere. It is what throws your risk assessment out the window because it tells you the position (Dr. Jekyll) is all that matters while the person (Mr. Hyde) is irrelevant. Likewise, it tells you that your dedicated, talented, truth teller needs to be positioned as a threat, and the unique person (Montgomery, Carle, Wilson, Macfarlane) is irrelevant. Both those workplace scenarios are tragic for individuals and for the institution.

In Montgomery's case, he was reduced to a student number. It is easy to put people in the out-group when they are *not* individuals. It's easy to see them as happy majority versus unhappy minority. The minority can be stripped of their individuality so quickly it results in traumatic shock. But think about it: we are seeing a shift in focus from the altruist right hemisphere of the brain to the opportunist left. We're moving from empathy and the "interconnectedness of things" to grasping, getting, and feeding.[41] McGilchrist sees our Western world as marching down this well-trod path into the world conjured up by the opportunist where the altruist, with its connection to all others and the planet, is seen as irrelevant.

This is a world where there's a war on truth that becomes a post-truth era because the left-hemisphere opportunist does not care about the truth. Spectacle, confabulation, illusion, alternative truths, fictional masks, lies, manipulations are the name of the game played with psychopathic fascination. Our planetary home is simply seen as an object to exploit and destroy if it fuels the driving need of the opportunist to get, grasp, and feed. This is a society where whole categories of people are seen as exploitable and expendable, dismissed with the easily applied category of rival, loser, enemy who are positioned as threats. This reversal or substitution is one of the most sickening and cruel as it results in war, exclusion, suffering, and potentially death for whole populaces.

When the altruist right hemisphere cries out about this crisis of imbalance, the left hemisphere cannot hear it, denies it made a sound, scorns it for weakness. The opportunist left hemisphere wants power, which silences others including the right hemisphere of the brain, which knows we are part of a complex, ever-changing, miraculous, connected whole. The altruist right hemisphere knows that we are interdependent both on one another's and on the planet's health. It willingly sacrifices power and the desire to be a hero to recognize the essence of diversity that creates a whole world from flora and fauna and humanity, the planet and the galaxy.

Notably, McGilchrist calls the right hemisphere "an anomaly detector."[42] This is an interesting way to think about whistle-blowers. It's as if they notice something's amiss with Dr. Jekyll, something's not right with the accounting, the technology seems off and might be unsafe, the way a perpetrator is acting reveals a worrisome problem or trend, the tendency of others to look away suggests a pending crisis. These resources of the altruist right hemisphere may feel like they endanger the party line and threaten the institution's master narrative, but it is better to hear from within that an anomaly has been detected than wait for it to blow up publicly. The altruist right hemisphere leads us to walk in others' shoes. It keeps us from asserting our own point of view and makes us listen closely to someone else. It opens the door to debate, dialogue, and diverse points of view.[43] The altruist right hemisphere has self-awareness, empathy, identification with others, and sensitivity to intersubjective processes. Notice what a richer, more in-depth, and more greatly nuanced vision this produces of reality than the rigid categories that rule the opportunist left hemisphere's vision. When the lies of bullying and gaslighting surface, this more complex view will better serve leaders, managers, and HR regardless of the impulse to assert command and control, generate a coherent narrative, and reestablish the status quo. It's truly concerning that the left hemisphere can lead us away from this more encompassing view that the right hemisphere offers.

Tilting to the Opportunist Model

McGilchrist summarizes the seductive world of the opportunist. "First, the left hemisphere view is designed to aid you in grabbing stuff. Its purpose is utility and its evolutionary adaptation lies in the service of grasping and amassing 'things.'"[44] The intense spotlight of focus, the specialty of the opportunist, is needed for getting and feeding. It's an intense survival impulse, but when it rules unchecked, when it gets out of balance with the altruist right hemisphere, then we are in a workplace and in a world that normalizes abuses of all kinds. We see dictators and billionaires honored and adored as they grasp and amass "things." McGilchrist applies his in-depth knowledge from neuropsychological research to world history, philosophy, art, and poetry, and his insights apply in striking ways to today's workplace, especially one grappling with the lies of bullying, gaslighting, and institutional complicity:

> the decline of civilisation has been associated, not just with more left hemisphere ways of thinking, but appropriately with forms of military or economic imperialism, and a consequent overextension of administration, a coarsening of values, and a failure of vitality, vision and integrity.[45]

The workplaces that set out to crush Montgomery, Carle, Wilson, and Macfarlane demonstrate a failure of vitality, vision, and integrity. As McGilchrist expresses, the left-hemisphere vision of the world can dominate an individual brain, just as it can dominate a populace. So, to talk about this way of thinking, deciding, and acting as infectious, as influential, as developing into an opportunist model of leadership is realistic. When a coarsening of values enters an individual, institution, or nation it puts its energy into categories, not individuals. It objectifies others and the world itself. It creates what Hedges ominously called an "Empire of Illusion."

As Kahneman showed us, and McGilchrist reinforces, "the left hemisphere view offers simple answers. Its mode of thinking prizes consistency above all, and claims to offer the same mechanistic models to explain everything that exists."[46] This helps us understand the need for "overextension of administration," what Amos Guiora calls an "army of enablers"; and they, too, have lost individuality to the point of becoming faceless bureaucrats. When asked in court why they hurt innocent men, women, and children, they simply respond, "I was obeying orders."

McGilchrist says that the way the opportunist left hemisphere thinks is common to "implementers of bureaucratic systems." And when "this sort of thinking encounters a problem in reconciling apparent irreconcilables . . . it simply denies that one element or the other exists. That's very convenient."[47] We saw this denial in the case studies where Montgomery, Carle, Wilson, and McFarlane all found their irreconcilable track records—that documented their trustworthy, talented, exceptional pasts—denied as irrelevant, erasable. We saw it where a wife denies that her husband could ever be Mr. Hyde because she only knows him as Dr. Jekyll; a mother cannot fathom that her entrepreneurial son would ever utter an "untruth" when he's lied so much, he's now in jail; a hospital cannot imagine that a nurse trained to save lives would ever take lives. These convenient denials can devastate targets. Regardless, the opportunist left hemisphere is adept at denial.

The opportunist left hemisphere is more vocal than the right, and it's very interested in constructing a coherent master narrative and issuing it. McGilchrist writes, "The left hemisphere's world view is easier to articulate. The left hemisphere is the speaking hemisphere: the right hemisphere has literally no voice."[48] This division echoes Kahneman's depiction of the vocal remembering self and the silent experiencing self. This ability of the opportunist—whose narrow focus not only is for grasping, getting, and feeding but also shines the spotlight of attention on its own heroic self, to articulate and confabulate and tell stories—makes it adept at drowning out the more complex, empathic, individual, emotionally and naturally interconnected realms of the altruist right hemisphere. It's challenging to bring interconnectedness and a sense of deep connection into the world of mechanistic categories. It is easy to take the altruist right-hemisphere side of the story and simply suppress it. The opportunist left hemisphere's vision is self-reflexive, like a mirror. The world it envisions is meant to reflect its own heroic status, and it feels nothing in its hermetically sealed chamber when others are shattered, and the world goes up in flames.

According to McGilchrist, "it is as if the left hemisphere, which creates a sort of self-reflexive virtual world, has blocked off the available exits, the ways out of the hall of mirrors, into a reality which the right hemisphere could enable us to understand."[49] The blocked exits from the hall of mirrors worry McGilchrist and should worry all of us. We need to fight back against this tendency of our brain to objectify, create categories, make mistakes, and fall for manipulations. If our workplace becomes like the opportunist left-hemisphere vision—what McGilchrist calls "the enclosed system of the self-conscious mind"—then we lose our bearings. We get so good at articulating the coherent master narrative that everything's fine, bullying doesn't happen here, there are no victims, no mistakes were made, no one got hurt, safety is a given, I'm the decent hero in a story about integrity, and so on, that we lose a way to discern between truth and lies. We start filling irreconcilable gaps with confabulation. We become accustomed to reversals, substitutions, and reducing individuals to categories to find the least expensive and most self-aggrandizing way to solve problems. We take the easy brain way out.

We focus on keeping ourselves at the center of the story as a decent hero, forgetting about the painful, humbling truths of experience and instead, shining our spotlight on our own future memories. In this way, we put ourselves individually and institutionally at risk of becoming divided, a Dr. Jekyll frantically covering up Mr. Hyde. What does this feel like? McGilchrist says, "An increasingly mechanistic, fragmented, decontextualized world, marked by unwarranted optimism, mixed with paranoia and a feeling of emptiness, has come about, reflecting, I believe, the unopposed action of a dysfunctional left hemisphere."[50] While the opportunist left hemisphere concentrates on preserving the future memories of her legacy, her experiencing self must tune out the youth mental health crisis that tells the *whole story* of the future, not just the fabricated tale that positions her as a decent hero. Her future memories must tune out environmental degradation that tells an encompassing story of the actual future. Her future memories especially need to tune out suffering individuals from bullied and gaslit targets all the way to whole populaces who are targeted by military attacks. Do you think youth today are so unwell because they feel trapped in an increasingly mechanistic, fragmented, decontextualized world, marked by unwarranted optimism, mixed with paranoia and a feeling of emptiness? Is that a description of how the online virtual world has replaced the actual world of organic, holistic, contextualized environments, nuanced by the deeper emotions of suffering and melancholy, mixed with feelings of security and fulfillment? The world we have created sounds hellish when the world we are guardians of is heavenly.

It's a lot of work to be a guardian, to fight for the altruistic right hemisphere's vision, but the encompassing vision of connection and community returns us to one another and to nature. In contrast, the opportunist left hemisphere is seductive in that it provides so much power, the power to be a totalitarian dictator in an objectified, fragmented world, where one's own optimistic happiness trumps the paranoia and emptiness of all others. Heartless conduct on repeat, mechanistic approach to life that demands others act like robots, eroded empathy, are all symptoms of psychopathology. The opportunist left hemisphere's default to language and cognition parallels its lack of empathy and emotion. It isn't a balanced or healthy brain.

McGilchrist worries that "as a society, we are becoming more like individuals with right hemisphere deficits."[51] We are drowning in toxic positivity and look away to ignore many who are slipping beneath rising water.

THE OPPORTUNIST DIVIDES TO CONQUER

We learned from Baron-Cohen (chapter 7) that individuals who present with borderline personality disorder, narcissism, and psychopathology suffer from empathy erosion. They become split personalities that we have used Dr. Jekyll and Mr. Hyde to describe as a kind of shorthand. With the research and insights of Iain McGilchrist, we've gone through an uncomfortable process of examining our own potential as an individual and as a workplace community—or even a populace and civilization—to develop erosion or deficits in our right hemisphere. This means that we are losing ground as the respectful healer and caregiver Dr. Jekyll and succumbing to the grasping, getting, and feeding impulses of Mr. Hyde. When we recall our case studies, it is apparent that too many workplaces enable this potentially destructive approach when leadership is not balanced by the altruist right hemisphere, which is empathic, deeply connected to the planet, and cares greatly for our social bonds with one another.

We flourish as holistic beings that attain balance or homeostasis, according to Stephen and Seth Porges (chapter 11). Before we look more closely at the implications of erosion or deficits of our altruist hemisphere, as it is dominated by our opportunist hemisphere, let us take a moment to remember Merzenich's research that teaches us that if we have neurological deficits, we are able to repair them (chapter 9). If we have eroded empathy, if we have a workplace tipping into believing the destructive lies of bullying and the manipulative lies of gaslighting, which we cover up through institutional complicity, we can turn that ship around. Neuroplasticity means that we can work our way back to balance and homeostasis by putting in time at the brain gym, learning how our brains work, being vigilant about shortcuts (chapter 13), and not taking the easy way out (chapter 12). We can discover why and how we're blind to betrayal (chapter 5). We can build nuanced vocabularies to articulate emotion concepts for actual gifts and manipulative gifts (chapter 10). We can put on progressive lenses so as not to fall for the position and fail to see the person (chapter 12).

What's striking in McGilchrist's description of right-hemisphere deficits is how it sounds like someone who tells pathological lies, at the same time as it sounds like someone who has been gaslit. When we factor in that the Dark Triad often come from backgrounds of abuse and neglect, we see once again the contagion of the divided self and how much the true risk is the way it infects others. We would be wise to protect ourselves and our institutions from this insidious illness at all costs. McGilchrist examines "the fragmentation of what should be experienced as a whole—the mental separation of components of experience that would ordinarily be processed together, again suggesting a right hemisphere problem."[52] From a psychological perspective, McGilchrist depicts dissociation, a profound fragmentation of the self, which can put one's life at risk. The opportunist sees with a narrow, intense focus necessary for survival, but that can become what we referred to as tunnel vision; it could also be described as dissociation from one's holistic self and one's place in a complex web of connections. When we suffer shattering, fragmentation, or dissociation, we lose a sense of wholeness, the domain of the altruist right hemisphere. Along with not being able to see the big picture, the one where we are part of an empathic, caring social community, at home on a planet where we, with all other species belong, we lose homeostasis, the ability to balance, critical for our ability to repair and attain optimum health.

McGilchrist continues in his description of the impact of fragmentation: "Core features of dissociation include amnesia for autobiographical information, identity disturbances, depersonalisation and derealisation."[53] Is this why the track records of targets are ignored through institutional amnesia? Targets' autobiographical past—specifically, as they worked for the institution—is simply missing in the equation. The perpetrators have clear identity disturbances; by the time they are done with the targets, they, too, are often infected. Health is gone, and in its place, we have mental and physical illness. Carle could no longer see herself in the mirror, and she notes that none of her past supporters could either. Wilson says he felt "crazy" and suffered suicidal ideation, a clear indication of "depersonalization." Macfarlane's life was put at risk due to her mother's negligence and bullying, overlaid on multiple sexual assaults, being repeatedly exposed to her partner's violence only to find herself in a workplace that was covering up and enabling sexual assault by a law professor. Toxic abuse flourishes in our world despite the attempts of "toxic positivity" to assure us that all is well. Montgomery, Carle, Wilson, and Macfarlane survived fragmentation by never letting go of their altruistic right hemisphere's knowledge of their holistic selves.

When you have been gaslit by bullying, gaslighting, and institutional complicity, your own feelings and sense of reality seem unreal, as if they don't belong to you. Your unique identity slips away. The world beyond also recedes as you can't tell whether the lights are up or dimming, whether there's a sound in the attic or it's silent, are you stealing from others or are you being robbed. As you lose trust in your erased past and yourself, you become more dependent on the version of yourself constructed on what you may have once recognized as lies, through silencing and confabulation. I speak from the experiencing self.

McGilchrist documents that these neurological responses are identical to subjects who have "right hemisphere damage." These patients describe "a change in, and a foreignness of, the self, which is disconnected from the world, a loss of feeling of belonging in the world. At times they report having become insensible automata, puppets, or mere spectators, devoid of feelings and cut off from the surrounding world."[54] The target of bullying and gaslighting is much like a puppet with the perpetrator pulling the strings. Nuanced feelings disappear when one is being subjected to the lies of bullying and gaslighting. Targets find themselves in a state of fight, flight, freeze, and fawn; homeostasis a distant dream. Emotion concepts collapse into survival responses such as "under threat," "humiliated," "at risk," "ostracized," and so on. The brain's ability to gather more information, seek justice, look at the complexity, draw on the deliberation of the slow brain is met with the shocking substitutions, reversals, and intuitive shortcuts of the fast brain. One wonders whether deficits in the altruist right hemisphere have contributed to burnout, a disengagement with work, a lack of motivation, and a general malaise, not to mention a youth mental health crisis of epic proportions that swerves from violence to numbness.

We have more than enough brain science to fix these crises.

Institutions that walk away from the outdated model for handling bullying and gaslighting with institutional complicity will pave the way for workplaces that prioritize brain health and balance. They will educate their employees on neuroplasticity and make everyone accountable for carving out thirty minutes a day for brain fitness. They will hold training sessions and workshops on developing nuanced emotion concepts that are unique to their community and reinforce their values. They'll teach employees about our brains' threat detection system and the way our bodies and brains react to stress with fight, flight, freeze, and fawn. They will commit to an emphasis on connection and coregulation—to establish the health benefits of "socioception"—that will naturally follow. They will steer clear of myopic vision that only sees Dr. Jekyll and ignores Mr. Hyde. They will be wary of the brain's tendency to use shortcuts and take the time for slow thinking. They will never let the opportunist left hemisphere ignore and overwhelm the altruist right hemisphere. Included in this community, listened to and respected, will be whistle-blowers. They'll be understood as allies, not enemies of the institution. These workplaces, as documented in research, will attain greater productivity and profitability.

These lessons will lead to workplaces that champion homeostasis and support those who are stressed and need extra intervention and care. A foundation of safety for brain and body will lead to innovation and creativity from dishabituation entrepreneurs who observe workplace minefields and produce ways to navigate around them or send in the sappers to dismantle them. The future workplace will strive to avoid the power-fueled self as decent hero, along with avoiding command-and-control leadership models that default to the intuitive shortcuts of fast thinking. Instead, leaders, managers, and HR will strive to do slow thinking, gather the information needed, deliberate, debate, and discuss to ensure a fair and healthy outcome for the institution and those it employs. The healthy workplaces of the future will strive for a balance in left and right hemisphere approaches. They will not let the left hemisphere dominate and drown out the vitally important right hemisphere. The opportunist has its place, but it will not be allowed to usurp the altruist who cares about connection, community, and the planet.

Notes

1. Iain McGilchrist, *The Master and His Emissary: The Divided Brain and the Making of the Western World* (New Haven, CT, and London: Yale University Press, 2009), xxi.
2. McGilchrist, *The Master and His Emissary*, 21.
3. Paul Babiak and Robert Hare, *Snakes in Suits: When Psychopaths Go to Work* (New York: Harper, 2006), 128.
4. Chris Hedges, *Empire of Illusion: The End of Literacy and the Triumph of Spectacle* (Toronto: Random House, 2010), 33.
5. McGilchrist, *The Master and His Emissary*, 85.
6. McGilchrist, *The Master and His Emissary*, 22.
7. McGilchrist, *The Master and His Emissary*, 22.
8. McGilchrist, *The Master and His Emissary*, 93.
9. McGilchrist, *The Master and His Emissary*, 236.
10. McGilchrist, *The Master and His Emissary*, 93.
11. Babiak and Hare, *Snakes in Suits*, 46.
12. McGilchrist, *The Master and His Emissary*, 85.
13. McGilchrist, *The Master and His Emissary*, 85.
14. McGilchrist, *The Master and His Emissary*, 85.
15. McGilchrist, *The Master and His Emissary*, 93.

16. McGilchrist, *The Master and His Emissary*, 59.
17. McGilchrist, *The Master and His Emissary*, 61.
18. McGilchrist, *The Master and His Emissary*, 71.
19. McGilchrist, *The Master and His Emissary*, 28.
20. McGilchrist, *The Master and His Emissary*, 25.
21. McGilchrist, *The Master and His Emissary*, 25.
22. McGilchrist, *The Master and His Emissary*, 28.
23. McGilchrist, *The Master and His Emissary*, 28.
24. McGilchrist, *The Master and His Emissary*, 25.
25. Babiak and Hare, *Snakes in Suits*, 250.
26. McGilchrist, *The Master and His Emissary*, 28.
27. McGilchrist, *The Master and His Emissary*, 28.
28. McGilchrist, *The Master and His Emissary*, 62.
29. McGilchrist, *The Master and His Emissary*, 63.
30. McGilchrist, *The Master and His Emissary*, 31.
31. McGilchrist, *The Master and His Emissary*, 31.
32. McGilchrist, *The Master and His Emissary*, 31.
33. McGilchrist, *The Master and His Emissary*, 93.
34. McGilchrist, *The Master and His Emissary*, 93.
35. McGilchrist, *The Master and His Emissary*, 93.
36. McGilchrist, *The Master and His Emissary*, 93.
37. McGilchrist, *The Master and His Emissary*, 81.
38. McGilchrist, *The Master and His Emissary*, 81.
39. McGilchrist, *The Master and His Emissary*, 81.
40. McGilchrist, *The Master and His Emissary*, 51.
41. McGilchrist, *The Master and His Emissary*, 57.
42. McGilchrist, *The Master and His Emissary*, 52.
43. McGilchrist, *The Master and His Emissary*, 57.
44. McGilchrist, *The Master and His Emissary*, xxii.
45. McGilchrist, *The Master and His Emissary*, xxii.
46. McGilchrist, *The Master and His Emissary*, xxiii.
47. McGilchrist, *The Master and His Emissary*, xxiii.
48. McGilchrist, *The Master and His Emissary*, xxiii.
49. McGilchrist, *The Master and His Emissary*, 6.
50. McGilchrist, *The Master and His Emissary*, 6.
51. McGilchrist, *The Master and His Emissary*, xxii.
52. McGilchrist, *The Master and His Emissary*, 236.
53. McGilchrist, *The Master and His Emissary*, 236.
54. McGilchrist, *The Master and His Emissary*, 236.

Conclusion

An Ounce of Prevention Is Worth a Pound of Cure

THE WORKPLACE NEEDS TO MAKE A SIGNIFICANT SHIFT FROM IDLING AT trauma informed; it's time to become trauma preventative. Why do we ignore how our brains have created a dysfunctional culture that normalizes the telling of lies, makes manipulation seem like a triumph, and looks the other way when human and environmental suffering is exploding? How can we look ourselves in the mirror when our youth populations have succumbed to widespread, profound mental illness, including a shocking rise in suicides? We have reached a moment of crisis, which demands that we change or continue at our peril. Instead of pouring more and more resources into trying to repair traumatic damage, which is overwhelming our doctors, nurses, first responders, and mental health professionals, we can harness our neuroplasticity and psychological research to bring about healthy change. It costs a lot less than trying to pick up the shattered lives that the lies of bullying, gaslighting, and institutional complicity cause.

Montgomery put the bullying and gaslighting he suffered at school in the rearview mirror. He walked away. Although going to University of Oregon was a cathartic way to start fresh with a community constructed on truth, it was not enough to repair the scars. They were not on his body; they were on his brain.[1]

Institutional complicity left him with nightmares, anxiety, depression becoming so severe at one point that he went to the mental health center at the university to seek counseling. He had worked previously with an excellent sports psychologist who had unpacked for him the debilitating fear he had been forced to cope with while trying to play his sport, but his PTSD from institutional betrayal, being labeled a liar for telling the truth, was far bigger than the basketball court. When those in positions of power, credibility, and social standing drop their masks and show you manipulative, inhumane faces, it's not easy to recover, especially when you're young.

The university mental health center ensured that he was not suicidal, but it had such an enormous backlog of college students needing mental health support that he couldn't get an appointment with a counselor for six months. That shocked me. Thirty years earlier, when I was working for my PhD at the University of Toronto, after the abuse I had endured at the hands of teachers for years, I asked for help and was seen by psychiatrists that week. There was no backlog, no waiting list. I was not suicidal, but I had an eating disorder and was cutting—not exactly crisis level, but the point being, the mental health system wasn't overwhelmed. Our vision hadn't been reduced to the mirror of a phone, drawing us to gaze at Facebook, Snapchat, TikTok, Instagram, X with their rampant manipulation, exploitation, and disinformation. We hadn't entered the unregulated hall of mirrors that replaced authentic communication with algorithms. Lying publicly, repeatedly, had not yet become normal for society's leaders. We had not yet devolved into a war on truth. Children weren't having their empathy narrowed into myopia. Most young brains weren't confused, overwhelmed, anxiety ridden, distracted, and depressed. Suicide wasn't occurring at shockingly rapid rates.

Let's recall the gut-wrenching statistic from the CDC: from 2000 to 2018 youth suicide in those aged ten to twenty-four increased 57 percent.[2] If you found psychiatrist Iain McGilchrist's concerns alarming, this statistic should make his serious concerns a priority. These young people are the new employees. They will create the future workforce, and they are not well. They are suffering in life-threatening ways, and their illness is reaching pandemic proportions. We need to turn this ship around, and the adults, the leaders, managers, and HR can do so.

Preventing Trauma

An important first step is to become trauma informed, but getting informed about a global pandemic won't stop it. Recognizing the symptoms, talking about them, and sharing information about them won't stop them. Medical professionals stopped the spread of COVID-19. Governments put in place a whole series of new laws, taking all measures they could to save people. They made mistakes, but they were simply human. Regardless of what they got right or wrong, those in power tried to act urgently and effectively in a quickly evolving and escalating crisis. We wore masks; we stayed home; we established safe distances; we took newly made vaccines with all the fear that comes with such an intervention; we traced potentially infected individuals; we quarantined those infected. In the scheme of things, we saw a shocking number of deaths, a shocking amount of illness, and now long-term illness, but the pandemic was almost completely stopped.

Science was at the center of saving lives. A vaccine can cause unexpected reactions in certain individuals, just as a food or medicine can. It does not mean that the vaccine, food, or medicine should *not* be delivered to the many individuals it can save. It does *not* mean that the scientists failed. Vaccines can prevent, and their intervention essentially shut down the spread of COVID-19, as they have prevented many other afflictions that used to take or harm many lives.

We have a bullying epidemic in our society. It infects far more individuals than COVID-19 did. It leads to many more illnesses and deaths. But instead of trying to prevent it, we wait until the bullying and gaslighting lies have done their destructive harm, *then* we try to heal it with psychological, psychiatric, and medical interventions. Bullying and gaslighting have become so normalized and are spreading so rapidly, our mental health and health professionals can't keep up. Our workplaces are struggling with the trauma. It is not surprising that education and health-care professionals are suffering burnout at higher and higher rates, which puts those suffering at higher risk. Few can afford to spend hours, weeks, months, and years with mental health professionals. Many working with a psychologist or psychiatrist have been blessed to slowly but surely regain their balance and health. I have been lucky enough to do that, but what about those who can't afford one-on-one treatment or even small-group therapy?

In recent years, the waitlists for mental health counseling have become utterly untenable. Young people even at risk of serious mental suffering can't see professionals for months or more. Practitioners with their dedication to healing and saving individuals are unable to meet an impossible demand. All these issues converged for me and resulted in three pressing questions that drove the writing of *The Gaslit Brain*:

- What if we *prevented* trauma caused by perpetrators who bully at work in the first place?
- What if we stopped trauma from intensifying with the lies of gaslighting, which in too many professions are a normalized part of our work lives?
- What do we need to learn to make trauma prevention a new way of conducting ourselves at work?

A viable response to these three questions is psychological research that specifically teaches us how our brains identify the lies of workplace bullying and gaslighting that traumatize *before* they shatter us. Institutions can use brain science to avoid the complicity trap with those who tell lies that hurt others.

Psychology teaches us strategies to identify and prevent the trauma from bullying and gaslighting lies. It teaches us that harming others through abuse and neglect at home and at work leads to internal and external division that tears us apart. It's not normal, and the brain's confusion and susceptibility to falsehoods should never let us drop our guard and normalize the divide-and-conquer methods of Dr. Jekyll and Mr. Hyde. And finally, what we need to learn, our most important takeaway, is that we *create* reality. This knowledge empowers us to choose a future that is either dominated by getting, grasping, and feeding, or a future that includes the bigger picture of our humanity, our social connection, our deep-seated knowledge that this planet and our lives—all of us together—are inextricably entwined. We can be destroyers or guardians of one another and of the planet. It's our choice.

We can choose a future where we have unfit brains or a future where we all strive for brain fitness that leads to healthy, higher-level thinking and problem-solving. We can choose a future where we lack a nuanced vocabulary to describe our rich world of emotion concepts or one where we build a shared vocabulary to capture the wealth of information that our bodily systems provide, and our culture creates. We can choose a future where we simply react (fight, flight, freeze) when we feel unsafe or one where we become well-versed in our nervous system's need for homeostasis grounded in our caring relationships with one another.

We can choose to have our brains and bodies bathed in the stress hormone cortisol or in the bonding, healing hormone oxytocin. We can choose to see what is before our eyes, oftentimes placed there by those who want to manipulate us like Dr. Jekyll, or we can look beyond, look twice, be aware of our brain's capacity to put on progressive lenses and see the danger of Mr. Hyde in his many forms. We can choose a future where we default to intuitive shortcuts, or we can think slowly and sidestep the faster, easier route as we know it puts us and others at risk. We can choose to see the world only through the lens of the opportunist or we can balance this left hemisphere with the right hemisphere's altruism.

THE IMPACT OF TRUTH AND LIES

The Gaslit Brain focuses on prevention. It contains strategies to protect yourself and your workplace from the infectious spread of trauma that comes from the lies of bullying, gaslighting, and institutional complicity. *The Bullied Brain* focused on recovery and repair. It examined how the brain is physically harmed by bullying and abuse with the overarching goal of outlining evidence-based practices to heal neurological damage and the resulting scars. *The Gaslit Brain* describes the danger we face in the workplace when exposed to the Dark Triad. It shares six brain science–informed ways—proven ways—to stay safe and sane. If we want our workplaces to flourish, to be high performers, to be trustworthy, we need to face up to divisive lies and learn how they unbalance and destabilize our institutions. *The Gaslit Brain* lays out a new brain-informed way of thinking for leaders, managers, and HR to create workplaces that *prevent* trauma. The overarching goal is to stop trauma *before* it can infect the institution and its employees.

If your institution can afford to lose talent, upend succession planning, cause disengagement, lack productivity and profitability; if your institution doesn't need to worry about negative media or reputation, lawsuits, or penalties, then don't apply the insights of *The Gaslit Brain*. However, if you want to retain talent, have your top employees mentor others with their skills and experience, if you want positive media coverage and care about your institution's reputation and keeping it secure and safe from lawsuits and penalties, this book has applicable insights for you to apply.

One of our most ancient Western texts shows us a satanic force succeed at breaking our sense of reality that was scripted by a Creator, making us doubt ourselves, leading us astray to believe his lies, and resulting in the loss of our connection to the divine garden of our planet and to something bigger than our limited minds. We are at a turning point again. With neuroscience, we face a choice. Do we trust the self-serving personification of evil that manipulates us into believing his violence against facts and truth, or do we stand strong in our relationship to reality constructed by a more encompassing altruistic vision with one another and our planet, not against one another and against our natural planetary home?

We saw in the case studies that this is a critical choice facing today's institutions. Too often in workplaces, it's become normal to privilege lies over truth. It's become normal to respond to those who report bullying with gaslighting. It's become normal to protect those who jeopardize honesty, health, and safety while ousting those who try—at great personal risk—to protect these values. What are we seeing in response to this habituation? Burnout, disengagement at work, despair in youth populations, a lack of security and safety on global and environmental levels. Too many of us are caught on a merry-go-round of dizzying reversals that sow confusion, destabilize brains, and produce those who fearfully follow rather than rebel.

As we have seen in *The Gaslit Brain*, one way to unite is by listening to those who rebel, who speak up, who are willing to protect the institution regardless of the risks by being a whistle-blower. Dr. Jekyll insists that those who see Mr. Hyde and report on his destructive role are liars, but never forget that despite his fancy suit, his sheep's clothing, his insistence that he's a prophet, Dr. Jekyll's modus operandi is to commit violence against targets, facts, and truth. When he calls someone a liar because they are cutting through the bullying and gaslighting lies, are *not* silenced by him, have the intestinal fortitude to speak up, ask yourself why it is that you choose to believe Dr. Jekyll. Is it because of his power, credibility, and social standing? As we've seen, that's a dangerous mistake.

BELL THE CAT

Leaders, managers, and HR can do a far better job of informing, preparing, and having employees stay safe from the manipulations of the Dark Triad. Keeping them ignorant of the threat posed by the confusing lies of Dr. Jekyll and Mr. Hyde is a major risk. It opens the doors to manipulation, fraud, and abuse. It brings the Trojan horse right through the gates, making your workplace susceptible to wide-scale harm. Worst of all, it may put you in the position of becoming complicit with wrongdoing, all the while believing that you're doing it for the right reasons. Case studies and information from the neuroscience chapters showed that our brains can lead us astray. They have faulty approaches to how they construct reality. Ignorance about how our brains work makes us extremely vulnerable to internal and external manipulation. Our society encourages a one-sided approach: we talk endlessly about Dr. Jekyll but steer clear of the challenges and discomfort that come from admitting the existence, let alone the statistical reality, of Mr. Hyde.

An ideal analogy in society is the way we approach marriage. It's a multibillion-dollar industry that starts early in wiring children and young people's brains to believe in romance. However, if we look at facts and truth rather than a feel-good facade, it's a pretty sobering reality. We teach young adults about marriage by showing them rom-coms rather than educating them about the very real possibility of divorce. Why not prepare them to fully understand the risks that divorce presents: the financial implications, the cost of the legal system, the toll on emotions and health, the trauma to children? Why not ensure that people marry from a place of wisdom, not ignorance? Every person who marries should be trained on domestic abuse: Why does it happen? How can you anticipate financial, psychological, and physical abuse? What do the psychological experts know? How can the impulse to harm be stopped before it destroys marriages and children? What are the statistics on femicide? What resources are available?

These marital questions are highly relevant to institutional culture because those who manipulate use identical techniques with those who hire them, work with them, and lead them. They lie on their résumés. They lie in their interviews. Once in the institutional door, the games begin. They are ravenous for victims, and they hunt dressed in sheep's clothing. They speak prophecies that are believed, even though they are false. They don masks that change depending on who they are grooming and seducing. They love bomb. They keep Mr. Hyde's face carefully covered until he strikes the unwitting targets while playing innocent with higher-ups. They lie to those they bully. They lie to those they gaslight. They tell you what you want to hear. They wear beautiful suits as they climb the institutional ladder that becomes complicit at covering up their cold reptilian brains, brains that lack affective empathy. They reflect to you all your own desires and vulnerabilities until they have power over you. The mirror turns, and you must reflect them in such a way that their power is unlimited. In marriage, this can mean repeat assaults or even a violent death. In the institution, it can mean extensive harm to targets, productivity, profitability, and even the death of victims, whistle-blowers, or the institution itself. If a violent or suicidal death isn't extracted, a significant amount of trauma occurs in many lives that act as a slow death.

The Gaslit Brain has brought together leaders in the field of bullying, gaslighting, and institutional complicity with leaders in the field of psychology, specifically in terms of how our brains construct reality. That combination helps us develop a plan of action based on proven strategies to replace manipulative illusions with truth, remove our blinders to look through progressive lenses, become well-versed in the textbook ways that the Dark Triad play their game in the workplace and ruin individuals and institutions. Importantly, it educates us about how our own brains can fall prey to falsehoods due to lack of brain fitness; how our own brains can make prediction errors due to limited emotion concepts; how our own brains are vulnerable to disconnection and stress, leading us out of homeostasis and into a state that makes us easy to manipulate; how our own brains tend to see the position we're told to see while we fail to notice the person behind the facade; how our own brains can replace careful thinking with biased frameworks and intuitive shortcuts; and most concerning, how our own brains can succumb to a self-aggrandizing and grasping opportunist left hemisphere that lords over others and the world. The left hemisphere creates its own reality that has the potential to ruin individuals, institutions, and the planet itself. It's worth understanding and avoiding by proactively, intentionally tapping into the power of the altruist right hemisphere.

THE COURAGE TO FEEL SADNESS

There's a striking feature in the testimonies by Montgomery and the other students about the abuse they were enduring and wanted stopped. Many of them commented on how the most painful part of their ordeal was witnessing the humiliation and harm done to their peers. In the extensive national media coverage of the abuse and cover-up on the part of the school and government regulator, the newspaper's opening lines showcased the pain Montgomery felt for his fellow victims.

> *VICTORIA—Sleep had long since abandoned Montgomery Fraser-Brown by the winter of 2012.*
>
> *Lying awake at 2 a.m. on a cold December morning, the high school basketball star, then 17, opened his computer and wrote a note to his parents as they slept down the hall in their Victoria home.*
>
> *"When I lay in my bed all I can think about is images on and off the court seeing friends humiliated and embarrassed," he wrote. "I know I will struggle with these feelings for a long time."*[3]

Our present-day society worries a great deal—and rightly so—about depression in youth. It worries about young people's feelings, their addiction to a virtual world, their anxiety about the financial future, their loss of work opportunities due to technology, their isolation and loneliness, their inability to connect through love and the way this blockage turns violent, their suffering from bullying that can turn into an impulse to harm, their despair about environmental degradation and global warming. But what if these feelings were a sign of flickering health?

If we can stop for just a moment our normalizing, even worshipping of the brain's left-hemisphere vision—the opportunist who is motivated to grasp, get, and feed—and instead see our world and our future from the right-hemisphere vision—the altruist—who privileges social connection and a deep sense of responsibility to be a guardian of the natural world we have been graced to live within, perhaps we can rethink young people's sadness. McGilchrist, expert in mental health, explains:

> *If there is a tendency for the right hemisphere to be more sorrowful and prone to depression, this can, in my view, be seen as related not only to being more in touch with what's going on, but more in touch with, and concerned for, others. "No man is an island": it is the right hemisphere of the human brain that ensures we feel part of the main. The more we are aware of and empathically connected to whatever it is that exists apart from ourselves, the more we are likely to suffer. Sadness and empathy are highly correlated.*[4]

Montgomery and the other victims of abuse were deeply sorry about the harm done to one another. They were prone to depression. Why? Because they were young enough not to be cut off and cutthroat. They were more in touch with what was going on and concerned for one another. They were empathically connected to each other and therefore, more likely to suffer. Their sadness is a warning for older people in the workplace. We don't have to continue until we crash on the rocks or find ourselves drowning. If we strive to keep the affective empathy alive and well in our youth, they can help us turn the workplace ship around. They are the future.

How many leaders, managers, and HR, let alone employees, know about the left and right hemispheres of the brain and how they see the world? Instead of knowing their value, we put on blinders to avoid them. What if we found the courage to know that our brain is one of our most humane gifts because it keeps our affective empathy healthy and well. What should make us deeply afraid is delight at suffering, a rush of personal power at the idea of revenge, excitement about ousting those we have put in the out-group. What should make us terrified is violence against facts and truth because they are the bulwark against individual and collective insanity. When we no longer know if what we see is an illusion of our own making or a verifiable reality, we are lost.

McGilchrist's book analyzes the way in which neuroscience—and philosophy, poetry, and art—have taught us throughout the ages about our dual brains. In his honoring of sorrow and depression, he quotes from the seventeenth-century metaphysical poet John Donne who writes that "No man is an island" as he notes our connection to "the continent / A part of the main." To quote McGilchrist, the right hemisphere of the human brain ensures that we feel "part of the main." When we become divided within, divided against one another, cut off from our relationship to the land, we slip in destructive ways into the limited world of the opportunist left hemisphere.

In John Donne's day, when a death occurred, the church bells would toll. In our modern workplaces, in our modern world, we need to allow ourselves to feel the sadness of every death, for it takes with it a part of our own humanity. Don't let the left hemisphere fool you into thinking that the more you grasp, get, and feed, the more you fully pursue "reality." The truth is, it's only a part, as Donne illuminates:

> Any man's death diminishes me,
> Because I am involved in mankind.
> And therefore never send to know for whom the bell tolls;
> It tolls for thee.

NOTES

1. Jennifer Fraser, *The Bullied Brain: Heal Your Scars and Restore Your Health* (Essex, CT: Prometheus, 2022).

2. Sally Curtin, "State Suicide Rates among Adolescents and Young Adults Aged 10–24: United States, 2000 to 2018," *National Vital Statistics Reports* 69, no. 11 (September 11, 2020), https://www.cdc.gov/nchs/data/nvsr/nvsr69/nvsr-69-11-508.pdf.

3. Robert Cribb, "Teachers' Bullying Scarred Us, Say Student Athletes," *Toronto Star*, March 14, 2015, https://www.thestar.com/news/canada/teachers-bullying-scarred-us -say-student-athletes/article_446e01ba-543b-5a01-8280-e5003dcd1c4b.html.

4. Iain McGilchrist, *The Master and His Emissary: The Divided Brain and the Making of the Western World* (New Haven, CT, and London: Yale University Press, 2009), 85.

ACKNOWLEDGMENTS

I AM BLESSED TO HAVE JOHN WILLIG AS MY LITERARY AGENT. HE IS SO respected by editors and publishers that he opens all doors. Not only that, but we share a commitment to truth telling even when it is hard and risky. When my approach falters, John coaches me until the book can reach readers. He has the benefit of experience and insight, coupled with an exceptional sensitivity to words. I am also blessed to have Jonathan Kurtz as my editor and publisher. He allows me time to navigate challenges and maintains an unwavering faith in the project until it is truly ready to share. I greatly appreciate the fine work of production editor Felicity Tucker, copy editor Joanne Foster, marketer Anthony Pomes, and publicist Lianne Castelino.

I am thankful to Megan Carle, Jonathan Wilson, and Julie Macfarlane. They are exceptional individuals who took the bullying, gaslighting, and institutional betrayal done to them and transformed it into powerful action to help others. The three have risen from the ashes of cruelty and abandonment even stronger and brighter. It was an honor to work within their remarkable stories and use them to showcase the brain science.

A special shout-out to Mary Inman, who generously shared her experience and knowledge about whistle-blowers who are Davids fighting Goliaths and are lucky to have a lawyer like Mary by their sides. I'd like to honor intrepid and feisty Pamela Forward, cofounder and leader of the Whistleblowing Canada Research Society; along with veteran and tireless policy and program expert Jackie Garrick, founder of Whistleblowers of America; and thought leader Georgina Halford-Hall, CEO of WhistleblowersUK and Secretariat to the All-Party Parliamentary Group for Whistleblowing. These leaders fight for truth telling in a "post-truth era." Our world is in desperate need of a cure from the virus of lying. I am full of gratitude to all the individuals out in the world who fight for the truth and resist the onslaught of disinformation.

As with *The Bullied Brain*, in *The Gaslit Brain* I stand on the shoulders of giants. The chapters of this book are full of the life-changing science and scholarship of brilliant minds. As an educator and storyteller, I am grateful for the opportunity to share this knowledge with the world. It is information that can protect the health and integrity of the workplace. For individuals this information can protect their mental health, prevent harm to their physical health, and save lives at risk, yet for many of us it seems out of reach. I have done my very best to bring the psychology and brain science about manipulation and deception into a readable and applicable format. Any and all errors are mine.

Once again, my work has benefited from the expertise of Dr. Michael Merzenich. He receives more than a hundred emails every day because the world refuses to let geniuses retire, and yet he carved out time to ensure that the brain science was correct before my book was published. I admire him more than I can say. I have learned invaluable knowledge from his research, and I am humbled by his support for my work.

My husband works in a high-stress environment doing emergency preparedness for the provincial government. He daily provides me with an exemplar of someone who cares deeply about the communities he serves and will do everything in his power to prepare them and protect them. He is known at work for his integrity. His combination of empathy and ethics helps me see at all times as I work on empathy erosion and corruption that there is another, better way for all of us.

My younger son, Angus-James, suffers from a rare genetic condition that causes him chronic illness and utterly devastating chronic pain. He sees me more than anyone else as I read, research, and write. He, too, is a writer and understands on a meaningful level the challenge of taking one's thoughts, feelings, and ideas and striving to articulate them into stories that are meaningful for others. Having him be part of my isolated world of writing a book that takes years has been an enormous gift to me.

My father, sister, brother, sisters-in-law, and brother-in-law always have my back; and having us rally this year when my glorious mother died has been a saving grace. My friend Katy Slakov has read the manuscript for *The Gaslit Brain* and every other manuscript that has become one of my books, and she encourages me every step of the way. Her support is invaluable.

The Gaslit Brain is dedicated to my older son, Montgomery. When I find myself in despair at the state of the world, observing Montgomery and learning from him gives me hope. He belongs to a generation in which I continue to have faith while my own has left me profoundly concerned. Montgomery is fearless in speaking truth to power. He cannot be manipulated. He refuses to believe lies. And he cares deeply about others and won't stand by while they are harmed. He is the antidote in *The Gaslit Brain* to bullying, gaslighting, and institutional complicity.

REFERENCES

Achor, Shawn. *The Happiness Advantage: The Seven Principles of Positive Psychology That Fuel Success and Performance at Work*. New York: Random House, 2010.

Babiak, Paul and Robert Hare. *Snakes in Suits: When Psychopaths Go to Work*. New York: Harper, 2006.

Baron-Cohen, Simon. *The Science of Evil: On Empathy and the Origins of Cruelty*. New York: Basic Books, 2011.

Barrett, Lisa Feldman. *How Emotions Are Made: The Secret Life of the Brain*. New York: Houghton Mifflin Harcourt, 2017.

Bashir, Manzar. "Six Signs That You Are Being Gaslighted and How to Break Free." *Forbes*, October 25, 2023. https://www.forbes.com/councils/forbescoachescouncil/2023/10/25/six-signs-that-you-are-being-gaslighted-and-how-to-break-free/.

Bekiempis, Victoria, and Dani Anguiano. "Caroline Ellison Says She Felt 'Relief Not to Have to Lie Anymore' after FTX Collapse." *The Guardian*, October 11, 2023. https://www.theguardian.com/business/2023/oct/11/caroline-ellison-testimony-sam-bankman-fried-trial.

Boydell, Carroll. "Best Practices in Whistleblower Legislation: An Analysis of Federal and Provincial Legislation Relevant to Disclosures of Wrongdoing in British Columbia." BC Freedom of Information and Privacy Association, 2018. https://fipa.bc.ca/wp-content/uploads/2018/11/FIPA_Whistleblower_Paper_web.pdf.

Burgo, Joseph. "All Bullies Are Narcissists." *The Atlantic*, November 14, 2013. https://www.theatlantic.com/health/archive/2013/11/all-bullies-are-narcissists/281407/.

Carle, Megan. *Walk Away to Win: A Playbook to Combat Workplace Bullying*. New York: McGraw-Hill, 2023.

CBC News. "B.C. Teachers Strike Boosted Private School Enrollment." CBC, February 12, 2015. https://www.cbc.ca/news/canada/british-columbia/b-c-teachers-strike-boosted-private-school-enrolment-1.2955562.

Choudhury, Subrata. "Indian Police Fire Teargas at Hundreds Protesting over Kolkata Doctor's Rape, Murder." *Reuters*, August 27, 2024. https://www.reuters.com/world/india/indian-police-fire-teargas-hundreds-protesting-over-kolkata-doctors-rape-murder-2024-08-27/.

Connor, Tracy. "Larry Nassar Complains It's Too Hard to Listen to Victim Stories." NBC, January 18, 2018. https://www.nbcnews.com/news/us-news/larry-nassar-complains-it-s-too-hard-listen-victim-stories-n838731.

Crawshaw, Laura. *Grow Your Spine and Manage Abrasive Leadership Behavior: A Guide for Those Who Manage Bosses Who Bully*. New York: Executive Insight Press, 2023.

Creswell, Julie, Kevin Draper, and Rachel Abrams. "At Nike, Revolt Led by Women Leads to Exodus of Male Executives." *New York Times*, April 28, 2018. https://www.nytimes.com/2018/04/28/business/nike-women.html.

Cribb, Robert. "Teachers' Bullying Scarred Us, Say Student Athletes." *Toronto Star*, March 14, 2015. https://www.thestar.com/news/canada/2015/03/14/teachers-bullying-scarred-us-say-student-athletes.html.

Curtin, Sally. "State Suicide Rates among Adolescents and Young Adults Aged 10–24: United States, 2000 to 2018." *National Vital Statistics Reports* 69, no. 11 (September 11, 2020). https://www.cdc.gov/nchs/data/nvsr/nvsr69/nvsr-69-11-508.pdf.

Dathan, Matt. "Women Not Reporting Crimes to 'Broken' Police." *The Times*, July 3, 2023. https://www.thetimes.com/uk/law/article/women-not-reporting-crimes-to-broken-police-rhx8v9ktj.

Dhillon, Amrit. "India's Supreme Court Issues Handbook against Use of Archaic Terms for Women." *The Guardian*, August 18, 2023. https://www.theguardian.com/world/2023/aug/18/indias-supreme-court-issues-handbook-against-use-of-archaic-terms-for-women.

Fraser, Jennifer. *The Bullied Brain: Heal Your Scars and Restore Your Health*. Essex, CT: Prometheus, 2022.

Fraser, Jennifer. "Is Your Bully Abusive or Just Abrasive?" *Psychology Today*, May 8, 2023. https://www.psychologytoday.com/intl/blog/the-bullied-brain/202305/is-your-bully-abusive-or-just-abrasive.

Fraser, Jennifer. "Cruelty of Workplace Bullying Grabs the Attention of Mass. Lawmakers." *Boston Globe*, January 16, 2024. https://www.bostonglobe.com/2024/01/16/opinion/letters-to-the-editor-workplace-bullying/.

Freyd, Jennifer, and Pamela Birrell. *Blind to Betrayal: Why We Fool Ourselves We Aren't Being Fooled*. Hoboken, NJ: Wiley, 2013.

Garrett, Neil, Stephanie Lazzaro, Dan Ariely, and Tali Sharot. "The Brain Adapts to Dishonesty." *Nature Neuroscience* (December 19, 2016): 1727–32. https://pmc.ncbi.nlm.nih.gov/articles/PMC5238933/.

Gillard, Michael, and Fiona Hamilton. "Senior Met Officer Claims He Was Shut Out over Bullying Complaint." *The Times*, July 9, 2023. https://www.thetimes.com/uk/article/senior-met-officer-claims-he-was-shut-out-over-bullying-complaint-xwtvj3nlg.

Gladwell, Malcolm. "In Plain View." *New Yorker*, September 17, 2012. https://www.newyorker.com/magazine/2012/09/24/in-plain-view.

Guiora, Amos N. *Armies of Enablers: Survivor Stories of Complicity and Betrayal in Sexual Assault*. Saratoga Springs, NY: American Bar Association, 2020.

Hedges, Chris. *Empire of Illusion: The End of Literacy and the Triumph of Spectacle*. Toronto: Random House, 2010.

Horton, Adrian. "'Kafka-esque Nightmare': What Many Women Face When Reporting Rape." *The Guardian*, May 20, 2023. https://www.theguardian.com/film/2023/may/20/netflix-documentary-victim-suspect-women-rape.

Huizen, Jennifer. "Examples and Signs of Gaslighting and How to Respond." *Medical News Today*, March 22, 2024. https://www.medicalnewstoday.com/articles/gaslighting.

Pennsylvania Office of Attorney General. "Western Pennsylvania Nurse Sentenced to Consecutive Life Sentences after Pleading Guilty to Killing and Attempting to Kill Patients." May 2, 2024. https://www.attorneygeneral.gov/taking-action/western -pennsylvania-nurse-sentenced-to-consecutive-life-sentences-after-pleading -guilty-to-killing-and-attempting-to-kill-patients/.

Porges, Stephen, and Seth Porges. *Our Polyvagal World: How Safety and Trauma Change Us.* New York: Norton, 2023.

Reiss, Helen. *The Empathy Effect: Seven Neuroscience-Based Keys for Transforming the Way We Live, Love, Work, and Connect across Differences.* Boulder, CO: Sounds True, 2018.

Sarkis, Stephanie. *Gaslighting: Recognize Manipulative and Emotionally Abusive People— And Break Free.* Boston: Da Capo Lifelong Books, 2018.

Schofield, Hugh. "Woman Describes Horror of Learning Husband Drugged Her So Others Could Rape Her." BBC, September 5, 2024. https://www.bbc.com/news/ articles/cd9dwxexp77o.

Sharot, Tali, and Cass Sunstein. *Look Again: The Power of Noticing What Was Always There.* London: Bridge Street Press, 2024.

Sherman, Ted. "'Gaslighting, Retaliation and Intimidation' Forced Me to Leave Seton Hall, Former President Says." NJ.com, February 6, 2024. https://www.nj.com/edu cation/2024/02/gaslighting-retaliation-and-intimidation-forced-me-to-leave -seton-hall-former-president-says.html.

Simpson, Ian. "Sandusky's Wife Claims He's Innocent, Victims Manipulated." Reuters, March 12, 2014. https://www.reuters.com/article/sports/sanduskys-wife-claims -hes-innocent-victims-manipulated-idUSBREA2B0ZU/.

"The Sleep of Reason: Met Boss Turned 'Blind Eye' to Bullying." The Upsetter, 2023. https://theupsetterstrikes.substack.com/p/the-sleep-of-reason.

Slovo, Gillian. "The People of Grenfell Knew the Truth Before the Fire. It's We Who Must Learn from Them Now." *The Guardian,* 2024. https://www.theguardian .com/commentisfree/article/2024/sep/07/the-people-of-grenfell-knew-the-truth -before-the-fire-its-we-who-must-learn-from-them-now.

Solnit, Rebecca. "Feminism Taught Me All I Need to Know about Men Like Trump and Putin." *The Guardian,* February 25, 2023. https://www.theguardian.com/comment isfree/2023/feb/25/feminism-men-putin-trump-abusive-men-dictators.

Squires, David. "David Squires on . . . Luis Rubiales and the Gaslighting Scandal in Spanish Football." *The Guardian,* August 29, 2023. https://www.theguardian.com/ football/ng-interactive/2023/aug/29/david-squires-on-luis-rubiales-and-the-gas lighting-scandal-in-spanish-football.

Stubben, Stephen, and Kyle Welch. "Evidence on the Use and Efficacy of Internal Whistleblowing Systems." *Journal of Accounting Research,* March 4, 2020. https:// onlinelibrary.wiley.com/doi/10.1111/1475-679X.12303.

Suskind, Dorothy. "Whistleblowers: Speaking Up for Justice." *Psychology Today,* August 6, 2020. https://www.psychologytoday.com/ca/blog/bully-wise/202008/whistle blowers-speaking-up-for-justice.

Suskind, Dorothy. "Workplace Bullying: A Three-Part Degradation Ceremony." *Psychology Today,* April 2, 2021. https://www.psychologytoday.com/ca/blog/bully-wise/ 202104/workplace-bullying-a-three-part-degradation-ceremony.

Svoboda, Elizabeth. "What Makes Whistleblowers Speak Up while Others Stay Silent about Wrongdoing." *Washington Post*, July 13, 2017. https://www.washington post.com/news/speaking-of-science/wp/2017/07/13/what-makes-whistleblowers -speak-out/.

Sweet, Paige. "How Gaslighting Manipulates Reality: Gaslighting Isn't Just between People in a Relationship—It Involves Social Power, Too." *Scientific American*, October 1, 2022. https://www.scientificamerican.com/article/how-gaslighting -manipulates-reality/.

Travers, Mark. "Obvious Signs of 'Workplace Gaslighting,' from a Psychologist." *Forbes*, May 7, 2024. https://www.forbes.com/sites/traversmark/2024/05/07/2-obvious -signs-of-workplace-gaslighting-from-a-psychologist/.

Upsetter. "The Upsetter Strikes." *Substack*. https://theupsetterstrikes.substack.com/.

Valenti, Jessica. "Bill Cosby's Wife Wants to Know Who the Real Victim Is. There Are All Too Many Options." *The Guardian*, December 16, 2014. https://www.theguardian. com/commentisfree/2014/dec/16/bill-cosby-wife-camille-who-the-real-victim-is.

van der Kolk, Bessel. *The Body Keeps the Score: Mind, Brain, and Body in the Transformation of Trauma*. New York: Penguin, 2015.

Van Natta, Don, Jr. "Video Shows Mike Rice's Ire." ESPN, April 2, 2013. https://www .espn.com/espn/otl/story/_/id/9125796/practice-video-shows-rutgers-basketball -coach-mike-rice-berated-pushed-used-slurs-players.

Ward, Paula. "'She Is Evil Personified': Victims' Families Face Killer Nurse Heather Pressdee in Court." TRBLive, May 2, 2024. https://triblive.com/local/regional/ ex-nurse-pressdee-pleads-guilty-to-killing-nursing-home-patients/.

Welch, Kyle, and Stephen Stubben. "Throw Out Your Assumptions about Whistle-blowing." *Harvard Business Review*, January 14, 2020. https://hbr.org/2020/01/ throw-out-your-assumptions-about-whistleblowing.

"Western Pennsylvania Nurse Sentenced to Consecutive Life Sentences after Plead-ing Guilty to Killing and Attempting to Kill Patients." Pennsylvania Office of Attorney General, May 2, 2024. https://www.attorneygeneral.gov/taking-action/ western-pennsylvania-nurse-sentenced-to-consecutive-life-sentences-after-plead ing-guilty-to-killing-and-attempting-to-kill-patients/.

Westover, Jonathan. "How to Avoid and Counteract Gaslighting as a Leader." *Forbes*, October 28, 2021. https://www.forbes.com/sites/forbescoachescouncil/2021/10/28/ how-to-avoid-and-counteract-gaslighting-as-a-leader/.

"Word of the Year 2022: 'Gaslighting,' plus 'Sentient,' 'Omicron,' 'Queen Consort,' and Other Top Lookups of 2022." Merriam-Webster Dictionary. https://www.merriam -webster.com/wordplay/word-of-the-year-2022.

www.ingramcontent.com/pod-product-compliance
Lightning Source LLC
Chambersburg PA
CBHW021952090426
42811CB00041B/2413/J